FOURTH EDITION

THE HANDY BOOK

FOR

GENEALOGISTS

REVISED AND ENLARGED

State and County Histories

Maps

Libraries

Bibliographies of Genealogical Works

Where to Write for Records, etc.

By

George B. Everton, Sr.

and

Gunnar Rasmuson

Published by

THE EVERTON PUBLISHERS

526 North Main   Logan, Utah

Lithographed U. S. A.
Publishers Press

Binding
Mountain States Bindery

FOREWORD
Fourth Edition The Handy Book For Genealogists

In the preface of the 1949 "Handy Book for Genealogists" Walter M. Everton wrote, "Answering genealogical queries occupied the major part of my time during the last six years. It began in the Sutro Branch Library in San Francisco in 1943." This was the beginning not only of "The Handy Book for Genealogists" but also "The Genealogical Helper" and "The How Book for Genealogists."

From queries received and answers formulated, he gradually planned outlines of general procedures necessary for genealogical researchers. These instructions were mimeographed for specific geographical areas in order to save time and effort. At first he only sent the sheet or sheets pertaining to a specific question, but as the instruction sheets increased he finally decided to publish and bind them so those interested could have all the helps in a convenient form. This first publishing effort he called "The How Book for Genealogists."

All 500 copies of this mimeographed effort were gone within a week or two after they were announced. He then engaged a professional printing shop for the next edition. Eventually he sold more than 16,000 of that little 46-page booklet.

His success with the "How Book" revealed to him the great need of most people for guidance in their search for ancestors. To be of help to these people, he continued to gather and arrange as much general information as possible. He also consulted many books written to aid genealogists. Naturally he formed many plans for future publications.

In 1947 he originated "The Genealogical Helper," a quarterly magazine with news and aids for progenitor searchers. By 1949 he had gathered a great deal more information which he felt should be published in book form. He had also formulated the first "Genealogists' Exchange" which he advertised, inviting genealogists to list their surname research interests so all others interested in those lines could cooperate and corroborate. This exchange material was published in the "1949 Handy Book for Genealogists." Also incorporated in that book was all information previously published in the "How Book" besides new information gathered to assist genealogists in their search for unknown ancestors. Ten thousand copies of the 1949 "Handy Book were printed and sold.

Almost as soon as the book was off the press he realized that the "Exchange" material ought to be published at least every year, as progenitor interests change each time a point is proved and new ancestors come into sight, while the general information on where to search for records is much more permanent. So preparations were made to make the December 1950 issue of "The Genealogical Helper" an "Exchange Edition" and then to make that innovation an annual affair.

This plan was announced in the summer of 1950 and immediately he began to receive registrations. He was busily engaged in arranging the material and making publication plans when he was suddenly stricken with a heart attack and died 20 December 1950.

His wife, Pearl Knowles Everton, who had assisted him in his genealogical activities, and his eldest living son, George Baugh Everton, took over and continued his work. Mrs. Everton died 3 March 1952.

Gunnar Rasmuson, former editor of The Herald-Journal, a daily newspaper of Logan, Utah, and an ardent genealogist, was then asked to help in carrying on the publications started by Mr. Everton. He assisted with the 1953 and the third edition of the "Handy Book" and with this new fourth edition as co-author. His writings have also significantly influenced "The Genealogical Helper" for good.

This edition comes to you with many additions, changes and corrections. A questionnaire was sent to every county clerk in the U.S. asking for information about the vital records held by them - dates of commencement, etc. They were also asked to check the information printed in the third edition of the "Handy Book" for accuracy and to indicate any changes that should be made to give genealogists correct and up-to-date data about their county. Some of these questionnaires were not returned and some that were returned gave no additional light. The rest form the basis for what is hoped will be another substantial aid to genealogists - a listing of county records with starting dates.

In this edition will also be found "A Genealogists' Check List of the Historical Records Survey." This was originally published in the June 1961 issue of "The Genealogical Helper." It is a compilation of parts of a survey made by the Works Progress Administration (WPA) during the years 1936 to 1943. It includes only records of interest to genealogists. More information regarding this addition how to use it etc. is shown on page VIII.

New maps of all the states are printed in this edition. They give the latest information on county boundaries, being taken from the U. S. Department of Commerce map "County Boundaries as of April 1, 1960." These maps show not only the counties of each state but also the counties of each bordering state, thus enabling the researcher to trace migrations from county to county and state to state with much greater ease.

Many errors of past editions have been corrected but undoubtedly some still remain. One difficulty in getting the dates of formation of counties correct is due to the fact that "date of formation" is interpreted in different ways. Sometimes there may be as much as 20 or 30 years between the time a county was formed or set up by legislative act and the time it was actually functioning. In seeking these records of counties you will find some authorities have used the formation date, others the organization date and still others the date the records were started. This has led to considerable confusion in the past. In the present edition we have tried to use the formation date - the date the boundaries were outlined by legislative act. So you will naturally find most counties starting their records at later dates. You may also occasionally find a county with records starting before formation because the people could not wait for the legislature to act. Also you may find records pre-dating the formation date because of change of status, etc.

It is sincerely hoped that readers finding errors in this edition will call them to our attention, as many have done in past editions, which has been greatly appreciated. You may help your neighbor or friend by helping us eliminate errors.

The introduction following this forward is also a new feature. Here you will find instructions on how to use the information about the counties and states. Once a person learns how to use that information he will seldom if ever turn back to the introduction. Many will find it a great help in getting started. Even those who have used former editions until they were threadbare may find pointers to assist them.

George B. Everton, Sr.
Gunnar Rasmuson

April 1, 1962

INTRODUCTION

As you start to gather information for your family tree you will undoubtedly find that your American ancestors migrated from place to place. It is a rare thing to find even two or three generations of a family at one location. If they were not in one of the mass movements from Europe to America or from the eastern seaboard on west, they were nevertheless looking for greener pastures and changed their abodes - sometimes so often it is extremely difficult to follow their trails.

As they moved from one country, state or county to another they usually left records. You must find those records to verify births, deaths, marriages and many other facts regarding their lives and loves. You must follow their trails sometimes backwards and forward. It is not unusual for genealogists to work on both ends of the trail, finally closing the gap, making a complete record of their movements and many other interesting facts about their lives.

When you start your search for their records you may find some in one state and some in another. It is also possible you will find some of your progenitors living in one place for many years, yet their records are scattered in several counties. This may have been caused by their original counties being divided and subdivided again and again. How to search for these records at one time presented a great challenge, but "The Handy Book for Genealogists" gives answers to thousands of these questions quickly, easily.

Many of the older genealogists have said they wished they had had this aid when they started research. They had to dig the facts regarding the dates of organization of counties and their parent counties from history books, county commission and legislature minute books and many other kinds of archival material. By trial and error they found where records were kept, what they revealed, etc. These facts must be known in practically all cases before you can get the information needed to establish your connections.

Knowing what records are available and who to contact for extracts or copies also presents a tremendous problem as each country, state and county may have different record keeping systems. The county clerk may have the records you need in one county, the city clerk in another, the clerk of the court in another, and the state health department in another. With this book you can quickly decide where to write for what records.

To assist you in the use of the information you have in this volume let us illustrate with some hypothetical cases:

1. STATE HISTORIES

Tradition holds that one of your great grand parents was born in Missouri in 1811. You check the history of Missouri in "The Handy Book" and find it did not become a territory until 1812 - that from 1805 to 1812 it was part of Louisiana Territory. Therefore it would be unlikely that Missouri would have a record about him or his parents in 1811. If you wanted to start a search, the place to look would be in the Louisiana records. Of course, you might find he was not born in Missouri or in 1811 - that his parents brought him from another state as a babe or any one of a dozen other possibilities. One sure thing, you would know that the Territory of Missouri was not created until 1812, one year after his traditional birth, and prior to that time that section belonged to the Territory of Louisiana.

2. COUNTY HISTORIES

Suppose you had a progenitor who was one of the first settlers at Key West, Florida. He took his family there in 1822 but died in 1823 leaving his wife and children. You want to know if there is a will, record of real estate, or any other contemporary record about him in the county records. You find that Key West is the county seat of Monroe County, but none of their records help you. You wonder if something might be found in adjoining counties but your search is fruitless in six or eight neighboring counties. Finally you learn about the "Handy Book for Genealogists." You turn to page 27 and find that Monroe County was formed in 1824 from St. John County, one year after the death of your forfather. A further check reveals that St. Augustine is the county seat of St. John County and it is almost on the other side of the state, over 375 miles from Key West. you go to the records at St. Augustine and there find just what you want.

Next you search for the records of a forebearer who lived and died in Ford County, Illinois. He was 75 years old at his death in 1869 - making his birth date ca. 1794. You have reason to believe he was born at or near his place of death and would like to know everything possible about him from the county records. You check Ford County on page 40 of "The Handy Book" and find it was formed in 1859 from Clark County. Going back you find that Clark was formed in 1859 from Crawford which was formed from Edwards in 1815. In turn Edwards was formed in 1814 from Madison and Gallatin, they being formed in 1812. St. Clair, which was formed from the N. W. Territory in 1790, was the parent county of Madison. Randolph, formed from St. Clair and the N. W. Territory in 1795, was the parent county of Gallatin.

You must search the records of six or seven counties to be sure you have all that can be found about a man who supposedly lived all his life within the confines of one county: Ford 1869-1814; Clark 1850-1819; Crawford 1819-1815; Edwards 1815-1814. Then Madison 1814-1812; St. Clair 1812-1795 or Gallatin 1814-1812; Randolph 1812-1795. It might pay to do further investigating to establish whether your research should go to Madison or Gallatin Counties. It undoubtedly would not be both.

3. LIBRARIES

One of your ancestors came from Connecticut. What library might have records on his life? You check the list of libraries on page 20 and find quite a number you can write to for information. You also find several books listed which could be extremely helpful in your progenitor search.

4. MAPS

You are searching the records for an early pioneer of Colorado County, Texas. You note this county was created in 1836 but on writing to the County Clerk, he informs you that the county was not finally organized until 40 years later, 1876, and practically none of their records go beyond the organization date. You look at the map of Texas and find that Austin, Fayette, Fort Bend, Jackson, Lavaca and Wharton Counties surround Colorado County and a further check shows they were all created about the same time or shortly after Colorado. It might be well to check with neighboring county clerks to ascertain if they have some record of your ancestor. Occasionally persons would travel to an adjoining county for a marriage or other important business if it could not be taken care of in their own county.

A new feature of this edition is that the maps of all the states show the adjoining counties in neighboring states. Thus you can follow migrations with much greater ease than heretofore.

You follow the trail of one of your ancestors in his westward trek through Virginia. It starts at James City with a year or two or three stop in each of the following counties: Henrico, Buckingham, Roanoke and Scott. Here you loose the trail. You have reason to believe he moved across the line to Tennessee. You locate Scott County on the map and you find bordering it on the south the Tennessee counties of Hancock, Hawkins and Sullivan - the three counties you will have to search to pick up the trail again.

5. COUNTY RECORDS

A questionnaire was sent to every county clerk or clerk of court in the U. S. asking for information about the records in their custody. About half of them returned the questionnaire. Many gave information which should be helpful in searching county records. This information is included in this edition with the other county data. For instance you turn to Arkansas on page 8 and find that Arkansas County is the first county listed. Under this county you find: (Co Clk has pro rec from 1809; Cir Clk has div & civ ct rec from 1803, war ser discharge from 1917.) Interpreted this says: County Clerk has probate records from 1809; Circuit Clerk has divorce and civil court records from 1803 and war service discharges from 1917. The explanations of abbreviations of any words you might have difficulty with are listed on page X. If this feature proves to be helpful, let us know and we'll try to expand it in our next issue.

6. GENEALOGISTS' CHECK LIST OF HISTORICAL RECORDS SURVEY.

Surveys of public record archives were conducted in most states during 1936 to 1943 by the Works Progress Administration (WPA), a government agency. For example, inventories were made of the federal archives in all the states, of state, some county and municipal archives, transcripts of some public archives, directories of church archives and religious publications, guides to public vital statistics records and depositories of manuscript collections, check lists of American imprints, and various other surveys and listings of records and archives of interest to different types of researchers.

A great many of these records, as you will note, are vital to genealogical research. But very few of the WPA publications give full transcripts - they only name the records available in the respective archives. Quite often they tell the condition of the records, where they were stored when the survey was made, and dates of commencement and conclusion of the records. The records themselves must be examined to gain the information.

However, you may save a lot of time in your data search by first consulting the check list, and then the survey, inventory or transcript to find out the existence of buried or piled up records in some county courthouse basement or attic, which may give contemporary evidence regarding the life of your ancestor.

Of course, only a small portion of all available records and archives were surveyed, but that which was completed is a great help in locating records for research - finding what may be available - what the records contain, etc.

Many times one will find unusual and extremely valuable records for genealogical research in county or other archives which are not common. A search should be made in each place to see if such records as naturalization papers, apprenticeship records, special tax assessments, and many other out-of-the-ordinary records are available, as well as the usual wills, deeds, court and vital records.

From the Genealogists Check List of the Historical Records Survey you can quickly determine if a survey was made by the WPA. Then you should consult the survey to ascertain what records are available in that archive - the usual and the unusual. You will then know what to look for if you can visit the place personally or what to write for if you can't.

A check list of these publications was published by the WPA according to the type of publication. Sometimes it takes a lot searching to find all the records which might be listed of one state or locality. Many of the publications are of little or no value to genealogists since they pertain to such things as reports and records of the Treasury department and other federal agencies none of which have any personal records. They are of no value to the genealogist.

At the suggestion of Meredith B. Colket, Jr., for many years director of the Institute for Genealogical Research, sponsored by the American University and the National Archives, George B. Everton, Sr. of The Everton Publishers undertook the assignment of making a rearranged check list of these WPA publications. Almost 2000 books were examined and evaluated as to their genealogical value. The ones of no value to genealogists were eliminated from the list. Then the list was rearranged according to states, putting all publications of a state together. Thus, if you are searching for records of Missouri you can now find them all grouped together, making it possible to quickly determine if the records of any particular county, city, church or federal agency in Missouri was surveyed for records of a genealogical nature. If so, then you should try to get the publication to determine if any records might be available which would assist you.

Of course, as with most records, you will find some of the listed publications of greater value than others. For instance, Ship Registers and Enrollments have only a slight value to genealogists. Nevertheless, the names of the owners and captains of these ships are easy to check in the good indices and at times this may prove to be the only record you can find of these people. You may also find clues as to where other records may be found. So don't be discouraged if some of the publications don't produce the information you need. Persistence is a virtue no genealogist can afford to overlook.

Every state or region had a designated depository of unpublished material which also may have many of the publications. An exchange was made at the time of printing whereby copies were supposed to be sent to each region or state depository. The depositories of unpublished materials - that which was in preparation for publication at the time the project was abandoned - are listed in the rearranged check list. Many libraries also have fair collections of the WPA Historical Records Survey Publications. At one time the Library of Congress acted as an exchange station, distributing surplus copies to other libraries and depositories. The staff of the National Archives Library, Washington 25, D. C., under the direction of Miss

Grace Quimby have also endeavored to gather a complete set, but still lack some numbers. They also have a few surplus copies they would be happy to exchange with other libraries or depositories, especially if they could fill in the ones they lack.

So you may find a copy of the publication you need close by, or you may have to do some searching. Check with your local library first and extend your search from there. If you can locate the publications pertinent to the area and time of your ancestor you may save many hours of tedious labor, as they will quickly show you what records are available in each archive where surveys were made.

7. ABBREVIATIONS

The following abbreviations have been used to save space - making it possible for us to give you more information.

adpt - adoption; Am - American or America; arch - archives; assn - association; b - birth; Bap - Baptist; bd - board; bk - book; bur - burial; ca - about; cal - calendar; cat - catalog; cen - census; ch - chapter; CH - court house; chr - church; cir - circuit; civ - civil; clk - clerk; co - county; col - collection; cor - correspondence; ct - courts; cts - courts

depo - depository; dept - department; dir - directory; dist - district; div - divorce; doc - document; fed - federal; gen - general; gov - government or governmental; his - historical or history; incom - incomplete; inv - inventory; jour - journal; lib - library;

m, mar - marriage; mat - material; mem - memorial; min - minutes; ms - manuscript; mss - manuscripts; mun - municipal; mus - museum; nat - naturalization; navig - navigation; ord - ordinances; Ord - Ordinary; org - organization; par - parish; pre - preliminary; pro - probate; Prot - Protestant; pub - public; publ - published or publisher; RC - Roman Catholic; rec - record; reg - register; rel - religious; rev - revision or revised;

soc - society; stat - statistics; sup - supplementary, supplement or Superior; syn - synagogue; terr - territory; tn - town; tran - transcription; unpubl - unpublished; U or univ - university; US - United States; vit - vital; vol - volume.

Alabama

The first permanent white settlers to establish homes in Alabama came there in 1702, although some historians say 1699. About one hundred seventy four years earlier the Spanish explorers De Narvaes and Cabeza de Vaca passed through the section on their exploration trips. The first white settlers to move into the territory were Spanish and French. They established Mobile in 1702 as the first community.

To evade participation in the Revolutionary War many British sympathizers living in Georgia moved westward into the Alabama section in 1775. They were followed in 1783 by other planters from Georgia, Virginia and the Carolinas. A group of Scotch-Irish who had tried farming in Tennessee in 1809 settled in the northern part of Alabama, in the rich Tennessee Valley district. In the early 1800s former Carolinians and Virginians came into the central part of the territory. Other groups from the same section came to the western part of Alabama along the Tombigbee and the Black Warrior rivers. But it was not until the end of the War of 1812 that Alabama saw a real influx of settlers. The conclusion of that war was the beginning of a gigantic southward and westward movement which resulted in statehood for four territories between 1816 and 1819. Alabama was the last of the four to gain statehood.

Previously the territory of Alabama had been created from the Territory of Mississippi on March 3, 1817. St. Stephens became the capital of the territory. In November 1818 Cahaba, a community existing only in the blue-print stage, with out buildings or a population, was made the capital.

So great had been the influx of people into that south-western section that two years and four months after Alabama had become a Territory a political convention prepared a state constitution. This gathering was held on July 5, 1819 in the temporary state capital, Huntsville, the seat of Madison county, located between the Tennessee River and the southern boundry of the state of Tennessee. Representatives were present from the then existing twenty-two counties of Alabama, namely, Autaga, Baldwin, Blount, Cabela which in 1820 became Biggs, Clarke, Conecuh, Cotaco which in 1821 became Morgan, Dallas, Franklin, Lauderdale, Lawrence, Limestone, Madison, Marengo, Marion, Montgomery, Monroe, St. Clair, Shelby, Tuscaloosa, and Washington.

Alabama officially became a state on December 14, 1819.

The official census reports show the Alabama population to be 127,901 in 1820, 309,527 in 1830, 590,756 in 1840, and 771,623 in 1850. It passed the million mark sometime in the 1870-1880 period, and in 1950 had surpassed the three million mark, of which two-thirds was white. All but eight counties of Alabamas' first census, taken in 1820, has been lost. All other census records are intact. Less than ten thousand of the 1950 population were foreign born, coming mainly from Italy, Germany, England, Russia, and Greece.

At present Alabama has sixty-seven counties.

The Bureau of Vital Statistics, Department of Public Health, Montgomery 4, Alabama, has birth and death records since 1908 and incomplete records prior to 1908. The cost of a certified copy is $1.00, the short form $.50. Similar records prior to 1908 are kept in the office of some county clerks. Marriage records are in counties where the Probate Courts also have old records of deeds and wills. Some Alabama counties have court houses in cities or towns in addition to the county seats. The records in those places must be searched as well as those at the county seat. Undoubtedly the Alabama Department of Archives and History, Montgomery, Alabama, may be able to furnish some information or give directions to other sources.

Although not so large as in some states, the Alabama Department of Archives and History, Montgomery, Alabama, has a considerable collection of genealogy and biography pertaining to the south. Copies of the federal census of Alabama are also deposited there.

Among books dealing with Alabama individuals are the following which can be found in many libraries throughout the nation.

Brewer, Willis: "Alabama, Her History and Public Men, 1872."

Owen, Thomas M., Director Alabama Dept. of Archives and History, "Revolutionary Soldiers in Alabama," 132 pp.

1

Montgomery Ala., The Brown Printing Co., 1911.

Owen, Thomas M. "Our State, Alabama". 1927.

Alabama Society of the SAR, "Roster and Roll of Honor, 1903-1952" (Contains names of 263 Revolutionary Soldiers.)

A partial list of Alabama libraries -- Anniston, (Calhoun), Carnegie Library; Birmingham, (Jefferson), Public Library, 700 N.. 21st St; Florence, (Lauderdale), Muscle Shoals Regional Library, 210 N. Wood Ave.; Gadsden, (Etowah), Public Library, Forest Ave.; Mobile, (Mobile), Public Library, 701 Government St.; Montgomery, (Montgomery), 131 S. Perry St.

Alabama County Histories

(Population figures to nearest thousand -- 1960 Census)

Name	Map Index	Date Formed	Pop. By M	Census Reports Available	Parent County	County Seat
Autauga	D3	1818	19	1830-80	Montgomery	Prattville
(Judge of Pro has m, pro, adpt, and land deed rec)						
Baker (See Chilton)						
Baldwin	F1	1809	49	1820-80	Washington, part of Fla.	Bay Minette
Barbour	D4	1832	25	1840-80	Creek Cession 1812	Clayton & Eufaula
(Judge of Pro has m rec; Clk of cir ct has civ ct rec)						
Benton (see Calhoun)						
Bibb	C2	1818	14	1830-80	Monroe, Montgomery	Centreville
(changed from Cabela 1820)						
Blaine (see Etowa)						
Blount	B3	1818	25	1830-80	Cherokee Cession, Montgomery	Oneonta
Bullock	D4	1866	13	1870-80	Barbour, Macon,	
(Cir ct Clk has div & civ Ct rec)					Montgomery, Pike	Union Springs
Butler	E3	1819	25	1830-80	Conecuh, Montgomery	Greenville
(CH burned April 1853 - Judge of Pro has rec since then).						
Cabela (see Bibb)						
Calhoun	B3	1832	96	1860-80	Creek Cession of 1832	Anniston
(Name changed from Benton Jan 29, 1858)						
Cataco (see Morgan)						
Chambers	C4	1832	38	1840-80	Creek Cession of 1832	La Fayette
Cherokee	B4	1836	16	1840-80	Cherokee Cession 1835	Centre
Chilton	C2	1868	26	1880	Autauga, Bibb, Perry, Shelby	Clanton
(Changed from Baker 1874)						
Choctaw	D1	1847	18	1850-80	Sumter, Washington	Butler
Clarke	E1	1812	26	1830-80	Washington	Grove Hill
Clay	C3	1866	12	1870-80	Randolph, Talladega	Ashland
Cleburne	B4	1866	11	1870-80	Calhoun, Randolph, Talladega	Heflin
Coffee	E3	1841	31	1850-80	Dale	Elba and Enterprise
(Judge of Pro has m rec from 1876, pro rec from 1850)						
Colbert	A1	1867	47	1870-80	Franklin	Tuscumbia
Conecuh	E2	1818	18	1820-80	Monroe	Evergreen
Coosa	C3	1832	11	1840-80	Creek Cession of 1832	Rockford
Cotaco (see Morgan)						
Covington	E3	1821	36	1830-80	Henry	Andalusia
Crenshaw	E3	1866	15	1870-80	Butler, Coffee, Covington,	
					Lowndes, Pike	Luverne
Cullman	B2	1877	46	1880	Blount, Morgan, Winston	Cullman
Dale	E4	1824	31	1830-80	Covington, Henry	Ozark
(Pro Judge has m rec from 1885, pro rec from 1885; Co Clk has civ ct & div rec from 1885; Co Health dept has bur rec)						
Dallas	D2	1818	57	1820-80	Montgomery	Selma
DeKalb	A3	1836	41	1840-80	Cherokee Cession of 1835	Fort Payne
Elmore	C3	1866	31	1870-80	Autauga, Coosa,	
					Montgomery, Tallapoosa	Wetumpka
Escambia	E2	1868	34	1870-80	Baldwin, Conecuh	Brewton
Etowah	B3	1868	97	1870-80	Blount, Calhoun, Cherokee, Dekalb,	
(Changed from Blaine 1868)					Marshall, St. Clair	Gadsden

Fayette   B1   1824   16   1830-80   Marion, Pickens, Tuscaloosa . . . Fayette
Franklin   A1   1818   22   1830-80   Cherokee & Chickasaw
                                             Cession of 1816 . . . . Russellville
   (Co Clk has civ & crim ct rec from 1923; Pro Judge has m & pro rec from 1896)
Geneva   E3   1868   22   1870-80   Dale, Henry, Coffee . . . . Geneva
Greene   C1   1819   14   1830-80   Marengo, Tuscaloosa . . . . Eutaw
Hale   C2   1867   20   1870-80   Greene, Marengo,
                                             Perry, Tuscaloosa . . . . Greensboro
   (Pro Judge has m, div, pro, civ ct, deeds, and mtg rec from 1868)
Hancock (see Winston)
Henry   E4   1819   15   1830-80   Conecuh . . . . Abbeville
Houston   E4   1903   51   Dale, Geneva, Henry . . . . Dothan
Jackson   A3   1819   37   1830-80   Cherokee Cession of 1816 . . . . Scottsboro
Jefferson   B2   1819   635   1830-80   Blount . . . . Birmingham
Jones (see Lamar)
Lamar   B1   1867   14   1880   Marion, Fayette, Pickens . . . Vernon
   (Jones co formed Feb 4 1867, abol Nov 3 1867 & ret to parent cos. Sanford Co
   org Oct 8 1868 from orig Jones, name changed to Lamar 1877. Co Clk has pro
   rec from 1886 and will rec from 1880)

Lauderdale   A1   1818   62   1830-80   Cherokee & Chickasaw
   (Pro Judge has m & pro rec)   Cession in 1816 . . . . Florence
Lawrence   A2   1818   25   1830-80   Cherokee & Chickasaw
                                             Cession 1816 . . . . Moulton
   (Pro Judge has incom b & d rec 1881 to 1912, m, div, pro & deed rec from 1810,
   also cen of Conf sol)
Lee   C4   1866   50   1870-80   Chambers, Macon,
                                             Russell, Tallapoosa . . . . Opelika
Limestone   A2   1818   37   1820-80   Cherokee & Chickasaw
                                             Cession 1816 . . . . Athens
Lowndes   D3   1830   15   1830-80   Butler, Dallas, Montgomery . . . Hayneville
Macon   D4   1832   27   1840-80   Creek Cession of 1832 . . . . . . Tuskegee
Madison   A3   1808   117   1830-80   Cherokee & Chickasaw
                                             Cession 1806-7 . . . . Huntsville
Marengo   D1   1818   27   1830-80   Choctaw Cession of 1816 . . . . . Linden
Marion   B1   1818   22   1830-80   Tuscaloosa . . . . Hamilton
Marshall   A3   1836   48   1840-80   Blount, Cherokee Cession 1835,
                                             Jackson . . . . Guntersville
Mobile   F1   1817   314   1830-80   West Florida . . . . Mobile
   (Clk of pro ct has m rec from 1813, pro rec from 1809 and will books 1 to 44)
Monroe   E2   1815   22   1830-80   Creek Cession 1814,
                                             Washington . . . . Monroeville

Montgomery D3   1816   169   1830-80   Monroe . . . . Montgomery
   (Clk of Bd of Revenue has m & pro rec from 1817, div rec from 1852, deeds &
   mtg from 1817, civ ct rec from 1917)
Morgan   A2   1818   60   1830-80   Cherokee Turkeytown Cession . . . Decatur
   (Name changed from Cotaco 1821. Judge of Pro has m and pro rec from 1818)
Perry   C2   1819   17   1830-80   Montgomery . . . . Marion
Pickens   C1   1820   22   1830-80   Tuscaloosa . . . . Carrollton
Pike   E3   1821   26   1830-80   Henry, Montgomery . . . . Troy
   (Co Clk has m & pro rec from 1830, deeds from 1828)
Randolph   C4   1832   19   1840-80   Creek Cession 1832 . . . . Wedowee
Russell   D4   1832   46   1840-80   Creek Cession 1832 . . . . Phenix City
   (Some rec at Seale)
Sanford (see Lamar)
St. Clair   B3   1818   25   1820-80   Shelby . . . . Pell City
Shelby   C2   1818   32   1820-80   Montgomery . . . . Columbiana
Sumter   C1   1832   20   1840-80   Choctaw Cession of 1830 . . . . Livingston
Talladega   C3   1832   65   1840-80   Creek Cession of 1832 . . . . . . Talladega
Tallapoosa   C4   1832   35   1840-80   Creek Cession of 1832 . . . . . . Dadeville

Tuscaloosa C2 1818 109 1830-80 Cherokee & Choctaw
                              Cesssion 1816 . . . . Tuscaloosa
  (Judge of Pro has m & pro rec from 1823)
Walker B2 1823 54 1830-80 Marion, Tuscaloosa . . . . Jasper
  (Judge of Pro has m & pro rec)
Washington E1 1800 15 1830-80 Mississippi Terr., Baldwin . . . Chatom
Wilcox D2 1819 19 1820-80 Dallas, Monroe . . . . Camden
Winston B2 1850 15 1860-80 Walker . . . . Double Springs
  (Name changed from Hancock 1858)

Note – All 1820 Census records are missing except for eight Counties. More information may be had about this census from the State Archivist, Montgomery, Ala. The eight counties are as follows: Baldwin, Conecuh, Dallas, Franklin, Limestone, St. Clair, Shelby and Wilcox.

County Map of Alabama

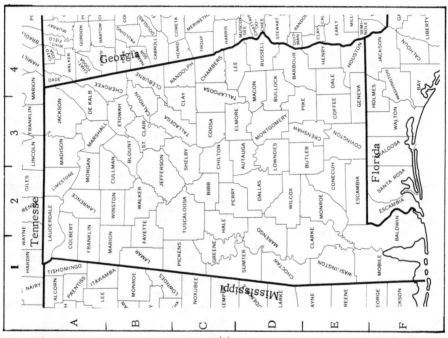

Genealogists' Check List of the Historical Records Survey, Alabama (see page VIII)

Fed Cts; Inv of Co Arch - Clay, Colbert, Conecuh, Cullman, Greene, Hale, Lauderdale, Lowndes, Madison, Marengo, Sumter, Talladega, Wilcox, Winston; Guide to Pub Vit Stat Rec; Guide to Vit Stat Rec - Chr Arch; See La for navig casualties; Inv of chr arch of Ala - Prot Episcopal Chr; Check List of Ala Imprints, 1807-1840; Depo of unpub mat, Dept of Arch & Hist, Montgomery, Ala.

Alaska

Capital, Juneau - Territory 1912 - State 1959 (49th)

Alaska was purchased from Russia 30 March 1867. At first a district (or unorganized territory), then a Territory in 1912 and a state in 1959. The first federal census was taken in 1880.

First Judicial Dist. . . . . Juneau
Second Judicial Dist. . . . . Nome
Third Judicial Dist. . . . . Anchorage
Fourth Judicial Dist. . . . . . . Fairbanks

Arizona

The first white people to come to Arizona were attracted there by the tale of the fabulous "Seven Cities of Cibola" which they had heard time and again in Mexico City. As early as 1539 the first European explorer came into the region but it was about one hundred fifty years later before Catholic missions were started among the Indians. Tucson became a village about the time the American colonies along the Atlantic coast were fighting their mother country in the Revolutionary War. As a section of New Mexico, Arizona came under the ownership and guidance of Mexico in 1821.

At the close of the Mexican War in 1848, a new dispute arose relative to the ownership of a tract of land at the international border. To alleviate any further difficulties the United States minister to Mexico, James Gadsen, negotiated a deal very unpopular in Mexico, by which the United States paid ten million dollars for slightly less than 50,000 square miles of land, lying south of the Gila River and extending east from the California border to the Rio Grande River.

From the beginning the new territory attracted very few settlers. In 1870, seven years after Arizona became an organized territory, the entire state held less than ten thousand residents. In the forty year period that followed the Arizona population increased twenty fold, and the following half century more than trebled the 1910 population. The 1950 census placed Arizona with three quarters of a million inhabitants. Since then Arizona stands in the foremost ranks among the states with the highest growth percentage.

The foreign born population of Arizona comes in the following order: Mexico, Canada, England and Wales, Germany, Russia, Italy, Poland, Austria, Sweden, Greece, Ireland, Scotland, Yugoslavia, and Czechoslovakia.

Since 1850 many Mormon families from Utah have settled in Arizona. In fact, in several large agricultural districts, the Mormon population predominates.

Established in July 1909, the Division of Records and Statistics, State Department of Health, Phoenix, Arizona has birth and death records available since that date, and also similar records originating in the county seats since 1887.

Marriage records are on file with the Clerk of the Superior Court of county in which the license was issued.

Divorce actions are maintained by the Clerk of the Superior Court in county seat where the action was granted.

Citizenship or naturalization papers are filed in the district court of the county where examination was conducted; also in the office of the clerk of the United States district courts in Tucson, Tombstone, Phoenix, Prescott, and Solomonville.

All real estate records are on file in the office of the recorder of the county in which the land is located.

The 1850 and the 1860 census of Arizona were taken as part of New Mexico. A territorial census of 1864 is in the office of the Secretary of State in the capitol in Phoenix.

The best collection of Arizona history is at the Arizona State Department of Library and Archives in Phoenix at 309 Capitol Building where microfilm facilities are obtainable. No research is done by staff members. Other libraries with considerable Arizona and southwest history are in the Arizona State College Library, the Flagstaff Public Library and the Museum of Northern Arizona Library, PO Box 402, all of Flagstaff, Arizona; the Maricopa County Free Public Library 831 North First Ave., Phoenix; The Arizona Pioneers' Historical Society Library, University Stadium, Tucson, and the Genealogical Library, LDS Temple, Mesa. Names of professional researchers may be obtained from the latter if a self-addressed, stamped envelope is enclosed.

Among books of value to the researcher are the following:

American Guide Series (1940) "Arizona, a State Guide," gives bibliography on works on Arizona. Bancroft, Hubert Howe, "History of Arizona and New Mexico," (San Francisco 1889). Farish, Thomas E., "History of Arizona," 8 vols., (San Francisco 1915). McClintock, James Harvey, "Arizona, Prehistoric, Aboriginal, Pioneer, Modern," 3 vols., (Chicago 1916). Lockwood, Francis Cummins, "Pioneer Days in Arizona," (New York 1932).

A partial list of Arizona libraries. Flagstaff, (Coconino), Public Library, 212 W. Aspen; Mesa, (Maricopa), Public Library; Phoenix, (Maricopa), County Free

Public Library, 831 N. 1st Ave.; Prescott, Carnegi᷄ Free Library, 200 S. 6th Ave.
(Yavapai), Public Library; Tucson, (Pima)

Arizona County Histories

(Population figures to nearest thousand – 1960 Census)

Name	Map Index	Date Formed	Pop. By M	Census Reports Available	Parent County	County Seat
Apache	B4	1872	30	1880	Mohave	St. Johns
Cochise	F4	1881	55		Pima	Bisbee
Coconino	B3	1891	42		Yavapai	Flagstaff
Gila	D3	1881	26		Maricopa, Pinal	Globe

County Map of Arizona

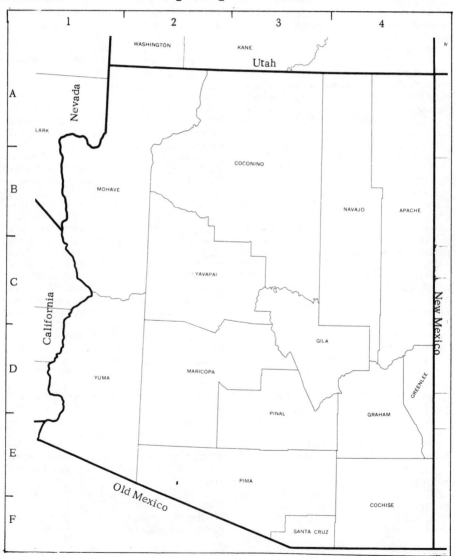

Graham	D4	1881	14		Apache, Pima	Safford
(Clk of Sup Ct has m, div, pro, and civ ct rec; Registrar of Vit Sta has b & d rec)

Greenlee	D4	1909	12		Graham	Clifton
Maricopa	D2	1871	664	1880	Yavapai, Yuma	Phoenix
Mohave	B1	1864	8	1870-80	Original county	Kingman

(Co Clk has m, div, pro and civ ct rec; Bureau of Vit Sta has b & d rec)

Navajo	B4	1895	38		Apache	Holbrook

(Clk of Sup Ct has m, div, pro and civ ct rec)

Pah Ute (disolved 1895 returned to Mohave)

Pima	E3	1864	266	1870-80	Original county	Tucson
Pinal	D3	1875	63	1880	Pima	Florence
Santa Cruz	F3	1899	11		Pima	Nogales
Yavapai	C2	1864	29	1870	Original county	Prescott

(Clk of Sup Ct has m, div, pro and civ ct rec)

Yuma	D1	1864	46	1870	Original county	Yuma

(Co Clk has m, div, pro and civ ct rec from 1863)

Additional U. S. Census Data: For the 1850 and the 1860 census figures of the following, see New Mexico: Bernalillo, Rio Arriba, Santa Ana, Soccoro, and Valencia.

Genealogists' Check List of the Historical Records Survey, Arizona (see page VIII)

Fed Cts (start 1912); Inv of Co Arch - Maricopa, Pima, Santa Cruz; 1864 Cen of Terr; Guide to Pub Vit Stat Rec; Dir of Chr. and Rel Org; Private Jour of George White-well Parsons; Jour of the Pioneer and Walker Dists; Check List of Ariz Imprints 1860-1890; Dist Cts of the Terr of Ariz 1864-1912; Depo of unpubl mat, Ariz State Lib & Arch, Phoenix, Ariz.

Arkansas

Capital Little Rock - Territory 1817 - State 1836 - (25th)

The Indians had free reign in Arkansas until after the United States completed negotiations with the French for the Louisiana Purchase in 1803. Off and on during the previous two hundred sixty two years several French explorers had come to the region with their parties in search of whatever loot they could find. They came today and were gone tomorrow.

With the land in the ownership of the United States it was immediately thrown open for settlement at attractive low prices. The new opportunities beckoned thousands of earlier settlers of the mideast and south-east sections. The first comers were mainly of English, Irish and Scottish stock. Many moved into the new section from nearby Kentucky and Tennessee.

What is now Arkansas became part of the Missouri Territory in 1812. When Missouri applied for statehood in 1819 Congress created the Arkansas Territory included in which was what is now Oklahoma. On June 15, 1836 Arkansas became the twenty-fifth state in the union.

When the Panic of 1837 drained most of the settlers in the older southern and eastern states many of them set out for the newly created state on the west to make a new start in life. Thirty years later the rich lands between the Arkansas and the White Rivers attracted large groups of South European emigrants. Many came direct from Poland to establish themselves in Pulaski County. Italians were attracted to the northwest section of the state where they engaged in fruit raising.

Lawrence County, in the northeast corner of the state, and Arkansas County, in the southeast corner, were settled before most of the other counties in the state.

The Bureau of Vital Statistics, State Health Department, State Health Bldg., Little Rock, Arkansas, has birth and death records from 1914 and marriage records from 1917. Clerks of counties where license was obtained also have marriage records. The County Clerks or the Clerks of Circuit Courts also have records of wills, deeds, divorces, and war service. Naturalization records are on file in the District Courts at Little Rock, Helena, Batesville, Fort Smith, and Texarkana.

All Arkansas federal census since 1830 are available. The 1820 census was also taken in the Arkansas Territory but the schedules are missing.

A continuously expanding collection of early Arkansas history and genealogy is to be found in the Public Library, 700 Louisiana Street, Little Rock. Other Arkansas collections are at the Carnegie City Library, 318 North 13th Street Fort Smith; Arkansas Agricultural, Mechanical and Normal College Library, Pine Bluff; Garland County Public Library, 200 Woodbine, Hot Springs; The University of Arkansas Library, Fayetteville, and the Arkansas History Commission, Little Rock.

State Land Office, State Capitol Bldg, has original plats of U. S. Government surveys of Arkansas and original field notes, also books showing original entries by Township and Range.

Among important books dealing with Arkansas and her people are the following: Josiah Shinn's "Pioneers and Makers of Arkansas," 1908 (recognized in some circles as the most valuable historical record of the state); David Y. Thomas' "Arkansas and Its People," 4 vols. (last two biographical), New York, 1931; Arkansas Historical Association's "Arkansas Historical Quarterly," Fayetteville 1942- ; W. F. Pope, "Early Days in Arkansas," 1895; similar to this in popular character, vast in bulk and loose in method, are the "Biographical and Pictorial Histories," covering the different sections of the state, (one volume by J. Hallum in 1887, four others compiled anoymously. 1889-1891.)

A partial list of Arkansas libraries – Fayetteville, (Washington), County Library, Court House; Hot Springs, (Garland), County Public Library, 200 Woodbine; Little Rock, (Pulaski), Public Library, 700 Louisiana St.; Pine Bluff, (Jefferson), County Public Library, 219 W. Fifth Ave.

Arkansas County Histories

(Population figures to nearest thousand - 1960 Census)

Name	Map Index	Date Formed	Pop. By M	Census Reports Available	Parent County	County Seat
Arkansas	C3	1813	23	1830-80	Original county	Stuttgart & De Witt

(Co Clk has pro rec from 1809, m rec from 1838; Cir Clk has div & civ ct rec from 1803, War ser discharge from 1917)

Name	Map Index	Date Formed	Pop. By M	Census Reports Available	Parent County	County Seat
Ashley	D3	1848	24	1850-80	Union, Drew	Hamburg
Baxter	A2	1873	10	1880	Fulton, Izard, Marion & Searcy	Mountain Home
Benton	A1	1836	36	1840-80	Washington	Bentonville
Boone	A2	1869	16	1870-80	Carrol, Madison	Harrison

(Co Clk has m & pro rec from 1869)

Name	Map Index	Date Formed	Pop. By M	Census Reports Available	Parent County	County Seat
Bradley	D3	1840	14	1850-80	Union	Warren
Calhoun	D2	1850	6	1860-80	Dallas, Ouachita	Hampton

(Co Clk has m, div, pro, civ ct rec)

Name	Map Index	Date Formed	Pop. By M	Census Reports Available	Parent County	County Seat
Carroll	A1	1833	11	1840-80	Izard	Berryville & Eureka Springs
Chicot	D3	1823	19	1830-80	Arkansas	Lake Village

(Co Clk has m & pro rec from 1839; Cir Clk has civ ct rec from 1824)

Name	Map Index	Date Formed	Pop. By M	Census Reports Available	Parent County	County Seat
Clark	C2	1818	21	1830-80	Arkansas	Arkadelphia
Clay	A4	1873	21	1880	Randolph, Green	Corning & Pigott

(Co Clk has m, div, pro, civ ct rec from 1893)

Name	Map Index	Date Formed	Pop. By M	Census Reports Available	Parent County	County Seat
Cleburne	B3	1883	9		White, Van Buren, Independence	Heber Springs
Cleveland	C2	1873	7	1880	Dallas, Bradley, Jefferson, Lincoln	Rison

(Changed from Dorsey 5 March 1885)

Name	Map Index	Date Formed	Pop. By M	Census Reports Available	Parent County	County Seat
Columbia	D2	1852	26	1860-80	Lafayette, Hempstead, Ouachita .	Magnolia
Conway	B2	1825	15	1830-80	Pulaski	Morrilton

(Co Clk has incom m rec from 1851, pro rec from 1846; Cir clk has div rec from 1842, civ ct rec from 1865, Deed rec from 1825, will rec from 1861)

Name	Map Index	Date Formed	Pop. By M	Census Reports Available	Parent County	County Seat
Craighead	A4	1859	47	1860-80	Mississippi, Greene, Poinsett . .	Jonesboro and Lake City

(Co Clk has m, co ct & pro rec from 1878)

Name	Map Index	Date Formed	Pop. By M	Census Reports Available	Parent County	County Seat
Crawford	B1	1820	21	1830-80	Pulaski	Van Buren

(Co Clk has m, div, pro, civ ct and crim ct rec 1883 for eastern dist of co only)

Name	Map Index	Date Formed	Pop. By M	Census Reports Available	Parent County	County Seat
Crittenden	B4	1825	48	1830-80	Phillips	Marion
Cross	B4	1862	20	1870-80	Crittenden, Poinsett, St. Francis . . .	Wynne
Dallas	C2	1845	11	1850-80	Clark, Bradley	Fordyce
Desha	C3	1838	21	1840-80	Arkansas	Arkansas City
Dorsey (see Cleveland)						

Drew   D3 1846 15 1850-80 Arkansas, Bradley .... Monticello
Faulkner   B2 1873 24 1880   Pulaski, Conway .... Conway
(Co Clk has m, pro, co ct rec from 1873)
Franklin   B1 1837 10 1840-80 Crawford ...... Charleston and Ozark
Fulton   A3 1842   7 1850-80 Izard .... Salem
(Part attached from Fulton 1855)
Garland   C2 1873 47 1880   Montgomery, Hotsprings,
                                   Saline .... Hot Springs N.P.
Grant   C2 1869   8 1870-80 Jefferson, Hotsprings, Saline .. Sheridan
Greene   A4 1833 25 1840-80 Lawrence .... Paragould
Hempstead   D1 1818 20 1830-80 Arkansas .... Hope
Hot Springs C2 1829 22 1830-80 Clark .... Malvern
(Co Clk has m & pro rec from 1845; Cir Clk has div & civ ct rec)
Howard   C1 1873 11 1880   Pike, Hempstead, Polk, Sevier .. Nashville
Independence A3 1820 20 1830-80 Lawrence, Arkansas .... Batesville
(Co Clk has M & pro rec from 1824)
Izard   A3 1825   7 1830-80 Independence .... Melbourne
(Line between Izard & Sharp changed 9 Mar 1877. Co Clk has m, div, pr, civ ct
rec from 1889)
Jackson   B3 1829 23 1830-80 Woodruff .... Newport
(Co Clk has m rec 1846, pro rec 1845; Cir Clk has div & civ ct rec from 1845)
Jefferson   C3 1829 81 1830-80 Arkansas, Pulaski .... Pine Bluff
Johnson   B2 1833 12 1840-80 Pope .... Clarksville
(Co Clk has m rec from 1855, div & civ ct rec from 1865, pro rec from 1844,
Deed books from 1836, and will rec from 1844)
Lafayette   D1 1827 11 1830-80 Hempstead .... Lewisville
Lawrence   A3 1815 17 1830-80 New Madrid, Mo. .... Powhatan
                                                       Walnut Ridge (1)
Lee   C4 1873 21 1880   Phillips, Monroe, Crittenden,
(Co Clk has m & pro rec from 1873) St. Francis .... Marianna
Lincoln   C3 1871 14 1880   Arkansas, Bradley, Desha, Drew,
                                   Jefferson .... Star City
(Co Clk has m, pro, and tax rec from 1871)
Little River D1 1867   9 1870-80 Hempstead .... Ashdown
Logan   B1 1871 16 1880   Pope, Franklin, Johnson, Scott,
                                   Yell .... Booneville & Paris (1)
Lonoke   B3 1873 25 1880   Pulaski, Prarire .... Lonoke
Lovely   1827   Abolished 1828
Madison   A1 1836   9 1840-80 Washington .... Huntsville
Marion   A2 1836   6 1840-80 Izard .... Yellville
Miller   D1 1820 32 1880   Abolished 1836 & ret to Arkansas
                                   Re-established 1874 ...... Texarkana
Mississippi A4 1833 70 1840-80 Crittenden ...... Blytheville & Osceola
Monroe   C3 1829 17 1830-80 Phillips, Arkansas .... Clarendon
(Co Clk has m rec from 1851 and pro rec from 1830; Cir Clk has div rec from
1851, Civ ct rec from 1830)
Montgomery C1 1842   5 1850-80 Hotsprings .... Mount Ida
Nevada   D2 1871 11 1880   Hempstead, Columbia, Ouachita . Prescott
(Co Clk has m, div, pro & Civ ct rec from 1871)
Newton   A2 1842   6 1850-80 Carroll .... Jasper
(Co Clk has m rec from 1867, Deed rec from 1870)
Ouachita   D2 1842 32 1850-80 Union .... Camden
Perry   B2 1840   5 1850-80 Conway .... Perryville
(Co Clk has m, div, pro, & civ ct rec from 1884)
Phillips   C4 1820 44 1830-80 Arkansas, Hempstead .... Helena
Pike   C1 1833   8 1840-80 Clark, Hempstead .... Murfreesboro
(Co Clk has m, div, pro & civ ct rec from 1895)
Poinsett   B4 1838 31 1840-80 Greene, St. Francis ..... . Harrisburg
Polk   C1 1844 12 1850-80 Sevier .... Mena
(Co Clk has m rec from 1887, pro rec from 1889, & Co ct rec from 1873; Cir Clk
has div rec from 1907, Crim ct rec from 1873, & deed rec from 1882)
Pope   B2 1829 21 1830-80 Crawford .... Russellville
(Co Clk has m & pro rec from 1835)

Prairie   B3   1846   11   1850–80   Pulaski ...... Des Arc & De Valls Bluff
Pulaski   C3   1818   243   1830–80   Arkansas .... Little Rock
   (Co Clk has m rec from 1838, pro rec from 1840, will rec from 1820, civ ct rec
   from 1846; Cir Clk has deed rec from 1820)
Randolph   A3   1835   13   1840–80   Lawrence .... Pocahontas
   (Co Clk has m & pro rec from 1836, div rec from 1841)
St. Francis   B4   1827   33   1830–80   Phillips .... Forrest City
Saline   C2   1835   29   1840–80   Pulaski, Hempstead .... Benton
Scott   B1   1833   7   1840–80   Pulaski, Crawford, Pope .... Waldron
   (Co Clk has m, div, pro & civ ct rec from 1882)
Searcy   A2   1838   8   1840–80   Marion .... Marshall
   (Co Clk has m, div, pro & civ ct rec from 1881, deed rec from 1866)
Sebastian   B1   1851   67   1860–80   Scott, Polk .... Fort Smith & Greenwood
Sevier   C1   1828   10   1830–80   Hempstead, Miller .... De Queen
   (Co Clk has m rec from 1839, pro rec from 1830)
Sharp   A3   1868   6   1870–80   Lawrence ..... Evening Shade & Hardy
   (Line between Sharp & Izard changed 1877)
Stone   A3   1873   6   1880   Izard, Independence, Searcy,
                                           Van Buren .... Mountain View
   (Co Clk has m, div, pro & civ ct rec from 1873)
Union   D2   1829   50   1830–80   Hempstead, Clark .... El Dorado
   (Co Clk has m rec from 1864, also Co ct rec)
Van Buren   B2   1833   7   1840–80   Independence, Conway, Izard ... Clinton
Washington   A1   1828   56   1830–80   Crawford .... Fayetteville
White   B3   1835   33   1840–80   Pulaski, Jackson .... Searcy
Woodruff   B3   1862   14   1870–80   Jackson, St. Francis ...... Augusta
   (Co Clk has m & pro rec from 1865)
Yell   B2   1840   12   1850–80   Pope, Scott ... Danville & Dardanelle (1)

County Map of Arkansas

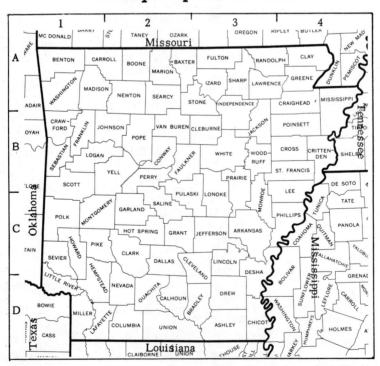

Genealogists' Check List of the Historical Records Survey, Arkansas (see page VIII)

Fed Cts (start 1819); Inv of Co Arch - Baxter, Benton, Carroll, Cleburne, Cleveland, Cross, Faulkner, HotSprings, Izard, Jackson, Madison, Monroe, Montgomery, Polk, Saline, Scott, Searcy; Guide to Vit Stat Rec - Chr Arch; Inv of the Chr Arch of Ark, Chr of Christ Scientists; Dir of Chr & Religious Org; Check list of Ark Imprints, 1821-1876; Union list of Ark Newspapers, 1819-1942, a partial inv of Ark newspaper files available in offices of publs, lib and private col; Depo of unpub mat, Univ of Ark Lib, Fayetteville, Ark.

California

Capital Sacramento - State 1850 - (31st)

Various expeditions from Mexico, Spain, Russia and England visited California from 1540 to 1792. Spain controlled until 1822 when Mexico came into possession and held power until 1848. It then ceded California to the United States. The fever that struck all sections of the United States and every country of Europe with the finding of gold at Sutter's Mill brought people to California from all parts of the world. The Gold Rush increased the population from 15,000 to 250,000. In 1957 the population was more than eleven million. About one tenth of the population is foreign born.

The foreign born residents of California, listed in point of numbers, originated in the following countries: Mexico, Canada, Italy, England & Wales, Russia, Germany, Sweden, Ireland, Scotland, Poland, Austria, France, Denmark, Norway, Switzerland, Portugal, Greece, Yugoslavia, Hungary, Netherlands, Spain, Finland, Czechoslovakia, Rumania, Lithuania, and Belgium. Records of births and deaths since 1905 on record in office of the Bureau of Records and Statistics. State Department of Health, 631 J. Street, Sacramento, Calif. Many of the health offices of the larger cities have similar records prior to July 1, 1905, as have also the recorders of the various counties, or the county clerks. The Department of Health in San Francisco has early death and cemetery records.

The Bureau of Records and Statistics, address as above, and all County Clerks have records of marriage licences issued in the respective counties.

Divorce records are available in the office of the Clerk of the Superior Court in the county in which the proceedings were conducted.

Many of the County Recorders have early birth and marriage records. County Clerks have divorce, probate, civil court and other records of interest to genealogists.

Naturalization records are kept in the county offices of the Superior Courts, and also in the United States Circuit Courts in Los Angeles and San Francisco.

Deeds for real estate and lands are filed in the office of the County Recorder in the county in which the land concerned is located.

A communication from the Chief of the Bureau of Records and Statistics and the Chief of the Vital Records Section of the Department of Public Health says, "In the case of a request for a search for an unknown event, we require a fee of $1.00 (may be more now) per hour of search, paid in advance. An example of this kind of a record search is when a person was last known to be alive on a given date, and we are asked to search for a death record of the person from that date forward.

"There are certain items of information which we require in order to make a search of our records. These items vary with the type of record sought and the time period involved.

'As we now have over ten million records on file, duplication of names is common. It is therefore desirable that secondary identifying data be furnished."

The largest genealogical library on the west coast is that of the Public Library, 630 West Fifth Street, Los Angeles 17. No research is done by staff members. The next largest genealogical collection on the coast is found in the Sutro Branch of the California State Library. Other California libraries may borrow books from the Sutro Branch for their clients. Names of professional genealogists may be obtained from the library in question if inquiry is made in writing and a self addressed, stamped envelope is enclosed.

Other valuable genealogical collections are located in California Genealogical Society Library, 2029 Pacific Ave., San Francisco 9; California Historical Society

Library 2090 Jackson St., San Francisco, 9; Society of Mayflower Descendants Library, 926 DeYoung Bldg., 690 Market St., San Francisco 4; Society of California Pioneers Library, 456 McAllister St., San Francisco 2; Sons of the American Revolution Library, 926-928 de Young Bldg., 690 Market St., San Francisco 4; Swedish American Hall Library, 2174 Market St., San Francisco 14; Stockton and San Joaquin County Library, Market and Hunter Sts., Stockton 4: Public Library, 2090 Kittredge St., Berkeley 4; General Library, University of California, Berkeley 4; Public Library, 425 E. Olive Ave., Burbank; County Library, 322 S. Broadway Los Angeles 13; Library, University of California at Los Angeles, 405 Hilgard Ave., Los Angeles 24; Public Library,

659 - 14th St., Oakland 12; Public Library, Hamilton at Bryant, Palo Alto; State Library, Sacramento 9; County Free Public Library, 364 Mt. View Ave., San Bernardino; Whittier College Library, Whittier; Long Beach Public Library, Long Beach; Sons of Revolution, Hope St., Los Angeles.

Books on California: H. H. Bancroft, "History of California 1542-1890," 7 vols., San Francisco 1884-90; T. H. Hittell "History of California," 4 vols., San Francisco 1885-97; C. E. Chapman, "A History of California," The Spanish Period," New York, 1921; J. W. Caughey, "California," New York 1940; R. G. Cleland, "From Wilderness to Empire," New York 1944; R. G. Cleland, "California in Our Time," New York 1847; State of California, Secretary of State, "California Blue Book," Sacramento, irregularly.

California County Histories

(Population figures to nearest thousand - 1960 Census)

Name	Map Index	Date Formed	Pop. By M	Census Reports Available	Parent County	County Seat
Alameda	C2	1853	906	1860-80	ContraCosta & Santa Clara ...	Oakland
Alpine	C2	1864	397	1870-80	Eldorado, Amador, Calaveras .	Markleeville
Amador	C2	1854	10	1860-80	Calaveras	Jackson
Butte	B2	1850	82	1850-80	Original county	Oroville
Calaveras	C2	1850	10	1850-80	Original county	San Andreas
Colusa	C2	1850	12	1850-80	Original county	Colusa
Contra Costa	C2	1850	409	1860-80	Original county	Martinez
Del Norte	A1	1857	18	1860-80	Klamath	Crescent City
El Dorado	C2	1850	29	1850-80	Original county	Placerville & Rescue
Fresno	D2	1856	366	1860-80	Merced, Mariposa	Fresno
(Co Rec has b, d & bur rec from 1900, m, div, pro & civ ct rec from 1860)						
Glenn	B2	1891	17		Colusa	Willows
Humboldt	B1	1853	105	1860-80	Trinity	Eureka
Imperial	G4	1907	72		San Diego	El Centro
(Co Rec has b, m, d rec from 1907; Co Clk has div, pro & civ ct rec from 1907)						
Inyo	E3	1866	12	1870-80	Tulare	Independence
(Co Clk has div, pro & civ ct rec from 1866)						
Kern	E3	1866	292	1870-80	Tulare, Los Angeles	Bakersfield
(Co Clk has div, pro & civ ct rec from 1866; Co Rec has b, m & d rec)						
Kings	E2	1893	50		Tulare, Fresno	Hanford
(Co Clk has div, pro, civ ct, crim, Juvenile, and voting reg from 1893; Co Rec has b, m, & d rec from 1893)						
Lake	C1	1861	14	1870-80	Napa	Lakeport
Lassen	B2	1864	14	1870-80	Plumas, Shasta	Susanville
Los Angeles	F3	1850	6039	1850-80	Original county	Los Angeles
(Co Rec has b, m, & d rec from 1875)						
Madera	D2	1893	40		Fresno	Madera
Marin	C1	1850	147	1850-80	Original county	San Rafael
Mariposa	D2	1850	5	1850-80	Original county	Mariposa
Mendocino	B1	1850	51	1850-80	Original county	Ukiah
(Co Clk has m rec 1893, div rec 1880, pro rec 1859, civ ct rec 1880)						
Merced	D2	1855	90	1860-80	Mariposa	Merced
Modoc	A3	1874	8	1880	Siskiyou	Alturas

Mono   D3   1861   2   1870–80 Calaveras, Fresno . . . . Bridgeport
(Co Clk has b & d rec from 1925, m rec from 1861, div rec from 1880, & pro &
civ ct rec from 1875)
Monterey   D2   1850   198   1850–80 Original county . . . . Salinas

County Map of California

Napa   C2   1850   66   1850-80   Original county . . . .   Napa
(Co Clk has div, pro, civ ct rec from 1850)
Nevada   C2   1851   21   1860-80   Yuba . . . .   Nevada City
Orange   F3   1889   704   Los Angeles . . . .   Santa Ana
Placer   C2   1851   57   1860-80   Yuba, Sutter . . . .   Auburn
Plumas   B2   1854   12   1860-80   Butte . . . .   Quincy
(Co Clk has div, pro, & civ ct rec from 1860)
Riverside   F4   1893   306   San Diego, San Bernardino . . Riverside
(Co Clk has div, pro & civ ct rec from 1893; Co Rec has b, m & d rec from 1893)
Sacramento   C2   1850   503   1850-80   Original county . . . .   Sacramento
San Benito   D2   1874   15   1880   Monterey . . . .   Hollister
San Bernardino F4 1853   504   1860-80   Los Angeles . . . . Mentone & San Bernardino
(Co Clk has m lic rec from 1887, div & pro rec from 1856, Civ & crim ct rec
from 1853, Insanity & Inebriate rec from 1887, Guardianship rec from 1856)
San Diego   G3   1850 1033   1850-80   Original county . . . .   San Diego
(Co Clk has div, pro & civ ct rec from 1855)
San Francisco Cl 1850   743   1860-80   Original county . . . .   San Francisco
San Joaquin   C2   1850   250   1850-80   Original county . . . .   Stockton
(Co Clk has div, pro & civ ct rec 1850, Art of Inc & Naturalization rec 1851)
San Luis Obispo E2 1850   81   1850-80   Original county . . . . San Luis Obispo
                                                                          & Templeton
San Mateo   D1   1856   444   1860-80   San Francisco . . . .   Redwood City
(Co Clk has div, pro & civ ct rec from 1856)
Santa Barbara E2   1850   169   1850-80   Original county . . . .   Santa Barbara
Santa Clara   D2   1850   642   1860-80   Original county . . . .   San Jose
Santa Cruz   D1   1850   84   1850-80   Original county . . . .   Santa Cruz
(Co rec has b & d rec 1873, m rec 1852; Co Clk has div, pro & civ ct rec 1850)
Shasta   B2   1850   59   1850-80   Original county . . . .   Redding
Sierra   C2   1852   2   1860-80   Yuba . . . .   Downieville
(Co Clk has b, m, d, div, pro & civ ct rec from 1852)
Siskiyou   A2   1852   33   1860-80   Shasta, Klamath . . . .   Yreka
(Co Clk has div, pro & civ ct rec from 1852)
Solano   C2   1850   135   1850-80   Original county . . . .   Fairfield
Sonoma   C1   1850   147   1850-80   Original county . . . .   Santa Rosa
Stanislaus   D2   1854   157   1860-80   Tuolumne . . . .   Modesto
(Co Clk has div, pro & civ ct rec from 1854)
Sutter   C2   1850   33   1850-80   Original county . . . .   Yuba City
(Co Clk has div, pro & civ ct rec from 1850)
Tehama   C2   1856   25   1860-80   Colusa, Butte, Shasta . . . . . Red Bluff
Trinity   B1   1850   10   1860-80   Original county . . . .   Weaverville
(Co Clk has b, m, d, div, pro & civ ct rec from 1890)
Tulare   E2   1852   168   1860-80   Mariposa . . . .   Visalia
(Co Clk has div, pro & civ ct rec from 1852)
Tuolumne   C2   1850   14   1850-80   Original county . . . .   Sonora
(Co Clk has div, pro, civ ct rec from 1850, voting reg from 1866; Co Rec has m
rec from 1850, d rec from 1857)
Ventura   F2   1872   199   1880   Santa Barbara . . . .   Ventura
                                                                          (San Buenaventura)
(Co Clk has div, pro and civ ct rec from 1873)
Yolo   C2   1850   66   1850-80   Original county . . . .   Woodland
(Co Clk has div, pro & civ ct rec from 1850)
Yuba   C2   1850   34   1850-80   Original county . . . .   Marysville
(Co Clk has m rec from 1865, div, pro & civ ct rec from 1850, Voting rec 1866)

Genealogists' Check List of the Historical Records Survey, California (see page VIII)

Fed Cts (Start 1850); Ship Reg and Enrolments Port of Eureka, 1859-1920; Inv of Co Arch - Alameda, Fresno, Kern, Los Angeles (4 Vol), Marin, Mono, Napa, San Benito, San Bernardino, San Diego, San Francisco, San Luis Obispo, San Mateo, Santa Barbara, Santa Clara, Ventura; Guide to Pub Vital Rec, Vol 1 Births, Vol 2 Deaths; Guide to Chr Vit Stat Rec, Six Denominations; Dir of Chr & Rel Org in Alameda Co, San Francisco, Los Angeles Co, San Diego Co; Cal of the Major Rink Snyder Col of

Mss Col in the US, Calif; Cal of the Montana Papers in the William Andrews Clark Mem Lib, U of C at Los Angeles; Cal of the Francis Bret Harte Letters in the William Andrews Clark Mem Lib, U of C at Los Angeles; Inv of the Bixby Col in the Palos Verdes Lib and Art Gallery; List of the letters and Mss of Musicians in the William Andrews Clark Mem Lib U of C at Los Angeles; List of the Letters and Doc of Rulers and Statesmen in the William Andrews Clark Mem Lib, U of C at Los Angeles; Check List of Calif Non-Documentary Imprints, 1853-1855; Depo of unpubl mat, State Arch (No. Calif mat), Sacramento, & Los Angeles Co Mus (So. Calif mat), Los Angeles,

Colorado

Capital Denver - Territory 1861 - State 1876 - (38th)

Dr. LeRoy R. Hafen, for many years executive director of the State Historical Society of Colorado and the author of several works on Colorado, says, "Colorado was named for the great river that raises in the snowbanks of her western slope. The musical Spanish word meaning 'red' was bestowed on the river by Spanish explorers a century before it was applied to Colorado Territory."

Early Spanish explorers who came to Mexico heard the natives tell exciting tales of cities of gold and silver to the northward. To find the precious metals many of these fortune hunters pressed northward, some of them coming into sections of the present New Mexico, Arizona, Utah, and Colorado. Some of these adventurers were the first white men to see the Grand Canyon of the Colorado, the Rio Grande Valley, and other sections of the Rocky Mountain Territory. Escalante the Catholic priest who tried to find a short cut from Santa Fe to the Pacific Coast, came through there on his unsuccessful trip in the summer of 1776.

About fifty years later these sections swarmed with competing trappers and fur traders working for the various large fur companies of eastern United States and Canada.

The real settlers of Colorado didn't come until 1858, thus making the state the last to be occupied by permanent settlers. Many of the first-comers were attracted there by the discovery of gold and other metals. Not too successful in their fortune hunt, they turned to the land and the ranges for their livelihood.

The territory of Jefferson was voted by the residents in 1859 but was never recognized by congress. Thus some of the counties have organization dates and records prior to 28 February 1861 when the Territory of Colorado was recognized.

The 1860 Census showed a population of about 33,000 men, and 1,500 women. This was taken when Colorado was still a part of Kansas.

Colorado was admitted to statehood August 1, 1876. It was called the Centennial State because it became part of the union 100 years after the formation of the United States.

The first territorial assembly created the first 17 counties in September 1861. They were Arapahoe, Boulder, Clear Creek, Costilla, Douglas, El Paso, Fremont, Gilpin, Guadalupe (later named Conejos), Huerfano, Jefferson, Lake, Larimer, Park, Pueblo, Summit and Weld.

A few birth records before January 1907 may be obtained from the respective county clerks, after January 1907 from the State Bureau of Vital Statistics, Denver, Colo.

A few death records before January 1900 may be obtained at the office of the county clerks, after January 1900 at the Bureau of Vital Statistics.

Marriage records are kept by the county clerks. Marriages were not recorded generally until after 1881, but some counties have marriage records as early as 1860.

Probate matters and wills are on file in the office of the county clerk.

All land titles, deeds, mortgages, leases, etc. are kept by the county recorder.

An efficient and congenial staff of librarians is ready to assist all researchers in the rapidly growing genealogical section of the Public Library, 1357 Broadway, Denver 3. Rocky Mountain region history and lore is available at the university of Colorado Library, Boulder; Public Library, 21 W. Kiowa St., Colorado Springs; McClelland Public Library, 100 Abriendo Ave., Pueblo. Information regarding professional researchers may be obtained by sending self-addressed envelopes to libraries.

Colorado County Histories

(Population figures to nearest thousand – 1960 Census)

Name	Map Index	Date Formed	Pop. By M	Census Reports Available	Parent County	County Seat
Adams	B2	1902	120		Arapahoe	Brighton
Alamosa	D4	1913	10		Costilla, Conejos	Alamosa

(Co Clk has m & land title rec from 1913)

Arapahoe	C2	1861	113	1870-80	Original county	Littleton

(First formed in 1855 as Territorial Co. For Arapahoe 1860 U.S. Census figures see Kansas 1860)

Archuleta	E4	1885	3		Conejos	Pagosa Springs
Baca	A4	1889	6		Las Animas	Springfield
Bent	B4	1874	7	1880	Greenwood	Las Animas
Boulder	C2	1859	74	1870-80	Original county	Boulder

(Co Clk has m rec from 1866)

Chaffee	D3	1879	8	1880	Lake	Salida
Cheyenne	A3	1889	3		Bent, Elbert	Cheyenne Wells
Clear Creek	D2	1859	3	1870-80	Original county	Georgetown
Conejos	D4	1861	8	1880	Original county	Conejos
Costilla	C4	1859	4	1870-80	Original county	San Luis
Crowley	B3	1911	4		Bent, Otero	Ordway
Custer	C3	1877	1	1880	Fremont	Westcliffe
Delta	E3	1883	16		Gunnison	Delta
Denver	C2	1902	494		Arapahoe	Denver

(Has annexed terr from Arapahoe, Adams & Jefferson Co on several occasions)

Dolores	F4	1881	2		Ouray	Dove Creek
Douglas	C2	1859	5	1870-80	Original county	Castle Rock
Eagle	D2	1883	5		Summit	Eagle

(Co Clk has m rec from 1883)

Elbert	B2	1874	4	1880	Douglas, Greenwood	Kiowa
El Paso	C3	1859	144	1880	Original county	Colorado Springs

(Co Clk has m rec from 1860)

Fremont	C3	1859	20	1870-80	Original county	Canon City

(Co Clk has m rec from 1860)

Garfield	E2	1883	12		Summit	Glenwood Springs
Gilpin	C2	1861	.7	1880	Original county	Central City
Grand	D2	1874	4	1880	Summit	Hot Sulphur Spr.

(Co Clk has m rec from 1893)

Gunnison	E3	1874	5	1880	Lake	Gunnison
Hinsdale	E4	1874	.2	1880	Conejos	Lake City

(Co Clk has m rec from 1876, b & d rec from 1900, deed rec from 1874)

Huerfano	C4	1861	8	1870-80	Original county	Walsenburg
Jackson	D1	1891	2		Grand	Walden
Jefferson	C2	1861	128	1870-80	Original county	Golden

(Co Clk has m rec from 1861)

Kiowa	A3	1889	2		Cheyenne, Bent	Eads

(Co Clk has m rec from 1889, b & d rec from 1941)

Kit Carson	A2	1889	7		Elbert	Burlington
Lake	D2	1861	7	1870-80	Original county	Leadville
La Plata	E4	1874	19	1880	Conejos, Lake	Durango
Larimer	C1	1861	53	1870-80	Original county	Fort Collins

(Co Clk has m rec from 1865, b & d rec from 1915)

Las Animas	B4	1866	20	1880	Huerfano	Trinidad

(Co Clk has m rec from 1867)

Lincoln	B3	1889	5		Elbert	Hugo

(Co Clk has m rec from 1889)

Logan	B1	1887	20		Weld	Sterling

(Co Clk has m rec from 1887)

Mesa	F3	1883	51		Gunnison	Grand Junction

(Co Clk has m rec from 1883)

County Map of Colorado

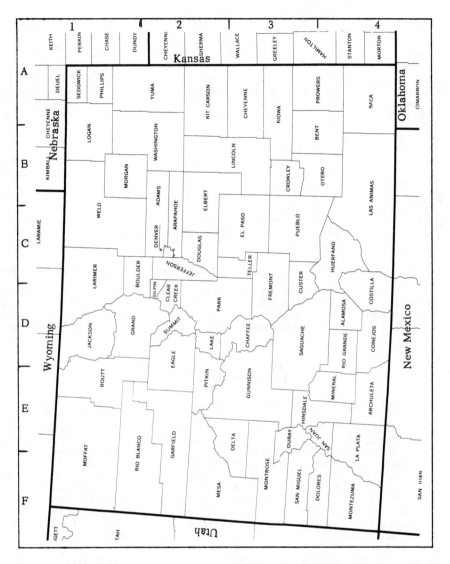

Mineral	E4	1893	.4	Hinsdale . . . . Creede
Moffatt	E1	1911	7	Routt . . . . Craig
(Co Clk has m rec from 1911)				
Montezuma	F4	1889	14	La Plata . . . . Cortez
Montrose	F3	1883	18	Gunnison . . . . Montrose
Morgan	B1	1889	21	Weld . . . . Fort Morgan
(Co Clk has m, div, pro, civ ct rec from 1889)				
Otero	B4	1889	24	Bent . . . . La Junta
(Co Clk has m rec from 1892, Real Estate rec from 1889)				
Ouray	E3	1877	2 1880	Hinsdale . . . . Ouray
Park	D2	1861	2 1870-80	Original county . . . . Fairplay
(Co Clk has m rec from 1893)				
Phillips	A1	1889	4	Logan . . . . Holyoke
(Co Clk has m rec from 1889)				

Pitkin	D2	1881	2		Gunnison . . . . Aspen
Prowers	A4	1889	13		Bent . . . . Lamar
Pueblo	C3	1861	119	1880	Original county . . . . Pueblo
Rio Blanco	E2	1874	5		Summit . . . . Meeker

(Co Clk has m rec from 1874 also early day Agriculture & stock rec, Bounty Books Brand rec registered as Summit Co, Garfield Co, and finally Rio Blanco)

Rio Grande	D4	1874	11	1880	Conejos, Costilla . . . . Del Norte
Routt	E1	1877	6	1880	Grand . . . . Steamboat Springs
Saguache	D3	1870	4	1880	Costilla . . . . Saguache
San Juan	E4	1876	.8	1880	La Plata . . . . Silverton
San Miguel	F3	1883	3		Ouray . . . . Telluride

(Co Clk has b & d rec from 1910, m rec from 1883)

Sedgwick	A1	1889	4		Logan . . . . Julesburg

(Co Clk has m rec from 1889)

Summit	D2	1861	2	1870-80	Original county . . . . Breckenridge
Teller	C3	1899	2		El Paso . . . . Cripple Creek

(Co Clk has m rec from 1899)

Washington	B2	1887	7		Weld, Arapahoe . . . . Akron

(Co Clk has m rec from 1887)

Weld	B1	1861	72	1870-80	Original county . . . . Greeley
Yuma	A2	1889	9		Washington, Arapahoe . . . . Wray

(Co Clk has m rec from 1900)

Genealogists' Check List of the Historical Records Survey, Colorado (see page VIII)

Fed Cts (start 1861); Inv of Co Arch, Alamosa, Arapahoe, Bent, Conejos, Costilla, Fremont, Garfield, Hinsdale, Larimer, Logan, Morgan, Phillips, Prowers, San Miguel, Washington, Yuma; Guide to Vit Stat, Vol 1 Pub Arch, Vol 2 Church Arch; Inv of the Chr & Syn Arch, Jewish; Depo of unpubl mat, State Hist Soc, Denver.

Connecticut

Capital Hartford - Ninth Colony - State 1788 - (5th)

The settlement of Connecticut began in 1635 by former Massachusetts colonists. Some of them left Massachusetts on order of narrow religious leaders, and others because they had become weary of the intolerant attitude displayed by those leaders. The green Connecticut valley had beckoned them with abundant evidences of opportunities for material prosperity. Most of the settlers in the Massachusetts towns of Newtown, Watertown and Dorchester, all near Boston, moved their families and all of their belongings to the central part of Connecticut, where along the Connecticut River they established three new communities which later came to be called Windsor, Hartford and Wethersfield. It was an attack of these three communities that later caused the Pequod Indian War.

As early as 1614 a Dutch seafarer, Adriaen Block, sailed up the broad river, which he named the Varsche River. The first knowledge of the fertile section of Connecticut the early settlers of Massachusetts learned from the Indians who gave them a highly painted word picture of the section. It was this that brought about the settlement of the three communities mentioned above. Late in 1635 about fifty persons left what is now Cambridge, then called Newtown, and established themselves at Suckiaug, now Hartford. New migrations continued throughout the next few years. While the Dutch remained at the trading posts or forts, the English spread all over the territory.

From 1635 to 1644 another English colony flourished at Saybrook, near the mouth of the Connecticut, but then faded away. In 1643, New Haven was extended as a colony to include Milford (1639), Guilford (1639), and Stamford (1641).

During the ten year period from 1640 to 1650, there was a heavy influx of settlers into Connecticut. The new settlers came almost entirely direct from England. The following forty years saw a tremendous migration away from the newly settled district. The movement was generally westward where fertile fields beckoned those anxious to secure their independence.

In many instances the entire population of some of the towns participated in the migration and established themselves again among their old neighbors in a new environment.

In 1772 about 30 English families under the leadership of the Reverend Richard Mosely left Litchfield, Connecticut, for the Kingsborough Patent, Fulton County, New York. (See The Genealogical Helper Vol. 14-4 page 213)

The 1790 Census of Connecticut shows a population of 232,236. All of them with the exception of three and eight-tenths per cent, or 223,437 had come from England proper. Scotland was represented with two and eight-tenths per cent, or 6,425; Ireland with seven-tenths per cent, or 1,589; France, two tenths per cent, or 512; Holland, one-tenth per cent, or 258. There were also five Hebrew, four German, and six from other countries.

During the early days of the American colonies Connecticut had more home indurstries than any other colony. All kinds of household gadgets were invented and manufactured in the homes. These early necessities were carried all over the eastern section of the present United States, even down to New Orleans, by the so called "Yankee Pedlars". With the heavy migration in the latter part of the eighteenth century away from the state, Connecticut sent lavish invitations to Europe for more familes to settle there.

About that time a severe potato crop failure in Ireland brought four million people to the verge of starvation. It didn't take many inducements for them to accept suggestions or invitations to make their home in Connecticut. Thousands of them came in the late 1840's although many had come for ten years previously. It is estimated that more than 70,000 Irish came during that period who with their descendants now number more than 200,000.

Since 1880 it is estimated that more than 80,000 Germans have sought residence in various sections of the state. Unlike many other nationalities the Germans seldom live in solid nationality groups but are more intermingled with the already existing population.

Canada has always contributed freely to the population of Connecticut. The English-Canadians have generally come to Hartford or some of the other larger cities in the state, while the French-Canadians have been satisfied to cross over the border separating them from the United States and settle down in some of the Northeastern industrial cities where upwards of seventy thousand of them have been employed in the textile industry.

During the past eighty years a heavy influx of Scandinavians has been registered in Connecticut. The earlier migration was much heavier than the later. It is estimated that upwards of fifty-five thousand persons have come from those nations to the Nutmeg State, about eight per cent from Norway, eleven per cent from Denmark, and eighty-one per cent from Sweden. The majority of them have engaged in the mechanical arts, while some have engaged in gardening and farming.

The Italians have been coming to Connecticut in quite a solid stream over the past eighty years. The greatest influx was during the first sixteen years of the twentieth century. The first and second generation of Italians number approximately more than 300,000 in Connecticut today. While good-sized colonies of them live in many of the cities, most of them are centered around Hartford.

With about an equal distribution in agricultural and industrial pursuits there are about 150,000 former residents of Poland in Connecticut. They have concentrated especially around Bridgeport and New Britain. The factories and industrial plants of Waterbury have employed most of the 40,000 Lithuanians who have come here over the years, while about an equal number from Czechoslovakia have centered around the Bridgeport plants. About 30,000 Magyars (Hungarians) are also established in the state, about nine thousand foreign born living there in 1950.

Unlike most states the town clerk, rather than the county clerk, is the custodian of marriage licenses and records, marriage and death records, and land records. Long before the counties were organized, the town clerks were recording these statistics. Record of wills, inventories and administrations of estates are in the probate districts. These are not always identical with the town.

The Church records are still in the respective churches. If information is desired from them, it may be best to write the town clerk and ask him to help you decide where to seek the data desired.

The census records of the state are all complete. The 1790 census is printed in book form and can be found in most libraries. The later census records are in the National Archives in Washington, D. C. and are available for research. In doing research in the Archives, it may be to your advantage to employ a professional researcher. Write to the National Archives, Washington, D. C. state your problem and ask for suggestions how to proceed.

Some Connecticut towns had a census taken in 1776. Information concerning this may be obtained from the Connecticut State Library, Hartford, Conn.

Bureau of Vital Statistics, State Department of Health, State Office Bldg., Hartford 15, Conn., has birth, death and marriage records since July 1, 1897. Earlier similar records are on file in the city or town offices of the respective communities.

Information on divorces may be obtained for a fee in the office of the clerk of the Superior Court in the county where the proceedings were heard.

Naturalization records are on file in the office of the United States Circuit court in Hartford, or in the county offices of the Superior Courts.

The Lutheran and the Episcopal churches have available besides the vital statistics, the christening, baptism, confirmation, entrance and departure dates and burials.

The town clerks also have custody of the land records.

The district courts of the counties are the custodians of wills, inventories and administrations of estates: Sometimes a town constitutes a district. Sometimes several smaller towns are grouped into one probate district. There are 118 districts and 169 towns.

Almost every city or town in the state have printed histories containing a great deal of genealogy especially concerning the early inhabitants. Many family genealogies have also been printed.

A wealth of information on early day families of Connecticut may be found in almost every library. Many books have been published, giving the names of the participants in all of the American wars. Numerous family histories have been printed and are available at most of the libraries, and most of the towns and cities have valuable histories of their founding, growth and progress. Many of the family histories in the libraries are in manuscript form. Many of them have been indexed to facilitate research activities. Information regarding these indexes may be obtained from the libraries if self-addressed, stamped envelopes accompany the request. No research is done by library staff members, but information regarding professional researchers may be given by the libraries.

Town and vital records and genealogical information pertaining to the early

days of the state may be obtained from the Public Library, 925 Broad St., Bridgeport 4; Public Library, 215 Greenwich Ave., Greenwich; Connecticut Historical Society, 1 Elizabeth St., Hartford 5; State Library, Capitol Ave., Hartford 1; Public Library, 624 Main St., Hartford 3; Curtis Memorial Public Library, 175 E. Main St., Meriden; Free Public Library, 133 Elm St., New Haven 11; Yale University Library, 120 High St., New Haven; The Public Library, New London; Otis Public Library, Norwich; Ferguson Public Library, Broad and Bedford Sts., Stamford; Wilbur L. Cross Library, University of Connecticut, Storrs; Silas Bronson Public Library, 267 Grand St., Waterbury 2.

Among books about Connecticut and its people are the following: John Warner Barber, "Historical Collections," 1836; Edgar L. Heermance, "Connecticut Guide" Samuel Peters, "General History of Connecticut," 1781.

The various counties of Connecticut are at present divided into the following townships: **Fairfield:** Bethel, Bridgeport, Brookfield, Darien, Danbury, Easton, Fairfield, Greenwich, Monroe, New Canaan, New Fairfield, Newtown, Norwalk, Redding, Ridgfield, Sheldon, Sherman Stamford, Stratford, Trumbull, Weston, Westport, Wilton.

Hartford: Avon, Berlin, Bloomfield, Bristol, Burlington, Canton, East Granby, East Hartford, East Windsor, Enfield, Farmington, Glastonbury, Granby, Hartford, Hartland, Manchester, Marlborough, New Britain, Newington, Plainville, Rock Hill, Simsbury, Southington, South Windsor, Suffield, West Hartford, Wethersfield, Windsor, Windsor Locks.

Litchfield: Barkhamsted, Bethlehem, Bridgewater, Canaan, Colebrook, Cornwall, Goshen, Harwinton, Kent, Litchfield, Morris, New Hartford, New Milford, Norfolk, North Canaan, Plymouth, Roxbury, Salisbury, Sharon, Thomaston, Torrington, Warren, Washington, Watertown, Winchester, Woodbury.

Middlesex: Chester, Clinton, Cromwell, Deep River, Durham, East Haddam, East Hampton, Essex, Haddam, Killingworth, Middlefield, Middletown, Old Saybrook, Portland, Westbrook.

New Haven: Beacon Falls, Bethany, Branford, Cheshire, Derby, East Haven, Guilford, Hamden, Madison, Meriden, Middlebury, Milford, Naugatuck, New Haven, North Branford, North Haven Orange, Oxford, Prospect, Seymour, Southbury, Wallingford, Waterbury, West Haven, Woodbridge, Woolcot.

New London: Bozrah, Colchester, East Lynne, Franklin, Griswold, Groton, Lebanon, Ledyard, Lisbon, Lyme, Montville, North Stonington, Norwich, Old Lyme, Preston, Salem, Sprague, Stonington, Waterford.

Tolland: Andiver, Bolton, Columbia, Coventry, Ellington, Hebron, Mansfield, Somers, Stafford Tolland, Union, Willington.

Windham: Ashford, Brooklyn, Canterbury, Chaplin, Hampton, Eastford, Killingly, Plainfield, Pomfret, Putnam, Scotland, Sterling, Thompson, Windham, Woodstock.

Connecticut Towns organized before 1800:

Fairfield County — Brookfield 1788; Danbury 1684; Fairfield 1639; Greenwich 1640; Huntington 1788; New Fair-

County Map of Connecticut

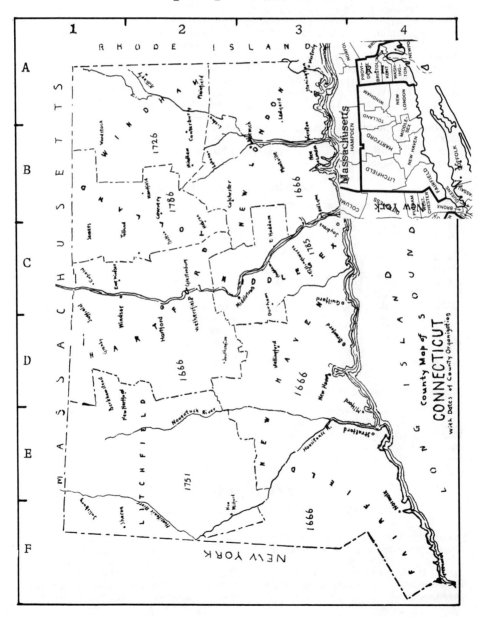

field 1740;Newton 1700; Norwalk 1649; Redding 1757; Ridgefield 1709; Stamford 1648; Stratford 1639; **Trumbull** 1798; Weston 1717.

Hartford County — Berlin 1785; Bristol 1747; Canton 1740; East Windsor 1680; Enfield 1681; Farmington, 1640; Glastonbury 1690; Grandby 1786; Hartford 1635; Hartland 1753; Simsbury 1670; Southington 1779; Suffield 1674; Wethersfield 1635; Windsor 1633.

Litchfield County — Barkhamsted 1746; Bethlehem 1787; Canaan 1739; Colebrook 1779; Cornwall 1740; Goshen 1739; Harwinton 1731; Kent 1739; Litchfield, 1719; New Hartford, 1739; New Milford, 1712; Norfolk, 1744; Plymouth 1795; Roxbury, 1796; Salisbury, 1730; Sharon, 1732-3; Torrington, 1740; Washington, 1779; Warren, 1786; Watertown, 1780; Winchester, 1771; Woodbury, 1674.

Middlesex County — Chatham, 1767; Durham, 1698; E. Haddam, 1685; Haddem, 1662; Killingsworth, 1667; Middletown, 1653; Saybrook, 1635.

New Haven County — Branford 1644; Cheshire, 1723; Derby, S. 1675; Guilford, 1639; Hamden, 1786; Meriden, 1796; Millford, 1639; New Haven, 1638; North Haven, 1786; Oxford, 1798; Seymour, 1672; Southbury, 1672; Wallingsford, 1669; Waterbury, 1686; Walcott, 1796; Woodbridge, 1786.

New London County — Bozrah, 1786; Colchester, 1703; Franklin, 1786; Groton, 1705; Lebanon, 1700; Lisbon, 1786; Lyme, 1664; Montville, 1786; New London, 1646; Norwich, 1660; Preston, 1687; Stonington, 1649.

Tolland County — Bolton, 1716; Coventry, 1709; Ellington, 1786; Hebron, 1704; Mansfield, 1713; Somers, 1734; Stafford, 1718; Tolland, 1700; Union, 1727; Vernon ,1716; Willington, 1720.

Windham County — Ashford, 1710; Brooklyn, 1786; Canterbury, 1690; Hampton, 1786; Killingly, 1700; Plainfield, 1699; Pomfret, 1686; Sterling, 1794; Thompson, 1715; Voluntown, 1696; Windham, 1689; Woodstock, 1749.

Connecticut County Histories

(Population figures to nearest thousand - 1960 Census)

Name	Map Index	Date Formed	Pop. By M	Census Reports Available	Parent County	County Seat
Fairfield	F4	1666	654	1790-80	Original county . . . Danbury & Bridgeport	
Hartford	D2	1666	690	1790-80	Original county .. Hartford & New Britain	
Litchfield	E2	1751	120	1790-80	Hartford, Fairfield . . . . . . Litchfield & Winsted	
Middlesex	C3	1785	89	1790-80	Hartford, New London, New Haven . . . . Middletown	
New Haven	E3	1666	660	1790-80	Original county . . Waterbury & New Haven	
New London	B3	1666	186	1790-80	Original county . . New London & Norwich	
Tolland	B2	1786	69	1790-80	Windham . . . . Rockville	
Windham	A2	1726	69	1790-80	Hartford, New London . . . . . . Putnam & Willimantic	

Genealogists' Check List of the Historical Records Survey, Connecticut (see page VIII)

Fed Cts (start 1789); Inv of Mun & Tn Arch - Avon, Berlin, Bloomfield, Newington, North Branford, North Haven, Orange, Oxford, Prospect, Seymour, Southbury, Weston; Guide to Vit Stat in Chr Rec; Inv of the Chr Arch of Conn - Lutheran, Prot Episcopal; Pre Check List of Am Portraits 1620-1825, found in Conn; Depo of unpubl mat, State Lib, Hartford, Conn.

Delaware

Capital Dover - First State - State 1787 - (1st)

Late in August 1609, Henry Hudson a British seacaptain and adventurer in the service of the Dutch West India Company, visited the Delaware section en route to the Hudson River in search of a northwest passage.

During a six-year period between 1614 and 1620 a group of sailors under the captaincy of Cornelius Hendricksen, a Dutch navigator, visited the section. As a result of information brought back to Holland by these sailors the Dutch West India

Company was organized in 1621. In 1629 this company adopted a charter to grant land in the new world to feudal lords. The following year the company bought land adjoining the Delaware River, and in 1631 David Pietersen de Vries established a camp on Lewes Beach.

Hearing how other European monarchs fostered expeditions and settlements in the new world, the Swedish rulers encouraged the New Sweden Company in outfitting an expedition of two boats, "The Kalmar Nyckel" and "Grip". They arrived at Jamestown, Va., in March 1638, remained there ten days and then continued to Delaware. They established settlements in the rich section south of the present Wilmington, in the extreme north of the colony. They were attacked by the Dutch at different times from 1651 to 1655 when the Swedes were routed from Fort Christina, named after the then twenty-one year old Queen Kristina, daughter of Gustaf Adolf, who lost his life on the battlefield at Lutzen, Germany, in 1632.

The first Finnish colonists came to Delaware in 1656 aboard a Swedish Ship.

The British forces took possession of the Delaware Colony and Amsterdam (New York) in 1664. Two years later a large influx of English people from Virginia, Maryland, New Jersey, New York and Europe made their homes among the Swedes and the Dutch in Delaware. From then on conditions among the colonists greatly improved and more unity was established.

Most of the colonists came to the New World for religious as well as material or financial purposes. Churches were among the first buildings erected as each new community was established. The Swedes brought with them religious desires of their groups. The Dutch settlers had in their companies priests of the Reformed church who functioned in chapels erected by their flocks. Many Irish who came after 1698 for the right of worshiping in accordance with the Presbyterian faith gave an early impetus to that body. As early as 1730 many staunch Roman Catholics established themselves in the northern part of Delaware, where the first Catholic chapel was built in 1772 on the Lancaster Pike, going northeast from Wilmington to Philadelphia. Another influx of Catholics came in 1790 when several French families sought rescue here from the West Indies uprisings. Among them were some who since then have played important parts in the financial development of the United States.

Many settlers who first arrived in the northern part of Delaware spread from there into Pennsylvania, Maryland and New Jersey.

When Delaware ratified the Constitution of the United States on December 7, 1787, it became the first state in the Union.

During the Civil War, although a slave state, Delaware was on the side of the regular government.

Because of the slow transportation methods in the early days, the state's three counties were divided into districts, called hundreds. The hundreds correspond to a township.

Among the foreign born the Italians, Poles, Russians, Irish, Germans and English predominate in that order.

The early colonial records of Delaware are scattered. Some are in the archives of the state of New York. After 1681 they were stored in the Archives of Pennsylvania. As the counties exercised full powers as government, not all of the colonial records went to Pennsylvania. Some are to be found in the Delaware Archives in Dover. Land records after 1785 will be found in the county courthouses and wills also after 1800.

In the Bureau of Vital Statistics, State House, Dover, will be found a record of births, deaths and marriages since 1881. There are some marriages recorded as early as 1847. A record of births was kept from 1861 to 1863.

The State Archivist said in June 1952, "All extant public records of Delaware and its political subdivisions dated before 1873, other than deeds and mortgages, are in the custody of The Public Archives Commission. Original vital statistics entries to 1913 are also in our custody. It is not possible to list a specific fee for service on these records, since most requests are for photostatic or microfilm copies. Our scale of prices for these is based on the size and number of pages to be copied, and is in line with commercial rates in the area.

"Vital statistics since 1913 are in the custody of the Bureau of Vital Statistics, Dover, Delaware.

"Deeds and mortgages are in the custody of the respective Recorders of New Castle, Kent and Sussex Counties in courthouses in Wilmington, Dover, and Georgetown, Delaware. All service on such records is through those offices.

"The Historical Society of Delaware has a small file of birth, death and marriage records culled from newspaper files which does not in all instances duplicate our own.

"Before 1790 all extant marriage records are from unofficial sources. So also are birth and death records before the Civil War period. Before 1913 coverage was not complete in all catagories for each year."

All Delaware Census records are available with the exception of the entire 1790 Census which is missing.

Books on Delaware:

Israel Acrelius, Swedish Lutheran minister, wrote history of New Sweden about 1714-1791.

Finck, "Lutheran Landmarks and Pioneers in America."

Benjamin Farris, "A History of the Original Settlements on the Delaware."

&c," Wilson and Heald, Wilmington, 1846, 312 p.

J. M. Runk & Co., "Biographical and Genealogical History of the State of Delaware" Chambersburg, Pa., 1899, 2 vols.

Amandus Johnson, "The Swedish Settlements on the Delaware, Their History and Relations to the Indians, Dutch and English, 1638-1664," N. Y., U. of Pa. Press per D. Appleton & Co., Agents, 1911, 2 vols.

Christopher Ward (Longstreth), "Dutch and Swedes on the Delaware 1609-1664," Philadelphia, University of Pa. Press, 1930, 393 p.

See, "Delaware, The American Guide Series," 1938, pp. 537, 538 for histories of Delaware cities, towns and villages.

Delaware County Histories

(Population figures to nearest thousand - 1960 Census)

Name	Map Index	Date Formed	Pop. By M	Census Reports Available	Parent County	County Seat
Kent	B5	1682	66	1800-80	St. Jones, Name ch in 1682	Dover
New Castle	B5	1673	307	1800-80	Original county	Wilmington
Sussex	C5	1682	73	1800-80	Early 17th Century Horrekill District	Georgetown

See Maryland for Map

Genealogists' Check List of the Historical Records Survey, Delaware (see page VIII)

Fed Cts (start ca 1790) (Del has some lists of NJ); Inv of Co Arch - Newcastle; Inv of the Chr Arch of Del - Preprint of Sec 22. Lutheran Chr & 29. Prot Episcopal; Dir of Chr & Rel Org in Del; Depo of unpubl mat, Dept of Arch, State U, Dover, Del.

District of Columbia

Territory of Washington D. C. organized 1790, Seat of Government 1800

The capital of the United States covers about seventy square miles on the northeast side of the Potomac River, about 38 miles southwest of Baltimore.

The Bureau of Vital Statistics, Health Department, D. C., 300, Indiana Ave., N. W., Washington, D. C., is the custodian of births from 1871 to the present, and deaths from 1855 to the present, except 1861 and 1862. Custodian of marriages is the Clerk, U. S. District Court for the District of Columbia, Fourth and E Streets, N. W., Washington, D. C. Custodian of wills is the Register of Wills, Fifth and E Streets, N. W. In charge of all real estate records and land titles is the Recorder of Deeds, Sixth and D. Streets, N.W., Census records may be obtained from the U. S. Bureau of the Census, Washington 25, D. C. Taxpayer lists are at the office of the Tax Collector, District of Columbia, District Bldg., Washington, D. C. All cemetery records are kept at the individual cemeteries.

"In 1800," says a historian, "Washington, the new capital, had been recently occupied. It was hardly a village, except on paper, and contained only the Capitol, the White House, two departmental Buildings, and a few boarding houses. The public buildings were still uncompleted. Mrs. Adams (the wife of President John Adams) found the audience room of the White House convenient for drying clothes, and the representatives met in a temporary building erected in the middle of the unfinished Capitol."

Public buildings in the city were burned by the British during the War of 1812.

The first U. S. Census of the District of Columbia was taken in 1800, but is incomplete. All of the 1810 census records of the district are missing. 1820 and subsequent censuses are available.

The National Society, Daughters of the American Revolution, (DAR) 1176 D. St. N. W. Washington, D. C. maintain a library of over 40,000 vols., many manuscripts and genealogical records.

The Genealogical Department of the Library of Congress and the National Archives, both Washington 25, D. C. are two of the richest sources of genealogical material in the U. S.

The National Genealogical Society, 1921 Sunderland Place, Washington, 6, D. C. also has considerable material helpful to genealogists.

Genealogists' Check List of the Historical Records Survey, D. C. (see page VIII)

Inv of the Chr Arch - Prot Episcopal Chr Dio Vol 1, Washington Cathedral Vol 2, RC Chr Preprint of Inv of St Patrick's Chr and School; Dir of Chr & Rel org in D of C 1939; Cal of Alexander Graham Bell Cor in the Volta Bureau, Wash, DC; Cal of the Letters and Doc of Peter Force on the Mecklenburg Declaration of Independence in the Loomis Col; Cal of the Writings of Frederick Douglass in the Frederick Douglass Mem Home, Anacostia, DC; Bio-Bibliographical Index of Muscians in the US from Colonial Times; Depo of unpubl mat, Library of Congress, Wash 25, DC.

Florida

Capital Tallahassee - Territory 1822 - State 1845 - (27th)

Maps existing in Spain for nearly five centuries indicate that the contours of the American continent were already then known there. Ponce de Leon, the intrepid Spanish explorer, reached the Florida coast as early as 1513. Landing there on Easter Sunday, he called the new land Florida, from the Spanish name for Easter, Pascua Florida. Attempts to locate Spanish settlers in the new region a few years later failed when the colony was routed by the Indians.

Efforts by the French Huguenots to establish colonies on the south bank of the St. John's river in 1564 had an encouraging beginning but ended in disaster in a couple of years.

In the 1763 peace treaty of Paris, which ended the Seven Years' War, in which the British and the Prussians fought France, Spain and Austria, all her North American possessions east of the Mississippi were ceded by France to Britain. In the same treaty Spain traded Florida to Britain for Havana.

That same year a proclamation by the King of England established among other American provinces, East and West Florida. The two sections were divided by the Chattahoochee and the Appalachicola rivers.

Twenty years later, the Florida sections were returned to Spain in the treaty ending the Revolutionary War in 1783.

West Florida was taken by the United States in 1810 and 1812, and, after many efforts, finally succeded in 1819 in getting Florida by promising to pay indemnities to her citzens who had been damaged by Spain. The section embracing West Florida was added to Louisana, Mississippi, and Alabama.

In 1821 about eight thousand whites lived in Florida, most of them Spaniards, although there were a goodly number of Anglo-Saxons. As early as 1740 many British, Scotch and Irish populated the Cumberland and the Shenandoah valleys and spread through every southern state east of the Mississippi. The early population in the Deep South was predominantly of Irish ancestry. They were the "Okies" of the early days. They built Jacksonville in 1822, Quincy in 1825, Monticello in 1828, Marianna and Apalachicola in 1829, and St. Joseph in 1836. Many wealthy people established their homes in Florida, but their bad treatment of the Indians caused the Seminole wars during 1835-42.

A considerable number of Greeks from southern Greece and the Dodecanese Islands moved into Florida as early as 1820. As expert sponge-divers they have established themselves as energetic and successful citizens. Religiously they are affilated with the orthodox Greek Catholic Church.

The first railroad in the state was built in 1831 and extended from Tallahassee to St. Marks. The middle section of Florida was settled about 1820 by former settlers from Virginia, North Carolina, and South

Carolina. Most of the people who came to East Florida from 1845 to 1860 had lived in Georgia, Alabama, and North and South Carolina.

Florida became a territory of the United States on March 30, 1822, from which time her county records begin. She became a state on March 3, 1845, the twenty-seventh state to join the Union.

During the eighteen-forties the population of Florida increased about fifty six per cent. The census of 1860 shows the white population to have increased to seventy-eight thousand. At that time there were in the state seventy-seven plantations embracing more than one thousand acres each. The 1860 census also showed that about half the population was native born while twenty-two per cent had come from Georgia, eleven per cent from South Carolina and five per cent from North Carolina.

In 1912 a large group of Lutheran Slovaks moved from Cleveland, Ohio, onto a large tract of land they had purchased in Seminole county where they established a communal agricultural and poultry business.

The Bureau of Vital Statistics, State Board of Health, P.O. Box 210, Jacksonville, Florida, is custodian of the following records: incomplete records of births from 1865 to 1917, and births from 1917 to date; incomplete records of deaths from 1877 to 1917, and deaths from 1917, to date; marriages from June 1927 to date; divorce records also available there.

Some birth and death records are in the city or county health departments from 1893 to 1913 in Jacksonville; from 1897 to 1916 in Pensacola; prior to 1917 in St. Petersburg, and varied records in Ocala, in custody of H. C. Sistrunk, Box 502, Ocala, Fla.

The office of the County Judge of the bride's home county has marriage records prior to June 1927. These offices also have the records of wills of their constituents.

Divorce records before 1927 are filed in the office of the clerk of the Circuit Court where divorce was granted; similar records before or after 1927 in the mentioned office of the Bureau of Vital Statistics.

Naturalization records are in the federal circuit and district courts at Pensacola and Jacksonville.

Well-indexed records of land claims prior to Florida's statehood are at the Land Office, Department of Agriculture, Tallahassee, Florida.

The first U. S. Census of Florida was taken in 1830. Two census records taken by the state in April 1935 and April 1945 are in the office of the Commissioner of Agriculture, Tallahassee, Florida.

Libraries: Fort Lauderdale, (Broward), Public Library; Jacksonville, (Duval), Free Public Library, 101 E. Adams St.; Miami, (Dade), Public Library, 1 Biscayne Blvd.; Orlando, (Orange), Albertson Public Library, 165 E. Central Ave.; Tallahasse, (Leon), Florida State Library, Supreme Court Bldg.; Tampa (Hillsborough), Public Library, 7th Ave. & Franklin St.

Florida County Histories

(Population figures to nearest thousand - 1960 Census)

Name	Map Index	Date Formed	Pop. By M	Census Reports Available	Parent County	County Seat
Alachua	B4	1824	74	1830-80	Duval, St. John	Gainesville
Baker	B4	1861	7	1870-80	New River	MacClenny
Bay	A2	1913	67		Calhoun, Washington	Panama City
(Co Clk has div & civ ct rec from 1913)						
Benton		1843		1850	Alachua (Now Hernando)	
Bradford	B4	1861	12	1870-80	"New River" up to 1861	Starke
(Co Clk has div & civ ct rec from 1875)						
Brevard	C5	1855	111	1860-80	"St. Lucas" up to 1855	Titusville
Broward	E5	1915	334		Dade, Palm Beach	Ft. Lauderdale
(Co Judge has m & pro rec from 1915; Clk cir ct has div & civ ct rec from 1915; Clk Ct of Rec has crim rec from 1915)						
Calhoun	A2	1836	7	1840-80	Franklin, Washington, Jackson .	Blountstown
Charlotte	D4	1921	13		DeSoto	Punta Gorda
(Co Clk has div & civ ct rec from 1921)						
Citrus	D4	1887	9		Hernando	Inverness
Clay	B4	1858	20	1860-80	Duval	Green Cove Springs
Collier	E4	1923	16		Lee, Monroe	Naples
Columbia	B4	1832	20	1840-80	Alachua	Lake City
Dade	E5	1836	935	1840-80	Monroe, St. Lucie (1855)	Miami

County	Code	Year	No.	Range	Formed from	Seat
DeSoto	D4	1887	12		Manatee	Arcadia
Dixie	B3	1921	4		Lafayette	Cross City
Duval	B4	1822	455	1830–80	St. John	Jacksonville

(Clk civ ct has div, civ ct rec and deeds & mtg from 1921, Soldiers & Sailors rec book from 1920)

County	Code	Year	No.	Range	Formed from	Seat
Escambia	A1	1821	174	1830–80	One of two original counties . .	Pensacola
Flager	B5	1917	5		St. John, Volusia	Bunnell

(Co Clk has div and civ ct rec from 1917; Co Judge has m and pro rec from 1917)

County	Code	Year	No.	Range	Formed from	Seat
Franklin	B2	1832	7	1840–80	Jackson	Apalachicola
Gadsden	A3	1823	42	1830–80	Jackson	Quincy
Gilchrist	B4	1925	3		Alachua	Trenton
Glades	D4	1921	3		DeSoto	Moore Haven
Gulf	B2	1925	10		Calhoun	Wewahitchka

(Co Clk has div and civ ct rec from 1925)

County	Code	Year	No.	Range	Formed from	Seat
Hamilton	A4	1827	8	1830–80	Duval	Jasper
Hardee	D4	1921	12		DeSoto	Wauchula
Hendry	D4	1923	8		Lee	LaBelle
Hernando	C4	1850	11	1870–80	Alachua (formerly Benton)	Brooksville
Highlands	D4	1921	21		DeSoto	Sebring
Hillsborough	C4	1834	398	1840–80	Alachua, Monroe	Tampa
Holmes	A2	1848	11	1850–80	Walton, Washington, Calhoun . . .	Bonifay
Indian River	C5	1925	25		St. Lucia	Vero Beach
Jackson	A2	1822	36	1830–80	Escambia	Marianna

(Co Clk has m, div, pro & civ ct rec from 1850)

County	Code	Year	No.	Range	Formed from	Seat
Jefferson	A3	1827	10	1830–80	Leon	Monticello
Lafayette	B3	1856	3	1860–80	Madison	Mayo
Lake	C4	1887	57		Orange, Sumter	Tavares
Lee	D4	1887	55		Monroe	Ft. Myers
Leon	A3	1824	74	1830–80	Gadsden	Tallahassee
Levy	B4	1845	10	1850–80	Alachua, Marion	Bronson
Liberty	B2	1855	3	1860–80	Franklin, Gadsden	Bristol
Madison	A3	1827	14	1830–80	Jefferson	Madison
Manatee	D4	1855	69	1860–80	Hillsboro	Bradenton
Marion	B4	1844	52	1850–80	Alachua, Hillsboro, Mosquito	Ocala
Martin	D5	1925	17		Palm Beach, St. Lucie	Stuart

(Clk of cir ct has deeds & mtg from 1925)

County	Code	Year	No.	Range	Formed from	Seat
Monroe	E5	1824	48	1830–80	St. Johns	Key West
Mosquito	C3	1824		1830–40	(Changed to Orange 1845)	
Nassau	A4	1824	17	1830–80	Duval	Fernandina Beach
New River		1858		1860	(Changed to Bradford 1861)	
Okaloosa	A1	1915	61		Santa Rosa, Walton	Crestview
Okeechobee	D5	1917	6		Osceola, Palm Beach, St. Lucie .. Okeechobee	
Orange	C5	1824	264	1850–80	(changed from Mosquito, 1845),	

(Co Clk has div rec from 1864) Sumpter (1871) . . . . Orlando

County	Code	Year	No.	Range	Formed from	Seat
Osceola	C5	1887	19		Brevard, Orange	Kissimmee
Palm Beach	D5	1909	228		Dade	West Palm Beach
Pasco	C4	1887	37		Hernando	Dade City
Pinellas	C4	1911	375		Hillsboro	Clearwater
Polk	C4	1861	195	1870–80	Brevard, Hillsboro (Boundries changed 1871	Bartow
Putnam	B4	1849	32	1850–80	Alachua, Marion, Orange, St. Johns	Palatka
St. Johns	B5	1821	30	1830–80	One of two original cos. . . .	St. Augustine
St Lucas		1844			(changed to Brevard 1855)	
St. Lucie	D5	1844	39	1850	Brevard	Fort Pierce
Santa Rosa	A1	1842	30	1850–80	Escambia	Milton

(Clk of cir ct has b, div, & civ ct rec from Jul 15, 1869; Co Judge has m rec from 1869) (Ct House burned 1869)

County	Code	Year	No.	Range	Formed from	Seat
Sarasota	D4	1921	77		Manatee	Sarasota
Seminole	C5	1913	55		Orange	Sanford

(Co Clk has civ ct rec from 1915)

Sumter   C4   1853   12   1860-80   Marion, Orange . . . .   Bushnell
   (Clk of cir ct has div and civ ct rec 1900; Co Judge has m and pro rec 1900)
Suwannee   B4   1858   15   1860-80   Columbia . . . .   Live Oak
   (Co Clk has div and civ ct rec from 1858)
Taylor   B3   1856   13   1860-80   Madison . . . .   Perry
Union   B4   1921   6   Bradford . . . .   Lake Butler
Volusia   B5   1854   125   1860-80   St. Lucas . . . .   DeLand
Wakulla   B3   1843   5   1850-80   Leon . . . .   Crawfordville
   (Co Clk has div & civ ct rec from 1843)
Walton   A2   1824   16   1830-80   Jackson . . . .   De Funiak Springs
Washington A2   1825   11   1830-80   Jackson, Walton . . . .   Chipley

County Map of Florida

Genealogists' Check List of the Historical Records Survey, Florida (see page VIII)

Fed Cts (start 1821); Inv of Co Arch – Charlotte, Clay, Collier, Duval, Flagler, Hardee, Hendry, Leon, Okaloosa, Pinellas, Sarasota, Wakulla; Tran of St Augustine, Ord and Min of City, 1821-1827 (no index); Guide to Pub Vit Stat Rec; Guide to Sup Vit Stat from Chr Rec – Vol 1 Alachu, Vol 2 Gilchrist, Vol 3 Orange; See La for navigation casualties; Inv of the Chr Arch of Fla Baptists Bodies – Black Creek Bap Assn, Lake Co Bap Assn, Northeast Fla Bap Assn, Northwest Coast Bap Assn, Okaloosa Bap Assn, Orange Blossom Bap Assn, Palm Lake Bap Assn, Pinellas Co Bap Assn, Seminole Bap Assn, Southwest Bap Assn, Florida State Assn of Old Line Bap Composed of Missionary Bap Chrs; Translation and Tran of Chr Arch of Fla, RC Rec, St Augustine Par White Baptisms 1784-1792; A pre list of Rel Bodies in Fla; Guide to Dep of Ms Col in the US – Fla, A list of the Mat in the Austin Carey Mem Col in the U of Fla; A Pre Short-Title Check List of Books, Pamphlets and Broadsides Printed in Fla 1784-1860; Check List of Rec Required of Co Officials duly appointed or elected; Check list of Rec Required by Law in Fla Cos; Spanish Land Grants in Fla, Vol 1 Unconfirmed Claims, Vol 2 Confirmed Claims A-C, Vol 3 Confirmed Claims D-J, Vol 4 Confirmed Claims K-R, Vol 5 Confirmed Claims S-Z: Depo of unpubl mat, Dept of Arch, Tallahassee, Fla.

Georgia

Capital Atlanta - State 1788 - (4th)

For one hundred sixty years or more the French and the Spanish were playing a gigantic game of chess with the dominance of Georgia as the prize. This continued from 1540 to about early in 1700. When South Carolina became a royal province, the land between the Savannah and the St. Mary's rivers was set aside for a new British colony.

It was the practise in England at that time to imprison individuals unable to pay their debts. This practise irked a humanitarian army officer and member of Parliament, James Oglethorpe, who conceived the idea of rehabilitating these poor people by taking them to the New World, giving them a tract of land and assisting and guiding them in establishing their homes. He induced King George II to grant to him and twenty other men the English territory south of the Savannah.

With thirty-five families he arrived there in 1733 and established a community at the mouth of the Savannah, which he named after the river. Halfway between the mouth of that river and the southern border of South Carolina, they established Augusta in 1734. In the meantime persecuted Protestants in Europe had been invited to come to the colony. At first Roman Catholics were refused to enter the new country.

About 1738 Swiss, German, Italian, Scottish Highlanders, Salzburger, and Moravian settlers had arrived in Georgia. In 1739 another community called Frederica was established on the south banks of the Altamaha. Two years later Georgia was divided into two counties - north of the Altamaha was called Savannah, and south of that river Frederica.

Many of the Moravians had come from North Carolina to Spring Place and New Echota. Unsuccessful in their desire to convert the Indians to their faith, the Moravians later moved from Georgia to Pennsylvania, where they increased rapidly in Bethlehem and Nazareth.

Many of the Presbyterians who came to Georgia as Scottish Highlanders settled in Darien, which they renamed New Inverness. In 1752 a group of Massachussetts Puritans came to Midway.

Georgia became a royal province in 1752. The colony claimed all of the land between North Carolina and Florida, and the Atlantic and the Mississippi.

The first counties in Georgia were formed in 1777. These counties covered only a fraction of the land claimed by the province. They covered the section between the Savannah River and the Oconee and the Altamaha Rivers, and a strip about thirty five miles wide extending from the Altamaha to the Florida border. In 1790 there were eleven counties as follows, from north to south: Franklin, Wilks, Greene, Richmond, Burke, Washington, Effingham, Chatham, Liberty Glyn, and Camden. These counties included the area now occupied by the present counties, as follows:

Franklin: the south three-fourths of Stephens, Franklin, Banks, Jackson, all of Oconee but the southern most tip, all of Clarke but the southern' fourth, all of Madison but the southeast tip, Hart and Elbert.

Wilks: the southern tip of Clarke, Oglethorpe, the southeastern tip of Madison, Wilkes, Lincoln, Columbia, McDuffie, Glascock, Warren, all but west fourth of Taliaferro, and small piece of east corner of Greene.

Greene: small south corner of Oconee, small west corner of Oglethorpe, all of Greene but small north triangle, west fourth of Taliaferro, all of Hancock but south fourth, triangular small northeast corner of Baldwin.

Richmond: triangular northeast fourth of Jefferson and Richmond.

Burke: all of Jefferson but southwest triangular quarter of northeast triangular quarter, Burke, all of Jenkins but southwest third, and northern triangular half of Screven.

Washington: south fourth of Hancock, triangular small southeast corner of Baldwin, Washington, southwest quarter of Jefferson, Johnson, east third of Laurns, east triangular half of Montgomery, Emanuel, southeast quarter of Jenkins, Bulloch, Bryan, and west half of Tattnall, and Toombs.

Effingham: the southern half of Screven, and Effingham.

Chatham: Chatham, and southern half of Bryan.

Liberty: eastern half of Tattnall, Liberty Long, and McIntosh.

Glyn: eastern half of Wayne, Glynn, and northeastern third of Brantley.

Camden: southeastern third of Brantley,

eastern half of Charlton, and Camden.

Today Georgia has 159 counties. Only nineteen states have a larger area.

In 1798 the Territory of Mississippi was created from the western half of Georgia. Later that territory was formed into the states of Alabama and Mississippi.

Georgia ratified the federal consitiution on January 2, 1788 and thus became the fourth state in the union.

Many settlers in Virginia and the Carolinas were attracted to Georgia by the early land lotteries. Families who had lived in the territory for at least one year were permitted to draw for acreages as large as 400 acres. Such lotteries, the participant lists of which are now in the office of the Secretary of State, were held in 1803, 1806, 1819, 1827, and 1832.

Division of Vital Statistics, State Department of Public Health, 1 Hunter St., S. W., Atlanta 3, Ga., has on file birth and death records since Jan. 1, 1919. Atlanta and Savannah city health offices similar records of earlier dates.

The county clerk or the clerk of the Ordinary Court have records of marriages performed in that county.

Records of divorce actions are kept by Superior Court clerk in county where granted. They also have Civil Court records.

Naturalization records are filed in the office of the Superior Court in county where hearing was held. Similar records in the office of the clerk of the federal district courts in Atlanta and Savannah.

The deeds to lands are recorded in the office of the Court of Ordinary where land is located. Abstracts of land grants are furnished for a fee in the office of the clerk of the Secretary of State.

Wills are recorded in the office of the clerk of the Court of Ordinary in county where testator resided.

Libraries: Albany, (Dougherty), Carnegie Public Library, 215 No. Jackson St.; Atlanta, (Fulton), Public Library, 126 Carnegie Way, (Genealogy); Georgia State Dept. of Archives and History Library, Rhodes Memorial Hall, 1516 Peachtree Rd. has thousands of valuable early records, deeds, and marriage certificates, and personal histories of early residents, also many volumes of Georgia colonial history; Columbus, (Muscogee), W. C. Bradley Memorial Library, (Chattahoochee Valley History); Macon, (Bibb), Washington Memorial Library, 1190 Washington Ave.; Savannah (Chatham), Georgia Historical Society Library, 501 Whitaker St.; Savannah Public Library, 2002 Bull St.

Georgia County Histories

(Population figures to nearest thousand – 1960 Census)

Name	Map Index	Date Formed	Pop. By M	Census Reports Available	Parent County	County Seat
Appling	D3	1818	13	1820-80	Creek Indian Lands	Baxley
(Rec begin 1879; some 1859)						
Atkinson	E3	1917	6		Coffee, Clinch	Pearson
(Clk of sup ct has div, pro & civ ct rec from 1919; Clk Ord has b & d rec from 1928, m rec from 1919)						
Bacon	D3	1914	8		Appling, Pearce, Ware	Alma
Baker	E1	1825	5	1830-80	Early	Newton
(Rec begin 1874)						
Baldwin	C2	1803	34	1820-80	Creek Indian Lands	Milledgeville
(Co clk has b, m, d, bur, div, pro, civ ct rec from 1861)						
Banks	A2	1858	6	1860-80	Franklin, Habershaw	Homer
Barrow	B2	1914	14		Jackson, Walton, Guinett	Winder
Bartow	A1	1861	28	1870-80	Changed from Cass 1861	Cartersville
(Some rec dest CW)						
Ben Hill	D2	1906	14		Irwin, Wilcox	Fitzgerald
Berrien	E2	1856	12	1860-80	Lowndes, Coffee, Irwin	Nashville
Bibb	C2	1822	141	1830-80	Jones, Monroe, Twiggs, Houston	Macon
Bleckley	C2	1912	10		Pulaski	Cochran
Brantley	E3	1920	6		Charlton, Pierce, Wayne	Nahunta
(Co Clk has b, m, d, bur, div, pro and civ ct rec from 1921)						
Brooks	E2	1851	15	1860-80	Lowndes, Thomas	Quitman
Bryan	D4	1793	6	1820-80	Effingham, Liberty	Pembroke
(Ord Ct rec lost 1866)						
Bulloch	C4	1796	24	1820-80	Franklin	Statesboro
(Rec believed complete)						

Burke   C3 1777   21 1820-80 St. George Parish . . . . Waynesboro
(Fire 1870; one will bk, one deed bk saved)
Butts   B2 1825   9 1830-80 Henry, Monroe . . . . Jackson
Calhoun   D1 1854   7 1860-80 Baker & Early . . . . Morgan
(Early rec lost; first m rec begin 1880)
Camden   E4 1777   10 1820-80 St. Mary, St. Thomas . . . . Woodbine
(Fire 1870 - all rec lost)
Campbell   B1 1828   1830-80 Carroll, Coweta - Merged Fulton 1932 . . . .
Candler   C3 1914   7   Bulloch, Emanuel, Tattnall . . . . Metter
Carroll   B1 1826   36 1830-80 Indian Lands . . . . Carrollton
Cass   1832   1840-60 Changed to Bartow 1861
Catoosa   A1 1853   21 1860-80 Walker, Whitfield . . . . Ringgold
Charlton   E3 1854   5 1860-80 Camden, Ware . . . . Folkston
Chatham   D4 1777   188 1820-80 St. Phillip, Christ Church Parish . Savannah
Chattahoochee C1 1854   13 1860-80 Muscogee, Marion . . . . Cusseta
Chattooga   A1 1838   20 1840-80 Floyd, Walker . . . . Summerville
Cherokee   A2 1832   23 1840-80 Cherokee Lands, Habersham, Hall . Canton
(Deeds comp except Bk Q; Wills bks A & B lost)
Clarke   B2 1801   45 1820-80 Jackson, Green . . . . Athens
(Clk of Sup Ct has div, deeds & civ ct rec from 1801; Co Dept of Health has b, d
& bur rec from 1920; Ord Ct has m and pro rec from 1801)
Clay   D1 1854   5 1860-80 Early, Randolph . . . . Ft. Gaines
Clayton   B2 1858   46 1860-80 Fayette, Henry . . . . Jonesboro
Clinch   E3 1850   7 1850-80 Ware, Lowndes . . . . Homerville
(Clk of Sup Ct has m & div rec from 1868, pro & civ ct rec from 1872, b, d &
bur rec from 1919; Fires 1856 & 1867)
Cobb   B1 1832   114 1840-80 Cherokee . . . . Marietta
(Fire 1864; rec lost previously)
Coffee   D3 1854   22 1860-80 Clinch, Irwin, Ware, Telfair . . . . Douglas
(Fire 1864 - all lost)
Colquitt   E2 1856   34 1860-80 Lowndes, Thomas . . . . Moultrie
(Fire 1881 - all lost)
Columbia   B3 1790   14 1820-80 Richmond . . . . Appling
Cook   E2 1918   12   Berrien . . . . Adel
Coweta   B1 1826   29 1830-80 Indian Lands . . . . Newman
Crawford   C2 1822   6 1830-80 Houston, Marion, Talbot, Macon . Knoxville
Crisp   D2 1905   18   Dooly . . . . Cordele
(Clk Sup Ct has div & civ ct rec from 1905)
Dade   A1 1837   9 1840-80 Walker . . . . Trenton
Dawson   A2 1857   4 1860-80 Lumpkin, Gilmer . . . . Dawsonville
Decatur   E1 1823   25 1830-80 Early . . . . Bainbridge
DeKalb   B2 1822   257 1830-80 Fayette, Gwinett, Newton, Henry . Decatur
(Clk of Sup Ct has div & civ ct rec from 1842; Ct of Ord has m & pro rec from
1842; CH burned 1842 & 1916)
Dodge   D3 1870   16 1880   Montgomery, Pulaski, Telfair . . Eastman
Dooly   D2 1821   11 1830-80 Indian Lands . . . . Vienna
(Clk of Sup Ct has div & civ ct rec 1846; Fire dest early rec few m left 1848)
Dougherty   D2 1852   76 1860-80 Baker . . . . Albany
(Clk Sup Ct has div & civ ct rec from 1856)
Douglas   B1 1870   17 1880   Carroll, Campbell . . . . Douglasville
Early   E1 1818   13 1820-80 Creek Indian Lands . . . . Blakely
(many rec lost; first m bk 1854)
Echols   E3 1858   2 1860-80 Clinch, Lowndes . . . . Statenville
(Most rec burned 1897)
Effingham   C4 1777   10 1820-80 St. Mathews, St. Phillips . . . . . Springfield
(Ct of Ord has b & d rec from 1927, m & pro rec from 1790; Clk of Sup Ct has
div & civ ct rec from 1777; Some rec lost CW and fire 1890)
Elbert   B3 1790   18 1820-80 Wilkes, Madison . . . . Elberton
Emanuel   C3 1812   18 1820-80 Montgomery, Bulloch . . . . . Swainsboro
(Rec believed complete)
Evans   D4 1914   7   Bulloch, Tattnall . . . . Claxton
Fannin   A2 1854   14 1860-80 Gilmer, Union . . . . Blue Ridge

Fayette   B2   1821   8   1830–80   Indian Lands, Henry .... Fayetteville
Floyd   A1   1832   69   1840–80   Cherokee, Chattooga, Palding .... Rome
Forsyth   A2   1832   12   1840–80   Cherokee, Lumpkin .... Cumming
Franklin   A2   1784   13   1830–80   Cherokee Lands .... Carnesville
    (Rec believed complete; prior to 1850 in Ga. Archives)
Fulton   B1   1853   556   1860–80   DeKalb, Campbell .... Atlanta
    (Clk of Sup Ct has div & civ ct rec from 1854)
Gilmer   A2   1832   9   1840–80   Cherokee, Union .... Ellijay
Glascock   B3   1852   3   1860–80   Warren, Jefferson .... Gibson
Glynn   E4   1777   42   1820–80   St. David, St. Patrick .... Brunswick
    (Co Bd of health has b, d & bur rec from 1925; Ct of Ord has m rec from 1845,
    Adminsitrators, Guardianship & pro rec from 1792; Clk of Sup Ct has div &
    civ ct rec from 1792; Deeds 1824–1829 burned, all rec to 1818 damaged)
Gordon   A1   1850   19   1850–80   Cass, Floyd .... Calhoun
    (Rec destroyed 1864)
Grady   E2   1905   18   Decatur, Thomas .... Cairo
Greene   B3   1786   11   1820–80   Washington, Oglethorpe,
                                         Wilkes .... Greensboro
    (Clk of Sup Ct has div and civ ct rec from 1786)
Gwinnett   B2   1818   44   1820–80   Cherokee Lands, Jackson .. Lawrenceville
    (CH burned 1871; only few rec saved)
Habersham   A2   1818   18   1820–80   Cherokee Lands, Franklin ... Clarkesville
Hall   A2   1818   50   1820–80   Cherokee Lands, Jackson,
                                         Franklin .... Gainesville
    (Tornado leveled CH 1936; many rec lost; deeds saved)
Hancock   B3   1793   10   1820–80   Greene, Washington .... Sparta
    (Ct of Ord has b, m, & d rec from 1927)
Haralson   B1   1856   15   1860–80   Carroll, Polk .... Buchanan
Harris   C1   1827   11   1830–80   Muscogee, Troup .... Hamilton
Hart   A3   1853   15   1860–80   Elbert, Franklin .... Hartwell
Heard   B1   1830   5   1840–80   Carroll, Coweta, Troup ...... Franklin
    (Ct of Ord has b & d rec from 1927 and m & pro rec from 1894; Fire 1894)
Henry   B2   1821   18   1830–80   Indian Lands, Walton ..... McDonough
    (Some early rec lost; first m 1837)
Houston   C2   1821   39   1830–80   Indian Lands .... Perry
    (Clk of Sup Ct has div & civ ct rec from 1822; Ct of Ord has b, d & bur rec
    from 1927 and m rec from 1822)
Irwin   D2   1818   9   1820–80   Indian Lands, Coffee, Telfair ..... Ocilla
Jackson   B2   1796   18   1820–80   Franklin .... Jefferson
Jasper   B2   1812   6   1820–80   Baldwin .... Monticello
Jeff Davis   D2   1905   9   Appling, Coffee .... Hazelhurst
    (Clk of Sup Ct has div and civ ct rec from 1905)
Jefferson   C3   1796   17   1820–80   Burke, Warren .... Louisville
    (Rec not complete; deeds 1797–1802; 1865)
Jenkins   C3   1905   9   Bullock, Burke, Emanuel, Screven .. Millen
Johnson   C3   1858   8   1860–80   Emanuel, Laurens, Washington . Wrightsville
Jones   C2   1807   8   1820–80   Baldwin, Bibb, Putnam .... Gray
Kinchafoonee   Stewart, changed to Webster 1856
Lamar   C2   1920   10   Monroe, Pike .... Barnesville
Lanier   E3   1919   5   Berrien, Lowndes, Clinch ... Lakeland
Laurens   C3   1807   32   1820–80   Montgomery, Washington,
                                         Wilkinson .... Dublin
Lee   D2   1824   6   1830–80   Indian Lands .... Leesburg
    (All rec lost in CH fire 1858)
Liberty   D4   1777   14   1820–80   St. Andrew, St. James, St Johns . Hinesville
    (Early rec lost; first m rec 1819)
Lincoln   B3   1796   6   1820–80   Wilkes .... Lincolnton
Long   D4   1920   4   Liberty .... Ludowici
Lowndes   E2   1825   49   1830–80   Irwin .... Valdosta
    (Ordinary's office burned, all rec lost to 1869)
Lumpkin   A2   1832   7   1840–80   Cherokee, Habersham, Hall ... Dahlonega
McDuffie   B3   1870   13   1880   Columbia, Warren .... Thomson

McIntosh   D4   1793   6 1820-80 Liberty . . . . Darien
(Many rec lost during CW; CH fire 1931)
Macon   C2   1837   13 1840-80 Houston, Marion . . . . Oglethorpe
(CH burned 1857; all rec lost)
Madison   B3   1811   11 1820-80 Clarke, Elbert, Franklin, Jackson,
                                      Oglethorpe . . . . Danielsville
Marion   C1   1827   5 1830-80 Lee, Muscogee, Stewart . . . . Buena Vista
(CH fire 1845; all rec lost)
Meriwether   C1   1827   20 1830-80 Troup . . . . Greenville
Miller   E1   1856   7 1860-80 Baker, Early . . . . Colquitt
(CH fire 1873; all rec lost)
Milton   B1   1857   1860-80 Cobb, Cherokee, Forsyth
                                      Merged Fulton 1911 . . . .
Mitchell   E2   1857   20 1860-80 Baker . . . . Camilla
(CH fire 1869; Sup Ct rec and some others saved)

Monroe   C2   1821   10 1830-80 Indian Lands . . . . Forsyth
(Co health center has b rec from 1928 & d rec from 1942; Ct of Ord has m and
pro rec from 1824)
Montgomery   D3   1793   6 1820-80 Washington, Laurens, Tattnall,
                                      Telfair . . . . Mt. Vernon
(Ct of Ord has b & d rec from 1918, m rec from 1807, pro rec from 1793)
Morgan   B2   1807   10 1820-80 Baldwin, Jasper . . . . Madison
Murray   A1   1832   10 1840-80 Cherokee . . . . Chatsworth
(Ct of Ord has b & d rec from 1924, m rec from 1842, pro rec from 1890; Clk of
Sup Ct has civ ct rec from 1834)
Muscogee   C1   1826 159 1830-80 Creek Lands, Harris, Lee,
                                      Marion . . . . Columbus
Newton   B2   1821   21 1830-80 Henry, Jasper, Morgan, Walton . . Covington
(Clk of Sup Ct has div, civ ct & land deeds 1822, also Army and Navy rec 1917)
Oconee   B2   1875   6 1880   Clarke . . . . Watkinsville
Ogelthorpe   B3   1793   8 1820-80 Clarke, Green, Wilkes . . . . . Lexington
(CH fire 1941; Ord and other rec saved; deeds complete)
Paulding   B1   1832   13 1840-80 Cherokee Lands, Carroll, Cobb . . Dallas
(m rec from 1832; wills 1865; deeds from 1848)

Peach   C2   1924   14   Houston, Macon . . . . Fort Valley
Pickens   A2   1853   9 1860-80 Cherokee, Gilmer . . . . Jasper
(Clk of Sup Ct has div, pro, & criminal ct rec from 1854)
Pierce   E3   1857   7 1860-80 Appling, Ware . . . . Blackshear
(Ct of Ord has b rec from 1926, m rec from 1875, d rec from 1924; Clk of Sup
Ct has div & civ ct rec from 1875; CH fire 1874)
Pike   C2   1822   7 1830-80 Monroe, Upson . . . . Zebulon
Polk   B1   1851   28 1860-80 Paulding . . . . Cedartown
Pulaski   D2   1808   8 1820-80 Laurens, Dodge, Dooly,
                                      Houston . . . . Hawkinsville
Putnam   B2   1807   8 1820-80 Baldwin . . . . Eatonton
Quitman   D1   1858   2 1860-80 Randolph, Stewart . . . . Georgetown
(Rec apparently lost; first m 1919)
Rabun   A2   1819   7 1830-80 Cherokee Lands, Habersham . . Clayton
Randolph   D1   1828   11 1830-80 Baker, Lee . . . . Cuthbert
Richmond   B3   1777 136 1820-80 St. Paul Parish . . . . Augusta
Rockdale   B2   1870   11 1880   Henry, Newton . . . . Conyers
Schley   D2   1857   3 1860-80 Marion, Sumter . . . . Ellaville
Screven   C4   1793   15 1820-80 Burke, Effingham . . . . Sylvania
(First m list 1822; some deeds 1793; minute bks 1811)
Seminole   E1   1920   7   Decatur, Early . . . . Donalsonville
Spalding   B2   1851   35 1860-80 Fayette, Henry, Pike . . . . Griffin
Stephens   A2   1905   18   Franklin, Habersham . . . . Toccoa
Stewart   D1   1830   7 1840-80 Randolph . . . . Lumpkin
(Ct of Ord has b, d & bur rec from 1927 & m rec from 1828; Clk of Sup Ct has
div, pro & civ ct rec from 1830)
Sumter   D2   1831   25 1840-80 Lee . . . . Americus

Talbot   C1   1827   7   1830-80   Crawford, Harris, Marion, Macon,
                                         Muscogee . . . . Talbotton
Taliaferro   B3   1825   3   1830-80   Green, Hancock, Oglethorpe,
                                         Warren, Wilkes . . . . Crawfordville
   (Ct of Ord has b rec from 1927, m & pro rec from 1826, d rec from 1920, Land
   grants from 1750, Church rec from 1802; Clk of Sup Ct has div & civ ct rec 1826)
Tattnall   D3   1801   16   1820-80   Montgomery, Liberty . . . . Reidsville
Taylor   C2   1853   8   1860-80   Crawford, Macon, Marion,
                                         Talbot, Monroe . . . . Butler
Telfair   D3   1807   12   1820-80   Wilkinson, Appling . . . . McRae
Terrell   D2   1856   13   1860-80   Lee, Randolph . . . . Dawson
Thomas   E2   1825   34   1830-80   Baker, Decatur, Irwin,
                                         Lowndes . . . . Thomasville
   (Co health dept has b rec from 1920 Ct of Ord has them prior to 1920; Co Health
   dept has d rec from 1920; Ct of ord has pro rec from 1825; Clk of Sup Ct has
   div & civ ct rec from 1826)
Tift   D2   1905   23   Berrien, Irwin, Worth . . . . Tifton

County Map of Georgia

Toombs   D3 1905   17   Emanuel, Tattnall, Montgomery . . . Lyons
  (Ct of Ord has b, m, d, bur & pro rec from 1905; Clk of Sup ct has div and civ ct
  rec from 1905)
Towns   A2 1856   5 1860-80 Rabun, Union . . . . Hiawassee
Treutlen   C3 1917   6   Emanuel, Montgomery . . . . . Soperton
Troup   C1 1826   47 1830-80 Indian Lands . . . . LaGrange
Turner   D2 1905   8   Dooly, Irwin, Wilcox, Worth . . . . Ashburn
Twiggs   C2 1809   8 1830-80 Wilkinson . . . . Jeffersonville
Union   A2 1832   7 1840-80 Cherokee Lands, Lumpkin . . . Blairsville
Upson   C2 1824   24 1830-80 Crawford, Pike . . . . Thomaston
Walker   A1 1833   45 1840-80 Murray . . . . LaFayette
  (Clk of the Sup Ct has div & civ ct rec from 1883; CH fire 1883)
Walton   B2 1803   20 1820-80 Cherokee Lands . . . . Monroe
Ware   E3 1824   34 1830-80 Appling . . . . Waycross
  (Rec burned 1854)
Warren   B3 1793   7 1820-80 Columbia, Richmond, Wilkes . . Warrenton
Washington C3 1784   19 1820-80 Indian Lands . . . . Sandersville
  (Fire dest all rec 1855; Sherman dest most all 1864)
Wayne   D4 1803   18 1820-80 Indian Lands, Appling, Glynn,
                                       Camden . . . . Jesup
Webster   D1 1856   3 1860-80 Changed from Kinchafoonee 1856 .. Preston
  (Rec apparently dest; first m 1914)
Wheeler   D3 1912   5   Montgomery . . . . Alamo
  (Clk of Sup Ct has div & civ ct rec from 1913)
White   A2 1857   7 1860-80 Habersham . . . . Cleveland
Whitfield   A1 1851   42 1860-80 Murray, Walker . . . . Dalton
  (Ct of Ord has b, m, d, bur & pro rec from 1852; Clk of Sup Ct has div & civ ct
  rec from ca 1852)
Wilcox   D2 1857   8 1860-80 Dooly, Irwin, Pulaski . . . . Abbeville
Wilkes   B3 1777   11 1820-80 Washington . . . . Washington
  (Early rec perhaps lost; first m rec 1792)
Wilkinson   C2 1803   9 1820-80 Creek Cession . . . . Irwinton
  (CH burned 1926)
Worth   D2 1852   17 1860-80 Dooly, Irwin . . . . Sylvester

Genealogists' Check List of the Historical Records Survey, Georgia (see page VIII)

Fed Cts (start 1789); Inv of Co Arch – to Pub Vit Stat Rec; Inv of the Chr and Syn
Chatham, Clinch, Cook (includes Tn Arch Arch of Ga, Atlanta Assn of Bap Chrs,
within Co), Dougherty, Echols, Jefferson, Fairburn Missionary Bap Assn; Classified
Lee (Hist Sketch Vol 1, Rec entries Vol Inv of Ga Maps; Depo of Unpubl mat, U of
2), Muscogee, Richmond; Inv of Mun & Tn Ga, Athens, Ga.
Arch – Adel, Cecil, Lenox, Sparks; Guide

Hawaii

Capital Honolulu - Territory 1900 - State 1959 - (50th)

Hawaii, 2,100 miles west-southwest of
San Francisco, is a 390- mile chain of
islets and eight main islands - Hawaii
Kahoolawe, Maui, Lanai, Molokai, Oahu,
Kauai, and Niihau. It was discovered in
1778 by Captain James Cook, who named it
the Sandwich Islands. It was ruled by
native monarchs until 1893, thereafter as
a republic until 1898, when it ceded itself
to the U. S.

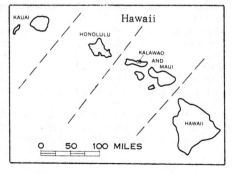

Idaho

Capital Boise - Territory 1863 - State 1890 - (43rd)

Idaho was the last state to be carved from the Oregon Territory. When Idaho became a territory on March 3, 1863, it included all of Montana and nearly all of Wyoming. Montana became a territory in 1864 and Wyoming in 1868. The six original counties of Idaho were formed between 1861 and 1865. It was admitted as a state July 3, 1890, the forthy-third state in the union.

The southern part of the state, which borders Utah was the first section to be settled. Mormon emigrants from northern Europe were the first to establish permanent settlements in the region.

A mining boom in 1860 attracted people from the East and Mid-West to the mountainous Idaho valleys. The later construction of large irrigation systems and districts around the long Snake River section about 1910 brought many western and midwestern farm families to take advantage of the farming opportunities in the new state.

Catholic and Protestant churches are represented in most Idaho communities, but more than half of its church membership belongs to the Church of Jesus Christ of Latter-day Saints.

The Division of Vital Statistics, Box 640, Boise, Idaho, has information on births and deaths from July 1, 1911.

The county recorder has records of marriages solemnized in his county. No marriage licenses were required before March 11, 1895.

The county clerk has records of births in that county since 1907. Wills and probate matters are also filed in the clerk's office.

All records pertaining to land transactions are in custody of the county recorder in the respective county court houses.

The first U. S. Census of Idaho was taken in 1870.

Libraries - Boise, (Ada), Public Library, 815 Washington St.; Nampa, (Canyon), Carneigie Library; Pocatello, (Bannock), Public Library; Twin Falls, (Twin Falls), Public Library, 434 Second St., E.

Idaho County Histories

(Population figures to nearest thousand - 1960 Census)

Name	Map Index	Date Formed	Pop. By M	Census Reports Available	Parent County	County Seat
Ada	E1	1864	93	1870–80	Boise	Boise
(Co Clk has m, div, and civ ct rec from 1864)						
Adams	D1	1911	3		Washington	Council
(Co Clk has m, div, & civ ct rec from 1911)						
Alturas		1863		1870–80	Original county; discontinued	
(Transferred to Lincoln?)						
Bannock	F4	1893	49		Oneida, Bear Lake	Pocatello
Bear Lake	F4	1875	7	1880	Oneida	Paris
Benewah	B1	1915	6		Kootenai	St. Maries
(Co Clk has m, div, & civ ct rec from 1915)						
Bingham	E3	1885	28		Oneida	Blackfoot
Blaine	E2	1895	5		Alturas	Hailey
(Co Clk has b & d rec from 1907 to 1911, m rec from 1865, div & civ ct rec 1890)						
Boise	E2	1863	2	1870–80	Original county	Idaho City
Bonner	A1	1907	16		Kootenai	Sandpoint
Bonneville	E4	1911	47		Bingham	Idaho Falls
Boundary	A1	1915	6		Bonner	Bonners Ferry
Butte	E3	1917	3		Bingham, Blaine, Jefferson	Arco
Camas	E2	1917	.9		Blaine	Fairfield
Canyon	E1	1892	58		Owyhee, Ada	Caldwell
(Co Clk has m, div, pro, & civ ct rec from 1891)						
Caribou	E4	1919	6		Bannock, Oneida	Soda Springs
(Co Clk has m, div, pro & civ ct rec from 1919)						
Cassia	F3	1879	16	1880	Oneida	Burley
(Co Clk has m, div & civ ct rec from 1879)						

County Map of Idaho

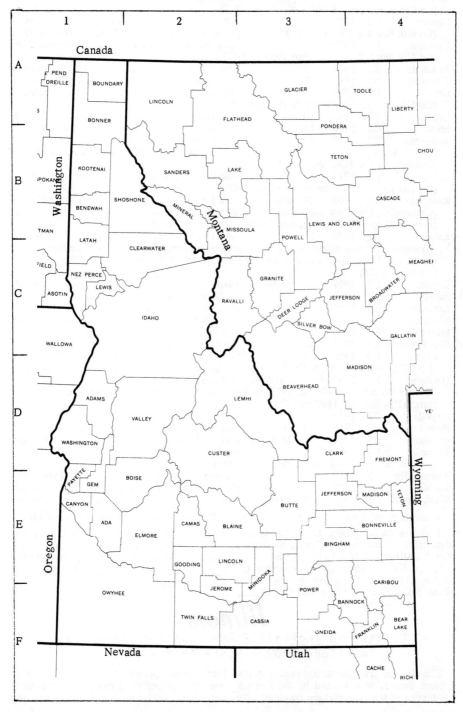

Clark   D3   1919   .9   Fremont . . . . Dubois
(Co Clk has m, div, pro & civ ct rec from 1919)
Clearwater   C2   1911   9   Nez Perce . . . . Orofino
(Co Clk has m, div, & civ ct rec from 1911)
Custer   D2   1881   3   Alturas . . . . Challis
(Co Clk has b & d rec 1907 to 1911, m, pro & civ ct rec from 1879, div rec 1881)
Elmore   E2   1889   17   Alturus, Ada . . . . Mountain Home
(Co Clk has b & m rec from 1910 to 1935)
Franklin   F4   1913   8   Oneida . . . . Preston
Fremont   D4   1893   9   Bingham, Lemhi . . . . St. Anthony
Gem   E1   1915   9   Boise, Canyon . . . . Emmett
(Co Clk has m, div, & civ ct rec from 1915)
Gooding   E2   1913   10   Lincoln . . . . Gooding
Idaho   C2   1862   14 1870-80 Original county . . . . Grangeville
Jefferson   E3   1913   12   Fremont . . . . Rigby
(Co Clk has m, div & civ ct rec from 1914, also Deeds and all rec where
property is involved from 1886)
Jerome   F2   1919   12   Gooding, Lincoln . . . . Jerome
(Co Clk has m, d & civ ct rec from 1919)
Kootenai   B1   1864   30 1880 Nez Perce . . . . Coeur d'Alene
(Created in 1864, but not organized or officered until 1881. Co Clk has b & d rec
from 1907 to 1912, m, div, pro & civ ct rec from 1881)
Latah   B1   1888   21   Nez Perce . . . . Moscow
(Created and organized by U. S. Congressional enactment, said to be the only
Co in the U. S. so created. Co Clk has b & d rec 1907 to 1911, m, div & civ ct
rec from 1888)
Lemhi   D3   1869   6   1870-80 Idaho . . . . Salmon
Lewis   C1   1911   4   Nez Perce . . . . Nez Perce
Lincoln   E2   1895   4   Alturas . . . . Shoshone
Madison   E4   1913   9   Fremont . . . . Rexburg
Minidoka   E3   1913   14   Lincoln . . . . Rupert
Nez Perce   C1   1861   28   Original county . . . . Lewiston
Oneida   F3   1865   4   Original county . . . . Malad City
(Co Clk has b rec 1907 to 1912, m rec 1866, pro rec 1879, div & civ ct rec 1880)
Owyhee   F1   1863   6   1870-80 Original county . . . . Murphy
(Co Clk has b & d rec 1907 to 1913, m rec from 1895, div & civ ct rec from 1864,
Naturalization rec 1893 to 1911)
Payette   E1   1917   12   Canyon . . . . Payette
Power   E3   1913   4   Bingham, Blaine, Oneida . . American Falls
Shoshone   B2   1861   21 1870-80 Original county . . . . Wallace
Teton   E4   1915   3   Madison, Fremont . . . . Driggs
(Co Clk has m, div & civ ct rec from 1916)
Twin Falls   F2   1907   42   Cassia . . . . Twin Falls
Valley   D2   1917   4   Boise, Idaho . . . . Cascade
Washington   D1   1879   8   1880 Boise . . . . Weiser

Genealogists' Check List of the Historical Records Survey, Idaho (see page VIII)

Fed Cts (start 1890); Inv of Co Arch - Bingham, Boundary, Clark, Kootenai, Lemhi, Minidoka, Nez Perce, Power, Teton; Co Gov in Idaho (Supplementing Inv of Co Arch); Guide to Pub Vit Stat Rec, State & Co; Dir of Chrs & Rel Org of Ida; A Check List of Idaho Imprints 1839-1890; A Short-Title Check List of Books, Pamphlets & Broadsides Printed in Idaho 1839-1890; Depo of unpubl mat, Secretary of State, Boise, Idaho.

Illinois
Capital Springfield - American Territory 1783
Territory 1809 - State 1818 - (21st)

Illinois, the transportation center of the United States, was visited by the French explorers in the late sixteen hundreds. Its fertile land appealed to members of various early expeditions passing through during their exploring or hunting or war activities. Many of them returned later and farmed the deep, rich soil along its many rivers and streams.

The southern part was the first to be occupied by permanent settlers. They came from the earlier southern states, including North Carolina, Virginia and Kentucky. Others came for Maryland and Pennsylvania. This condition existed until some years after Illinois had become a state.

Settlers began to arrive in the northern section about 1825. Generally they came from the New England states.

With the beginning of the industrial growth of Illinois, European emigrants flocked there by the thousands every month. They furnished the man-power for the factories and industrial plants that sprung up like mushrooms in the Lake Michigan section. That is one reason why more than forty per cent of the state population centers in that area. They came from Ireland, and the south European countries. Germans flocked there until they form about one-fourth of the population. They are closely crowded by the Poles, Italians, Swedes and Russians.

Illinois was part of the Northwest Territory which the United States obtained after the Revolutionary War from Great Britain to whom it had been ceded by France in 1763. It became part of the United States in 1783. It was organized as American territory in 1787. It included the land north and west of the Ohio River, east of the Mississippi, and south of Canada. Illinois became the third of five territories and eventual states formed from that area. That was in 1818.

St. Clair became the first county organized in the Illinois Territory. That was in 1790. It extended along the Kaskaskia River. Five years later another county was formed, Randolph, situated farther south along the Kaskaskia and the Mississippi. Farther east, along the Wabash, Edwards county, the third Illinois county, came into existance in 1814. And north of that county, Clark County, also along the Wabash, was formed in 1819. Those four counties were the forerunners of 98 others to be formed in Illinois. The last two of her present 102 counties were formed in 1859, Ford and Douglas.

A communication from the Department of Public Health at Springfield says "Illinois has no provisions for giving genealogical service from the official birth and death records. Our law authorizes the State Department of Public Health, the County Clerks, and the Local Registrars to issue a certified copy of a specified record at the statutory fee of $1.00 per copy. The law forbids us to issue any information from the records except by certified copy as described.

"Marriage records are in sole custody of the County Clerks. Births and deaths from 1877 to 1916 were registered (if at all) by the County Clerks. In a few counties there are some records existing prior to 1877, also in some cities.

"Afther 1916 all original birth and death certificates have been deposited with this department. A copy of each is deposited with the County Clerk of the county where the event occurred.

"Such genealogical research as is done in the State offices is done in the Illinois State Archives from its miscellaneous historical records. For further information about the services from the Archives communicate with The State Archivist, Archive Building, Springfield, Illinois.

"The best source of the kind of information you request is to be found in a publication by the Historical Records Survey Project of the W. P. A. in May, 1941, entitled, "Guide to Public Vital Statistics Records in Illinois," (137 pp. mimeographed)." (See page VIII)

The United States Census Records are intact from 1820 on. Some schedules are in the State Library in Springfield.

Counties with a population of more than 70,000 have probate courts, in other counties probate matters and wills are handled by the County Clerk. Matters pertaining to real estate are in the offices of the County Recorder of Deeds.

The War Veterans Graves Registration Files contain names of about 350,000 veterans buried in the State of Illinois. It is in alphabetic order, by veterans names, broken down by wars. Also a cemetery listing set up by counties, on which veterans' burials are listed and cemeteries in alphabetic order by county. The files carry only those veterans buried within the state. The records are within ninety per cent, possibly more, for veterans buried in Illinois. Each card gives name of veteran, serial, claim, rank, organization, enlistment, discharge, date and place of birth, date and place of death, cemetery where buried, name of town, county, grave description, next of kin and address. A seprate index file is carried on peace time soldiers, whose names are not listed on the cemetery listings; also those with service unknown but thought to have had military service. Address: Illinois Veterans Commission,

State Office Bldg., 400 Spring St., Springfield, Illinois.

The Newberry Library in Chicago one of the largest in the west, has valuable genealogical volumes. In Springfield the State Historical library is second only to the Newberry Library in genealogical material in Illinois. In most of the counties in the state are libraries with more or less genealogical information.

Libraries: Bloomington, (McLean), Withers Public Library, 202 E. Washington St.; Chicago, (Cook), Chicago Histroical Society Library, North Ave. & Clark St.;

Public Library, 78 E. Washington St.; A. N. Marquis Co Library, 210 E. Ohio, (Biographical records); Newberry Library 60 W. Walton; U. S. Railroad Retirement Board Library, 844 Rush St.; University of Chicago Library, Zone 37; Decatur (Macon), Public Library, 457 N. Main St.; East St. Louis, (St. Clair), Public Library, 9th & State St.; Peoria, (Peoria), Public Library, Ill. No. Monroe St.; Rockford, (Winnebago), 215 N. Wyman St.; Springfield (Sangamon), Illinois State Historical Library, Centennial Bldg., (Genealogy).

Illinois County Histories

(Population figures to nearest thousand - 1960 Census)

Name	Map Index	Date Formed	Pop. By M	Census Reports Available	Parent County	County Seat
Adams	C1	1825	68	1830–80	Pike	Quincy
Alexander	E3	1819	16	1820–80	Johnson	Cairo
Bond	D2	1817	14	1820–80	Madison	Greenville
(Co Clk has b, d, pro & civ ct rec from 1877, m rec from 1817)						
Boone	A3	1837	20	1840–80	Winnebago	Belvidere
Brown	C2	1839	6	1840–80	Schuyler	Mt Sterling
Bureau	B2	1837	38	1840–80	Putnam	Princeton
(Co Clk has incom b & d rec 1848 to 1916, com 1916, m, pro & civ ct rec 1837)						
Calhoun	C1	1825	6	1830–80	Pike	Hardin
Carroll	A2	1839	20	1840–80	Jo Daviess	Mt. Carroll
Cass	C2	1837	15	1840–80	Morgan	Virginia
(Co Clk has b rec 1860, m & pro rec 1837, d rec 1878, civ ct rec 1849)						
Champaign	C3	1833	132	1840–80	Vermillion	Urbana
(Co Clk has b & d rec from 1916, m & pro rec from 1833)						
Christian	C3	1839	37	1840–80	Sangamon, Shelby	Taylorville
(Formerly Dane)						
Clark	C4	1819	17	1820–80	Crawford	Marshall
(Co Clk has b & d rec from 1877, m rec from 1820)						
Clay	D3	1824	16	1830–80	Wayne, Lawrence, Fayette	Louisville
Clinton	D2	1824	24	1830–80	Washington, Bond, Fayette, Crawford	Carlyle
Coles	C3	1830	43	1840–80	Clark, Edgar	Charleston
Cook	A4	1831	5130	1840–80	Putnam	Orland Park & Chicago
Crawford	D4	1815	21	1820–80	Edwards	Robinson
Cumberland	C3	1843	10	1850–80	Coles	Toledo
Dane		1839			Name changed in 1840 to Christian County.	
DeKalb	A3	1837	52	1840–80	Kane	Sycamore
DeWitt	A3	1839	17	1840–80	Macon, McLean	Clinton
(Co Clk has b & d rec from 1877, m rec from 1839)						
Douglas	C3	1859	19	1860–80	Coles	Tuscola
(Co Clk has b rec from 1870, m, d, pro, civ ct rec from 1859)						
DuPage	A3	1839	313	1840–80	Cook	Wheaton
Edgar	C4	1823	23	1830–80	Clark	Paris
Edwards	D3	1814	8	1820–80	Madison, Gallatin	Albion
(Co Clk has m & civ ct rec from 1814, pro rec from 1815, b & d rec from 1877)						
Effingham	D3	1831	23	1840–80	Fayette, Crawford	Effingham
Fayette	D3	1821	22	1830–80	Bond, Wayne, Clark, Jefferson	Vandalia
Ford	B3	1859	17	1860–80	Clark	Paxton
(Co Clk has m, pro, civ ct rec from 1859, b & d rec from 1878)						
Franklin	E3	1818	39	1820–80	White, Gallatin	Benton
(Co Clk has b & d rec from 1877, m rec from 1836, pro & civ ct rec from 1838)						

Fulton   B2 1823   42 1830-80 Pike .... Lewistown
Gallatin   E3 1812   8 1820-80 Randolph .... Shawneetown
  (Co Clk has b rec 1879, m rec 1830, d rec 1880, pro rec 1860)
Greene   C2 1821   17 1830-80 Madison .... Carrollton
  (Co Clk has b & d rec from 1877, m rec from 1821)
Grundy   B3 1841   22 1850-80 LaSalle .... Morris
  (Co Clk has incom b rec from 1877, incom d rec from 1878, m rec from 1841,
  pro rec from 1854)
Hamilton   D3 1821   10 1830-80 White .... McLeansboro
Hancock   B1 1825   25 1830-80 Pike, Unorg. Terr. .... Carthage
Hardin   E3 1839   6 1840-80 Pope .... Elizabethtown
Henderson   B1 1841   8 1850-80 Warren .... Oquawka
  (Co Clk has b & d rec from 1877, m, pro & civ ct rec from 1841)
Henry   B2 1825   49 1830-80 Fulton .... Cambridge
  (Co Clk has b & d rec from 1877, m rec from 1843, bur rec from 1839)
Iroquois   B3 1833   34 1840-80 Vermillion .... Watseka
Jackson   E2 1816   42 1820-80 Randolph, Johnson .... Murphysboro
Jasper   D3 1831   11 1840-80 Clay, Crawford .... Newton
  (Co Clk has b & d rec from 1877, m & pro rec from 1835)
Jefferson   D3 1819   32 1820-80 Edwards, White .... Mt. Vernon
Jersey   D2 1839   17 1840-80 Greene .... Jerseyville
Jo Daviess A2 1827   22 1830-80 Henry, Mercer, Putnam ...... Galena
Johnson   E3 1812   7 1820-80 Randolph .... Vienna
Kane   A4 1836 208 1840-80 LaSalle .... Geneva
Kankakee   B3 1853   92 1860-80 Iroquois, Will .... Kankakee
  (Co Clk has b rec from 1876, m & pro rec from 1853, d rec from 1870)
Kendall   A3 1841   18 1850-80 LaSalle, Kane .... Yorkville
  (Co Clk has b & d rec from 1878, m rec from 1841)
Knox   B2 1825   61 1830-80 Fulton .... Galesburg
  (Co Clk has b & d rec from 1878, m rec from 1835, pro & civ ct rec from 1832)
Lake   A3 1839 294 1840-80 McHenry .... Waukegan
LaSalle   B3 1831 111 1840-80 Putnam, Vermillion .... Ottawa
Lawrence   D4 1821   19 1830-80 Crawford, Edwards ..... Lawrenceville
Lee   A3 1839   39 1840-80 Ogle .... Dixon
  (Co Clk has b & d rec from 1916, pro and civ ct rec from 1839)
Livingston B3 1837   40 1840-80 LaSalle, McLean .... Pontiac
Logan   C2 1839   34 1840-80 Sangamon .... Lincoln
McDonough   B2 1830   29 1830-80 Schuyler .... Macomb
McHenry   A3 1836   84 1840-80 Cook .... Woodstock
McLean   B3 1830   84 1840-80 Tazewell, Unorg. Terr. .... Bloomington
Macon   C3 1829 118 1830-80 Shelby .... Decatur
Macoupin   C2 1829   44 1830-80 Madison, Greene .... Carlinville
  (Co Clk has b & d rec from 1877, m rec from 1829)
Madison   D2 1812 225 1820-80 St. Clair .... Edwardsville
  (Co Clk has b & d rec from 1868 to 1916, m rec from 1813)
Marion   D3 1823   39 1830-80 Fayette, Jefferson .... Salem
  (Co Clk has b, m, d, pro, civ ct rec from 1850)
Marshall   B2 1839   13 1840-80 Putnam .... Lacon
Mason   C2 1841   15 1850-80 Tazewell .... Havana
Massac   E3 1843   14 1850-80 Pope, Jefferson .... Metropolis
Menard   C2 1839   9 1840-80 Sangamon .... Petersburg
  (Co Clk has b & d rec from 1877, m, pro & civ ct rec from 1839)
Mercer   B2 1825   17 1830-80 Unorg. Terr., Pike .... Aledo
Monroe   D2 1816   16 1820-80 Randolph, St. Clair .... Waterloo
  (Co Clk has b rec 1865, m rec 1816, d rec 1878, pro rec 1845, civ ct rec 1843)
Montgomery C2 1821   31 1830-80 Bond, Madison .... Hillsboro
  (Co Clk has b & d rec from 1877, m & pro rec from 1821)
Morgan   C2 1823   37 1830-80 Sangamon .... Jacksonville
Moultrie   C3 1843   14 1850-80 Shelby, Macon .... Sullivan
Ogle   A3 1836   38 1840-80 Jo Daviess .... Oregon
  (Co Clk has b rec from 1860, m rec from 1837, d rec from 1878)

Peoria   B2   1825   189   1830–80   Fulton .... Peoria
   (Co Clk has b, m, civ ct rec from 1878, m rec from 1825)
Perry   E2   1827   19   1830–80   Randolph, Jackson .... Pinckneyville
   (Co Clk has incom b rec 1850, incom d rec 1827, m, pro & civ ct rec 1827)
Piatt   C3   1841   15   1850–80   DeWitt, Macon .... Monticello
Pike   C1   1821   21   1850–80   Madison, Bond, Clark ...... Pittsfield
Pope   E3   1816   4   1820–80   Gallatin, Johnson .... Golconda
   (Co Clk has b rec from 1875, m rec from 1816, d rec from 1878, pro rec 1820)
Pulaski   E3   1843   10   1850–80   Johnson .... Mound City
Putnam   B3   1825   5   1830–80   Fulton .... Hennepin
   (Co Clk has b & d rec from 1878, m, pro & civ ct rec from 1831)

County Map of Illinois

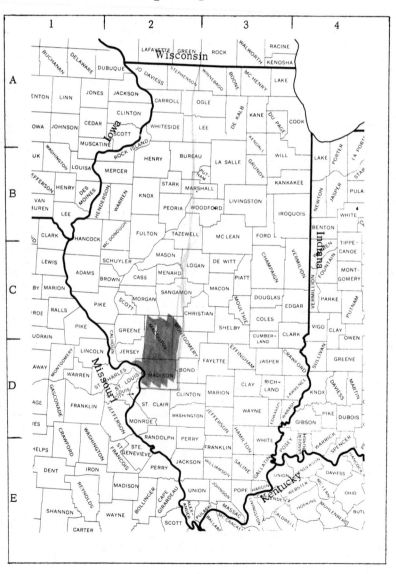

Randolph   E2   1795   30   1820-80   NW Territory, St. Clair . . . . . Chester
(Co Clk has b & d rec 1877, m, pro & civ ct rec from 1809)
Richland   D3   1841   16   1850-80   Clay, Lawrence . . . . Olney
(Co Clk has b rec from 1878, m rec from 1841)
Rock Island B2   1833   151   1840-80   Jo Daviess . . . Rock Island & Carbon Cliff
(Co Clk has b & d rec from 1877, m rec from 1833)
St. Clair   D2   1790   263   1820-80   NW Territory . . . . Belleville
Saline   E3   1847   26   1850-80   Gallatin . . . . Harrisburg
(Co Clk has b, m, d, bur, pro rec from ca 1890)
Sangamon   C2   1821   147   1830-80   Bond, Madison . . . . Springfield
(Co Clk has b & d rec from 1877, m rec from 1821)
Schuyler   C2   1825   9   1830-80   Pike, Fulton . . . . Rushville
(Co Clk has b rec from 1877, m rec from 1827)
Scott   C2   1839   6   1840-80   Morgan . . . . Winchester
(Co Clk has b, m, d, pro & civ ct rec from 1839)
Shelby   C3   1827   23   1830-80   Fayette . . . . Shelbyville
(Co Clk has b rec from 1879, m rec from 1827, d rec from 1878, pro rec 1839)
Stark   B2   1839   8   1840-80   Knox, Putnam . . . . Toulon
Stephenson   A2   1837   46   1840-80   Jo Daviess, Winnebago . . . . . . Freeport
(Co Clk has m & d rec from 1878, m rec from 1837, pro & civ ct rec from 1894)
Tazewell   B2   1827   100   1830-80   Sangamon . . . . Pekin
(Co Clk has b & d rec from 1878, m & pro rec from 1827, civ ct rec from 1840)
Union   E3   1818   18   1820-80   Johnson . . . . Jonesboro
Vermilion   C4   1826   96   1830-80   Unorg. Terr., Edgar . . . . . . Danville
Wabash   D4   1827   14   1830-80   Edwards . . . . Mt. Carmel
(Co Clk has b & d rec from 1878, m & pro rec from 1857)
Warren   B2   1825   22   1830-80   Pike . . . . Monmouth
(Co Clk has b & d rec from 1875, m rec from 1830, pro & civ ct rec from 1825)
Washington   D2   1818   14   1820-80   St. Clair . . . . Nashville
(Co Clk has   b & d rec from 1877, m rec from 1832, pro rec from 1850)
Wayne   D3   1819   19   1820-80   Edwards . . . . Fairfield
White   D3   1816   19   1820-80   Gallatin . . . . Carmi
Whiteside   A2   1839   60   1840-80   Jo Daviess, Henry . . . . Morrison
Will   B3   1836   192   1840-80   Cook, Iroquois . . . . Joliet
(Co Clk has b rec from 1836, m & d rec from 1877)
Williamson   E3   1839   46   1840-80   Franklin . . . . Marion
Winnebago   A3   1836   210   1840-80   Jo Daviess . . . . Rockford
(Co Clk has b & d rec from 1877 & m rec from 1837)
Woodford   B3   1841   25   1850-80   Tazewell, McLean . . . . Eureka
(Co Clk has b & d rec from 1877, m & pro rec from 1841)

Genealogists' Check List of the Historical Records Survey, Illinois (see page VIII)

Fed Cts (start before 1850. Fire 1871 destroyed most of rec up to that time); Inv of Co Arch - Adams, Brown, Carroll, Champaign, Clark, Cumberland, De Witt, Douglas, Effingham, Fayette, Franklin, Jackson, Jo Daviess, Knox, Livingston, Logan, Macon, Macoupin, Menard, Montgomery, Morgan, Moultrie, Ogle, Peoria, Piatt, Pike, Rock Island, Saline, Sangamon Scott, Shelby, St Clair, Stephenson, Vermilion; Guide to Pub Vit Stat Rec; Guide to Chr Vit Stat Rec; Inv of Chr Arch of Ill, Presbytery of Springfield, Cumberland Presbytery of Cairo, Presbytery of Springfield, Cumberland Presbyterian Chr; Dir of Negro Bap Chr in the US, two vol; Guide to Dep of Mss Col in Ill; Cal of the Robert Weidensall Cor 1861-1865, at George Williams College, Chicago, Ill; Cal of the Ezekiel Cooper Col of Early Am Methodist Mss 1785-1839; Check list of Chicago Ante-Fire Imprints 1851-1871; Check List of the Kellogg Col of "Patent Inside," Newspapers of 1876; Depo of unpubl mat, U of Ill, (Lincolniana); State Hist Lib, (Inv of Ms Col); State Arch (All other materials.)

Indiana

When the French explorers first came into the Indiana region about 1679, the entire territory was more or less a wilderness inhabited by a few Indians. During most of the 1700's, the only white men there were some fur traders.

The first counties to be settled were Knox, Harrison, Switzerland and Clark, in the extreme south end. Settlers in those counties came from Virginia, Kentucky and the Carolinas, although a group of Swiss emigrants established themselves in the southeast part of the state. The Wabash and the Ohio river sections drew many of the first settlers. Many Germans and Irish came there about 1830. About twenty years later New Englanders established themselves in the northern counties. The central part of the state was the last to be settled. Less than seventy years after the settlement of the state, the population had reached more than a million and a half. Abhoring slavery Quakers left Tennessee and the Carolinas and established themselves in Wayne and Randolph counties along the Ohio border mid-way north and south in Indiana.

With the development of the industrial area of the Calumet section, adjacent to the South Chicago area in the northwest part of the state many Central Europeans flocked there to man the rapidly increasing factories.

The marriage records are kept by the clerk of each county where the ceremony was performed.

Birth records before October, 1907 are in the office of the county health officer in the respective county seats; after October, 1907, in the office of the state health department, division of vital records, Indianapolis, Ind.

Death records before October, 1899 should be in the office of the county health officer; after October 1899, in the office of the division of vital records in Indianapolis

Records of wills and all probate matters are in the custody of the Clerk of the Circuit Court or County Clerk in most County Seats.

Real estate records, land titles, etc., are in the office of the county recorder in the various counties.

The first U. S. Census taken in Indiana was in 1800.

Libraries: Evansville, (Vanderburgh), Public Library, 22 S. E. Fifth St.; Indianapolis, (Marion), Indiana Historical Society, William Henry Smith Memorial Library, 140 N. Senate Ave. (Northwest Territory data); Public Library, Meridian & St. Clair Sts. (Genealogy); Muncie, (Delaware), Public Library, 301 E. Jackson St.; South Bend, (St. Joseph), Northern Indiana Historical Society, 112 S. Lafayette Blvd.

Lists of a score or more early day histories of the state and its people may be obtained in most libraries in the state. Most of the census records may be obtained at the State Library.

Highly valuable in all research activities in Indiana is a compilation by the Indiana State Library 140 No. Senate Ave., Indianapolis 4, of "A Consolidated Index to Thirty-two Histories of Indianapolis and Indiana, 1820-1830". It also has many volumes, microfilm records and manuscripts from the older counties of Indiana.

For a detailed account of the early settlements of the state, the reader is referred to the 1932 Year Book of the Society of Indiana Pioneers in which Charles Nebeker Thompson has an article dealing with "The Pioneer Period in Indiana."

Indiana County Histories

(Population figures to nearest thousand - 1960 Census)

Name	Map Index	Date Formed	Pop. By M	Census Reports Available	Parent County	County Seat
Adams	B3	1838	25	1840–80	Allen	Decatur
Allen	A3	1823	232	1830–80	Randolph	Fort Wayne
Bartholomew	C3	1821	48	1830–80	Indian Lands	Columbus
Benton	B2	1840	12	1850–80	Indian Lands	Fowler
Blackford	B3	1834	15	1840–80	Jay	Hartford City
Boone	B2	1830	28	1830–80	Indian Lands	Lebanon
Brown	C2	1836	7	1840–80	Morgan, Johnson, Monroe, Lawrence	Nashville

Carroll	B2	1828	17	1830–80	Indian Lands	Delphi
Cass	B7	1828	41	1830–80	Indian Lands, Allen	Logansport
Clark	D3	1801	63	1820–80	Knox	Jeffersonville
Clay	C2	1825	24	1830–80	Indian Lands	Brazil
Clinton	B2	1830	31	1830–80	Indian Lands	Frankfort
Crawford	D2	1818	8	1820–80	Orange	English
Daviess	C2	1817	27	1830–80	Indian Lands	Washington
Dearborn	C3	1803	29	1820–80	Original county	Lawrenceburg
Decatur	C3	1821	20	1830–80	Indian Lands	Greensburg
DeKalb	A3	1836	28	1840–80	Allen, Lagrange	Auburn
Delaware	B3	1827	111	1820–80	Henry	Muncie

(Co Clk has m, div, pro & civ ct rec from 1827)

| Dubois | D2 | 1817 | 27 | 1820–80 | Orange, Perry .... | Jasper |
| Elkhart | A3 | 1830 | 107 | 1830–80 | Indian Lands, Allen .... | Goshen |

(Co Clk has m rec from 1831, div, pro & civ ct rec from 1830)

Fayette	C3	1819	24	1820–80	Wayne	Connersville
Floyd	D3	1819	51	1820–80	Harrison, Clarke	New Albany
Fountain	B2	1826	19	1830–80	Montgomery	Covington
Franklin	C3	1811	17	1820–80	Wayne, Ripley	Brookville
Fulton	A2	1836	17	1840–80	Indian Lands, Allen	Rochester

(Co Clk has m, div, pro & civ ct rec from 1836)

| Gibson | D1 | 1813 | 30 | 1820–80 | Knox .... | Princeton |

(Co Clk has m rec from 1813, div, pro & civ ct rec from 1820)

Grant	B3	1831	75	1840–80	Delaware	Marion
Greene	C2	1820	26	1830–80	Knox	Bloomfield
Hamilton	B2	1823	40	1830–80	Hancock, Marion	Noblesville
Hancock	B3	1828	27	1830–80	Madison	Greenfield

(Co Clk has m rec from 1828, div, pro & civ ct rec from 1840)

| Harrison | D2 | 1809 | 19 | 1820–80 | Northwest Territory .... | Corydon |

(Co Clk has m, div, pro & civ ct rec from 1809)

Hendricks	C2	1824	41	1830–80	Indian Lands	Danville
Henry	B3	1822	49	1830–80	Indian Lands	New Castle
Howard	B2	1844	70	1850–80	Indian Lands (Originally Richardville County)	Kokomo
Huntington	B3	1834	34	1840–80	Allen	Huntington
Jackson	C2	1815	31	1820–80	Washington	Brownstown
Jasper	A2	1838	19	1840–80	Indian Lands	Rensselaer
Jay	B3	1837	23	1840–80	Randolph	Portland
Jefferson	C3	1810	24	1820–80	Indian Lands	Madison
Jennings	C3	1816	17	1820–80	Indian Lands	Vernon
Johnson	C2	1822	44	1830–80	Indian Lands	Franklin
Knox	C2	1787	42	1820–80	Northwest Territory	Vincennes

(Co Clk has m rec from 1807, pro rec from 1806, div & civ ct rec from 1796)

Kosciusko	A3	1835	40	1840–80	Indian Lands, Allen	Warsaw
Lagrange	A3	1832	17	1840–80	Unorganized Territory, Allen ..	Lagrange
Lake	A2	1837	513	1840–80	Porter, Newton	Crown Point

(Co Clk has m, div, pro, civ ct, crim ct rec from 1837)

LaPorte	A2	1832	95	1840–80	Indian Lands	LaPorte
Lawrence	C2	1818	37	1820–80	Orange	Bedford
Madison	B3	1823	126	1830–80	Fayette	Anderson
Marion	C2	1821	698	1830–80	Indian Lands	Indianapolis
Marshall	A2	1836	32	1840–80	Indian Lands, Allen	Plymouth

(Co Clk has m, div, pro, civ ct rec from 1836; Co public health office has b, d & bur from 1882)

Martin	C2	1820	11	1820–80	Indian Lands	Shoals
Miami	B2	1834	38	1840–80	Cass	Peru
Monroe	C2	1818	59	1820–80	Orange	Bloomington
Montgomery	B2	1823	32	1830–80	Indian Lands	Crawfordsville
Morgan	C2	1822	34	1830–80	Delaware	Martinsville
Newton	A2	1857	12	1860–80	Jasper	Kentland
Noble	A3	1836	28	1840–80	Elkhart, Lagrange	Albion

Ohio   C3   1844   4   1850-80   Dearborn . . . .   Rising Sun
   (Co Clk has m rec from 1882, div, pro, civ ct rec from 1844)
Orange   D2   1816   17   1820-80   Washington . . . .   Paoli
   (Co Clk has div & civ ct rec from 1874, pro rec from 1817)
Owen   C2   1818   11   1820-80   Indian Lands . . . .   Spencer
Parke   C2   1821   15   1830-80   Indian Lands . . . .   Rockville
   (Co Clk has m, div, pro, civ ct rec from 1833, b rec 1902, d rec 1882)
Perry   D2   1814   17   1820-80   Harrison, Warrick . . . .   Cannelton
Pike   D2   1817   13   1820-80   Indian Lands . . . .   Petersburg
Porter   A2   1832   60   1840-80   Indian Lands . . . .   Valparaiso
   (Co Clk has m, div, pro, civ ct rec from 1832)
Posey   D1   1814   19   1820-80   Knox . . . .   Mount Vernon
Pulaski   A2   1839   13   1840-80   Cass . . . .   Winamac
   (Co Clk has m, div, pro & civ ct rec from 1839)
Putnam   C2   1821   25   1830-80   Indian Lands . . . .   Greencastle
   (Co Clk has m rec 1822, div & civ ct rec 1828, pro rec 1825, wills 1844)
Randolph   B3   1818   28   1820-80   Wayne . . . .   Winchester
   (Co Clk has m rec from 1819, div & civ ct rec from 1830, pro rec from 1836)
Richardville   (see Howard)

County Map of Indiana

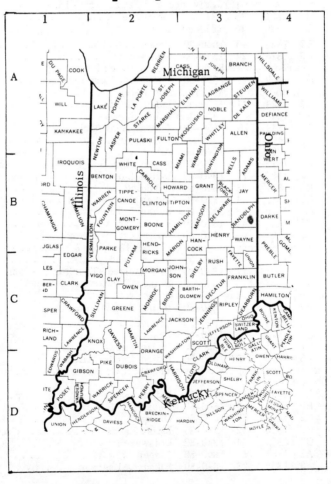

Ripley   C3 1817   21 1820-80 Indian Lands . . . . Versailles
(Co Clk has m, div, pro, civ ct rec from 1818)
Rush   C3 1821   20 1830-80 Franklin . . . . Rushville
Saint Joseph A2 1830 239 1830-80 Indian Lands, Allen . . . . . . South Bend
Scott   C3 1820   15 1820-80 Clark, Jackson . . . . Scottsburg
Shelby   C3 1821   34 1830-80 Indian Lands . . . . Shelbyville
Spencer   D2 1817   16 1820-80 Warrick . . . . Rockport
Starke   A2 1835   18 1840-80 Marshall . . . . Knox
(Co Clk has m rec from 1850, div, pro, civ ct rec from 1851)
Steuben   A3 1837   17 1840-80 Indian Lands, Allen . . . . Angola
Sullivan   C2 1817   22 1820-80 Unorganized Territory . . . . . . Sullivan
Switzerland   C3 1814   7 1820-80 Indian Lands . . . . Vevay
Tippecanoe   B2 1826   74 1830-80 Montgomery . . . . Lafayette
Tipton   B2 1844   16 1850-80 Hamilton . . . . Tipton
Union   C3 1821   6 1830-80 Wayne, Franklin . . . . Liberty
(Co Clk has m, div, pro & civ ct rec from 1821; Co health dept has b rec from
1882, d rec from 1907)
Vanderburgh D1 1818 166 1820-80 Indian Lands . . . . Evansville
(Co Clk has m, civ, pro & civ ct rec from 1835)
Vermillion   B2 1824   18 1830-80 Parke . . . . Newport
Vigo   C2 1818 108 1820-80 Indian Lands . . . . Terre Haute
Wabash   B3 1835   33 1840-80 Huntington . . . . Wabash
(Co Clk has m rec from 1835)
Warren   B2 1827   9 1830-80 Indian Lands . . . . Williamsport
(Co Clk has b rec 1882 to 1948, m, div, civ ct rec from 1828, pro rec from 1829)
Warrick   D2 1813   24 1820-80 Indian Lands . . . . Boonville
Washington   D2 1813   18 1820-80 Indian Lands . . . . Salem
(Co Clk has m rec 1815, div rec 1820, pro, civ ct rec 1814, wills 1821)
Wayne   B3 1810   74 1820-80 Indian Lands . . . . Richmond
(Co Clk has m rec from 1811, div & civ ct rec from 1873, pro rec from 1818)
Wells   B3 1835   21 1840-80 Huntington, Allen . . . . Bluffton
(Co Clk has m rec 1836, div rec 1850, pro rec 1837, civ ct rec 1853; Co health
dept has b rec 1904)
White   B2 1834   20 1840-80 Carroll . . . . Monticello
(Co Clk has m, div, pro, civ ct rec from 1834)
Whitley   A3 1828   21 1840-80 Huntington . . . . Columbia City

---

Genealogists' Check List of the Historical Records Survey, Indiana (see page VIII)

Fed Cts (start 1800); Inv of Co Arch – Allen, Blackford, Boone, Clay, Delaware, Fulton, Greene, Howard, Jay, La Porte, Marion, Marshall, Monroe, Morgan, Posey, St Joseph, Shelby, Tippecanoe, Tipton, Vanderburgh, Warrick, Wells; Guide to Pub Vit Stat Rec; Dir of Chrs & Rel Org in Ind, Vol 1 Marion Co, Vol 2 Calumet Region (Lake, Porter & La Porte Cos), Vol 3 Northern Ind Pt 1 Adventist Bodies & Mennonite Bodies, Pt 2 Methodist & YWCA; Check List of Ind Co Rec with Introduction on Co Gov Org; State Legislation pertaining to Arch and Rec – Sample Pages for Ind.

Microfilms were made of the following county records of Ind. (# indicates the roll number.)

Allen Co: #61 Deed Rec (A,B,C,D) 1824-1842, Commissioners Rec (A,B,C) 1824-1850; #62 Will Rec 1831-1855, Probate Order Book (A,B) 1825-1844, Civil Order Books (A,B) 1824-1839, Mar Rec (2 Vol) 1847-1856; #63, Mar Rec (5 Vol) 1857-1872; #64, Mar Rec (5 Vol) 1872-1880.

Clark Co: #17 Probate Order Book (Vol A) 1817-1828, Probate Order Book (Vol B) 1828-1835, Birth Rec 1882-1893, 1899-1907, 1882-1886, 1886-1890, 1888-1891, 1897-1899, 1900-1901, 1901-1907, Estray Book 1802-1818, Ct Common Pleas 1801-1805, 1806-1808, 1808-1810; #18, Order Book Ct Common Pleas 1810-1817, Ct Rec 1802-1813, Minute Book Ct Common Pleas 1801-1805, 1801-1803, 1803-1808, 1808-1814, Minute Book Circuit Ct & Commissioners Rec 1815-1820, Commissioners Rec 1820-1824, 1824-1828, 1832-1839; #19, Commissioners Rec 1839-1843, 1843-1845, 1845-1852, Seminary Rec 1830-1851, Alien Rec (Aliens to become Citizens of US) 1845-1852, Probate Order Book "C" (Estate of Jonathan Jennings) 1836, Appraisal and Estates of Jonathan Jennings Deceased 1833-1840; #58, Minutes Board Commissioners apportioning lands to Ill Regiment 1785-1820, Order Book Ct Quarter Sessions (2 Vol) 1801-1808, Ct Order Book 1807-1813.

Dearborn Co: #54, Mar Rec (Bks 8-13) 1846-1879; #54a, Mar Rec (2 Vol) 1880-1889; #55, Commissioners Rec (5 bks) 1826-1851, Surveyors Bk 1799-1805, Deed Rec Bk AA Prior to 1826; #56, Deed Rec (BB & CC) Prior to 1826 - (A to D) 1826-1830, Will Rec 1824-1832, Probate Ct Rec 1826-1830, Order Bk Circuit Ct (2 Vol) 1824-1829; #57, Birth Rec (7 Vol) 1882-1907.

Floyd Co: #13, Rar Rec 1819-1837, 1837-1845, 1845-1853, 1853-1857, 1858-1864, 1864-1871; #14, Mar Rec 1871-1878, 1878-1885, 1885-1891, Birth Rec 1882-1885, 1885-1887, 1887-1889, 1889-1891; #15, Birth Rec 1891-1894, 1894-1902, 1897-1903, 1904-1906, 1903-1907, 1900-1907, 1904-1907, Deed Rec (Vol A) 1818-1820, (Vol B) 1820-1825, (Vol C) 1825-1829, Will & Probate Rec (A) 1818-1829; #16, Mar Rec General Index No. 1 1808-1878, No. 2 1879-1897, Mar Rec (Vol A) 1808-1820, (Vol B) 1820-1828, (Vol C) 1828-1834 (Vol D) 1834-1841, Will Rec (Vol A) 1801-1817, (Vol B) 1817-1833.

Franklin Co: #48, Issue Docket 1811, Ct Common Pleas (Min of Bks B & C) 1811-1814, Apprentice Rec 1831-1853, Ct Common Pleas 1814, Will Rec (2 Vol) 1814-1831, Probate Order Bk 1827-1834, Probate Rec 1811-1829, Order Bk Circuit Ct (2 Vol) 1815-1819, (2 Vol) 1823-1828; #49, Order Bk Circuit Ct (4 Vol) 1819-1825, (3 Vol) 1828-1836, Minute Bk Circuit Ct 1815, Inv Estates 1811-1820, Fee Bk Circuit Ct 1811-1816; #50, Mar Rec (2 Vol, Index) 1811- 1824, (8 Vol) 1811-1868; #51, Mar Rec (4 Vol) 1868-1890, Birth Rec (4 Vol) 1882-1907, Brookville Birth Rec 1894-1907, Stock Brands 1811-1839, Estray Book 1811-1814, Min Bk Circ Ct 1815-1816, Reference Docket Circuit Ct 1815-1816, Execution Docket Circuit Ct 1811-1816; #52, Deed Rec (7 Vol) 1810-1830; #53, Mar Rec (Bks 1 to 7) 1826-1846.

Gibson Co: #34, Will Rec (3 Vol) 1813-1834, Probate Order Bk (A) 1817-1830, Order Bk Ct Common Pleas & Circuit Ct (A) 1813-1818, Order Bk Circuit Ct (B) 1820-1821, (C) 1821-1828, 1828-1839; #34, Common Pleas & Circuit Ct 1813-1820, Commissioners Rec 1835-1845; #35 Commissioners Rec 1845-1854, Birth Rec 1882-1907 #36, Princeton Birth Rec 1882-1907, Deed Rec (Vol A, B, C, D) 1813-1833, Co Tax List 1819-1826, #37, Mar Licenses (3 Vol) 1813-1868, Mar Rec (3 to 7) 1863-1890.

Harrison Co: #7, Estray Bk 1809-1817,

Tract Book 1807-1821, Deed Rec (Vol A) 1809-1817, (Vol B) 1817-1818, (Vol C) 1818-1822, (Vol D) 1822-1826, (Vol E) 1825-1829; # 8, Birth Rec (A) 1882-1886, (B) 1886-1888, (C) 1888-1890, (D) 1891-1893, (E) 1893-1897, (F) 1897-1900, (G) 1900-1904, (H) 1906-1907; Ms of William Mitchell 1725; Commissioners Rec (A) 1817-1824, (B) Letters of Corydon Branch Bank 1825-1830, (C) 1831-1838, (D) 1838-1844; #9, Commissioners Rec (Vol E) 1844-1849, (Vol F) 1849-1853, Will Rec Bk (A) 1809-1832, Seminary Rec (in possession of the Griffith Family, Corydon) 1827-1851, Ct Rec (partly Probate) 1815-1817, Probate Ct Rec 1817-1829, Ct Rec 1809-1816, 1814-1817, Circuit Ct Order Bk (B) 1820-1825, (C) 1817-1820; #10, Ct Rec 1817-1819, McClure Workingmens Institute 1855-1858, Account Bk of J.B. Slaughter 1818-1830, Min Bk Ct Common Pleas 1811-1814, Indices to Mar 1809-1817 & part 1842-1846, Mars 1809-1817, 1817-1832, Mar Rec (Vol B) 1826-1852, (Vol C) 1853-1859, (Vol E) 1859-1866; #11, Mar Affidavits (Vol 1) 1866-1875, Mar Rec (Vol F) 1866-1871, (Vol G) 1872-1875, (Vol H) 1876-1879, (Vol I) 1879-1882; # 12, Mar Rec (Vol J) 1882-1885, (Vol K) 1885-1888, (Vol L) 1888-1892.

Jefferson Co: #20, Will Rec (Vol A) 1811-1822, (Vol B) 1822-1827, (Vol C) 1827-1832 Civil Order Bk 1812-1818, Circuit Ct Rec 1811-1819, Treasurers Bk 1812, License Rec (by Treasurer) 1816-1837, Commissioners Rec 1817-1822, 1822-1832, 1836-1838; #21, Commissioners Rec 1832-1835, 1838-1840, 1840-1843, 1843-1847, 1847-1850, 1850-1854, Tax List 1827; #22, Birth Rec 1882-1896, 1897-1905, 1905-1907, 1882-1890, 1890-1896, 1893-1896, 1896-1900, 1901-1904, 1906-1907, Deed Rec Index for Vol "A" to "F" (inclusive 1811-1830), Deed Rec (Vol A) 1811-1817, (Vol B) 1816-1820; #23, Deed Rec (Vol C) 1820-1823, (Vol D) 1823-1827, (Vol E) 1827-1829 (Vol F) 1829-1830, Mar Rec 1811-1832, 1831-1836, 1836-1839; #24, Mar Rec 1839-1841, 1841-1845, 1845-1850, 1850-1853, Mar Rec Indices to Men (9 Vol) 1853-1891.

Jennings Co: #25, Birth Rec 1882-1884, 1885-1888, 1888-1893, 1893-1898 & 1903-1904, 1899-1902, 1904-1907, Circuit Ct 1817-1822, Will and Probate Rec 1818-1829, Probate Rec 1830-1836, Deed Rec (Vol A) 1817-1828, (Vol B) 1829-1833; #26, Commissioners Rec 1824-1836, 1836-1846, Index to Mar Rec 1818-1845, Mar Rec 1818-1830, 1830-1837, 1837-1845, 1845-1850; #27, Mar Rec 1850-1858, 1858-

1866, 1866-1873, 1873-1879, 1879-1887, Mar Returns 1881-1888.

Knox Co: #28, Reg of Negro Slaves 1805-1807, Minutes of Orphans Ct 1796-1805, Min of the Ct of Gen Quarter Sessions 1796 1801, 1801-1805, Chancery Appearance 1806-1810, Min Ct of Chancery 1807-1811, Ct Common Pleas 1790-1792, Min Ct Common Pleas 1796-1801, 1796-1799, 1801-1806, 1806-1810, 1807-1810, 1810-1813, Circuit Ct of Oyer & Terminer, General Jail Deliver, & Nisi Prius held by Fed Judge 1795, Min to Circuit Ct 1816-1818, Order Bk Common Pleas 1811-1813 and Order Bk Circuit Ct (A) 1814-1820 (B) 1817-1822; # 29, Order Bk Circuit Ct (Vol C) 1821-1825, (Vol D) 1825-1831, Will Rec 1806-1852, Probate Ct Rec 1790-1805, 1817-1829, 1829-1832, 1832-1839, Poor Relief Rec 1821-1832, Gen Index to Deeds 1814-1829 #30, Deed Rec (Vol A) 1814-1817, (B) 1817-1822, (C) 1822-1826, (D) 1826-1829, Ct of Claim 1814-1816 & Commissioners Rec 1817-1820, Commissioners Rec (Vol A) 1823-1839, (B) 1839-1847; #31, Commissioners Rec (Vol A 1827-1855, Birth Rec 1882-1886, 1886-1898, 1897-1899, 1899-1901, 1900-1902, 1902-1903, 1903-1904; #32, Birth Rec 1904-1905, 1905-1906, 1906 1907, Min Bd Trustees Vincennes U 1806-1836, Birth Rec (Vincennes) 1893-1903, 1903-1906, Mar Rec (Vol 4) 1838-1854, (Vol E) 1854-1860, (Vol F) 1860-1866; #33, Mar Rec (G,8,9,10) 1866-1883, Mar Returns 1881-1889, Estate Judge William Clarke 1802, Estate Moses Henry 1790, George Rogers Clark 1796, Jonathan Jennings 1807; #65, Borough of Vincennes: Trustees Proceedings 1815-1816, Ord 1816-1836, Treas Accounts 1819-1840, Common Rec 1818-1837, Jour of Borough Trustees 1820-1836, Misc Papers (Vincennes) 1784-1815c.

Perry Co: #59, Deed Rec 1815-1835, Circuit Ct (Complete Rec) 1817-1834, Commissioners Rec 1847-1851, Will Rec 1813-1843, Circuit Ct Order Bk (2 Vol) 1815-1832, Mar Rec (2 Vol) 1815-1861; #60, Mar Rec (4 Vol) 1861-1890, Birth Rec (3 Vol) 1889-1905.

Posey Co: #38, Deed Rec (Vol A to E) 1812-1832, Will Rec Index (A),(B) 1816-1852, Rec Circuit Ct & Probate Order Bk 1815-1827; #39, Probate Order 1828-1834, Circuit Ct Order Bk (A,B,C) 1815-1829, Gen Index Commissioners Rec to Vols A, B,C,D,E,F,G,H,I,J,K,L, 1817-1855, Commissioners Rec (A,B,C,D,E,F) 1817-1842; #40, Commissioners Rec (G,H,I,J,K,L) 1842-1855, Birth Rec (4 Vol) 1882-1900 a. Vol 1887-1893 contains rec of co Mt. Vernon & New Harmony; #41, Birth Rec (2 Vol) 1900-1907, Mar Rec Index Vols 1 & 2 1815-1846, Mar Rec (Vol 1-5) 1815-1868; #42, Mar Rec (Vol 6-8) 1868-1882, Mar Returns 1882-1887, 1887-1900.

Scott Co: #1, Deed Rec (A) 1819-1827, (B) 1826-1828, Land Entry Bk, Commissioners Rec (A) 1820-1840, (B) 1841-1851, Vol 1 1851-1865.

Washington Co: #5, Commissioners Rec (C) 1839-1846, (D) 1846-1855, Tract Bk deed Rec (Vol A) 1814-1817, (Vol B) 1817-1823, (Vol C) 1823-1826; #6, Deed Rec (Vol D) 1824-1828, (Vol E) 1827-1830, Will Rec 1821-1830, Circuit Ct Min Bk 1814-1818, Probate Order Bk (A) 1814-1824, (B) not photographed, (C) 1837-1841, Appraisement of Benjamin Parks Estate 1835, Sale Bill of Benjamin Parks Estate 1835.

Depo of unpubl mat, Indiana State Lib, Indianapolis, Ind.

Iowa

Capital Des Moines - Territory 1838 - State 1846 - (29th)

Outside of a few explorers and priests passing by on the Mississippi and some fur traders trapping along the rivers, no white man came to Iowa until about 1788.

Before Iowa became a territory in its own name in 1838, it had been part of the Missouri Territory, 1812-1821; unorganized territory, 1824-1834; the Michigan Territory, 1834-1836, and the Wisconsin Territory, 1836-1838.

Five years prior to becoming a Territory, Iowa had an influx of white settlers after a treaty with some of the numerous Indian tribes inhabiting the country had made it possible for settlements to be established. The first settlers came from the Eastern and the Southern states. Most of them were originally from the British Isles.

Among the thousands of immigrants who flocked to Iowa immediately prior to and after it had gained statehood were Scandinavians to the central and the western sections of the state, Hollanders to the south-central section, Germans along the Mississippi, Scotch and Welch to the mining towns of the southern counties, and many Czechs to the east-central section.

Iowa City, Johnson County, was the capital of Iowa until 1857 when it was moved about 110 miles west to Des Moines, Polk County.

The Division of Vital Statistics, State Department of Health, State Office Building, Des Moines 19, Iowa, has birth, marriage and death records. More or less incomplete birth records available up to 1897, less complete to January 1819. Death records available in some instances from 1880, and complete from 1905. Marriage records available since 1880.

The offices of the Clerk of the District Court in each County also have similar records of births, marriages and deaths; some marriage records on file since 1832; also records of all probate matters, wills and divorce proceedings of the cases handled in the respecitve counties.

The Court Auditor is the same as Court Clerk in most states, but the Clerk of the District Court has charge of most of the vital records.

Naturalization information may be obtained from the clerk of the United States Circuit Court in Des Moines and Dubuque, the Superior Courts of Council Bluffs and Cedar Rapids, and the district courts in the various county seats.

Real estate records are in the offices of the county recorder, taxpayers lists in the offices of the county treasurer.

The first federal census was taken in Iowa in 1840. Special state enumerations were taken in 1885, 1895, 1915 and 1925. They are on file at the Department of History and Archives, Historical Bldg., Des Moines Iowa.

War service records of Iowa participants in the Civil War, the Spanish-American War, World War I, and members of the National Guard from 1900 to date are in the office of the Adjutant General, State House, Des Moines, Iowa.

Libraries: Davenport, (Scott), Public Library, 321 Main St.; Des Moines, (Polk) Public Library, 100 Locust St., State Historical & Archive Dept. of Iowa; Iowa City, (Johnson), State Historical Society of Iowa Library; Sioux City, (Woodbury), Public Library, 6 & Jackson Sts.; Waterloo, (Black Hawk), 5th & Mulberry St.

Among books dealing with historical and genealogical information concerning Iowa are the following:

"Historical Atlas of State of Iowa", A. T. Andreas, Lakeside Press, 1875.

"Biographical History of Pottawattamie County, Iowa." The Lewis Publishing Company, 1891. 172 pp.

"Iowa Old and New" J. E. Briggs, University Publishing Company, 1939.

"Iowa; Its History and Its Foremost Citizens" Brigham Johnson

"History of Des Moines."

"Iowa; Through the Years" Cyrenus Cole, Iowa Historical Society. 1940 (Accurate historical account.)

"County Histories and Biographical Histories" every county, 99, in Iowa has had a history written about it, and its people, some counties have as many as five different books.

"Early Algona, The Story of Our Pioneers, 1854-1874" Florence Call Cowles, The Register and Tribune Company, Des Moines, Iowa 1929. 221 pp.

"Iowa Democracy, History of Politics" 1916, John D. Denison, S. J. Clarks Pub. Co.

"History of Iowa" 4 vol. Benjamin F. Gue, Century Historical Co of N. Y., 1903.

"Narrative, History of People of Iowa" Edgar R. Harlan, five vol. American Historical Soc. Chicago, 1931.

"Prominent Iowans" a Deluxe supplement to Iowa, Its History and Foremost citizens.

"Iowa History" Wm. J. Peterson, 4 vols, 1952, and genealogical histories.

"Hawkeye" Herbert Quick, Grosset, 1939. (Iowa life from 1857 to 1858)

"Ioway to Iowa" Irving Richman, Iowa State Historical Society, 1931. (Reliable history of early days in Iowa)

"Progressive Men of Iowa" 1899, "The First Census of the Original Counties of Dubuque and Demoine, Iowa, Taken in July 1836" Benjamin F. Shambaugh, The Historical Department of Iowa, Des Moines Iowa 1897. 93 pp.

"Notable Lawyers and Public men of Early Iowa to First and Second Generations" Edward Holcom Stiles, Des Moines Homestead Publ. Co 1916.

"Hawkeyes; a Biography of the State of Iowa" Phillip Duffield Stong, Dodd, 1940.

"An Illustrated History of the State of Iowa from its Exploration down to 1875" Charles R. Tuttle and Daniel S. Durrie, Richard S. Peale and Company 1876. Biographical sketches in the last fifty-five pages.

"U. S. Biographical Dictionary and Portrait Gallery" Iowa Volume 1878.

"Who's Who in Iowa" Iowa Press, 1940.

"A Guide to the Hawkeye State" Works Projects Adminstration, Viking, 1938. (American Guide Series)

Iowa County Histories

(Population figures to nearest thousand - 1960 Census)

Name	Map Index	Date Formed	Pop. By M	Census Reports Available	Parent County	County Seat
Adair	C2	1851	11	1860-80	Cass	Greenfield

(Clk of Dist Ct has b rec from 1880, m, div & civ ct rec from 1852)

| Adams | C2 | 1851 | 7 | 1860-80 | Taylor | Corning |
| Allamakee | A4 | 1847 | 16 | 1850-80 | Clayton | Waukon |

(Clk of Dist Ct has b, d, bur, div rec from 1880, m, civ ct & pro rec from 1850)

| Appanoose | C3 | 1846 | 16 | 1850-80 | Davis | Centerville |

(Clk of Dist Ct has b & d rec 1880 to 1935, m & pro rec 1846; div & civ ct rec 1848)

| Audubon | B2 | 1855 | 11 | 1860-80 | Cass, Black Hawk | Audubon |

(Clk of Dist Ct has b, d, bur rec from 1880, m rec from 1856, div rec from 1881, pro rec from 1869, civ ct rec from 1864)

Benton	B3	1846	23	1850-80	Indian Land Purchase	Vinton
Black Hawk	B3	1843	122	1850-80	Delaware	Waterloo
Boone	B2	1846	28	1850-80	Polk	Boone
Bremer	A3	1851	21	1860-80	Winnebago, Indian Reserve	Waverly
Buchanan	B3	1837	22	1850-80	Delaware	Independence

(Clk of Dist Ct has b & d rec from 1880, m, pro, civ ct rec from 1845)

| Buena Vista | A1 | 1859 | 21 | 1860-80 | Sac, Clay | Storm Lake |

(Clk of Dist Ct has b rec 1880, m rec 1878, d rec 1897, div, pro, civ ct rec 1887)

| Butler | A3 | 1853 | 17 | 1860-80 | Buchanan, Black Hawk | Allison |

(Clk of Dist Ct has b & d rec from 1880, m, div, pro, & civ ct rec from 1854)

Calhoun	B2	1855	16	1860-80	Formerly Fox County	Rockwell City
Carroll	B2	1854	23	1860-80	Guthrie	Carroll
Cass	C1	1853	18	1860-80	Pottawattamie	Atlantic

(Clk of Dist Ct has b & d rec from 1880, m rec from 1877, div rec from 1906, pro rec from 1870, Dist ct rec from 1865)

Cedar	B4	1838	18	1840-80	Wisconsin Territory	Tipton
Cerro Gordo	A3	1855	50	1860-80	Floyd	Mason City
Cherokee	A1	1857	19	1860-80	Crawford	Cherokee
Chickasaw	A3	1851	15	1860-80	Fayette	New Hampton

(Clk of Dist Ct has b rec from 1880, m, d, bur, div, pro, civ ct rec from 1854)

Clarke	C2	1846	8	1850-80	Lucas	Osceola
Clay	A1	1858	19	1850-80	Indian Lands	Spencer
Clayton	A4	1837	27	1840-80	Dubuque	Elkader
Clinton	B4	1839	55	1840-80	Dubuque	Clinton
Crawford	B1	1855	19	1860-80	Shelby	Denison

(Clk of Dist Ct has b, d, bur, div rec from 1880, m, pro, civ ct rec from 1855)

Dallas	B2	1847	24	1850-80	Polk	Adel
Davis	C3	1844	9	1850-80	Van Buren	Bloomfield
Decatur	C2	1850	11	1850-80	Appanoose	Leon

(Clk of Dist Ct has b, m, d, div, pro, civ ct rec from 1880)(Ct house burned 1880)

Delaware	B4	1837	18	1840-80	Dubuque	Manchester
Des Moines	C4	1836	45	1840-80	Wisconsin Terr.	Yarmouth & Burlington
Dickinson	A1	1857	13	1860-80	Kossuth	Spirit Lake

(Clk of Dist Ct has b, m, d, bur, div, pro & civ ct rec from 1880)

| Dubuque | B4 | 1835 | 80 | 1840-80 | Michigan Territory | Dubuque |

(Clk of Dist Ct has b & d rec 1880, m rec 1838, div & civ ct rec 1837, pro rec 1835, Land Transfers 1836)

Emmett	A2	1859	15	1860-80	Kossuth, Dickinson	Estherville
Fayette	A3	1850	29	1850-80	Clayton	West Union
Floyd	A3	1854	21	1860-80	Chickasaw	Charles City

(Clk of Dist Ct has b & d rec 1880, m & div rec 1860, pro & civ ct rec 1854)

Fox	(See Calhoun)					
Franklin	A3	1855	15	1860-80	Chickasaw	Hampton
Fremont	C1	1847	10	1850-80	Pottawattamie	Sidney
Greene	B2	1854	14	1860-80	Dallas	Jefferson

Grundy   B3   1856   14   1860-80   Black Hawk .... Grundy Center
Guthrie   B2   1851   14   1860-80   Jackson .... Guthrie Center
Hamilton   B2   1856   20   1860-80   Webster .... Webster City
   (Clk of Dist Ct has b & d rec from 1880, m, div, pro, civ ct rec from 1857)
Hancock   A2   1857   15   1860-80   Wright .... Garner
   (Clk of Dist Ct has b, d, bur rec from 1880, m rec from 1861, div rec from
   1873, pro rec from 1869, civ ct rec from 1865)
Hardin   B3   1853   23   1860-80   Black Hawk .... Eldora
   (Clk of Dist Ct has b, d, bur rec 1881 to 1921, m, div, pro, civ ct rec 1854)
Harrison   B1   1853   18   1860-80   Pottawattamie .... Logan
   (Clk of Dist Ct has b rec 1880, m, div, pro, civ ct rec 1853, d rec 1880 to 1910)
Henry   C4   1836   18   1840-80   Wisconsin Territory .... Mount Pleasant
Howard   A3   1855   18   1860-80   Chickasaw, Floyd .... Cresco
Humboldt   A2   1857   13   1860-80   Webster .... Dakota City
   (Clk of Dist Ct has b rec from 1880, m rec from 1858, d rec from 1895, div rec
   from 1890, pro rec from 1873, civ ct rec from 1892)
Ida   B1   1858   13   1860-80   Cherokee .... Ida Grove
Iowa   B3   1847   10   1850-80   Washington .... Marengo
Jackson   B4   1837   16   1840-80   Wisconsin Territory ...... Maquoketa
Jasper   B3   1846   21   1850-80   Mahaska .... Newton
   (Clk of Dist Ct has b, d, bur rec 1880, m, pro, civ ct rec 1849, div rec 1852)
Jefferson   C3   1839   35   1840-80   Indian Land Purchase .... Fairfield
   (Clk of Dist Ct has b, d, div, civ ct rec 1880, m rec 1839, pro rec 1850)
Johnson   B4   1838   16   1840-80   Des Moines .... Iowa City
Jones   B4   1837   54   1840-80   Wisconsin Territory .... Anamosa
   (Clk of Dist Ct has b & d rec from 1880, m rec from 1840, div rec from 1895)
Keokuk   C3   1844   21   1850-80   Washington .... Sigourney
Kossuth   A2   1855   15   1860-80   Webster .... Algona
   (Clk of Dist Ct has b & d rec from 1880, m div, pro, civ ct rec from 1857)
Lee   C4   1836   44   1840-80   Des Moines .... Ft. Madison & Keokuk
   (Clk of Dist Ct, Ft. Madison has b rec 1880 to 1921, d rec 1880 to 1919, m &
   civ ct rec 1837, pro rec 1883)(Clk of Dist Ct, Keokuk has most rec from 1880)
Linn   B4   1837   137 1840-80   Wisconsin Territory ..... Cedar Rapids
   (Clk of Dist Ct has b rec 1880, d rec 1941, m, div, pro, civ ct rec 1837)
Louisa   C4   1837   10   1840-80   Des Moines .... Wapello
   (Clk of Dist Ct has b & d rec from 1880, m, div, pro, civ ct rec from 1837)
Lucas   C2   1849   11   1850-80   Monroe .... Chariton
Lyon   A1   1851   14   1870-80   Woodbury .... Rock Rapids
Madison   C2   1850   12   1850-80   Polk .... Winterset
Mahaska   C3   1844   24   1850-80   Fox, Sac Indian Purchase ... Oskaloosa
   (Clk of Dist Ct has b & d rec from 1880, m, div, pro, & civ ct rec from 1844)
Marion   C3   1845   26   1850-80   Washington .... Knoxville
Marshall   B3   1849   38   1850-80   Jasper .... Marshalltown
   (Clk of Dist Ct has b & d rec from 1880, m, div, pro, civ ct rec from 1850)
Mills   C1   1851   13   1860-80   Pottawattamie .... Glenwood
   (Clk of Dist Ct has incom b rec 1880, d & div rec 1880, pro & civ ct rec 1851)
Mitchell   A3   1854   14   1860-80   Chickasaw .... Osage
   (Clk of Dist Ct has m rec from 1860, b, d, div, pro & civ ct rec from 1880)
Monona   B1   1854   14   1860-80   Harrison .... Onawa
Monroe   C3   1845   10   1850-80   Wapello .... Albia
   (Clk of Dist Ct has b & d rec from 1880, m rec from 1845, div & civ ct rec
   from 1869, pro rec from 1854)
Montgomery C1   1851   14   1860-80   Polk .... Red Oak
Muscatine   A4   1837   34   1840-80   Des Moines .... Muscatine
O'Brien   A1   1851   19   1860-80   Cherokee .... Primghar
Osceola   A1   1851   10   1870-80   Woodbury .... Sibley
   (Clk of Dist Ct has b, m, d, div, pro, civ ct rec from 1880)
Page   C1   1850   21   1850-80   Pottawattamie .... Clarinda
Palo Alto   A2   1858   15   1860-80   Kossuth .... Emmetsburg
Plymouth   A1   1858   24   1860-80   Woodbury .... Le Mars
   (Clk of Dist Ct has b, d, bur rec from 1880, m, div, pro & civ ct rec from 1871,
   nat rec from 1872)

Pocahontas A2 1859   14 1860–80 Humboldt, Greene .... Pocahontas
(Clk of Dist Ct has b & d rec from 1880, m rec from 1881, div & civ ct rec
from 1860, pro rec from 1872)
Polk   B2 1836 266 1850–80 Indian Lands .... Des Moines
Pottawattamie C1 1848   83 1850–80 Indian Lands .... Council Bluffs
Poweshiek   B3 1848   19 1850–80 Musquaka .... Montezuma
(Clk of Dist Ct has b, m, d, div, pro, civ ct rec from 1880)
Ringgold   C2 1855   8 1860–80 Taylor .... Mount Ayr
Sac   B1 1857   17 1860–80 Greene .... Sac City
(Clk of Dist Ct has b, m, d, bur, div, pro, civ ct rec from 1888, Ct house
burned in 1888)
Scott   B4 1837 119 1840–80 Wisconsin Territory ...... Davenport
Shelby   B1 1853   16 1860–80 Cass .... Harlan
Sioux   A1 1860   26 1860–80 Plymouth .... Orange City
(Clk of Dist Ct has b rec from 1880, m, d, div, pro, civ ct rec from 1870)
Story   B2 1853   49 1860–80 Jasper, Polk, Boone .... Nevada
(Clk of Dist Ct has b & d rec from 1880, m, div, pro, civ ct crim rec from 1854)
Tama   B3 1852   21 1850–80 Boone, Benton .... Toledo
(Clk of Dist Ct has b rec from 1880, m rec from 1853, d rec from 1880, div rec
from 1908, pro rec from 1895, civ ct rec from 1859)
Taylor   C2 1851   10 1850–80 Page .... Bedford
Union   C2 1855   14 1860–80 Clarke .... Creston
Van Buren   C3 1836   10 1840–80 Des Moines .... Keosauqua
Wapello   C3 1844   46 1850–80 Indian Lands .... Ottumwa
Warren   C2 1846   21 1850–80 Polk .... Indianola
(Clk of Dist Ct has b & d rec from 1880, m, div, pro rec from 1859)
Washington C4 1837   19 1840–80 Wisconsin Territory ...... Washington
(Clk of Dist Ct has b & d rec from 1880, m rec from 1846, div rec from 1906,
pro & civ ct rec from 1836)

County Map of Iowa

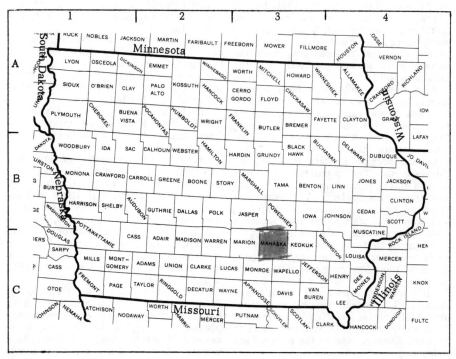

Wayne   C2   1850   10   1850–80   Appanoose . . . . Corydon
(Clk of Dist Ct has b & d rec from 1880, m rec from 1851, div rec from 1906,
pro rec from 1891, civ ct rec from 1875, cir ct rec from 1860, guardianship   1895)
Webster   B2   1852   48   1860–80   *Yell, *Risley . . . . Fort Dodge
                                    *Now known as Hamilton
Winnebago   A2   1857   13   1860–80   Kossuth . . . . Forest City
Winneshiek   A3   1847   22   1850–80   Indian Lands . . . . Decorah
(Clk of Dist Ct has b & d rec 1880, m, div, pro, civ ct rec from 1851)
Woodbury   B1   1851   108   1860–80   Indian Lands . . . . Sioux City
(Clk of Dist Ct has b & d rec 1880, m rec 1854, div, pro, civ ct rec 1857)
Worth   A3   1857   10   1860–80   Mitchell . . . . Northwood
Wright   A2   1855   19   1860–80   Webster . . . . Clarion

Genealogists' Check List of the Historical Records Survey, Iowa (see page VIII)

Fed Cts (start 1845); Inv of Co Arch - Col in Iowa; Diary of E.P. Burton, Surgeon, Carroll, Cherokee, Dallas, Dubuque, Ida, 7th Regiment, Ill; A Check List of Iowa Jasper, Montgomery, Polk, Sac, Taylor, Imprints, 1838-1860; Depo of unpubl mat, Woodbury; Guide to Pub Vit Stat Rec; Dir State Dep of Hist & Archives, DesMoines, of Chr & Rel org;   Guide   to Depo Iowa. of Mss Col in the US - Iowa; Guide to Mss

Kansas

Capital Topeka - Territory 1854 - State 1861 - (34th)

Kansas was part of the Louisiana Purchase when it became annexed to the United States in 1803. It was included in the Missouri Territory until 1821. For 33 years it was known as an unorganized territory, inhabited mainly by Indians. For many years there was constant trouble between them and the settlers, until the Indians were pushed gradually into the Oklahoma area.

Fort Levenworth became the first community in the area in 1827. To thousands en route to the valleys of Utah, the gold fields of California or the beckoning Oregon country, it was a welcome stopover outfitting place.

Kansas became a state in 1861, the thirty-fourth. The population then was about 110,000, consisting mostly of Southerners and New Englanders with a sprinkling from Missouri, Illinois, Indiana, Ohio, and Kentucky. Many Civil War veterans took up homesteads in Kansas following the war. Among the foreign born settlers many came from Germany, Russia, Sweden, and England. Many Mexicans also settled in the state.

Birth records since 1911, marriages since 1913, and death records since 1911 are obtainable at the office of Division of Vital Statistics, State Department of Health Topeka, Kansas. Most of the records are indexed.

The County Clerk in the county of occurance of birth and death has some records of these events.

The Probate Judge of each county has records of marriages in his county before 1913.

Records of divorces granted before 1951 are on file in the office of the clerk of the District Court handling the matter. Divorces granted after July 1951 are filled in the office of the above mentioned Division of Vital Statistics.

The Naturalization files are kept in the Topeka office of the United States Circuit Court and the district court in each of the counties in the state.

Probate matter and wills are handled by the Probate Judges who also have Civil Court records in most counties.

Real estate property is listed with the county recorder and county assessor in the county where land is located.

The Census Bureau, Memorial Bldg., Topeka, Kansas, has charge of all census records. The first Kansas federal census was taken in 1860. The State census of 1855 is alphabetized.

Libraries: Kansas City, (Wyandotte), Public Library, 6th & Minnesota Sts.; Lawrence, (Douglas), University of Kansas (Kansas History); Topeka, (Shawnee), Kansas State Historical Society Library, Memorial Bldg. (History and Genealogy);

Wichita, (Sedgwick), Public Library, 220 S. Main St., (Kansas History).

The Kansas State Historical Library in the Memorial Building, Topeka, Kansas, has more than 10,000 genealogical volumes including magazines, vital records, war records, family and local histories. Its newspaper collection is second only to that of the Library of Congress. Copies of the Federal Census for 1860, 1870 and 1880 are also there, together with the State Census records from 1855 to 1925, inclusive, at ten year periods.

Among books dealing with Kansas historical and genealogical information are the following:

"Biographical History of Central Kansas." The Lewis Publishing Company, New York and Chicago, 1902. Vol. I, 756 pp. Vol II, 877 pp.

Connelley, William Elsey. "History of Kansas, State and People." American Historical Society, 1928. History and biography.

Green, C. R. "Us and Our Neighbors." A historical and genealogical directory of more than 3,200 men, women and children who lived about Lyndon, Osage county, Kansas, as revealed by the assessor's returns for the years of 1896, 1897, and 1900. Compiled and published by C. R. Green, Lyndon, Kansas, June 1901. 299 pp.

"Genealogical and Biographical Record of North-eastern Kansas." The Lewis Publishing Company, Chicago, 1900. 755 pp

Isely, Bliss, and Richards, W. M. "Four Centuries in Kansas." McCormick-Mathers Company, Wichita, Kansas, 1936.

Works Projects Administration. "Kansas, a Guide to the Sunflower State. Viking 1939. American Guide Series.

Among available autobiographies or biographies of important Kansans are the following: Earl Browder, Walter P. Chrysler, John Steuart Curry, Charles Curtis, Amelia Earhart, Dwight D. Eisenhower, Dorothy Canfield Fisher, Frederick Funston, John James Ingalls, Hugh S. Johnson, Martin (Elmer) Johnson and Osa Helen Leighty Johnson, Edgar Lee Masters, Carry Amelia Moore Nation, Fred Andrew Stone, and William Allen White.

Kansas County Histories

(Population figures to nearest thousand - 1960 Census)

Name	Map Index	Date Formed	Pop. By M	Census Reports Available	Parent County	County Seat
Allen	A3	1855	16	1860-80	Original county	Iola
Anderson	A3	1855	9	1860-80	Original county	Garnett
Arapahoe	(Disorganized)			1860-80	(1870 census missing) (Inc. some of Colo.)	
Atchison	A2	1855	21	1860-80	Original county	Atchison
Barber	D4	1873	9	1880	Harper	Medicine Lodge
Barton	D2	1867	32	1870-80	Ellsworth	Great Bend
Bourbon	A3	1855	16	1860-80	Original county	Fort Scott
Breckenridge	(See Lyon)			1860		
Brown	A1	1855	13	1860-80	Original county	Hiawatha
Butler	B3	1855	38	1860-80	Original county	El Dorado
(Co Clk has b & d rec from 1890 to 1909 incom)						
Calhoun		1855			Name changed to Jackson after Civil War	
Chase	B3	1859	4	1860-80	Butler	Cottonwood Falls
(Co Clk has b rec 1886 - 1911 , d rec 1886 to 1910)						
Chautauqua	B4	1875	6	1880	Howard	Sedan
Cherokee	A4	1855	22	1870-80	Unorganized Territory	Columbus
Cheyenne	F1	1875	5	1880	Kirwin Land District	Saint Francis
Clark	E4	1873	3	1880	Ford	Ashland
(Co Clk has m rec from 1885)						
Clay	C2	1856	11	1860-80	Original county	Clay Center
Cloud	C2	1860	14	1870-80	Formerly Shirley County	Concordia
Coffey	B3	1855	8	1860-80	Original county	Burlington
(Co Clk has m rec 1859, div rec 1872, pro rec 1857, civ ct rec 1872)						
Comanche	D4	1875	3	1880	Kiowa	Coldwater
(Co Clk has b & d rec 1891 to 1908, m rec 1891 to 1913)						
Cowley	B4	1867	38		Formerly Hunter	Winfield
Crawford	A3	1867	37	1870-80	Bourbon	Girard
Davis		1871		1860-80	Riley - See Geary, Junction City	
Decatur	E1	1873	6	1880	Norton	Oberlin

Dickinson   C2   1855   22   1860-80   Original county . . . . Abilene
Doniphan   A1   1855   10   1860-80   Original county . . . . Troy
Dorn   1860   see Nesho
Douglas   A2   1855   44   1860-80   Original county . . . . Lawrence
Edwards   D3   1875   5   1880   Originial county . . . . Kinsley
Elk   B3   1875   5   1880   Howard . . . . Howard
    (Co Clk has b & d rec from 1885 to 1910)
Ellis   D2   1865   21   1870-80   Unorganized Territory . . . . Hays
Ellsworth   C2   1867   8   1870-80   Saline . . . . Ellsworth
Finney   F3   1884   16   Arapahoe, Foote, Sequoyah? . . Garden City
    (Pro Ct has m & pro rec from 1885; Co Reg has d rec from 1823; Clk Dist Ct
    has div & civ ct rec from 1885)
Foote   1880
Ford   E3   1873   21   1880   Unorganized Territory . . . . . Dodge City
Franklin   A2   1856   20   1860-80   Original county . . . . Ottawa
Garfield   (Annexed to Finney 1893)
Geary   B2   1889   29   Davis Co. 1875 to 1888 . . . Junction City
Godfrey   1860
Gove   E2   1880   4   1880   Unorganized Territory . . . . Gove
Graham   E2   1880   6   1880   Rooks . . . . Hill City
Grant   F3   1873   5   1880   Finney, Kearney . . . . Ulysses
    (Co Clk has b rec 1890 to 1909, d rec 1892 to 1921; Pro Ct has m rec 1892 to
    1921)
Gray   E3   1887   4   Finney, Ford . . . . Cimarron
Greeley   F2   1873   2   1880   Wichita . . . . Tribune
    (Pro Ct has m rec from 1888; Clk of Dist Ct has div rec from 1888; Co Clk has
    old newspapers from 1886)
Greenwood   B3   1855   11   1860-80   Original county . . . . Eureka
Hamilton   F3   1873   3   1880   Unorganized Territory . . . . . Syracuse
Harper   C4   1879   10   1880   Kingman . . . . Anthony
Harvey   C3   1872   26   1880   McPherson, Sedgwich . . . . Newton
Haskell   F3   1887   3   Finney . . . . Sublette
Hodgeman   E3   1879   3   1880   Indian Lands (Est. 1868) . . . . Jetmore
Howard   1875   Taken to form Elk and Chautauqua
Hunter (see Cowley)   1860
Jackson   B2   1855   10   1860-80   (See Calhoun) . . . . Holton
Jefferson   A2   1855   11   1860-80   Original county . . . . Oskaloosa
Jewell   C1   1870   7   1870-80   Mitchell . . . . Mankato
Johnson   A2   1855   144   1860-80   Original county . . . . Olathe
Kearny   F3   1873   3   1880   Finney . . . . Lakin
Kingman   C3   1874   10   1880   Unorganized Territory . . . . Kingman
Kiowa   D3   1886   5   Comanche, Edwards . . . . . . Greensburg
Labette   A4   1867   27   1870-80   Neosho . . . . Oswego
Lane   E2   1877   3   1880   Finney . . . . Dighton
Leavenworth A2   1855   49   1860-80   Original county . . . . Leavenworth
Lincoln   C2   1870   6   1870-80   Ellsworth . . . . Lincoln
    (Co Clk has m, d, pro rec from 1870)
Linn   A3   1855   8   1860-80   Original county . . . . Mound City
Logan   F2   1881   4   Wallace . . . . Russell Springs
    (Co Treas has tax receipts from 1890; Co Clk has Assessment rec from 1890;
    Reg of Deeds has deeds from 1890)
Lykins   1860   (See Miami)
Lyon   B2   1857   27   1870-80   Madison (See Breckenridge) . . . Emporia
    (Pro Ct has m rec from 1861, pro rec from 1859; Clk of Dist Ct has div rec
    from 1860, civ ct rec from 1858)
McGhee   1860   (See Cherokee)
McPherson   C3   1870   24   1870-80   Unorganized Territory . . . . . McPherson
    (Co Clk has b, m, d, bur rec from 1887)
Madison   1860   1860   Divided to Morris & Lyon Counties
Marion   C3   1860   15   1860-80   Chase . . . . Marion
    (Co Clk has b rec 1885 to 1911, m rec 1892 to 1899, d rec 1893 to 1903)
Marshall   B1   1855   16   1860-80   Original county . . . . Marysville

County Map of Kansas

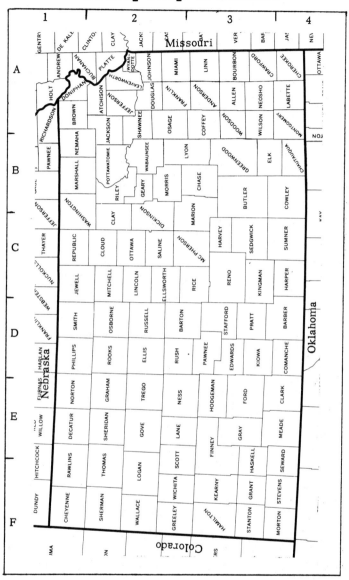

Meade	E4	1873	6	1880	Unorganized Territory .... Meade
Miami	A2	1855	20	1870-80	Formerly Lykins .... Paola
Mitchell	C2	1870	9	1870-80	Kirwin Land District .... Beloit
Montgomery	B4	1869	45	1870-80	Labette .... Independence

(Co Clk has b rec 1888 to 1911, m rec 1870 to 1888, d rec 1887 to 1911, div & pro rec from 1870, civ ct rec from 1871)

Morris	B2	1858	7	1860-80	Madison (Formerly Wise) .. Council Grove
Morton	F4	1881	3		Stanton .... Richfield
Nemaha	B1	1855	13	1860-80	Original county .... Seneca

(Co Clk has b, d, m rec 1885 to 1911, pro rec 1857, civ ct rec from 1859)

Neosho	A3	1855	19	1870-80	Labette .... Erie

(originally Dorn - name changed 1861)

Ness	E2	1873	5	1880	Hodgeman . . . . Ness City
Norton	D1	1872	8	1880	Unorganized Territory . . . . Norton
Osage	B2	1855	13	1860-80	Formerly Weller . . . . Lyndon
Osborne	D2	1867	8	1870-80	Mitchell . . . . Osborne
Otoe				1860	
Ottawa	C2	1866	7	1870-80	Saline . . . . Minneapolis
Pawnee	D3	1872	10	1880	Rush, Stafford . . . . Larned
Phillips	D1	1872	9	1880	Kirwin Land District . . . . . Phillipsburg
Pottawatomie	B2	1857	12	1860-80	Riley, Calhoun . . . . Westmoreland
Pratt	D3	1879	12	1880	Stafford . . . . Pratt

(Co Clk has b rec from 1887 to 1900)

Rawlins	E4	1873	5	1880	Kirwin Land District . . . . Atwood
Reno	C3	1877	59	1880	Sedgwick, McPherson . . . . Hutchinson
Republic	C1	1868	10	1870-80	Washington, Cloud . . . . Belleville
Rice	C3	1867	14	1870-80	Reno . . . . Lyons
Riley	B2	1855	42	1860-80	Unorganized Terr., Wabaunsee . Manhattan
Rooks	D2	1872	10	1880	Kirwin Land District . . . . Stockton
Rush	D2	1874	6	1880	Unorgǐnized Territory . . . . La Crosse

(Pro Ct has m rec from 1876)

Russell	D2	1867	11	1870-80	Ellsworth . . . . Russell
Saline	C2	1860	55	1870-80	Original county . . . . Salina
Scott	F2	1873	5	1880	Finney . . . . Scott City
Sedgwick	C3	1867	343	1870-80	Butler . . . . Wichita
Sequoyah				1880	
Seward	F4	1873	16	1880	Indian Lands . . . . Liberal
Shawnee	B2	1855	141	1860-80	Original county . . . . Topeka
Sheridan	E2	1873	4	1880	Unorganized Territory . . . . Hoxie.

(Co Clk has incom b rec 1887 to 1910, d rec 1887 to 1910, m, div, pro, civ ct rec from 1887)

| Sherman | F2 | 1873 | 7 | 1880 | Kirwin Land District . . . . Goodland |

(Co Clk has Newspaper files from 1898)

Shirley	(See Cloud)				
Smith	D1	1872	8	1880	Unorganized Territory . . . . Smith Center
Stafford	D3	1870	7	1880	Unorganized Territory . . . . Saint John
Stanton	F3	1873	2	1880	Reorganized . . . . Johnson
Stevens	F4	1873	4	1880	Indian Lands . . . . Hugoton
Sumner	C4	1867	25	1870-80	Cowley . . . . Wellington
Thomas	F2	1873	7	1880	Kirwin Land District . . . . Colby
Trego	E2	1879	5	1880	Ellis . . . . Wakeeney
Wabaunsee	B2	1855	7	1860-80	Riley, Morris . . . . Alma
Wallace	F2	1865	2	1870-80	Indian Lands (See Logan) . . Sharon Springs
Washington	C1	1856	11	1860-80	Original county . . . . Washington
Weller	(see Osage)				
Wichita	F2	1873	3	1880	Indian Lands . . . . Leoti
Wilson	B3	1855	13	1860-80	Original county . . . . Fredonia
Wise	(see Morris)				
Woodson	B3	1855	5	1860-80	Original county . . . . Yates Center
Wyandotte	A2	1856	185	1860-80	Original county . . . . Kansas City

Genealogists' Check List of the Historical Records Survey, Kansas (see page VIII)

Fed Cts (start 1854); Inv of Co Arch—Bourbon, Cherokee, Franklin, Gove, Graham, Gray, Greenwood, Johnson, Montgomery, Morris, Osage, Phillips, Seward, Shawnee; Guide to Pub Vit Stat Rec; Check List of Kansas Imprints 1854-1876; Depo of unpubl mat, Kansas State Hist Soc, Topeka, Kansas.

Kentucky

Capital Frankfort - State 1792 - (15th)

The settling of Kentucky from the mid-seventeen-hundreds to the early parts of the eighteen-hundreds included some of the most . hazardous and bloody events of

America. Several thousand of those early settlers lost their lives in skirmishes with Indians, determined to protect their hunting grounds from the encroachments of the white man.

Long before any white man had explored the entire Kentucky area, it was claimed by Virginia as part of her Augusta County. It was included in the Virginia County of 1584.

Daniel Boone, born in Pennsylvania of English paretns, moved his family in September 1773 into the Kentucky area from Rowan County, North Carolina, on the Yadkin River. However, he had previously explored that section some seven years earlier. Neither was Boone the first to investigate the possibilities of Kentucky. The eastern section of the area was explored by Dr. Thomas Walker as early as 1750. Twenty-five years later the Transylvania Company was organized under the leadership of Col. Richard Henderson of North Carolina. From Indian tribes he purchased almost half of what is now the state of Kentucky, all of the land between the Kentucky River, in the central part of the state, and the Cumberland River, in the extreme western part. A multiplicity of law suits and the Revolutionary War completed the activities of the Henderson enterprise in a dismal failure.

Previous to these explorations all of Kentucky had been made part of Fincastle county, Virginia. During Boone's activities in the section, Kentucky was designated as Kentucky County, Virginia. This designation was made in December, 1776. In 1780 it was divided into three counties, Fayette, Jefferson, and Lincoln, In 1790 those three counties were subdivided into nine counties Mason, Bourbon, Woodford, Fayette, Madison, Jefferson, Mercer, Nelson, and Lincoln.

By 1900 those nine 1790 counties had been subdivided into the following present counties:

MASON: The east six-seventh of Pike, Floyd, Martin, Johnson; the east half of each of Magoffin and Morgan; Lawrence, Elliott, Rowan, Carter, Boyd, Greenup, Lewis, Fleming, Mason, Robertson, Bracken, Campbell, and the east third of Pendleton.

BOURBON: East four-fifths of Harlan, Letcher, west one-seventh of Pike, Knott, Perry, east half of Leslie, Breathitt, west half of each of Magoffin and Morgan, Wolfe, north half of each of Lee and Estill, Bath Powell, Manifee, Montgomery, east half of Clark, Bourbon, Nicholas, east three-fourths of Harrison, and triangular shaped

south one-fifth of Pendleton.

WOODFORD: Woodford, Scott, east half of Franklin, Owen, Grant, Boone, Gallalin and east half of Carroll.

FAYETTE: Fayette, Jessamine and west half of Clark.

MADISON: Madison, east half of Garrard south half of Estill, Jackson, north-east third of Rockcastle, Owsley, south half Lee, Clay, west half of Leslie, and west one-fifth of Harlan.

JEFFERSON: North half of each of Spencer and Bullit, Jefferson, Shelby, Oldham, Henry, North-west corner of Anderson, Trimble, and west half of Carroll.

MERCER: Triangular south third Franklin, east half of Anderson, Mercer, north two-thirds of Boyle, and northwest third of Garrard.

NELSON: Washington, Marion, Taylor, north half of each of Green, Hart, Edmonson, Butler, and McLean; Ohio, Davies, Hancock, Breckinridge, Meade, Hardin, south half of each of Bullitt and Spencer; Nelson, Larue, and Grayson.

LINCOLN: Henderson, Webster, Hopkins, south half of McLean; Muhlenberg; south half of Butler; Warren, south half of each of Edmonson, Hart and Green, Adair, Casey, Lincoln, west of Garrard, southwest two-thirds of Rockcastle; Laurel, south one-third of Boyle, Knox, Bell, Whitley, Pulaski, Wayne, Russell, Clinton, Cumberland, Metcalf, Monroe, Barren, Allen, Simpson, Logan, Todd, Christian, Trigg, Caldwell, Lyon, Marshall, Calloway, Graves, Fulton, Hickman, Carlisle, Ballard, McCracken, Livingston, Crittenden and Union.

The extreme western tip of Kentucky, surrounded on three sides by water – the Mississippi River on the west, the Ohio and the Tennessee Rivers on the north, and the Kentucky Reservior on the east is sometimes referred to as the Jackson Purchase Region from the fact that it was purchased in 1818 from the Chickasaw Indians during the presidency of Andrew Jackson. It includes the following eight counties, sometimes included in the old Lincoln county: Calloway, Marshall, McCracken, Graves, Fulton, Hickman, Carlisle, and Ballard.

The descriptions of the Kentucky counties carved out of the nine counties existing in 1790 given in earlier paragraphs follow the Kentucky map printed in "A Century of Population Growth - 1790-1900" by the Bureau of Census, Washington 25, D. C. In several instances these descriptions do not harmonize with those on a map arranged by Bayless Hardin of Kentucky State Historical Society and published in Heineman and Brumbaugh's "First Census of Kentucky, 1790" (Kentucky Taxpayers of the Time.) This map is printed on page 45 of the 1953 Handy Book. Those interested may compare the two maps in question.

On June 1, 1792, Kentucky became the fifteenth state admitted into the union.

It took courageous men and women to make their homes in a country as full of danger and excitement as existed in Kentucky in its early days. They came mostly, to begin with, from Maryland, North Carolina, Pennsylvania, Tennessee, and Virginia. Originally they were of German, English, Irish and Scottish descent. As new territories, new states were carved from the large American expanse, many of them were settled by the descendants of the original Kentuckians. With the increased European migration many people have also come to Kentucky from Russia, Italy, Poland and Austria.

Division of Vital Records, State Department of Health, 620 South Third Street, Louisville 2, Ky., has birth and death records from the beginning of 1911. The City Health Department in some of the larger cities have still earlier records.

Records of births and deaths from some counties as early as 1851 are in the library of the Kentucky Historical Society, Frankfort, Ky.

County Clerk of county where transaction was completed may have wills, probate, marriage and divorce records.

Naturalization records are filed in the district courts in Bowling Green, Catlettsburg, Covington, Frankfort, London, Louisville, Owensboro, and Paducah. They may also be obtained in the office of the clerk of the Circuit Court in the various county seats in the state.

Quite complete records of birth, marriages, death, wills, etc., on file on microfilms and written and printed records at the Genealogical Society of Utah, Salt Lake City, Utah. Also the complete 1810 census.

Mimeographed copies of the 1810 Census by counties, and vital statistics by counties may be obtained from Mrs. Anne Walker Burns, P. O. Box 6183 Apex Station, Washington, D. C.

The federal census records of 1790 and 1800 are missing, but the so called "First Census of Kentucky", supplies a list of taxpayers of those years.

Libraries: Bowling Green (Warren), Western Kentucky State College Library, (Southern and Western History; Covington, (Kenton), Public Library, Scott &

Robbins Sts.; Frankfort, (Franklin), Kentucky Historical Society Library, Old State House; Lexington, (Fayette), Public Library, 2nd & Market Sts. (old newspapers); University of Kentucky Library, (historical manuscripts); Louisville (Jefferson) Filson Club Library, 118 W. Breckenridge St., (Ky. and Ohio Valley collections); Free Public Library, 301-333 Library Place, (Southern lore).

Among books dealing with Kentucky history and genealogy are the following:

ARDERY, MRS. WM. BRECKENRIDGE. *Kentucky Records — Early Wills and Marriages*. The Keystone Printery, Lexington, Ky., Vol I, 206 pp. 1926; Vol. II, 1932.

BIGGS, NINA MITCHELL AND MACKOY, MABEL LEE. *History of Greenup County, Ky*. The Franklin Press, Louisville, Ky., 1951, 345 pp.

Biographical Encyclopedia of Kentucky of the Dead and Living Men of the Nineteenth Century. O. J. Armstrong Company, 1873.

BURNS, ANNIE WALKER, P. O. Box 6183, Washington, D. C. *Kentucky Genealogies and Historical Recorder*. Eleven mimeographed volumes.

Abstracts of Pension Records from most of the Kentucky counties.

CHERRY, THOMAS C., AND STICKLES, ARNDT M. *Story of Kentucky*. Heath, 1940.

CLARK, THOMAS DIONYSIUS, AND KIRKPATRICK, LEE. *Exploring Kentucky*. American Book Co., 1939.

CLIFT, G. GLENN. *History of Maysville and Mason County*. Transylvania Printing Company, Inc., Lexington, Ky., 1936. Vol I 461 pp.

"Second Census" of Kentucky, 1800. Frankfort. Ky., 1954. 333 pp. A privately compiled list of taxpayers in the forty-two counties of Kentucky of 1800.

COLLINS, LEWIS (1797-1870). *History of Kentucky*.

COLLINS, RICHARD H. *History of Kentucky*. 1924.

DARNELL, ERMINA JETT. *Forks of Elkhorn Church*. The Standard Printing Co., Inc., Louisville, Ky., 1946. 322 pp.

Daughters of Colonial Wars, Kentucky Society, Kentucky Pioneers and Their Descendants. Roberts Printing Company, Frankfort, Ky., 1950, 460 pp.

GREEN, THOMAS MARSHALL. *Historic Families of Kentucky*. Robert Clarke and Company. Cincinnati. 1889. 304 pp.

HALL, MITCHELL, *Johnson County, Kentucky*. The Standard Press, Louisville, Ky., 1928. Vol I, History and Genealogy. 552 pp. Vol. II Genealogy. 708 pp.

HEINEMANN, CHARLES BRINK. *First Census of Kentucky, 1790*. A privately compiled list of taxpayers appearing in the tax lists of Kentucky counties established at time of First Census. Southern Book Company, St. James Hotel. Charles Street at Center, Baltimore 1, Maryland. 1956. 118pp.

JENNINGS, KATHLEEN. *Louisville's First Families*. A series of genealogical sketches. The Standard Printing Company, Louisville, Ky. 1920. 176 pp.

JILLSON, WILLARD ROUSE. *The Kentucky Land Grants, 1782-1924*. The Standard Printing Company, Inc., Louisville, Ky., 1925. 1,844 pp.

Old Kentucky Entries and Deeds. The Standard Printing Company, Inc., Louisville, Ky., 1926. 571 pp. State land office records.

McADAMS, MRS. HARRY KENNETT. *Kentucky Pioneer and Court Records*. Abstracts of early wills, deeds and marriages from Anderson, Bourbon, Boyle, Clark, Estill, Fayette, Garrard, Harrison, Jassamine, Lincoln, Madison, Mercer, Montgomery, Nicholas, and Woodford counties. The Keystone Printery, Lexington, Ky. 1929. 382 pp. Indexed.

McGHEE, LUCY KATE, Box 7213, Washington, D. C. *Historical Records of Old Crab Orchard*, Lincoln., Ky. 117 pp.

Pension Abstracts of Maryland Soldiers of the Revelotion, War of 1812, and In-dian Wars Who Settled in Kentucky. Vol. I, 76 pp. Vol. II, 90 pp.

SCOTT, HATTIE MARSHALL. *Kentucky Court and Other Records*. Records from Bourbon, Nicholas, Estill, Fayette, Gallatin, Green, Harrison, Scott, and Woodford counties and other miscellaneous items. The Kentucky Historical Society, Frankfort, Ky.. 1953. 251 pp. Excellent index.

THOMPSON, ED PORTER. *History of the Orphan Brigade*. Information on about 5,675 particpiants in the Civil War. Lewis N. Thompson, Louisville, Ky., 1898. 1,104 pp. Excellent index.

TIBBALS, ALMA OWENS. *History of Pulaski County, Kentucky*. The Franklin Press, Louisville, Ky., 1952. 272 pp. Fine index.

VAN METER, BENJAMIN F. *Genealogies and Sketches of Some Old Families*. (Virginia and Kentucky) John P. Morton and Company, Louisville, Ky., 1901. 183 pp.

WELLS, J. W. *History of Cumberland County, Kentucky*. The Standard Printing Company, Louisville, Ky., 1947. 480 pp.

WOOD, EDITH. *Middletown's Days and Deeds*. (Jefferson County) 1946. 281 pp.

WORKS PROJECTS ADMINISTRATION. *Kentucky*. (American Guide Series) Check List of Historical Records Survey Publications. 1940.

Kentucky County Histories

(Population figures to nearest thousand – 1960 Census)

Name	Map Index	Date Formed	Pop. By M	Census Reports Available	Parent County	County Seat
Adair	C2	1801	15	1810–80	Green	Columbia
Allen	D3	1815	12	1820–80	Barren, Warren	Scottsville
(Co Clk	has	m &	pro	rec from	1902; Cir Ct Clk has div rec from 1902)	
Anderson	C2	1827	9	1830–80	Franklin, Mercer, Washington	Lawrenceburg
Ballard	F3	1842	8	1850–80	Hickman, McCracken	Wickliffe
Barren	D3	1798	28	1810–80	Green, Warren	Glasgow
(Co Clk has m rec from 1799)						
Bath	B2	1811	9	1820–80	Montgomery	Owingsville
Bell	B3	1867	35	1880	Knox, Harlan	Pineville
Boone	C1	1798	22	1810–80	Campbell	Burlington
(Co Clk has m & pro rec from 1799)						
Bourbon	B2	1785	18	1810–80	Fayette	Paris
(Co Clk has m rec from 1786)						
Boyd	A1	1860	52	1860–80	Carter, Lawrence, Greenup . .	Catlettsburg
Boyle	C2	1842	21	1850–80	Mercer, Lincoln	Danville
(Co Clk has m, pro, wills from 1842)						
Bracken	B1	1796	7	1810–80	Campbell, Mason	Brooksville
Breathitt	B2	1839	15	1840–80	Clay, Estill, Perry	Jackson
Breckinridge	D1	1799	15	1810–80	Hardin	Hardinsburg
Bullitt	C2	1796	16	1810–80	Jefferson, Nelson	Shepherdsville
Butler	D3	1810	10	1810–80	Logan, Ohio	Morgantown
Caldwell	E3	1809	13	1810–80	Livingston	Princeton
(Co Clk	has	m &	pro	rec from	1809; Clk Cir Ct has div rec from 1809)	
Calloway	E3	1822	21	1830–80	Hickman	Murray

Campbell   B1 1795   87 1810-80 Harrison, Mason, Scott .... Alexandria
(Co Clk has m & pro rec from 1795)   & Newport
Carlisle   F3 1886   6   Graves, Ballard .... Bardwell
Carroll   C1 1838   8 1840-80 Gallatin, Henry, Trimble ... Carrollton
(Co Clk has b & d rec 1911 to 1949, m & pro rec from 1838)
Carter   A1 1838   21 1840-80 Greenup, Lawrence .... Grayson
(Co Clk has b rec 1911 to 1954, m rec from 1838)
Casey   C2 1806   14 1810-80 Lincoln .... Liberty
(Co Clk has m & pro rec from 1809)
Christian   E3 1797   57 1810-80 Logan .... Hopkinsville
(Co Clk has m & pro rec from 1797)
Clark   B2 1792   21 1810-80 Bourbon, Fayette .... Winchester
Clay   B2 1806   21 1810-80 Madison, Floyd, Knox .... Manchester
Clinton   C3 1835   9 1840-80 Wayne, Cumberland .... Albany
(Co Clk has m, deeds, mtgs, wills from 1865)
Crittenden   E2 1842   9 1850-80 Livingston .... Marion
(Co Clk has m & pro rec from 1842)
Cumberland   C3 1796   8 1810-80 Green .... Burkesville
(Co Clk has some m rec from 1882)
Daviess   D1 1815   71 1820-80 Ohio .... Owensboro
Edmonson   D3 1825   8 1830-80 Grayson, Hart, Warren .... Brownsville
Elliott   A2 1869   6 1870-80 Carter, Lawrence, Morgan ... Sandy Hook
(Co Clk has b rec 1882 to 1926, m rec from 1934)
Estill   B2 1808   12 1810-80 Clark, Madison .... Irvine
Fayette   B2 1780 132 1810-80 Kentucky .... Lexington
Fleming   B1 1798   11 1810-80 Mason .... Flemingsburg
Floyd   A2 1799   42 1810-80 Fleming, Mason,
                                     Montgomery .... Prestonsburg
Franklin   C2 1794   29 1810-80 Woodford, Mercer, Shelby ... Frankfort
Fulton   F3 1845   11 1850-80 Hickman .... Hickman
Gallatin   C1 1798   4 1810-80 Franklin, Shelby .... Warsaw
Garrard   B2 1796   10 1810-80 Madison, Lincoln, Mercer ... Lancaster
Grant   C1 1820   9 1820-80 Pendleton .... Williamstown
(Co Clk has m & pro rec from 1820)
Graves   F3 1823   30 1830-80 Hickman .... Mayfield
Grayson   D1 1810   16 1810-80 Hardin, Ohio .... Leitchfield
Green   C2 1792   11 1810-80 Lincoln, Nelson .... Greensburg
(Co Clk has b & d rec 1911 to 1954, m, deeds, ct orders from 1793)
Greenup   A1 1803   29 1810-80 Mason .... Greenup
(Co Clk has m rec 1803, pro rec 1837; Clk of Cir Ct has div & civ ct rec 1803)
Hancock   D1 1828   5 1830-80 Daviess, Ohio, Breckinridge .. Hawesville
(Co Clk has m, pro, deeds from 1828)
Hardin   D1 1792   68 1810-80 Nelson .... Elizabethtown
Harlan   B3 1819   51 1820-80 Knox .... Harlan
(Co Clk has m rec from 1820)
Harrison   B1 1793   14 1810-80 Bourbon, Scott .... Cynthiana
Hart   D1 1819   14 1820-80 Hardin, Barren,
                                     possibly Green .... Mumfordville
Henderson   E2 1798   34 1810-80 Christian .... Henderson
Henry   C1 1798   11 1810-80 Shelby .... New Castle
Hickman   F3 1821   7 1830-80 Caldwell, Livingston .... Clinton
Hopkins   E2 1808   38 1810-80 Henderson .... Madisonville
Jackson   B2 1858   11 1860-80 Rockcastle, Owsley, Madison,
                                     Clay, Estill, Laurel .... McKee
Jefferson   C2 1780 611 1810-80 Kentucky Co. .... Louisville
Jessamine   C2 1798   14 1810-80 Fayette .... Nicholasville
(Co Clk has m & pro rec from 1799)
Johnson   A2 1843   20 1850-80 Floyd, Morgan, Lawrence .... Paintsville
Josh Bell   1870
Kenton   B1 1840 121 1840-80 Campbell .... Independence
Knott   A2 1884   17   Perry, Breathitt, Floyd
                                     Letcher .... Hindman

Knox	B3	1799	25	1810–80	Lincoln	Barbourville
Larue	C2	1843	10	1850–80	Hardin	Hodgenville
Laurel	B3	1825	25	1830–80	Whitley, Clay, Knox, Rockcastle .	London
Lawrence	A2	1821	12	1830–80	Floyd, Greenup	Louisa
Lee	B2	1870	7	1870–80	Owsley, Breathitt, Wolfe, Estill .	Beattyville
Leslie	B2	1878	11	1880	Clay, Harlan, Perry	Hyden
Letcher	A3	1842	30	1850–80	Perry, Harlan	Whitesburg
Lewis	B1	1806	13	1810–80	Mason	Vanceburg

(Co Clk has b & d rec from 1911, m, Inv of personal estates, pro rec from 1806)

County Map of Kentucky

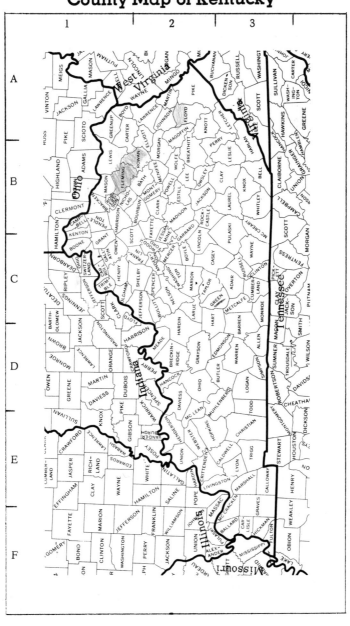

Lincoln	C2	1780	17	1810–80	Kentucky Co., Va.	Stanford

(Co Clk has m, div, pro, civ ct rec from 1792)

Livingston	E2	1798	7	1810–80	Christian	Smithland

(Co Clk has b rec from 1911, m, pro, surveys, ct orders, deeds, wills from 1800)

Logan	D3	1792	21	1810–80	Lincoln	Russellville

(Co Clk has m rec 1790, pro, real estate conveyances, early land grants & surveys from 1792)

Lyon	E3	1854	6	1860–80	Caldwell	Eddyville
Madison	B2	1785	34	1810–80	Lincoln	Richmond
Magoffin	A2	1860	11	1860–80	Floyd, Johnson, Morgan . . .	Salyersville

(Co Clk has m rec from 1860)

Marion	C2	1834	17	1840–80	Washington	Lebanon
Marshall	E3	1842	17	1850–80	Callaway	Benton
Martin	A2	1870	10	1880	Lawrence, Floyd, Pike, Johnson . .	Inez
Mason	B1	1788	18	1810–80	Bourbon	Maysville
McCracken	F3	1824	57	1830–80	Hickman	Paducah

(Co Clk has m & pro rec from 1825, b & d rec from 1911)

McCreary	B3	1912	12		Wayne, Pulaski, Whitley	Whitley City

(Co Clk has m, d, pro rec from 1912)

McLean	D1	1854	9	1860–80	Muhlenberg, Daviess, Ohio	Calhoun

(Co Clk has b & d rec 1911 to 1949, m, div, pro, civ ct rec, deeds from 1854)

Meade	D1	1824	19	1830–80	Hardin, Breckinridge	Brandenburg

(Co Clk has incom b & d rec 1852 to 1911, m, pro, civ ct rec from 1824)

Menifee	B2	1869	4	1870–80	Powell, Wolfe, Bath, Morgan, Montgomery	Frenchburg

(Co Clk has m rec from 1869; Clk of Cir Ct has div rec from 1869)

Mercer	C2	1785	15	1810–80	Lincoln	Harrodsburg
Metcalfe	C3	1860	8	1860–80	Monroe, Adair, Barren, Cumberland Green	Edmonton
Monroe	C3	1820	12	1820–80	Barren, Cumberland	Tompkinsville
Montgomery	B2	1796	13	1810–80	Clark	Mount Sterling

(Co Clk has m rec from 1864)

Morgan	B2	1822	11	1830–80	Floyd, Bath	West Liberty
Muhlenberg	D3	1798	28	1810–80	Christian, Logan	Greenville
Nelson	C2	1784	22	1810–80	Jefferson	Bardstown
Nicholas	B1	1799	7	1810–80	Bourbon, Mason	Carlisle
Ohio	D1	1799	18	1810–80	Hardin	Hartford
Oldham	C1	1823	13	1830–80	Henry, Shelby, Jefferson	LaGrange
Owen	C1	1819	8	1820–80	Scott, Franklin, Gallatin, Pendleton .	Owenton

(Co Clk has b rec 1911 to 1950, m & pro rec from 1819)

Owsley	B2	1843	5	1850–80	Clay, Estill, Breathitt	Booneville
Pendleton	B1	1798	10	1810–80	Bracken, Campbell	Falmouth
Perry	B2	1820	35	1830–80	Clay, Floyd	Hazard
Pike	A2	1821	68	1830–80	Floyd	Pikeville
Powell	B2	1852	7	1860–80	Clark, Estill, Montgomery	Stanton
Pulaski	C3	1798	34	1810–80	Green, Lincoln	Somerset & Dabney

(Co Clk has m rec from 1799)

Robertson	B1	1867	2	1870–80	Nicholas, Bracken, Mason, Fleming, Harrison	Mt. Olivet

(Co Clk has m, div, pro, civ ct, wills, deeds, settlement of Estates from 1867, Affidavit of descent from 1920)

Rockcastle	B2	1810	12	1810–80	Pulaski, Lincoln, Madison . .	Mount Vernon

(Co Clk has m rec from 1873; Cir Ct has div rec from 1873)

Rowan	B2	1856	13	1860–80	Fleming, Morgan	Morehead
Russell	C3	1825	11	1830–80	Cumberland, Adair, Wayne . . .	Jamestown

(Co Clk has m & pro rec from 1826; Cir Ct has civ ct rec from 1826)

Scott	C2	1792	15	1810–80	Woodford	Georgetown
Shelby	C2	1792	18	1810–80	Jefferson	Shelbyville
Simpson	D3	1819	12	1820–80	Allen, Logan, Warren	Franklin

(Co Clk has m rec from 1892)

Spencer	C2	1824	6	1830–80	Shelby, Bullitt, Nelson	Taylorsville
Taylor	C2	1848	16	1850–80	Green	Campbellsville

Todd	D3	1819	11	1820-80	Christian, Logan	....	Elkton
Trigg	E3	1820	9	1820-80	Christian, Caldwell	....	Cadiz
(Co Clk has m & pro rec from 1820)							
Trimble	C1	1836	5	1840-80	Henry, Oldham, Gallatin	......	Bedford
Union	E2	1811	15	1820-80	Henderson	....	Morganfield
Warren	D3	1796	45	1810-80	Logan	....	Bowling Green
Washington	C2	1792	11	1810-80	Nelson	....	Springfield
(Co Clk has m & pro rec from 1792)							
Wayne	C3	1800	15	1810-80	Pulaski, Cumberland	......	Monticello
Webster	E2	1860	14	1860-80	Hopkins, Union, Henderson	.....	Dixon
(Co Clk has m & pro rec from 1860)							
Whitley	B3	1818	26	1820-80	Knox	....	Williamsburg
Wolfe	B2	1860	7	1870-80	Owsley, Breathitt, Powell,		
					Morgan	....	Campton
(Co Clk has m rec from 1913)							
Woodford	C2	1788	12	1810-80	Fayette	....	Versailles

U. S. Census note: The Kentucky census figures for 1790 and 1800 are missing.

Genealogists' Check List of the Historical Records Survey, Kentucky (see page VIII)

Fed Cts (start 1789); Inv of Co Arch-Anderson, Breckenridge, Carlisle, Fayette, Jessamine, Knox, Laurel, McCreary, Meade; Guide to Pub Vit Stat Rec; Preliminary Bibliography of mat relating to Chrs in W. Va, Va, Ky and Southern Ohio; Check List of Ky Imprints 1787-1810; Check List of Ky Imprints 1811 1820; Sup Check List of Ky Imprints 1788-1820; Guide and Check List of Co Gov Org & Co Rec S ystem, Past and Present Cos; Depo of unpubl mat, Ky Lib, Lexington, Ky.

Louisiana

Capital Baton Rouge - Territory 1805 - State 1812 - (18th)

Ownership of the Louisiana sector for the first 250 or 300 years of its discovery zig-zagged between France and Spain, until it was sold to the United States as part of the Louisiana Purchase in 1803. Some of the quaint customs of the early French settlers have been perpetuated over the years and gives the state an atmosphere of antiquity.

Every school boy and girl remember with nostolgic feelings Longfellow's "Evangeline," the poetic story of the transfer of large groups of French settlers from Nova Scotia to Louisiana. Many descendants of these Acadians still live in Louisiana where they are known as Cajuns.

Rather than to fight against the Mother Country during the Revolutionary War, many loyal Britons moved their families at that time for the Atlantic states to Louisiana where they have perpetuated themselves.

On Oct. 1, 1804 Louisiana was divided into two parts by Congessional action. The upper portion was given the name "District of Louisiana" and the lower portion "Territory of Orleans". Immediately after the formation of the Territory of Orleans, large numbers of Americans from south of the Ohio moved into the new acquisition. In 1805 Louisiana was divided into 12 counties and in 1807 the Orleans Territory was partitioned into 19 parishes.

There is nothing different between a Lousiana parish and a county in any other state than the name. Otherwise everything is the same. Some of the early Church Parish records are now held by the Parish or Court Clerks.

For information regarding wills, deeds, divorces, civ court records and marriages write the clerk of the respective parishes.

The State Registrar, Bureau of Vital Statistics, State Dept. of Health, Civil Courts Bldg., New Orleans 7, La., has records of births since 1914, some since 1870 and deaths since 1914, some since 1899. The Bureau of Vital Statistics, City Health Dept. of New Orleans, 507 Carondelet St., has some birth, death and marriage records as far back as 1790.

Louisiana Libraries - Alexandria, (Rapides), Rapides Parish Library, P. O. Box 1032; Baton Rouge, (Baton Rouge), East Baton Rouge Parish Public Library 700 Laurel St.; Louisiana State University,

Hill Memorial Library, (Lower Mississippi Valley history); New Orleans (Orleans Parish), Public Library, 1031 St. Charles Ave.; Tulane University, Howard-Tilton Memorial Library, Audubon Place at Freret St. (Southern lore and archives); Shreveport, (Caddo), Shreve Memorial Public Library, 400 Edwards St.

Among available books dealing with Louisiana are the following:

ARTHUR, STANLEY C., *Old New Orleans, A History of the Vieux Carre, its Ancient and Historical Buildings.* 246 pp. New Orleans, 1936.

Baptismal, Marriage and Death Records of Christ Church Episcopal Cathedral, New Orleans. 1849-1900. Obtained at Southern Book Company, Baltimore, Md.

CURTIS, NATHANIEL C., *New Orleans, Its Old Houses, Shops and Public Buildings.* 267 pp. Philadelphia 1933.

DEILER, J. HANNO, *The Settlement of the German Coast of Louisiana and the Creoles of German Descent.* 136 pp. Philadelphia, 1909.

Guide to Public Vital Statistics Records in Louisiana.

Guide to Vital Statistics Records of Church Archives in Louisiana: Vol. I, *Protestant and Jewish Churches;* Vol. II, *Roman Catholic Churches.*

KING, GRACE. *New Orleans, The Place and the People.* 402 pp. New York 1922.

SAXON, LYLE. *Old Louisiana.* 388 pp. New York, 1941.

Louisiana Parish Histories

(Population figures to nearest thousand - 1960 Census)

Name	Map Index	Date Formed	Pop. By M	Census Reports Available	Parent Parish	Parish Seat
Acadia	C2	1886	50		Calcasieu, St. Landry	Crowley
Allen	C2	1913	20		Calcasieu	Oberlin
Ascension	C3	1802	28	1810-80	St. James	Donaldsonville
(Par Clk has m, div, pro, civ ct, conveyance, mtg, insanity, juvenile, army & navy discharges from 1767)						
Assumption	C3	1786	18	1810-80	Original Parish	Napoleonville
Attakaps				1810	Original Parish - Discontinued	
Avoyelles	C2	1763	38	1810-80	Original Parish - Reorg. 1873 . Marksville	
(Par Clk has m, div, pro, civ ct, conveyance, mtg from 1808)						
Beauregard	C1	1913	19		Calcasieu	DeRidder
Baton Rouge				1810		
Bienville	B2	1848	17	1850-80	Claiborne	Arcadia
Bossier	A1	1843	58	1850-80	Claiborne	Benton
Caddo	A1	1838	224	1840-80	Natchitoches	Shreveport
(Par Clk has m, div, pro, civ ct, mtg, conveyance rec from 1835)						
Calcasieu	C1	1840	145	1840-80	St. Landry	Lake Charles
(Par Clk has m, div, pro, and civ ct rec from 1910)						
Caldwell	B2	1838	9	1840-80	Catahoula	Columbia
(Par Clk has m, div, pro, civ ct, conveyance, mtg, leases from 1838)						
Cameron	C1	1870	7	1870-80	Calcasieu, Vermillion	Cameron
(Par Clk has m, div, pro, civ ct rec from 1870)						
Carroll				1840-70	See East and West Carroll	
Catahoula	B2	1808	11	1810-80		Harrisonburg
Claiborne	A2	1828	19	1830-80	Natchitoches	Homer
(Clk of Dist Ct has m, div, pro, civ ct rec from 1850)						
Concordia	B2	1807	20	1810-80	Catahoula, Avoyelles	Vidalia
De Soto	B1	1843	24	1850-80	Natchitoches	Mansfield
(Par Clk has m, div, pro, civ ct rec from 1843)						
East Baton Rouge	C3	1763	230	1820-80	Original Parish	Baton Rouge
East Carroll	A3	1877	14	1880	Carroll	Lake Providence
East Feliciana	C3	1824	20	1830-80	Seceded from Feliciana	Clinton
Evangeline	C2	1911	32		St. Landry	Ville Platte
(Par Clk has m, div, pro, civ ct rec from 1911)						
Feliciana				1820		
Franklin	B2	1843	26	1850-80	Catahoula	Winnsboro
(Par Clk has m, div, pro, civ ct rec from 1843)						

Grant	B2	1869	13	1870-80	Rapides, Winn	Colfax
Iberia	C2	1868	52	1870-80	St. Martin, St. Mary	New Iberia

(Par Clk has m rec from 1868, div, pro, civ ct rec from 1869)

Iberville	C3	1807	30	1810-80	Assumption, Ascension	Plaquemine
Jackson	B2	1845	16	1850-80	Winn	Jonesboro
Jefferson	D4	1825	209	1830-80	Orleans	Gretna

(Clk of Ct has m, div, pro, civ ct rec 1825, mtg rec 1892, conveyance rec 1827)

Jefferson Davis	C2	1913	30		Calcasieu	Jennings
Lafayette	C2	1823	85	1830-80	Attakapas (New Rapides), St. Landry	Lafayette

(Par Clk has m, div, pro, civ ct, property, crim ct rec from 1823)

Lafourche	D3	1807	55	1810-80	St. James, St. John, St. Charles	Thibodaux

(Par Clk has m, div, pro, civ ct rec from 1808)

LaSalle	B2	1910	13		Catahoula	Jena
Lincoln	A2	1873	29	1880	Bienville, Jackson, Union, Clairborne	Ruston

(Par Clk has m, div, pro, civ ct rec from 1873)

Livingston	C3	1832	27	1840-80	Baton Rouge, Ascension	Livingston
Madison	B3	1838	16	1840-80	Tensas	Tallulah

(Par Clk has m rec 1866, div rec 1839, pro rec 1850, civ ct rec 1882, deeds 1839, mtg 1865)

Morehouse	A2	1844	34	1850-80	Ouachita	Bastrop

(Par Clk has m, div, pro, civ ct rec 1870, conveyance & mtg 1844, some naturalization rec 1871 to 1895)

Natchitoches	B2	1763	36	1810-80	Original Parish	Natchitoches
Opelousas				1810		
Orleans	C4	1718	628	1810-80	Original Parish	New Orleans
Ouachita	A2	1800	102	1810-80	Original Parish	Monroe

(Par Clk has m, div, pro, civ ct rec from 1800)

Plaquemines	D4	1807	23	1810-80	Orleans	Pointe a la Hache
Pointe Coupee	C2	1807	22	1810-80	Feliciana, Avoyelles	New Roads
Rapides	B2	1763	111	1810-80	Original Parish	Alexandria

(Par Clk has m, div, pro, civ ct rec from 1864)

Red River	B1	1871	10		Caddo, Bossier, Bienville Natchitoches, DeSoto	Coushatta

(Clk of Ct has m & pro rec from 1871, div & civ ct rec from 1904)

Richland	A2	1868	24	1870-80	Ouachita	Rayville
Sabine	B1	1843	19	1850-80	Natchitoches	Many
St. Bernard	C4	1775	32	1810-80	Orleans	Chalmette
St. Charles	C3	1785	21	1810-80	Original Parish	Hahnville
St. Helena	C3	1845	9	1820-80	Livingston	Greensburg
St. James	C3	1785	18	1810-80	Original Parish	Convent
St John the Baptist	C3	1807	18	1810-80	Original Parish	Edgard
St. Landry	C2	1807	81	1820-80	Avoyelles, Rapides	Opelousas

(Par Clk has m rec from 1807, div, pro, civ ct rec from 1912)

St. Martin	C2,3	1807	29	1810-80	Original Parish	St. Martinville
St. Mary	D3	1811	49	1820-80	Assumption	Franklin
St. Tammany	C4	1811	39	1820-80	Orleans	Covington
Tangipahoa	C3	1869	59	1870-80	Livingston, St. Tammany	Amite
Tensas	B3	1843	12	1850-80	Concordia	St. Joseph
Terrebonne	D3	1822	61	1830-80	La Fourche	Houma
Union	A2	1838	18	1840-80	Ouachita, Claiborne	Farmerville
Vermillion	D2	1844	39	1850-80	Lafayette	Abbeville
Vernon	B1	1871	18	1880	Natchitoches, Rapides, Sabine	Leesville
Washington	C4	1819	44	1820-80	Original Parish	Franklinton
Webster	A1	1871	40	1880	Clairborne	Minden
West Baton Rouge	C3	1807	15	1820-80	Baton Rouge	Port Allen
West Carroll	A3	1877	14	1880	Carroll	Oak Grove
West Feliciana	C3	1824	12	1830-80	Feliciana	Saint Francisville
Winn	B2	1851	16	1860-80	Natchitoches	Winnfield

U. S. Census Note: Available are the following census reports from divided or discarded parishes: Attakaps, 1810; Baton Rouge, 1810; Carroll, 1840-1870; Feliciana, 1820; and Opelousas, 1810.

Parish Map of Louisiana

Genealogists' Check List of the Historical Records Survey, Louisiana (see page VIII)

Fed Cts (start 1804); Ships Reg & Enrollments of New Orleans - 6 Vol 1804-1870 - Index of names of owners and masters; Inv of Par Arch - Allen, Assumption, Beauregard, Bossier, Calcasieu, Grant, Jefferson Lafayette, Lafourche, Morehouse, Natchitoches, Orleans, Ouachita, Plaquemines, Sabine, St Bernard, St Charles, Terrebonne, Washington, Webster; Title Line Inv of Par Arch of La Parts 1 & 2 Acadia through Winn; Inv of Mun & Tn Arch - Franklinton, Thibodaux; Tran of Pub Arch-Iberville Par Police Jury Min, Vol 1 1850-1862, Vol 2 1880-1901, Vol 3 1901-1916, Vol 4 1916-1925, Vol 5 1925-1936, Gen Index 1850-1936; Tran of Pub Arch - Jefferson Par Police Jury Min, Vol 1 1834-

1843, Vol 3 1858-1870, Vol 3A 1871-1884, Vol 4 1870-1879; Tran of Pub Arch - St Bernard Par Police Jury Min, Vol 1 1870-1877, Vol 2 1880-1895, Vol 3 1895-1914, Vol 4 1914-1922, Vol 5 1922-1929, Vol 6 1929-1940; Guide to Pub Vit Stat Rec; Guide to Vit Stat Rec of Chr Arch - Vol 1 Prot & Jewish Chrs, Vol 2 RC Chrs;

A Rec of Casualties to Person & Vessels on the Mississippi River and Tributaries, US Customs Dist, Port of New Orleans 1873-1924; Navigation Casualties on the Mississippi River and Tributaries 1866-1910; East Baton Rouge Dist - Third Dist Ct Cases 1811-1848; Passenger Lists taken from Manifests of the Customs Service Port of New Orleans; New Orleans - Min

Bks of the US Dist Ct 1808-1876; Inv of the Chr & Syn Arch of La, Jewish Congregations and Org; Dir of Chrs & Rel Org in New Orlean.

Louisiana Mss Pub: Guide to Depo of Ms Col in La (in the La Hist Quarterly Vol 24, No. 2); Reprint (51p Apr 1941, 2nd Ed); Guide to Ms Col in La Dept of Arch, La State U, Vol 1 & Second Edition; Cal of Ms Col in La - Series I. The Dept of Arch - No. 1. Taber Col; An Inv of the Col of the Middle Am Research Institute - No. 1 Cal I. Fayssoux Col of William Walker Papers - No. 2 Cal of the Yucatecan Letters - No. 3 Maps in the Frederick L. Hoffman Col - No. 4 Maps in the

Lib of the Middle Am Research Institute; Trans of Ms Col of La - No. 1 The Favrot Papers, Vol 1 1695-1769, Vol 2 1769-1781, Vol 3 1781-1792, Vol 4 1793-1796, Vol 5 1796-1799, Vol 6 1799-1801, Vol 7 1801-1803, Vol 9 (1812)

Bibliography of the Official Publ of La 1803-1934; La Newspapers 1794-1940 - A Union List of La Newspaper Files in the Offices of Publishers, Lib and Private Col; Parish (Co) Boundairies in La; Microfilm-Birth Rec, City of New Orleans 1847-1901, New Orleans Bd of Health; Birth Rec, St Bd of Health, New Orleans, La 1911-1941 Depo of unpubl mat, Dept of Arch & Hist, La State U, Baton Rouge, La.

Maine

Capital Augusta - State 1820 - (23rd)

English and French explorers visited the present Maine region many times from 1798 to 1605. It was not until 1623 that the first permanent settlement was established. A community came into existance that year on the Saco River, in the extreme southwestern section. The settlers came into the district as English subjects and they brought with them the laws of England. They came with a permission granted them by the English rulers to create for themselves property in American lands.

One hundred Englishmen aboard two vessels left Plymouth on May 31, 1607. At the mouth of the Kennebec, then known as the Sagadahoc, they established a settlement which was disbanded the next year when the remaining settlers returned to England. Some historians maintain that not all of the settlers returned to England. Some, they say, appeared in the present Pemeaquid, Lincoln County, in 1608.

The appetite of many a hard-working low paid, stay-at-home Englishman was whetted by the description of the New Land by one of the returning explorers when he wrote, "Here are no hard landlords to rack us with high rents, or extorted fines to consume us. Here, every man may be master and owner of his own labor and land, or the greatest part, in a small time."

Various small groups brought over from England had settled along the coast of Maine where they engaged in fishing, but the first large contingent to come were the English Pilgrims or Puritans who arrived via Holland and Plymouth off Cape Cod in Massachusetts on November 11, 1620. Most of these so called dissenters came origi-

nally from Scrooby, Nottinghamshire.

In 1622 two members of the Plymouth Company in England, Sir Ferdinando Gorgas and Captain John Mason were granted all of the land between the Kennebec and the Merrimac rivers. It was about that time that Dover and Portsmouth in New Hampshire were established. Later the grant was divided, Mason taking the part that is now New Hampshire, and Gorgas the eastern section called Maine.

Late in sixteen hundred many communities existed along the coast of Maine and the many rivers in that section. Among them were Kittery, York, Kennebunk, Saco, Arundel (Kennebunkport), and several others which in that early period had a population of several thousand. Dissatisfaction among the early settlers toward the aristocratic regime of Gorges and his sons led to Maine's annexation to Massachusetts. After the death of King Charles in 1685, and the brief ascension of James II, Massachusetts suddenly lost all of its former legal standings, and landholders had to resecure their holdings at high fees. The new land titles were recorded in Boston, but Maine also established a special land office in York.

In those early days the population east of the Kennebec River was slim, indeed, most of the settlers gathering on the ocean shore or along the rivers between the Kennebec and the Piscataqua. Among the settlements of those early seventeen hundreds were Biddeford, opposite Saco on the southwest bank of the Saco River; Portland, then known as Falmouth Neck; Berwick, on the east side of the Piscataqua, which is the border between Maine and New Hampshire; Sanford and Alred, north of Berwick and west of Biddeford; and a long line of smaller communities extending north along the western state border, such as Hollis (Little Falls) Newfield (Hubbardstown), Waterborough, (Massabesic), Limington (Ossipee), Baldwin (Flintstown), Bridgton (Bridgetown), Fryeburg (Pequawkett), and Stow.

As a county of Maine, Yorkshire from 1716 until 1760, covered the entire state. In the latter year it was divided into three counties, Lincoln, Cumberland and York. At that time the population was about 17,000, of which 10,000 lived in the cities mentioned in the sixth paragraph above. Above Oxford county, the entire section was a wilderness into which few, if any, settlers, had dared to enter. For more than a hundred years transportation was one of the greatest handicaps of the settlements. Travel was mainly along the river courses. The extremely few roads then existing were in such terrible conditions that the limited number of cart roads were a dread to travelers. In many places they were almost impassable. To travel a distance less than sixty miles in those days required two long days. In the winter time when the roads were frozen, they were in better passable condition than in the summer. For many years after settlements were established in the Maine region, most of the roads, or trails, could be used only by the horseback riders.

In 1775 both York and Biddeford were county seats or shire towns of York shire, which at that time had a population of about 15,000 or about half the population of the state. Fryeburg, on the New Hampshire borderline about 65 miles north of Kittery, was made a deed registration office for the section north of the Ossipee River in 1799.

Like York county so Cumberland county had a string of fair sized communities along the coast in those early days, including Scarboro, Cape Elizabeth, Falmouth (Portland), and Yarmouth. These Cumberland County coast towns had a population of a little less than ten thousand. Among the inland plantations, running almost parallel with the coast from twelve to fifteen miles, were Gorham, Windham, New Gloucester, Gray (New Boston), Raymond, Turner (Sylvester Canada), and Harrison (Otisfield). Very few, if any, settlements existed then in the eastern part of the present Oxford County, not even a road or a trail. From the east boundary of Cumberland extended to the Canadian line, the rest of Maine formed the large county of Lincoln.

Only two towns were established along the ocean in all of that territory, Topsham in the west part of the present Sagadahoc County, and Belfast in the present Waldo County. About a dozen other small communities existed along the Kennebec River for a distance of about seventy miles from its mouth. Between the northernmost Norridgewock in the present Somerset County and the coast, some of the other towns then existing were Waterville, Winslow, Sidney, Hallowell, Gardiner (Pittstown), Richmond, and Bowdoinham. Pownalborough (Dresden) was the early county seat of Lincoln County.

Before the first federal census in 1790, the Maine census was taken twice – in 1764 and 1772. The 1764 census showed the population of the three counties to be York, 11,362; Cumberland, 8291, and Lincoln, 4,371. The 1772 census gave these figures, York, 13,398; Cumberland, 10,139, and Lincoln, 5,563.

From 1650 to 1819, Maine was under the jurisdiction of Massachusetts. After many attempts Maine finally succeeded in breaking away in 1819. A year later she was admitted into the union as the twenty-third state.

Although the early settlers were mainly from England, many Scotch-Irish and Huguenots came during the first century. Some German families came to Waldoboro, straight west from Rockland on the southeastern Atlantic shore line, from 1740 to 1800. During the nineteenth century many artisans came from England, Scotland and the Scandinavian countries to work in factories and ship yards. About 1870 many Swedes settled in the northeast corner of the state as indicated by such Swedish place-names as New Sweden, Stockholm, Jemtland, and Linneus. The large lumber camps in the northwest section of the state later beckoned many Finns.

Very early in their history, Maine towns began to keep records of births, marriages and deaths. Notwithstanding the many repeated governmental changes during the first two hundred years the vital statistics of the territory were disturbed but little. Many of the records have been printed and are now in genealogical libraries in most of the states. Unpublished information may be searched in the various city offices in the state. The large majority of the early communities still existing have printed their town histories. Most of those histories contain genealogical information about the early settlers.

Division of Vital Statistics, Department of Health and Welfare, Augusta, Maine, has records of birth, marriage, death, and divorce dating from 1892, adoption records from 1935, and about half a million birth, death, and marriage records of earlier dates. The state census records of 1850, 1860 and 1870 are also available there.

The city clerks of nearly five hundred towns and cities are in possession of the original records of vital statistics long before 1892. Authorities have reported that "the completeness of the early records varies all the way from absent to quite complete. Portland's records, for instance, are very complete and date from 1712."

In the sixteen offices of clerks of court are the records of land titles as well as the divorce records. The sixteen registrars of probate have the settlements of estates and the adoption records. They also have the 1880 census enumerations for their respective counties, but six of the sixteen, it is reported, have strangely mislaid them. The courts are located in the county seats of each county.

War service records, including graves registration, is under the office of the Adjutant General in Augusta.

The important libraries in the state are located in the following cities. Augusta (Kennebec Co.), Maine State Library, State House; Bangor (Penobscot Co.), Public Library, 145 Harlow St., (genealogies and town histories of Maine, N.H., Vt., and Mass.); Portland (Cumberland Co.), Guy Gannett Publishing Company, Press Herald-Express Library, 390 Congress St, (newspaper refrences); Portland Public Library, 619 Congress St.

The following reference books on Maine may help you in your research:

BANKS, CHARLES EDWARD, *Topographic-Dictionary of 2885 English Emigrants to New England*, 1620-1650. Publ. 1937. The homes of emigrants, parishes and counties were ascertained in numerous cases.

Documentary History of the State of Maine, 24 volumes, 1869-1916. Maine Historical Society.

HOUSE, CHARLES J., *Names of Maine Soldiers of the American Revolution*. Burleigh & Flynt, Augusta, Me., 1893. 50 pp.

LIBBY, CHARLES THORNTON; NOYES, SYBIIL AND DAVIS, WALTER GOODWIN, *Genealogical Dictionary of Maine and New Hampshire*, Five Volumes. Total pages. 795. Based largely on Col. Banks' two mammoth manuscripts, *Maine Genealogies*, which represent a life time of work in all the libraries over the country. The Southworth—Anthoensen Press, Portland, Me., 1928-38.

LIBBY, CHARLES THORNTON, Province and Court Records of Maine. Vol. I, 1928. Vol. II, 1931 (index).

LITTLE, GEORGE THOMAS, *Genealogical and Family History of the State of Maine*. About 6,000 individual biographies. Vol. I, 500 pp. Vol. II, 550 pp. Vol. III, 600 pp. Vol. IV, 633 pp. Lewis Historical Publishing Company, New York, 1909. (Commercial biographies should always be checked carefully.)

Maine 1790 Census. 105 pp. Bureau of the Census, Government Printing Office, Washington, D. C., 1908.

Maine Register and State Reference Book, 1852. Masters, Smith & Company, Hallowell. Me., 1852.

MARSHALL, J. M., *Buxton, Maine, Centennial Anniversary*, 288 pp. with 148 pp. of genealogy. Dresser, McLellan & Company, Portland, Me., 1874.

POPE, CHARLES HENRY, *Pioneers of Maine and New Hampshire*, 1623-1660, a descriptive list drawn from the records of the colonies, towns, churches, courts, and other contemporary sources. Alphabetically arranged. 1908.

SARGENT, WILLIAM MITCHELL, *Maine Wills*, 1640-1760. 953 pp. Four indexes: Testators, Other Persons, and Miscellaneous' Brown, Thurston & Company, Portland, Me., 1887.

SCALES, JOHN, *Piscataqua Pioneers*, 1623-1775. Sketches of early settlers and the first generation of their children, who lived on both sides of the Piscataqua River, including Dover, Oyster River, Kittery, Exeter, Brewick, and Portsmouth..

SPENCER, WILBUR DANIEL, *Pioneers on Maine Rivers*, with lists to 1651. 1930.

SPRAUGE'S *Journal of Maine History*, 14 vols. Printed 1913-1926.

The Maine Historical and Genealogical Recorder, 1884-1898. 8 vols. Reprint of vital records, family sketches, etc. (Valuable)

UNITED STATES, WORKS PROGRESS ADMINISTRATION, *Bibliography of Research Projects Reports*. Check list of historical records survey publications, 1940.

Maine Towns Organized Before 1800

ANDROSCOGGIN COUNTY — Durham, 1772; E. Livermore, 1780; Greene, 1780; Leeds, 1780; Lewiston, 1768; Lisbon, 1788; Livermore, 1779; Minot, 1769; Turner, 1772; Webster, 1774.

CUMBERLAND COUNTY — Bridgton, 1768; Brunswick, 1628; Cape Elizabeth, 1630; Casco, 1729; Cumberland, 1640; Deering, 1637; Falmouth, 1632; Freeport, 1658; Gorham, 1732; Gray, 1756; Harpswell, 1659; New Gloucester, 1735; Portland, 1632; Scarborough, 1631; Standish, 1763; Windham, 1735; Yarmouth, 1636.

FRANKLIN COUNTY — Avon, 1790; Chesterville, 1782; Farmington, 1794; Freeman, 1797; Industry, 1793-4; Jay, 1795; New Sharon, 1794; Philips, 1790; Wilton, 1792.

HANCOCK COUNTY — Blue Hill, 1762; Brookline S. 1688; Bucksport, 1764; Carline, O. 1626; Demariscotta, S. 1630; Deer Isle, O. 1789; Eastbrook, S. 1800; Eden, 1763; Ellsworth, S. 1763; Gouldsborough, S. 1700; Hancock, S. 1764-5; Penobscot, S. 1765; Fremont, S. 1613.

KENNEBEC COUNTY — Augusta, 1761-2; Harrington, 1797; Belgrade, 1774; Bingham, 1784; China, 1774; Clinton, 1775; Fayette, 1779; Hallowell, 1771; Litchfield, 1795; Manchester, 1774; Monmouth, 1777; Pittston bef. 1676; Vassalboro, 1760; Wayne, 1773; Waterville, 1760; Windsor, 1790; Winslow, 1771; Winthrop, 1771.

KNOX COUNTY — Camden, 1770; Cushing, 1789; Friendship, 1750; Hope, 1782; Rockland, 1767; St. George, 1635; Thomaston, 1770; Union, 1786; Vinal Haven, 1765; Warren, 1736.

LINCOLN COUNTY — Boothbay, 1630; Bremen, 1735; Dresden, 1649; Edgecomb, 1744; Jefferson, bef. Rev. New Castle, 1630 Pownalsborough, 1760; Waldoborough, 1733-40; Wiscasset, 1730.

OXFORD COUNTY — Ondover, 1789; Bethel, 1774; Brownsfield, 1770; Buckfield, 1776; Canton, 1790; Denmark, 1788-9; Dixfield, 1793; Fryeburg, 1763; Hanover, 1774; Hartford, aft. Rev. Hebron, 1778; Hiram, 1774; Lovell, 1777; Norway,

1786; Oxford, Dur. Rev. Oxford, 1780; Rumford, 1782; Waterford, 1775.

PENOBSCOT COUNTY—Bangor, 1769; Carmel, 1695; Charlestown, 1795; Corinth, 1796; Eddington, 1785; Hampden, 1767; Orono, 1770; Orrington, 1770.

SAGADAHOC COUNTY — Arrowsic, 1679; Bath, 1660; Bowdoin, previous Rev. Bowdoinham, 1762; Georgetown, 1716; Richmond, 1650; Sagadahoe, 1623; Topsham, 1658; Woolwich, 1638.

SOMERSET COUNTY — Anson, 1798; Athens, 1782; Cannaan, 1770; Concord, aft. Rev.; Cornville, 1794; Embden, 1779; Fairfield, 1774; Harmony, 1796; Norridgewock, aft. Rev.; Skowhegan, 1792; Palmyra, 1779; Pittsfield, 1794; Waterville, 1760.

WALDO COUNTY — Belfast, 1769; Frankfort, 1770; Freedom, 1794; Isleborough, 1769; Jackson, 1708; Monroe, 1760; Montville, 1778-9; Troy, 1778.

WASHINGTON COUNTY — Calais, bef. 1758; Cutler, 1785; Dennyville, 1786; Eastport, 1780-2; Edmonds, 1775; Harrington, 1762; Lunec, 1776; Machias, 1762-3; Pembroke, 1774.

YORK COUNTY — Acton, 1776; Alfred, 1764; Berwick, 1624; Biddleford, 1617-18; Buxton, 1772; Cornish, 1794; Dayton, 1664; Eliot, 1632; Hollis, 1753; Kennebunk, 1643; Kennebunkport, 1653; Kittery, 1623; Lebanon, 1746; Limerick, 1775; Lyman, 1778; N. Berwick, 1630; Parsonfield, 1772; Saco, 1653; Sanford, 1745; S. Berwick, 1624; Waterborough, 1768; Wells, 1640; York, 1663.

Maine County Histories

(Population figures to nearest thousand - 1960 Census)

Name	Map Index	Date Formed	Pop. By M	Census Reports Available	Parent County	County Seat
Androscoggin	D2	1854	86	1860-80	Cumberland, Oxford, Kennebec ..	Auburn
(Co Clk has civ ct rec from 1854)						
Aroostook	B2	1839	106	1840-80	Washington	Houlton
(Co Clk has div & civ ct rec from 1839)						
Cumberland	D2	1760	183	1800-80	York	Portland
Franklin	C1	1838	20	1840-80	Cumberland	Farmington
Hancock	C3	1789	32	1800-80	Lincoln . . . . Swans Island & Ellsworth
Kennebec	D2	1799	89	1800-80	Lincoln	Augusta
Knox	D2	1860	29	1860-80	Lincoln, Waldo	Rockland
Lincoln	D2	1760	18	1800-80	York	Wiscasset
Oxford	D1	1805	44	1810-80	York, Cumberland	So. Paris
Penobscot	C2	1816	126	1820-80	Hancock	Bangor
Piscataquis	C2	1838	17	1840-80	Penobscot, Somerset .. Dover & Foxcroft
Sagadahoc	D2	1854	23	1860-80	Lincoln	Bath
Somerset	C2	1809	40	1810-80	Kennebec	Skowhegan
(Co Clk has scattered m rec from 1800, div & civ ct rec from 1827, pro & property rec from 1809)						

Waldo   D2   1827   23   1830-80 Hancock .... Belfast
    (Co Clk has div & civ ct rec from 1827)
Washington   C3   1789   35   1800-80 Lincoln .... Lambert Lake & Machias
York (shire) E2   1638   99   1800-80 Original county reorg. 1658 .... Alfred
    (Part of 1800 census missing)

County Map of Maine

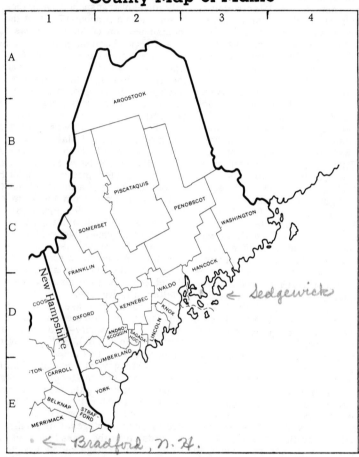

Genealogists' Check List of the Historical Records Survey, Maine (see page VIII)

Fed Cts; Inv of Mun & Tn Arch - Avon, Bar Harbor, Berlin, Brownville, Chesterville, Cranberry Isles, Coplin, Dallas, Eustis, Mt Desert, Seaville, Southwest Harbor, Tremont; Dir of Chr & Rel Org in Maine; Ship Reg & Enrollments of Machias 1780-1830 - Saco 1791-1915; Index to a Reference List of Mss Relating to the Hist of Maine - Part III in the Main Bulletin Vol XLIII No. 8; Am Portrait Inv found in the State of Me 1745-1850; Depo of unpubl mat, Works Progress Admin Warehouse, Portland, Maine.

Maryland

Capital Annapolis - State 1788 - (7th)

Depressed by the constant persecution in England of the members of the Roman Catholic church, with which he had become affiliated, Lord Baltimore (George

Calvert), a member of Parliament and Secretary of State of James I from 1609 to 1625, sponsored movements to establish colonies in America for the persecuted religionists in his homeland. Failing in his first attempt to build a colony in Newfoundland about 1620, he persuaded the King of England to grant him land for a colony farther south along the Atlantic coast. After the grant was made, but before the charter had been signed, Lord Baltimore died. King Charles I then transferred the grant to Lord Baltimore's son, Cecilius Calvert, the second Lord Baltimore.

The grant included all of the land between the fortieth parellel and the southern bank of the Potomac River. The first contingent of emigrants to be shipped to the new colony in 1634 consisted of about twenty Catholic gentlemen and two hundred Protestant laborers. They established a settlement about nine miles up the St George's river, which empties into the north side of the Potomac river, near its mouth.

Already occupying Kent Island in the Chesapeake Bay, just opposite the present site of Annapolis, were William Claiborne, a Virginia planter, and a large group of settlers he had brought there from Virginia several years ahead of the Calvert colonists. Continous warfare ensued between the two factions, as Claiborne refused to adhere to orders from the British King granting the territory to Lord Baltimore. It was not until Claiborne's death in 1677 that hostilities ceased.

The Maryland colony enjoyed a rapid growth. This was due, in a measure, to the pronouncement of its founder that religious toleration and protection would be extended to all Christians of whatever shade of religious belief who would come there to establish their homes. The Act Concerning Religion, passed by the colony in 1649, declared that "no person professing to believe in Jesus Christ shall henceforth be troubled or molested on account of religion."

This attracted a large group of Puritans who had become disgusted with the activities of the Church of England controlling Virginia. They left Virginia and came into Maryland. They settled and built up what is now Anne Arundel county. This influx increased the population of Maryland to about thirty thousand people.

In 1660 another migration brought many settlers to the so-called Eastern Shore, the land east of Chesapeake Bay. This movement was so great it necessitated the organization of Talbot county. About five years later with the migration continuing

steadily, Somerset county was formed south of Talbot.

During the first century of the settlement of Maryland, the settlers clung to the land along the many water courses, the rivers and the bays. No one ventured far away from the streams, which provided about the only mode of transportation in those days. It was not until about 1740 that the Appalachian section of Maryland was claimed by settlers. English, Scotch, and Scotch-Irish emigrants came up from St. Mary's, Charles, and Prince George's counties at that time. Joining with them shortly afterward were large groups of Germans who had come down from Pennsylvania. The population increased so rapidly that in 1748 Frederick county was organized in the northwest section of Maryland.

To Baltimore in 1755 came many Acadians driven from Nova Scotia. Less than forty years later another group of French people, upwards of a thousand, sought refuge in Baltimore from the race riots in Santo Domingo in 1793. From 1817 to 1847 thousands of Irish immigrants came to Baltimore as canal diggers. Later they established themselves as farmers and miners in the Appalachian section. Thousands of people who fled Germany after the 1848 Revolution in that country were given shelter in Baltimore.

The rapid increase in the Maryland population is indicated by the fact that eleven of her twenty-three counties were formed before 1700, and eight of the remaining before 1800.

Concerning vital records of Maryland, the Division of Vital Records and Statistics Department of Health, 2411 N. Charles St., Baltimore 18, Maryland, says, "This office is primarily issuing copies of births, deaths and marriages. Our birth and death records cover the years 1898 to the present time. Our marriage records begin June 1, 1951. Marriage records prior to that date may be obtained from the clerk of the Circuit Court in the county of marriages. Deeds may, in some cases, be found at the Clerk of Court's office in each county. Land grants are only in custody of the Land Office, Annapolis, Maryland. Wills are in the Register of Wills' Office in each county."

Libraries to be found in Maryland are as follows: Baltimore, (Baltimore), Maryland Historical Society Library, 201 W. Monument St.; Hagerstown, (Washington), Washington County Free Public Library, 21 Summit Ave.

The following books contain valuable genealogical information:

Archives of Maryland: Muster Rolls and Other Records of Service of Maryland Troops in the American Revolution, 1775-1783. 736 pp. Pub. 1900.

BALDWIN, JANE, (MRS. COTTON), *The Maryland Calendar of Wills.* 8 vols. Each volume indexed. 1635-1743. 2,579 pp.

BROMWELL, HENRIETTA ELIZABETH, *Old Maryland Families,* vital statistics, 1916.

BRUMBAUGH, GAIUS MARCUS, *Maryland Records,* Colonial, Revolutionary, County and Church, from Original Sources. Vital statistics. Valuable to researchers. Vol. 1, 513 pp. Williams & Wilkins Company, Baltimore 1915. Vol. II, 688 pp. Lancaster Press, Lancaster, Pa., 1928 (Genealogical Book Company, 521-23 St. Paul Place, Baltimore 2, Maryland.)

BURNS, ANNIE WALKER, *Maryland Genealogical and Historical Recorder.* Mimeographed. 13 vol.

............, *Abstract of Wills of Baltimore Co., 1791-1797,* 5 vols.

HAYES, JR., ROBERT F., *The Maryland Genealogical Bulletin,* 1930-44. Quarterly magazine.

JOHNSTON, CHRISTOPHER, *Genealogies of the Members and Record of Services of Ancestors, Society of Colonial Wars in the State of Maryland.* (Pedigrees of members.) 157 pp. Baltimore, 1905.

NEILL, REV. EDWARD D., *The Founders of Maryland.* 194 pp. Joel Munsell, Albany, 1878.

PARRAN, ALICE NORRIS, *Register of Maryland's Heraldic Families.* 1635 to 1935. Series I, 1935; Series II, 352 pp., 1938. Baltimore. (Genealogical Book Company, 521-23 St. Paul Place, Baltimore 2, Maryland.

U. S. BUREAU OF THE CENSUS, *First Census of United States, 1790, Maryland,* Government Printing Office, Washington, D. C., 1907.

Maryland County Histories
(Population figures to nearest thousand – 1960 Census)

Name	Map Index	Date Formed	Pop. By M	Census Reports Available	Parent County	County Seat
Allegany	A2	1789	84	1800-80	Washington	Cumberland
Anne Arundel	B4	1650	207	1790-80	Original county	Annapolis
Baltimore	B4	1659	492	1790-80	Original county . .	Fullerton & Towson
Baltimore City	B4	1729	939	1800-80	Baltimore	Baltimore
Calvert	C4	1650	16	1800-80	Original county	Prince Frederick
Caroline	B4	1773	19	1790-80	Dorchester, Queen Annes	Denton
Carroll	B3	1836	53	1840-80	Baltimore, Frederick	Westminster
Cecil	B4	1674	48	1790-80	Kent	Elkton
Charles	C3	1658	33	1790-80	Original county	La Plata
Dorchester	C4	1669	30	1790-80	Original county	Cambridge
Frederick	B3	1748	72	1790-80	Prince Georges	Frederick

(Clk of Cir Ct has m rec from 1778, div rec from 1807, civ ct & land rec 1748)

Garrett	A1	1872	20	1880	Allegany	Oakland

(Clk of Cir Ct has m, div, civ ct rec from 1872)

Harford	B4	1773	77	1790-80	Baltimore	Bel Air

(Clk of Cir Ct has m, div, civ ct rec from 1773)

Howard	B3	1851	36	1860-80	Baltimore, Anne Arundel . . .	Ellicott City
Kent	B4	1642	15	1790-80	Original county	Chestertown

(Clk of Cir Ct has m rec from 1796, div rec from 1853, land rec from 1656)

Montgomery	B3	1776	341	1790-80	Frederick	Rockville

(Clk of Cir Ct has m rec from 1799, div & land rec from 1776)(1830 census missing)

Prince Georges	B3	1695	357	1790-80	Charles, Calvert	Upper Marlboro

(Many rec with Clk of Cir Ct before 1785 – deeds complete – no fires)(1830 census missing)

Queen Annes	B4	1706	17	1790-80	Talbot	Centreville

(1830 census missing)

Saint Mary's	C4	1637	39	1790-80	Original county	Leonardtown

(1830 census missing)

Somerset	C4	1666	20	1800-80	Original county	Princess Anne

(1830 census missing)

Talbot	B4	1662	22	1790-80	Kent	Easton
Washington	A3	1776	91	1790-80	Frederick	Hagerstown
Wicomico	C5	1867	49	1870-80	Somerset, Worcester	Salisbury

(Clk of Cir Ct has m, div, civ ct rec from 1867)

Worcester	C5	1742	24	1790-80	Somerset	Snow Hill

(Clk of Cir Ct has m rec from 1866, div rec from 1900, civ ct rec from 1916)

County Map of Maryland and Delaware

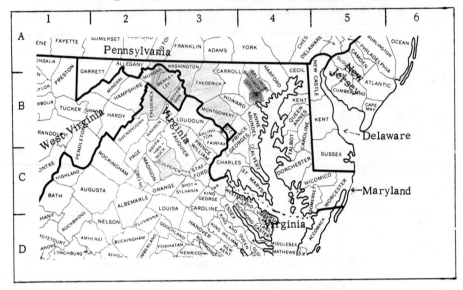

Genealogists' Check List of the Historical Records Survey, Maryland (see page VIII)

Fed Cts (start 1789); Inv of Co Arch - Allegany, Anne Arundel, Carroll, Garrett, Howard, Montgomery, Washington, Wicomico; Inv of Mun & Tn Arch - Accident, Annapolis, Arundel-on-the-bay, Barnesville, Barton, Boonsboro, Brooksville, Chevy Chase, Clearspring, Cumberland, Dear Park, Delmar, Ellicott City, Friendsville, Frostburg, Funkstown, Gaithersburg, Garrett Park, Glen Echo, Grantsville, Hagerstown, Hamstead, Hancock, Hebron, Keedysville, Kensington, Kitzmillersville, Laytonville, Loch Lynn, Lonaconing, Luke, Manchester, Mardela Springs, Midland, Mt Airy, Mountain Lake Park, New Windsor, Oakland, Poolesville, Rockville, Salisbury, Sharpsburg, Sharpstown, Smithburg, Somerset, Sykesville, Takoma Park, Taneytown, Union Bridge, Washington Grove, Westminster, Willards, Williamsport; Inv of the Chr Arch of Md - Prot Episcopal Chr - Diocese of Md; Ms Publ - Cal of the General Otho Hollard Williams Papers in the Md Hist Soc; Depo of unpubl mat, Hall of Rec, Annapolis, Md.

Massachusetts

Capital Boston - State 1788 - (6th)

It was on December 11, 1620, according to the calendar then in vogue, December 21, according to our calendar that Massachusetts came into existence with the landing of the Pilgrims on Plymouth Rock. Through the initiative of the Massachusetts Bay Company another colony was formed at Salem in 1628, and two years later more than a thousand colonists arrived founding the towns of Boston, Charleston, Roxbury, Dorchester, Watertown, and Newton, which later became Cambridge. Within ten years, more than 20,000 immigrants, almost entirely British, had landed in Massachusetts. For the first 200 years or more by far the larger number of immigrants were from England.

Disasters and political troubles of various kinds in Europe from 1850 on brought a large influx from Ireland, Germany and France. A few years later Italians, Russians, Poles, and Portuguese came into the state to work in its rapidly growing factories, mills and fisheries.

Families from Dorchester, England settled in Massachusetts and then migrated to South Carolina. Three separate settlements between Charleston and Georgetown, were settled by New England families.

The people of few states have been of

greater assistance to the genealogical researcher than have those of Massachusetts. From its earliest days, records of all vital statistics were kept and preserved. It is said that it is easier to trace genealogy in Massachusetts than in any other state. This because more records are available. Every town not only kept records from its earliest days, but has printed those records for the convenience of the researcher.

The birth and death records since 1850 may be obtained from Registrar of Vital Statistics, 272 State House, Boston 33, Massachusetts. Some records prior to 1850 are in the offices of the city or town clerks in localities where incidents happened. Similar records for Boston available since 1639 in the office of the City Registrar, Registry Division, Room 1004 City Hall Annex, Boston 8, Mass.

Partial marriage records from 1841, and complete from 1848 are in the office of the Division of Vital Statistics, The Secretary of State, Boston 33, Mass. Similar records in the offices of the city or town clerk where license was issued. Marriage bans may be found in respective churches in the city.

Divorce records are with the Clerk of the Superior Court or the Register of Probate in the county were divorce was granted

The state census records at five year intervals from 1850 to 1870, inclusive, are in the office of the Secretary of State.

The records of wills, deeds and land transactions are in the office of the Secretary of State.

The city or county assessors have all records of taxpayers.

The office of the Adjutant General controls all war service records.

Every town library in Massachusetts has vital statistical records from the adjoining communities and numerous biographical and historical books and manuscripts about early residents. Among the most important libraries in the state for genealogical purposes are the following: Boston, (Suffolk), Public Library, Copley Square, (biographies, New England family genealogies, English parish registers and records, heraldry from Great Britain, Ireland, Germany, Italy, Holland, France, and Belgium, early American and Civil War histories, old maps, old newspapers); Massachusetts Historical Society Library, 1154 Boylston St., (New England histories and genealogies); Massachusetts State Library, Beacon Hill, (history and newspapers); New England Historic Genealogical Society, 9 Ashburn Place. (170,000 volumes of history and genealogy, and manuscript family genealogies). Cambridge, (Middlesex), Public Library, 449 Broadway, (genealogical collection); Harvard University Library, (early American newspapers). Dedham, (Norfolk), Dedham Historical Society, (considerable number of historical and family histories and diaries in books and manuscripts, town histories, family genealogies, and newspapers from earliest days); Lowell, (Middlesex), City Library, Merrimac St., (Book and manuscript genealogies); Lynn, (Essex), Public Library, North Common St., (New England histories and genealogies); New Bedford. (Bristol), Free Public Library, Pleasant St., (southeastern Mass. family genealogies in books and manuscripts); Pittsfield, (Berkshire), The Berkshire Athenaeum, 44 Bank Row, (biography, Massachusetts history, New England genealogy); Salem, (Essex), Essex Institute Library, 132-134 Essex St., (town vital statistics, family histories, and genealogies, printed and in manuscript, and genealogical and historical magazines); Springfield, (Hampden), City Library Association, 220 State St., Westfield. (Hampden), Athenaeum, Elm St., (vital statistic records of the city, cemetery inscriptions, death notices from newspapers, family histories, printed and manuscript).

Among the many volumes available to ease the task of the researchers of Massachusetts genealogy are the following:

BANKS, CHARLES EDWARD. *The Planters of the Commonwealth.* A study of the Emigrants and Emigration in Colonial Times: to which are added Lists of Passengers to Boston and to the Bay Colony; the Ships which brought them; their English Homes and the Places of their Settlement in Mass. 1620-1640. 229 pp. Houghton Mifflin Company, Boston, 1930.

BOLTWOOD, L. M. *Genealogies of Hadley Families,* embracing early settlers of the towns of Hatfield, South Hadley, Amherst, and Granby. 168 pp. Metcalf & Company, Northampton, 1862.

First U. S. Census, 1790—Massachusetts, 363 pp. Government Printing Office, 1908.

HILLS, LEON CLARK. *Mayflower Planters and First Comers to Ye Olde Colonie,* 177 pp. Hills Publishing Company, Washington, D. C. 1936.

Massachusetts Encyclopedia of Biography and Genealogy, Vol. 1, 562 pp. Vol. 11, 410 pp.

Massachusetts Soldiers and Sailors of the Revolutionary War. 17 vols. of abt. 1,000 pp. each. Wright & Potter Printing Company, Boston, 1896-1908.

NASON, REV. ELIAS. *A Gazetteer of the State of Massachusetts*. Map and illustrations. 576 pp. B. B. Russel, Boston, 1874.

RAND, JOHN C. *One of a Thousand*. Biographies of Massachusetts Residents. 707 pp. First National Publishing Company, Boston, 1890.

STARK, JAMES H. *The Loyalists of Massachusetts and The Other Side of the American Revolution*. With names and biographies. Fully indexed. 510 pp. The Salem Press Company, Salem, Mass., 1910.

The cities and towns of no other state have so many published community histories and vital statistics as has Massachusetts. If your ancestors were there before 1850 it would be well to check with the libraries and town clerks to ascertain what information may be had from the printed records.

The present Massachusetts counties are divided into the following townships:

BARNSTABLE—Barnstable, Bourne, Brewster, Chatham, Dennis, Eastham, Falmouth, Harwich, Mashpee, Orleans, Provincetown, Sandwich, Truro, Wellfleet, and Yarmouth.

BERKSHIRE—Adams, Alford, Becket, Cheshire, Clarksburg, Dalton, Edgemont, Florida, Great Barrington, Hancock, Hinsdale, Lanesborough, Lee, Lenox, Monterey, Mount Washington, New Ashord, New Marlborough, North Adams, Otis, Peru, Pittsfield, Richmond, Sandisfield, Savoy, Sheffield, Stocksridge, Tyringham, Washington, West Stockridge, Williamstown, and Windsor.

BRISTOL—Acushnet, Attleboro, Berkley, Dartmouth, Dighton, Easton, Fairhaven, Fall River, Freetown, Mansfield, New Bedford, North Attleborough, Norton, Rynham, Rehoboth, Seekonk, Swansea, Taunton, and Westport.

DUKES—Chilmark, Edgartown, Gayhead, Gosnold, Oak Bluffs, Tidbury, and West Tidbury.

ESSEX—Andover, Amesbury, Beverly, Boxford, Danvers, Essex, Georgetown, Gloucester, Groveland, Hamilton, Haverhill, Ipswich, Lawrence, Lynn, Lynnfield, Manchester, Marblehead, Merrimac, Methuen, Middleton, Nahant, Newburyport, North Andover, Peabody, Rockport, Rowley, Salem, Salisbury, Saugus, Swampscott, Topsfield, Wenham, and West Newbury.

FRANKLIN—Ashfield Bernardston, Buckland, Charlemont, Colrain, Conway, Deerfield, Erving, Gill, Greenfield, Hawley Heath, Leverett, Leyden, Monroe, Montague, New Salem, Northfield, Or-

ange, Rowe, Shellburne, Shutesbury, Sunderland, Warwick, Wendell, and Whately.

HAMPDEN — Agawam, Blandford, Brimfield, Chester, Chicopee, East Longmeadow, Granville, Hampden, Holland, Holyoke, Longmeadow, Ludlow, Monson, Montgomery, Palmer, Russell, Southwick, Springfield, Tolland, Wales, Westfield, West Springfield, and Wilbraham.

HAMPSHIRE—Amherst, Belchertown, Chesterfield, Cummington, East Hampton, Goshen, Granby, Hadley, Hatfield, Huntington, Middlefield, Northampton, Pelham, Plainfield, South Hardely, Southampton, Ware, West Hampton, Williamsburg, and Worthington.

MIDDLESEX—Acton, Arlington, Ashby, Ashland, Ayer, Bedford, Belmont, Billerica, Boxborough, Burlington, Cambridge, Carlisle, Chelmsford, Concord, Dracut, Dunstable, Everett, Framingham, Groton, Holliston, Hopkinton, Hudson, Lexington, Lincoln, Littleton, Lowell, Malden, Marlborough, Medford, Melrose, Nation, Newton, North Reading, Pepperell, Reading, Sherborn, Shirley, Sommerville, Stoneham, Stow, Sudbury, Tewksbury, Townsend, Tyngsborough, Wakefield, Waltham, Watertown, Wayland, Westford, Weston, Wilmington, Winchester, and Woburn.

NANTUCKET—Nantucket.

NORFOLK—Avon, Bellingham, Braintree, Brookline, Canton, Cohasset, Dedham, Dover, Foxborough, Franklin, Holbrook, Medfield, Medway, Millis, Milton, Needham, Norfolk, Norwood, Plainville, Quincy, Randolph, Sharon, Stoughton, Walpole, Wellesley, Westwood, Weymouth, and Wrentham.

PLYMOUTH—Abington, Bridgewater, Brockton, Carver, Duxbury, East Bridgewater, Halifax, Hanover, Hanson, Hingham, Hull, Kingston, Lakeville, Marion, Marshfield, Mattapoisett, Middleborough, Norwell, Pembroke, Plymouth, Plympton, Rochester, Rockland, Scituate, West Bridgewater, Wareham, and Whitman.

SUFFOLK—Boston, Chelsea, Revere, and Winthrop.

WORCESTER—Ashburnham, Athol, Auburn, Barre, Berlin, Blackstone, Bolton, Boylston, Brookfield, Charlton, Clinton, Douglas, Dudley, East Brookfield, Fitchburg, Gardner, Grafton, Hardwick, Harvard, Holden, Hopedale, Hubbardston, Lancaster, Leicester, Leominster, Lunenburg, Mendon, Milford, Millbury, Millville, New Braintree, North Borough, Northbridge, North Brookfield, Oakham, Oxford, Paxton, Petersham, Phillipston,

Princeton, Royalston, Rutland, Shrewsbury, Southborough, South Bridge, Spencer, Sterling, Sturbridge, Sutton, Templeton, Upton, Uxbridge, Warren, Webster, Westborough, West Brookfield, West Boylston, Westminster, Winchendon, and Worcester.

Massachusetts Towns Organized Before 1800

BARNSTABLE COUNTY — Barnstable,, 1638; Chatham, 1712; Dennis, 1798; Eastham, 1651; Falmouth, 1694; Harwich, 1694; Nawsett, 1643; Orleans, 1747; Provincetown from Eastham, Sandwich, 1630; Suckanasset, 1670; Truro, 1709; Wellfleet, 1763; Yarmouth, 1639.

BERKSHIRE COUNTY — Adams, 1778; Alford, 1773; Becket, 1765; Chesshire, 1793; Clarksburg, 1798; Dalton, 1784; Egremont, 1760; Gagesborough, 1771; Great Barrington, 1761; Hancock. 1776; Lanesborough, 1765; Lee, 1777; Lenox, 1767; Loudon, 1773; Mount Washington, 1779; New Ashford, 1781; New Marlborough, 1759; Partridgefield, 1771; Pittsfield, 1771; Richmont, 1766; Richmond, 1785; Sandisfield, 1762; Savoy, 1797; Sheffield, 1733; Stockbridge, 1739; Tyringham, 1762; Washington, 1777; W. Stockbridge, 1774; Williamtown, 1765; Windsor, 1778.

BRISTOL COUNTY — Attleboro, 1694; Berkley, 1735; Dartmouth, 1652; Dighton, 1712; Easton, 1725; Freetown, 1683; Mansfield, 1770; New Bedford, 1787; Norton, 1710; Raynham, 1731; Rehobath, 1645; Somerset, 1790; Swansea, 1668; Taunton, 1639; Westport, 1787.

DUKES COUNTY — Chilmark, 1695; Edgartown, 1671; Tisbury, 1671, orig. Middletowne.

ESSEX COUNTY — Amesbury, 1668; name ch. fr. Salisbury-new-town; Andover, 1646; Beverly, 1668; Boxford, 1694; Bradford, 1675; Danvers, 1752; Gloucester, 1642; Hamilton, 1793; Haverhill, 1641; Ipswick, 1634; Lynn, 1637; Lynnfield, 1782; Manchester, 1645; Marblehead, 1633; Methuen, 1725; Middletown, 1728; Newbury, 1635; Newburyport, 1764; Rowley, 1639; Salem, 1630; Salisbury, 1640; Saugus, 1631, name ch. to Lynn; Topsfield, 1648; Wenham, 1643.

FRANKLIN COUNTY — Ashfield, 1765; Bernardstown, 1765; Buckland, 1779; Charlemont, 1765; Colrain, 1761; Conway, 1767; Deerfield, 1677; Gill, 1793; Greenfield, 1753; Hawley, 1792; Heath, 1785; Huntstown, 1736; Leverett, 1774; Leyden, 1784; Montague, 1754; New

Salem, 1753; Northfield, 1714; Orange, 1783; Rowe, 1785; Sherburne, 1786; Shutesbury, 1761; Sunderland, 1718; Warwick, 1763; Wendall, 1781; Whateley, 1771.

HAMPDEN COUNTY — Blandford, 1741, Orig. Glasgow; Brimfield, 1714; Chester, 1783; Orig. Murrayfield; Granville, 1754; Longmeadow, 1783; Ludlow, 1774; Monson, 1760; Montgomery, 1780; Murrayfield, 1765; Palmer, 1752; Russell, 1792; South Brimfield, 1762; Southwick, 1770; Springfield, 1641; Westfield, 1669; West Springfield, 1774; Wilbraham, 1763.

HAMPSHIRE COUNTY — Amherst, 1759; Belchertown, 1761; Chesterfield, 1762; Cummington, 1779; Easthampton, 1785; Goshen, 1781; Granby, 1768; Greenwich, 1754; Hadley, 1661; Hatfield, 1670; Middlefield, 1783; Northampton, 1656; Norwich, 1773; Pelham, 1743; Plainfield, 1785; Southampton, 1753; South Hadley, 1783; Ware, 1761; Westhampton, 1775; Williamsburg, 1771; Worthington, 1768.

MIDDLESEX COUNTY — Acton, 1755; Ashby, 1767; Bedford, 1729; Billerica, 1655; Boxborough, 1783; Burlington, 1799; Cambridge, 1630; Carlisle, 1780; Charlestown, 1630; Chelmsford, 1655; Concord, 1635; Dracut, 1702; Dunstable, 1680; E. Sudbury, 1780; Farmingham, 1675; Groton, 1655; Holliston, 1724; Hopkinston, 1715; Lexington, 1713; Littleton, 1715; Malden, 1649; Marlborough, 1660; Medford, 1630; Natick, 1661; Newton, 1691; Pepperell, 1733; Reading, 1644; Sherburn, 1674; Shirley, 1753; Stoneham, 1725; Stow, 1683; Studbury, 1639; Tewksbury, 1734; Townsend, 1732; Tynesborough, 1732; Waltham, 1738; Watertown, 1630; Westford, 1729; Weston, 1713; Wilmington, 1730; Woburn, 1642.

NANTUCKET COUNTY, Orig. 1695 (Island). Nantucket, 1795; Sherburn, 1687.

NORFOLK COUNTY — Bellingham, 1719; Braintree, 1640; Brookline, 1705; Canton, 1797; Cohasset, 1700; Dedham, 1636; Dorchester, 1630; Dover, 1784; Foxsborough, 1778; Franklin, 1778; Medfield, 1650; Medway, 1713; Milton, 1652; Needham, 1711; Quincy, 1792; Randolph, 1793; Roxbury, 1630; Sharon, 1783; Stoughton, 1726; Stoughtonham, 1765; Walpole, 1724; W. Roxbury, 1772; Weymouth, 1635; Wrentham, 1673.

PLYMOUTH COUNTY — Abington, 1712; Bridgewater, 1656; Carver, 1790; Duxbury, 1637; Halifax, 1734; Hanover,

1727; Hingham, 1635; Hull, 1644; Kingston, 1726; Marshfield, 1642; Middleborough, 1669; Pembroke, 1712; Plymouth, 1620; Plympton, 1707; Rexhame. 1642, name ch. to Marshfield. Rochester, 1686; Scituate, 1633; Wareham, 1739.

SUFFOLK COUNTY — Boston, 1630; Chelsea, S. 1739.

WORCESTER COUNTY — Ashburnham, 1765; Athol, 1762; Barre, 1776; Berlin, 1784; Bolton, 1738; Boylston, 1786; Brookfield, 1673; Charlton, 1755; Douglas, 1746; Dudley, 1732; Fitchburg, 1764; Gardner, 1785; Gerry, 1786; Grafton, 1735; Hardwick, 1739; Harvard,

1732; Holden, 1741; Hubbardtown, 1767; Hutchinson, 1774; Lancaster, 1653; Leicester, 1713; Leominster, 1740; Lunenberg, 1728; Mendon, 1667; Milford, 1780; New Braintree, 1751; New Sherburn, 1745; Northborough, 1766; Northbridge, 1772; Oakham, 1693; Oxford, 1693; Paxton, 1765; Petersham, 1754; Princeton, 1759; Royalston, 1765; Rutland, 1714; Shrewsbury, 1720; Southborough, 1727; Spencer, 1753; Sterling, 1781; Sturbridge, 1738; Sutton, 1714; Templeton, 1762; Upton, 1735; Uxbridge, 1727; Westborough, 1717; Western, 1742; Westminister, 1759; Winchenden, 1754; Worcester, 1684.

Massachusetts County Histories

(Population figures to nearest thousand – 1960 Census)

Name	Map Index	Date Formed	Pop. By M	Census Reports Available	Parent County	County Seat
Barnstable	B3	1685	70	1790–80	New Plymouth Colony	. . . . . . Barnstable

(Clk of Ct has div rec 1828 to 1928, civ ct rec from 1828)   & West Harwich

Berkshire	E2	1761	142	1790–80	Hampshire	Pittsfield
Bristol	C3	1685	398	1790–80	New Plymouth Colony . . . . . . ,Taunton

New Bedford, Fall River

(Bristol County, Taunton has all the old records as well as those to date for the northern part of the county, while the present records for the southern part of the county are at Fall River.)

Dukes	B4	1695	6	1790–80	(Martha's Vineyard)	Edgartown
Essex	C1	1643	569	1790–80	Original county	Salem
Franklin	E2	1811	55	1820–80	Hampshire	Greenfield
Hampden	E3	1812	429	1820–80	Hampshire	Springfield
Hampshire	E2	1662	103	1790–80	Middlesex	Northampton
Middlesex	C2	1643	1239	1790–80	Original county . . . Cambridge, Lowell

(The records from about 1890 or 1895 for the northern part of the county are at Lowell, while all the county records from 1643 to 1890 or 1895, and then up to the present for the southern part of the county are at East Cambridge.)

Nantucket	A4	1695	4	1790–80	Original county	Nantucket
Norfolk	C2	1793	510	1800–80	Suffolk	Dedham

(Originally part of the northeastern section of Massachusetts and some towns at present part of New Hampshire. The old records are now at Salem in Essex County which originally included most of Norfolk County.)

Plymouth	C3	1685	248	1790–80	New Plymouth Colony	Plymouth

(Clk of Ct has civ ct rec from 1700)

Suffolk	C2	1643	791	1790–80	Original county	Boston

(Part of 1800 Census missing.)

Worcester	D2	1731	583	1790–80	Suffolk, Middlesex	Worcester

Genealogists' Check List of the Historical Records Survey, Mass. (see page VIII)

Fed Cts (start 1789); Inv of Co Arch – Essex; Inv of Mun & Tn Arch - Agawam, Ashfield, Ashland, Athol, Auburn, Avon, Ayer, Barre, Bellingham, Berlin, Bernardston, Boston (Pt 5 & Pt 9), Braintree, Brookline, Buckland, Chicopee, Clinton, Hampden, Holbrook, Maynard, Pittsfield (Pt 1 & 2), Warwick; Guide to Pub Vit Stat Rec; Inv of the Chr Arch of Mass – Universalist Chrs; Ship Reg & Enrollments of Dist of Barnstable 1814-1913 – Boston & Charlestown 1789-1795 – New Bedford (3 Vol) 1796-1939 - Plymouth 1789-1808, Dighton - Fall River 1789-1938.

Indexes to Local News in the Hampshire Gazette, Northampton 1786-1937, Vol 1 part 1 Northampton A to M, Vol 2 part 1 Northampton N to Z - part 2 Hampshire & Franklin Cos except Northampton, Vol 3 part 3 Personal Section.

Abstract and Index of the Rec of the Inferior Ct of Pleas (Suffolk Co Ct) Held in Boston, 1680-1698; Index to Proclamations of Mass Issued by Govenors and other Authorities, Vol 1 1620-1775, Vol 2 1776-1936; Check List of Mass Imprints 1801 & 1802; Am Portraits Found in Mass 1620-1825 (2 Vol); Known Early Am Portrait

County Map of Massachusetts

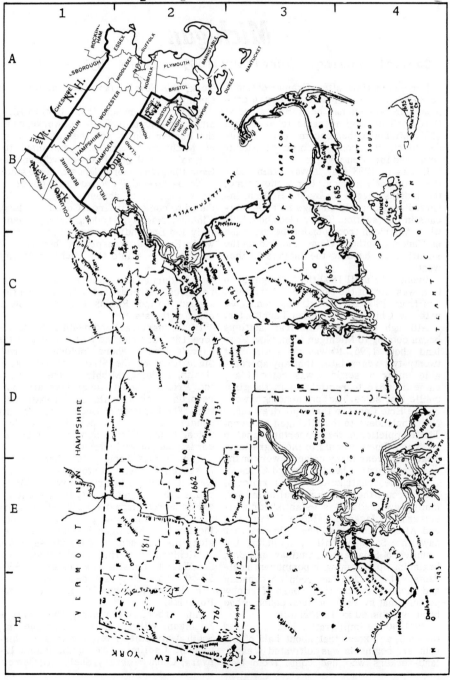

Painters before 1860

Ms Publ; Guide to Depo of Ms Cols in Mass; Guide to the Ms Colls in the Worces-Hist Soc; A Description of the Ms Cols in the Mass Diocesan Lib; Cal of the Ryder Col of Confederate Arch at Tufts College; Cal of the Gen Henry Knox Paper, Chamberlain Col, Boston Pub Lib; Cal of the Letters of Charles Robert Darwin to Asa Gray; Diary & Jour (1775-1807) of Seth Metcalf; Depo of unpubl mat, Forbes Lib, Northampton, Mass.

Michigan

Capital Lansing - Territory 1805 - State 1837 - (26th)

For some time after France obtained possession of American territory, a considerable outpost had been maintained at Detroit. This regime came to an end in 1763. Michigan then became part of Quebec territory, under which jurisdiction it remained for twenty years.

It was in 1783 that it was again under the claim of America. For a short time, the Indians, egged on by the British, inflicted considerable damage to the Americans in that section. This ended about 1795 when American troops under the command of General Anthony Wayne cleaned up the situation by herding the Indians farther west.

From 1787 until 1800 the Michigan section was part of the Northwest Territory, and from 1800 to 1805 it was connected with the Ohio and the Indian Territories. Although the first American settlers began coming to Michigan from New England about 1796, it was not until about twenty-two years later that any appreciable influx of settlers was noted. Many came in 1818 to participate in the first public land sales. The commencing of work on the Erie Canal in that year drew many New Englanders to the Michigan sections. The completion of that important canal in 1825 added new stimula to the migrations. That same year many came to work on the road construction headed toward Chicago.

With the construction of the territorial road through the Kalamazoo Valley in 1829, many New Englanders established themselves in the Jackson, Calhoun, Kalamazoo, and Allegan counties. The following year saw the Saginaw Valley, including the counties of Shiawassee, Saginaw and Bay, beginning to fill up with permanent residents. The growth had been so constant and rapid during the first years of the new century that by 1836 fourteen counties had been established in the territory.

By 1840 the immigration had increased to such an extent that about half of the southern peninsula was cultivated by eager land-seekers who had come from New York, the New England section, and from Germany.

A fifty year boom, from 1840 to 1890, attracted tens of thousands of workers into the lumber camps and the mining camps of Michigan, where they extracted the valuable and plentiful copper and iron ores from the rich mineral deposits of the state.

To secure the needed man-power to work these rich deposits men were induced to come there from Canada, Ireland, Finland, Norway, Sweden, Wales, Poland, Italy and England. The tin mines of Cornwall, England, transplanted hundreds of expert miners into the Michigan mining camps.

Also during that time large groups of religious refugees from Holland settled around Grand Rapids and the western coast of the state.

Birth, marriage, and death records before 1867 are handled by the Clerk of the Circuit Court where incident occured. Since then at the State Department of Health, Lansing, Michigan. The Clerk of the Probate Court supervises all court records, such as wills, and probate matters. The Register of Deeds of each county handles all matters pertaining to land titles. County Clerks have many vital records, see county histories.

The Detroit Society for Genealogical Research ℅ Burton Historical Collection, Detroit Public Library, Detroit 2, Mich., publish the Detroit Society for Genealogical Research Magazine which started as a monthly but later changed to a bimonthly. Inquiries on Michigan history and genealogy may be sent to the address above.

Michigan State Historical Society, 300 So. Walnut, Lansing has copies of 1830-50-60-70 and 80 census records.

Following is a partial list of Michigan libraries:

Ann Arbor, (Washtenaw), University of Michigan, William L. Clements Library, South University Ave., (early state histories); Cadillac, (Wexford), Public Library; County Library, Shelby St.; Detroit,

(Wayne), Public Library, 5201 Woodward Ave., (historical collections); Wayne County Public Library, 3661 Trumbull; Flint, (Genesee), Public Library, E. Kearsley & Clifford Sts.; County Library; Grand Rapids, (Kent), Public Library, Ill Library St., (state history, genealogical collection); County Public Library, 1961 Godfrey Ave., SW; Lansing, (Ingham), Public Library, 210 W. Shiawassee St.; State Library, State Office Bldg.; Wyandotte, (Wayne), Bacon Memorial Public Library, 2613 Biddle Ave., (local history).

Michigan County Histories

(Population figures to nearest thousand - 1960 Census)

Name	Map Index	Date Formed	Pop. By M	Census Reports Available	Parent County	County Seat
Alcona	C4	1869	6	1860-80	Alpena, Cheboygan	Harrisville

(Co Clk has b, m, d, bur, div, civ ct rec from 1869)

Alger	B2	1855	9		Schoolcraft	Munising
Allegan	E3	1835	58	1840-80	Kalamazoo	Allegan
Alpena	C4	1857	29	1860-80	Cheboygan	Alpena
Antrim	C4	1863	10	1860-80	Grand Traverse	Bellaire

(Co Clk has b, m, d, div rec from 1867, pro rec from 1863, civ ct rec from 1865)

Arenac	D4	1883	10		Bay, Saginaw	Standish

(Co Clk has b, m, d, div, civ ct rec from 1883, bur rec from 1952)

Baraga	B2	1875	7	1880	Houghton	L'Anse
Barry	E4	1839	32	1840-80	St. Joseph, Kalamazoo	Hastings
Bay	D4	1857	107	1860-80	Saginaw, Midland	Bay City
Benzie	C3	1869	8	1870-80	Grand Traverse, Leelanau	Beulah

(Co Clk has b & d rec from 1868, m & cir ct rec from 1869, div & pro rec from 1870, Naturalization rec from 1871, bur rec from 1934)

Berrien	E3	1831	156	1830-80	Cass	St. Joseph

(Co Clk has b & d rec from 1867, m rec from 1831, div rec from 1901, civ ct rec from 1933, bur rec from 1950)

Bleeker (See Menominee)

Branch	E4	1833	35	1840-80	St. Joseph, Lanawee	Coldwater
Calhoun	E4	1833	139	1840-80	St. Joseph, Kalamazoo	Marshall
Cass	E3	1829	37	1830-80	Lenawee	Cassopolis

(Co Clk has b & d rec from 1867, m rec from 1830, div & civ ct rec from 1831)

Charlevoix	C4	1869	13	1870-80	Emmet	Charlevoix
Cheboygan	C4	1853	15	1860-80	Mackinac	Cheboygan

(Co Clk has b, m, d, div, civ ct rec from 1867)

Chippewa	B4	1826	33	1830-80	Mackinac	Sault Ste. Marie
Clare	D4	1871	12	1870-80	Isabella, Midland, Mecosta	Harrison
Clinton	D4	1839	38	1850-80	Shiawssee, Kent	St. Johns

(Co Clk has b, m, d rec from 1867, div, civ ct rec from 1839)

Crawford	C4	1869	5	1820-80	Cheboygan, Antrim, Kalkaska	Grayling

(Co Clk has b, m, d rec from 1878, div rec from 1880)

Delta	B2	1861	34	1860-80	Mackinac	Escanaba
Des Moines		1834			Disorganized	
Dickinson	B2	1891	24		Marquette, Iron, Menominee	Iron Mountain

(Co Clk has m, b, d, div, civ ct, Naturalization rec from 1891)

Eaton	E4	1837	50	1840-80	St. Joseph, Kalamazoo, Calhoun	Charlotte

(Co Clk has b, m, d rec from 1867, div and civ ct rec from 1850)

Emmet	C4	1853	16	1860-80	Mackinac	Petoskey
Genesee	D4	1836	374	1840-80	Oakland	Flint

(Co Clk has b & d rec from 1867, m & div rec from 1836, civ ct rec from 1847)

Gladwin	D4	1875	11	1860-80	Saginaw, Midland	Gladwin
Gogebic	B1	1887	24		Ontonagon	Bessemer

(Co Clk has b, m, d, div, civ ct, Naturalization rec from 1887)

Grand Traverse	C3	1851	33	1860-80	Mackinac	Traverse City
Gratiot	D4	1855	37	1860-80	Saginaw, Clinton	Ithaca

(Co Clk has b, m, d, div, civ ct rec from 1867)

Hillsdale	E4	1835	35	1840-80	Lenawee	Hillsdale

Houghton   B1   1848   36   1850–80   Chippewa . . . . Houghton
(Co Clk has b, m, d, bur, div, civ ct rec from 1866)
Huron   D5   1840   34   1850–80   Saginaw, St. Clair, Sanilac . . . . Bad Axe
(rec prior 1867 destroyed by fire)
Ingham   E4   1838   211   1840–80   Washtenaw, Jackson . . . . Mason
Ionia   D4   1837   43   1840–80   Kent . . . . Ionia
Iosco   C4   1857   17   1860–80   Saginaw, Cheboygan . . . . Tawas City
(Co Clk has b, m, d, bur, div, civ ct rec from ca 1880)
Iron   B2   1885   17   Marquette, Menominee . . . Crystal Falls
(Co Clk has b, m, d, div, cir ct rec from 1885)
Isabella   D4   1859   35   1860–80   Saginaw, Midland . . . . . . Mt. Pleasant
Isle Royal   1875   1880   Disorganized 1897
(Attached 1885 to Houghton, 1897 to Keweenaw where records now are held.)
Jackson   E4   1832   132   1840–80   Washtenaw . . . . Jackson
(Co Clk has b & d rec from 1867, m rec from 1833)
Kalamazoo   E3   1830   170   1840–80   St. Joseph . . . . Kalamazoo
(Co Clk has b & d rec from 1867, m rec from 1831)
Kalkaska   C3   1871   4   1870–80   Grand Traverse, Antrim . . . . Kalkaska
(Co Clk has b, m, d, div rec from 1871)
Kent   D3   1836   363   1840–80   Kalamazoo . . . . Grand Rapids
Keweenaw   A2   1861   2   1870–80   Houghton . . . . Eagle River
Lake   D3   1871   5   1870–80   Oceana, Mason, Newaygo . . . . Baldwin
(Co Clk has b, m, d, bur, div, civ ct rec from 1876)
Lapeer   D5   1835   42   1840–80   Oakland . . . . Lapeer
(Co Clk has b & d rec from 1868, m, div, civ ct rec from 1835)
Leelanau   C3   1863   9   1860–80   Grand Traverse . . . . Leland
(Co Clk has b & d rec from 1867, m & civ ct rec from 1863, div rec from 1870)
Lenawee   E4   1826   78   1830–80   Wayne . . . . Adrian
(Ct house burned 1852, vital rec sketchy up to 1906)
Livingston   D4   1836   38   1840–80   Shiawassee, Washtenaw . . . . . . Howell
Luce   B3   1887   8   Chippewa, Mackinac . . . . Newberry
(Co Clk has b, m, d, div, pro, civ ct rec from 1887)
Mackinac   B3   1818   11   1820–80   Wayne and the French . . . . St. Ignace
(This Co first called Michilimackinac changed in 1849 to Mackinac. M & land
rec start 1821)
Macomb   D5   1818   406   1820–80   Wayne . . . . Mt. Clemens
(Co Clk has b & d rec from 1867, m rec from 1848, div & civ ct rec from 1835)
Manistee   C3   1855   19   1860–80   Mackinac, Ottawa, Oceana,
                                         Grand Traverse . . . . Manistee
Manitou   1855   1860–80   Disbanded 1895
Marquette   B2   1848   56   1860–80   Chippewa, Houghton . . . . Marquette
(Co Clk has b & d rec from 1867, m, div, civ ct rec from 1850)
Mason   D3   1855   22   1850–80   Ottawa, Oceana . . . . Ludington
Mecosta   D4   1859   21   1860–80   Kent, Newaygo . . . . Big Rapids
Menominee   C2   1861   25   1870–80   Marquette . . . . Menominee
(Organized in 1861 as Bleeker, name changed in 1863)
Midland   D4   1850   51   1850–80   Saginaw . . . . Midland
Missaukee   C4   1871   7   1870–80   Antrim, Grand Traverse . . . Lake City
(Some records destroyed in a fire in 1944)
Monroe   E5   1817   101   1820–80   Wayne . . . . Monroe
(Co Clk has b rec 1864, m rec 1818, d rec 1867, div rec 1897, civ ct rec 1857,
military dis from 1919, crim ct rec from 1859, naturalization from 1913)
Montcalm   D4   1850   36   1850–80   Ionia . . . . Stanton
Montmorency C4   1881   4   Cheboygan, Alpena . . . . Atlanta
(Most rec lost in fire 1942, still has vital rec others start 1943)
Muskegon   D3   1859   150   1860–80   Ottawa . . . . Muskegon
(Co Clk has b & m rec 1860, d rec 1871, div & pro rec 1867, cir ct rec 1859)
Newaygo   D3   1851   24   1850–80   Kent, Muskegon, Oceana . . . White Cloud
(Co Clk has b, m, d, div rec from 1867, civ ct rec from 1854)
Oakland   D5   1820   590   1820–80   Wayne . . . . Pontiac
(Co Clk has b & d rec from 1867, m & naturalization rec from 1827)

Oceana   D3 1851   17 1840-80 Ottawa .... Hart
   (Co Clk has b, m, d rec from 1867, div rec from 1897)
Ogemaw   C4 1875   10 1880   Cheboygan, Midland, Iosco .. West Branch
   (Co Clk has b, m, d, bur, civ ct rec from 1878, div rec from 1900)
Ontonagon   B1 1848   11 1850-80 Chippewa, Houghton .... Ontonagon
Osceola   D3 1869   14 1860-80 Mason, Newaygo, Mecosta .... Reed City
Oscoda   C4 1881   3 1870-80 Cheboygan, Alpena, Alcona .... Mio
Otsego   C4 1875   8 1880   Mackinac, Alpena, Cheboygan,
                                     Antrim .... Gaylord
Ottawa   D3 1837   99 1840-80 Kent .... Grand Haven
   (Co Clk has b & d rec from 1867, m & civ ct rec from 1847, div rec from 1863)
Presque Isle C4 1871   13 1860-80 Mackinac .... Rogers City
   (Co Clk has b & d rec from 1871, m rec from 1872, div rec from 1900)
Roscommon C4 1875   7 1880   Cheboygan, Midland .... Roscommon
   (Co Clk has b & d rec from 1874, m & civ ct rec from 1875, div rec from 1876)
Saginaw   D4 1835 191 1840-80 Oakland .... Saginaw
   (Co Clk has b rec 1866, m rec 1867, d rec 1868, div rec 1850, civ ct rec 1843)

County Map of Michigan

St. Clair	D5	1820	107	1830-80	Wayne	. . . .	Port Huron
St. Joseph	E4	1829	42	1830-80	Wayne	. . . .	Centreville
Sanilac	D5	1848	32	1850-80	Oakland, St. Clair, Lapeer	. . .	Sandusky
Schoolcraft	B3	1871	9	1850-80	Chippewa, Houghton, Marquette	.	Manistique
Shiawassee	D4	1837	53	1840-80	Oakland, Genesee	. . . .	Corunna

(Co Clk has b, m, d rec 1867, div & civ ct rec 1848, fire distroyed rec in 1867)

| Tuscola | D5 | 1850 | 43 | 1850-80 | Saginaw | . . . . | Caro |

(Co Clk has b & d rec 1866, m rec 1851, div rec 1884, civ ct rec 1887)

Van Buren	E3	1837	48	1830-80	Cass	. . . .	Paw Paw
Washtenaw	E4	1826	172	1830-80	Wayne	. . . .	Ann Arbor
Wayne	E5	1796	2666	1820-80	Original county	. . . .	Detroit
Wexford	C3	1869	18	1870-80	Manistee	. . . .	Cadillac

Genealogists' Check List of the Historical Records Survey, Michigan (see page VIII)

Fed Cts (start 1805); Inv of Co Arch - Alger, Alpena, Baraga, Bay, Calhoun, Cheboygan, Genesee, Iosco, Iron, Jackson, Marquette, Muskegon; Inv of Mun & Tn Arch, Detroit Recorders Ct, Muskegon List of City Offices; Vital Stat Holding by Gov Agencies - 1. Birth Rec, 2. Mar Rec, 3. Divorce Rec; Guide to Chr Vit Stat Rec, Wayne Co.

Trans of Pub Arch: Bucklin, Dearborn, Pepin - Min of Meetings of Townships, 1827-1857; Springwells 1861-1872; Hamtrack Min of Meetings, Charter Comm 1921-1922, Village Council 1901-1905 and index to both.

Guide to Ms Depo in the US - Mich; Guide to Ms Cols in Mich - Vol 1, Mich Hist Cols, Univ of Mich; Vol 2 Univ of Mich Cols; Calendar of the Bap Col of Kalamazoo College, Kalamazoo, Mich; Cal of John C Dancey Cor 1898-1910.

Inventory of the Chr and Syn Arch of Mich: African Methodist Episcopal Chr Mich Conference; Chr of the Nazarene Mich Dist Assembly; Chrs of God, Mich Assemblies; Dearborn Chrs; Evangelical & Reformed chr; Evangelical Chr, Mich Con; Jewis Bodies; Pilgrim Holiness Chr, Mich Dist; Presbyterian Chr in the USA - Presbytery of Detroit - Presbytery of Flint; Protestant Episcopal Chr - Diocese of Mich - Diocese of Northern Mich - Diocese of Western Mich; RC Chr - Diocese of Detroit; Salvation Army in Mich; Dir of Chrs and Rel Org in Greater Detroit.

Preliminary Check List of Mich Imprints; Depo of unpubl mat, Mich Hist Col, Univ of Mich, Ann Arbor, Mich.

Minnesota

Capital St. Paul - Territory 1849 - State 1858 - (32nd)

Minnesota, with its more than ten thousand lakes, began to attract sturdy Scandinavian settlers to its borders shortly after 1851 when the land west of the Mississippi was procured from the Indians. Several years prior to that, Yankees from the east and north-east, largely from Maine, had been pulled there by its infant lumber industry, which in succeeding decades drew thousands to its borders. When the Scandinavian influx began, it is estimated that less than 5,000 persons lived in the territory.

The earliest white people to visit the section were the Catholic missionaries and fur traders. Chief among the missionaries was Father Hennepin, who has been honored by having a county and one of the main streets in Minneapolis named after him. He came there about 1680 and floated down the Mississippi in a canoe.

When the northern iron mines began to be developed in the 1880's, Finns and Slavs came there by the tens of thousands. Poland, Lithuania and the Balkans furnished much of the labor for the rapidly growing packing plants around the Twin cities at the beginning of the present century.

The progenitors of the present Minnesota generation came mainly from Sweden, Norway, Denmark, Germany, Canada, Finland, Poland and Russia.

The first United States Census, a special enumeration, was taken in Minnesota in 1857, followed by the regular 1860 census. The State Archives, 117 University Ave., St. Paul Minnesota has the State census of 1865-1875-1885-1895 and 1905.

Birth and death records before 1900 and all marriage records are in the offices of the clerks of the District Court in the respective counties. The birth and death records after 1900 are in the office of State Department of Health, Division of Birth and Death Records, 469 State Office Bldg., St. Paul 1, Minn.

Records of wills, and all probate of estates are in the office of the clerk of the Probate Court in the county court house, while the records of deeds and mortgages are handled by the register of deeds in the county seat.

Some of the libraries of Minnesota which may give you assistance in your search of that area are:

Minneapolis, (Hennepin), Public Library, 1001 Hennepin Ave. (Scandinavian and local history); Northfield, (Rice), St. Olaf College, Rolvaag Memorial Library, (Norwegian collections); St. Paul, (Ramsey), Minnesota Historical Society Library (Minnesota, West, Northwest, Canadian collections, biography, genealogy, local history, Scandinavian-Americans); Public Library 4th & Washington Sts.; St. Peter, (Nicollet), Gustavus Adolphus College, Folke Bernadotte Memorial Library, (Swedish collections).

Books which may help you in your research are:

HOLCOMBE, MAJ. R. I. AND BINGHAM, WILLIAM H., *Compendium of History and Biography of Minneapolis and Hennepin County Minnesota*. Pub. 1914. Henry Taylor & Co. Minneapolis.

History of Steele and Wasega Counties, Minnesota. Pub. 1887 Union Publishing Co., Chicago, being an album of history and biography, embracing sketches of the villages, cities and townships, portraits of prominent citizens, old settlers, etc.

Minnesota County Histories
(Population figures to nearest thousand - 1960 Census)

Name	Map Index	Date Formed	Pop. By M	Census Reports Available	Parent County	County Seat
Aitkin	C3	1857	12	1860-80	Cass, Itasca	Aitkin
Anoka	D3	1857	86	1857-80	Ramsey	Anoka
(Clk of Dist Ct has b & d rec from 1870, m, div, pro, civ ct rec from 1857)						
Becker	C2	1858	24	1860-80	Indian Lands	Detroit Lakes
Beltrami	B2	1866	23	1870-80	Unorganized Territory	Bemidji
(was attached to Becker Co for many years for rec purposes)						
Benton	D2	1849	17	1850-80	Original county	Foley
(Clk of Dist Ct has b rec 1871, m rec 1850, d rec 1865, div & civ ct rec 1852)						
Big Stone	D1	1862	9	1870-80	Pierce	Ortonville
(unorganized until 1881)						
Blue Earth	F2	1853	44	1857-80	Unorganized Territory	Mankato
Breckenridge				1860	(see Clay, Toombs & Wilkin)	
Brown	E2	1855	28	1857-80	Nicollett, Blue Earth	New Ulm
Buchanan				1857-60	Discontinued	
Carlton	C3	1857	28	1857-80	Pine	Carlton
Carver	E3	1855	21	1857-80	Hennepin	Chaska
Cass	C2	1851	17	1857-80	Original county	Walker
Chippewa	E2	1862	16	1870-80	Pierce	Montevideo
Chisago	D3	1851	13	1857-80	Washington	Center City
Clay	C1	1862	39	1870-80	Breckenridge	Moorhead
(Clk of Dist Ct has b, m, d, div, civ ct rec from 1872)						
Clearwater	B2	1902	9		Beltrami	Bagley
Cook	B4	1875	3	1880	Lake	Grand Marais
(Clk of Dist Ct has b rec from 1879, m, d, div, civ ct rec from 1901)						
Cottonwood	F2	1857	16	1857-80	Brown	Windom
Crow Wing	C2	1857	32	1857-80	Cass, Aitkin	Brainerd
Dakota	E3	1849	78	1850-80	Original county	Hastings
(Clk of Dist Ct has b & d rec 1870, m rec 1857, div & civ ct rec 1853)						
Dodge	F3	1855	13	1857-80	Olmstead	Mantorville
Doty (see St. Louis & Lake)						
Douglas	D2	1858	21	1860-80	Todd	Alexandria
(attached to Sterns Co until 1866)						
Faribault	F2	1855	24	1857-80	Blue Earth	Blue Earth
(Clk of Dist Ct has b & d rec from 1870, m, div, civ ct rec from 1855)						
Fillmore	F4	1853	24	1857-80	Wabasha	Preston
Freeborn	F3	1856	38	1857-80		Albert Lea

Goodhue   E3 1853   33 1857–80 Wabasha .... Red Wing
Grant   D1 1868   9 1870–80 Stearns .... Elbow Lake
 (Clk of Dist Ct has b & d rec 1877, m rec 1869, div & civ ct rec 1883)
Hennepin   E3 1852 843 1857–80 Dakota .... Minneapolis
 (Clk of Dist Ct has b & d rec from 1870, m, div, civ ct rec from 1853)
Houston   F4 1854   17 1857–80 Fillmore .... Caledonia
 (Clk of Dist Ct has b & d rec from 1870, m, div, civ ct rec from 1859)
Hubbard   C2 1883   10   Cass .... Park Rapids
Isanti   D3 1857   14 1857–80 Anoka .... Cambridge
Itasca   B3 1850   38 1850–80 Original county .... Grand Rapids

County Map of Minnesota

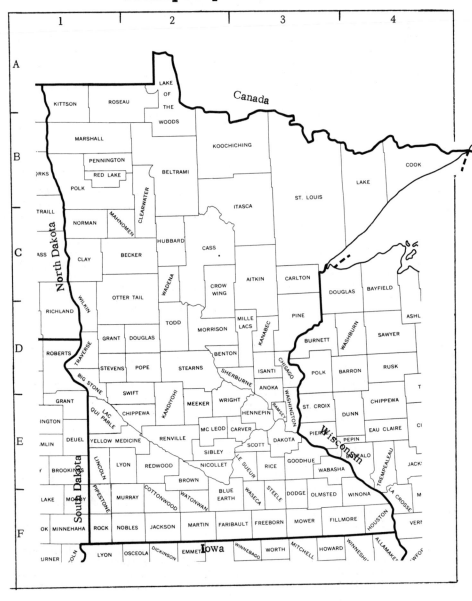

Jackson   F2   1857   16   1857-80   Unorganized Territory . . . . . . Jackson
Johnson   (see Wilkin)
Kanabec   D3   1858   9   1860-80   Pine . . . . Mora
(Clk of Dist Ct has b, m, d, bur, div, pro, civ ct, coroner's, naturalization rec
from 1883)
Kandiyohi   E2   1858   30   1860-80   Meeker . . . . Willmar
(Clk of Dist Ct has b, m, d, div, civ ct rec from 1870)
Kittson   A1   1879   8   1880   Unorganized Territory . . . . . . Hallock
Koochiching   B3   1907   18   Itasca . . . . International Falls
(Clk of Dist Ct has b, m, d, div, pro, and civ ct rec from 1907)
Lac Qui Parle E1   1863   13   1870-80   Formerly Toombs . . . . Madison
Lake   B4   1855   14   1857-80   Formerly Doty . . . . Two Harbors
Lake of the
 Woods   A1   1922   4   Beltrami . . . . Baudette
Le Sueur   E3   1853   20   1857-80   Unorganized Territory . . . . . . Le Center
Lincoln   E1   1873   10   1880   Lyon . . . . Ivanhoe
Lyon   E1   1871   23   1880   Redwood . . . . Marshall
McLeod   E2   1883   24   1857-80   Carver . . . . Glencoe
Mahnomen   C1   6   1857-80   Becker . . . . Mahnomen
Mankahta   1850   Discontinued
Marshall   B1   1878   14   1880   Kittson . . . . Warren
Martin   F2   1857   27   1857-80   Faribault, Brown . . . . Fairmont
(Clk of Dist Ct has b rec 1874, m rec 1864, d rec 1871, div rec 1880, civ ct rec 1870)
Meeker   E2   1856   19   1857-80   Wright, Stearns . . . . Litchfield
Mille Lacs   D3   1857   15   1860-80   Kanabec . . . . Milaca
Monongalia   1860-70   Discontinued
Morrison   D2   1856   27   1857-80   Benton, Stearns . . . . Little Falls
(Clk of Dist Ct has b & d rec from 1870, m, div, civ ct rec from 1860)
Mower   F3   1855   48   1857-80   Fillmore . . . . Austin
Murray   F2   1857   15   1857-80   Lyon . . . . Slayton
Nicollet   E2   1853   23   1857-80   Unorganized Territory . . . . . Saint Peter
Nobles   F2   1857   23   1857-80   Jackson . . . . Worthington
Norman   C1   1881   11   Polk . . . . Ada
(Clk of Dist Ct has b, m, d, div, civ ct rec from 1881)
Olmsted   F3   1855   66   1857-80   Unorganized Territory . . . . Rochester
(Clk of Dist Ct has incom b & d rec 1871, m rec 1855, div rec 1860, civ ct rec 1858)
Otter Tail   C2   1858   49   1860-80   Pembina, Cass . . . . Fergus Falls
Pembina   1850-70   discontinued
Pennington   B1   1910   12   Red Lake . . . . Thief River Falls
(Clk of Dist Ct has b, m, d, div, civ ct rec from 1910)
Pierce   1857-60   disorganized
Pine   D3   1857   17   1857-80   Unorganized Lands . . . . Pine City
Pipestone   F1   1857   14   1857-80   Murray . . . . Pipestone
Polk   B1   1858   36   1860-80   Indian Lands . . . . Crookston
Pope   D2   1862   12   1870-80   Pierce . . . . Glenwood
Ramsey   E3   1849   423   1850-80   Original county . . . . Saint Paul
(Clk of Dist Ct has b & d rec from 1870, m, div, civ ct rec from 1850)
Red Lake   B1   1897   6   Polk . . . . Red Lake Falls
Redwood   E2   1862   22   1870-80   Brown . . . . : . . Redwood Falls
(Clk of Dist Ct has b & d rec from 1870, m rec from 1865, div rec from 1871,
civ ct rec & citizenship rec from 1867)
Renville   E2   1855   23   1857-80   Unorganized Territory . . . . . . Olivia
Rice   E3   1853   39   1857-80   Original county . . . . Faribault
Rock   F1   1857   12   1857-80   Nobles as Unorg Co. Brown . . Luverne
(Clk of Dist Ct has b, m, d, div, civ ct rec from 1870)
Roseau   A1   1895   12   Kittson . . . . Roseau
(Clk of Dist Ct has b, m, d, div, civ ct rec from 1895, Pro Ct has pro rec 1895)
Saint Louis   B3   1855   232   1857-80   Doty (now Lake) . . . . . Duluth & Hibbing
Scott   E3   1853   22   1857-80   Dakota . . . . Shakopee
Sherburne   D3   1856   13   1857-80   Anoka . . . . Elk River
Sibley   E2   1853   16   1857-80   Unorganized Territory . . . . . . Gaylord
(Clk of Dist Ct has b & d rec 1870, m rec 1856, div & civ ct rec from 1860)

Stearns	D2	1855	80	1857-80	Indian Lands	Saint Cloud
Steele	F3	1855	25	1857-80	Unorganized Territory, Dodge .	Owatonna
Stevens	D1	1862	11	1870-80	Pierce, Big Stone	Morris
Swift	E1	1870	15	1880	Chippewa, Unorg. Lands	Benson

(Clk of Dist Ct has b & m rec from 1871, d rec from 1873)

Todd	D2	1856	23	1857-80	Stearns	Long Prairie
Toombs	(see Lac Qui Parle & Wilkin)				Disorganized	
Traverse	D1	1862	8	1870-80	Toombs	Wheaton
Wabasha	E3	1849	17	1850-80	Original county	Wabasha
Wadena	C2	1858	12	1870-80	Cass, Todd	Wadena

(Clk of Dist Ct has b, m, d, rec from 1873, div & civ ct rec from 1881)

Wahnata				1850	Disorganized	
Waseca	F3	1857	16	1857-80	Steele	Waseca

(Clk of Dist Ct has b & d rec from 1870, m, div, civ ct rec 1857, bur rec 1880)

Washington	E3	1845	52	1850-80	Original county	Stillwater

(Clk of Dist Ct has b & d rec from 1870, m rec from 1845, div & civ ct rec 1847)

Watonwan	F2	1860	14	1870-80	Brown	Saint James
Wilkin	D1	1858	11	1870-80	Cass, Toombs, Johnson . . .	Breckenridge

(Clk of Dist Ct has b rec from 1874, m & div rec from 1890, d rec from 1875)

Winona	F4	1854	41	1857-80	Unorganized Territory	Winona
Wright	E3	1855	30	1857-80	Hennepin	Buffalo
Yellow Medicine	E1	1871	16	1880	Redwood	Granite Falls

(Clk of Dist Ct has b, m, d, div rec from 1872)

Genealogists' Check List of the Historical Records Survey, Minnesota (see page VIII)

Fed Cts (start 1849); Inv of Co Arch – Aitkin, Anoka, Beltrami, Benton, Big Stone, Blue Earth, Cass, Chippewa, Dakota, Dodge, Douglas, Fairbault, Fillmore, Freeborn, Goodhue, Grant, Houston, Hubbard, Jackson, Kanabec , Lincoln, Marshall, Martin, Meeker, Mille Lacs, Morrison, Murray, Nicollet, Nobles, Olmstead, Otter Tail, Pipestone, Redwood, Renville, Rice, Rock, Scott, Sherburne, Stearns, Traverse, Wabasha, Washington, Wright, Yellow Medicine; Guide to Pub Vit Stat Rec; Guide to Chr Vit Stat Rec – Baptisms, Mar, Funerals; Dir of Chrs & Rel Org in Minn; Guide to Depo of Ms Col in the US – Minn; Minn Check list of Minn Imprints 1849-1865; General Legislation Concerning Cos in Minn; Guide to Historic Markers, Erected by the State Highway Dept Cooperating with the Minn Hist Soc; Minn Judicial Dists; The Cuyuna Range – A History of a Minn Iron Mining Dist; Depo of unpubl mat, State Historical Soc, St Paul, Minn.

Mississippi

Capital Jackson - Territory 1798 - State 1817 - (20th)

French and Spanish adventurers, less interested in establishing homes in the New World than in finding easy wealth to take home to their native lands, came to the Mississippi regions in the sixteenth century. Few evidences of their sojourn remain.

The French established colonies on the Gulf Coast at Old Biloxi in 1699 and on the Mississippi River at Natchez in 1716. The province was ceded to Great Britain in 1763 and the British settlers who followed established permanent homes. Land grants in the vicinity of Natchez to retired English army and navy officers spurred a migration of Protestants, land-loving set-

tlers who contrasted greatly with the remaining Roman-Catholic settlers of the French period. When the Thirteen Colonies revolted in 1766, the Natchez district remained loyal to the Crown, and a number of Tories of the seaboard colonies, unwilling to participate in the forced resistance, moved their families to the District. Between 1779 and 1781 Spain asserted her authority and took over the government of the Natchez District.

By 1798 pro-American sentiment had overthrown the rule of Spain and on April 7 of that year the Mississippi Territory was created by act of Congress. Natchez was the first Territorial capital, having served also as a seat of government for the District during the British and Spanish regimes.

The opening of the Mississippi River following the completion of the Louisiana Purchase in 1803 and the relinquishment of her claims to the western lands by the State of Georgia, brought about a land boom in the Mississippi Territory. Thousands of settlers came from the eastern and the northern states to claim the new lands. Petitions for statehood soon began and on December 10, 1817 the State of Mississippi was created, the eastern half of the Territory having been sheared off to create the Alabama Territory.

Another tremendous migration came in 1837 after the last of the Indian lands in Mississippi had been opened for settlement.

By 1850 Mississippi's population was more or less stabilized and is little changed basically today. The white people of the state are mostly Anglo-Saxons who trace their ancestry to the British Isles. Exceptions to this rule may be found in the families of southern European extraction who were brought to Biloxi as laborers in the fishing industry, and small colonies of thrifty Germans and Italians in various localities. In addition the Greek restaurateur is a fixture in almost every town of any size throughout the state and in the northwest section the Chinese grocer is an institution.

Genealogical information about Mississippi may be gained from records in the Mississippi Department of Archives and History at Dept. of Archives and History, War Memorial Bldg., 120 N. State St., Jackson, Miss., which has early censuses and tax rolls, newspaper files, microfilm copies of the Federal Censuses of Mississippi, records of Mississippi's Confederate soldiers and an excellent pamphlet "Research in the Mississippi Department of Archives and History." Many helpful suggestions given in foreign, territorial, state and federal archives. Wills, deeds and probate files are held by the Chancery Clerks of the various counties. Marriage records are kept by the Circuit Clerks. Records of births and deaths since 1912 are at the Bureau of Vital Statistics, State Board of Health, Jackson. Land grants are in the National Archives in Washington. The Evans Memorial Library, Aberdeen, has source records pertaining to Monroe County and surrounding territory.

The limited staff of the Department of Archives and History, Jackson, is happy to supply any information that is indexed or readily accessible but cannot undertake detailed research or microfilm census checking due to the time involved. They are glad to recommend persons outside of the Department who do this sort of work for a reasonable fee.

Incomplete birth and death records prior to 1912 are available in some counties at the office of the county clerk, where marriage records before 1926 also may be available. Wills, probate files and records of deeds and mortgages are in the office of the clerk of the Court of Chancery.

In several Mississippi counties the date of their formation doesn't necessarily coincide with the date of the available records. Some counties have valuable genealogical information dating way back earlier than their organization, while in other counties the records on file are of a much later date. Mrs. Margaret Scruggs Carruth, 3715 Turtle Creek Boulevard, Dallas 4, Texas, one of the leading southern researchers has given the following list of counties and the starting dates of their records, which you will note, are entirely different than their organization dates: Alcorn, 1842; Attala, 1870; Calhoun, Dec. 22, 1922; Chickasaw, 1863; Forest (formed 1906), 1876; Green 1875; Jackson, 1875; Jasper, 1932; Kemper, 1912; Newton, 1876; Neshola, 1836; Panola, 1870 (newspaper files since 1840); Tishamingo, 1877; Wayne 1892. Mrs. Carruth also says, "Since the Mississippi law forbids county clerks or anyone employed in their offices to do any research work, it is of no use to contact any of them by letter."

The Evans Memorial Library, Aberdeen, Miss., has a collection of tens of thousands of manuscripts, old church records, account books, letters, etc., all indexed in a card file. This is their announcement:

"The Manuscript Division of the Evans Memorial Library is inaugurating a "March of Monroe County Families". The object of this is to have every family represented with a collection of manuscript material in the files. By Manuscript is meant old letters, land grants, bills, paroles, clippings, diaries, account books, copied Bible records, scrapbooks, bulletins, old music, newspapers etc. A Collection can be two, two hundred or two thousand! Yes, we have some family collections containing over 2,000! The Gifts will be recorded, then placed in manila folders labeled with the family name which the donor prefers, then placed in locked steel filing cabinets. Authors, historians, research people who come to the library, study these materials for facts, descriptions, dates, names, etc., needed in their writing about the South. From time to time, certain items are placed on display in the locked museum case. These materials are never checked out but are used in the library."

Other Mississippi libraries: Jackson, (Hinds). Carneigie Public Library, 323 N. Congress St.; Meridian (Lauderdale), City and County Public Li-

brary, 628 25th Ave.

Books which have been published by genealogical and historical researchers may assist you in your Mississippi research:

HENDRICKS, MARY LOUISE FLOWERS, *Mississippi Court Records from the Files of the High Court of Errors and Appeals, 1799-1859.* Pub. 1950.

WELCH, ALICE TRACY, *Family Records Mississippi Revolutionary Soldiers,* Pub. 1953-56 by The Mississippi Society of the Daughters of the American Revolution. State Board of Management.

Mississippi County Histories

(Population figures to nearest thousand - 1960 Census)

Name	Map Index	Date Formed	Pop. By M	Census Reports Available	Parent County	County Seat
Adams	E1	1799	38	1820-80	Natchez District	Natchez
Alcorn	A4	1870	25	1870-80	Tippaw, Tishomingo, Wilkinson	Corinth
Amite	E1	1809	16	1820-80	Wilkinson	Liberty
Attala	C3	1833	21	1840-80	Choctaw Cession	Kosciusko
Benton	A3	1870	8	1880	Marshall, Tippah	Ashland

(Chancery Clk has div, pro, deeds, wills from 1871)

Bolivar	B1	1836	54	1840-80	Choctaw Cession	Rosedale & Cleveland
Calhoun	B3	1852	16	1860-80	Lafayette, Valobusha	Pittsboro
Carroll	B2	1833	11	1840-80	Choctaw Cession	Carrollton & Vaiden

(Co Clk has m, div, pro, civ ct, land rec from 1870)

Chickasaw	B3	1836	17	1840-80	Chickasaw Cession of 1832	Houston & Okolona
Choctaw	C3	1833	8	1840-80	Chickasaw Cession of 1832	Ackerman

(Co Clk has div rec from 1882, pro rec from 1890, civ ct rec from 1890; Co Health Dept has b & d rec from 1913; Cir Ct has m has m rec from 1881)

Claiborne	D1	1802	11	1820-80	Jefferson	Port Gibson

(Chancery Clk has m rec from 1816, div rec from 1856, pro & civ ct rec 1802)

Clarke	D4	1833	16	1840-80	Choctaw Cession	Quitman

(Chancery Clk has div & pro rec from 1875)

Clay	B4	1871	19	1880	Chickasaw, Lowndes, Monroe, Oktibbeha (Formerly Colfax)	West Point
Coahoma	A2	1836	46	1840-80	Chickasaw Cession 1836	Clarksdale
Colfax		1871			Name changed to Clay, 1876	
Copiah	D2	1823	27	1830-80	Hinds	Hazlehurst

(Co Clk has div, pro, civ ct, mort from 1823)

Covington	E3	1819	14	1820-80	Lawrence, Wayne	Collins
DeSoto	A2	1836	24	1840-80	Indian Lands	Hernando
Forrest	E3	1906	53		Perry	Hattiesburg
Franklin	E1	1809	9	1820-80	Adams	Meadville
George	F4	1910	11		Greene, Jackson	Lucedale
Greene	E4	1811	8	1820-80	Amita, Franklin, Wayne	Leakesville
Grenada	B2	1870	18	1870-80	Carrol, Yalobusha, Choctaw, Talahatchie	Grenada

(Chancery Clk has div & pro rec from 1870; Clk of Cir Ct has m rec from 1870)

Hancock	F3	1812	14	1820-80	Mobile District	Bay St. Louis
Harrison	F3	1841	119	1850-80	Hancock, Jackson	Gulfport
Hinds	D2	1821	187	1830-80	Choctaw Cession 1820	Jackson & Raymond
Holmes	C2	1833	27	1840-80	Yazoo	Lexington
Humphreys	C2	1918	19		Holmes, Washington, Yazoo, Sunflower	Belzoni
Issaquena	C1	1844	4	1850-80	Washington	Mayersville

Itawamba A4 1836 15 1840-80 Chickasaw Cession 1832 . . . . Fulton
Jackson F4 1812 56 1820-80 Mobile District . . . . Pascagoula
(Chancery Clk has div and pro rec from 1875)
Jasper D3 1833 17 1840-80 Indian Lands . . . Bay Springs & Paulding
(Co Clk has div, pro, civ ct rec from 1906)
Jefferson E1 1799 10 1820-80 Natchez, originally Pickering ... Fayette
Jefferson
  Davis E2 1906 14 Covington, Lawrence . . . . . . Prentiss
Jones E3 1826 60 1830-80 Covington, Wayne ... Ellisville & Laurel
Kemper C4 1833 12 1840-80 Choctaw Cession, 1832 . . . . DeKalb
(Chancery Clk has div, pro, civ ct rec from 1912)
Lafayette A3 1836 21 1840-80 Chickasaw Cession . . . . Oxford
Lamar E3 1904 14 Marion, Pearl River . . . . Purvis
Lauderdale D4 1833 67 1840-80 Choctaw Cession . . . . Meridian
Lawrence E2 1814 10 1820-80 Marion . . . . Monticello
Leake C3 1833 19 1840-80 Choctaw Cession . . . . Carthage
Lee A4 1866 41 1870-80 Itawamba, Pontotoc . . . . Tupelo

County Map of Mississippi

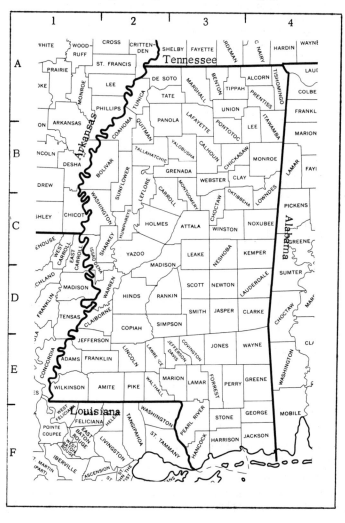

Leflore	B2	1871	47	1880	Carroll, Sunflower, Tallahatchie . Greenwood
Lincoln	E2	1870	27	1870-80	Franklin, Lawrence, Copiah, Pike,
					Amite .... Brookhaven

(Chancery Clk has div, pro, civ ct rec from 1893; Clk Dist Ct has m rec 1893)

Lowndes	C4	1830	47	1830-80	Monroe .... Columbus
Madison	C2	1828	32	1830-80	Yazoo .... Canton
Marion	E2	1811	23	1820-80	Amite, Wayne, Franklin .... Columbia
Marshall	A3	1836	25	1840-80	Chickasaw Cession of 1832 .. Holly Springs

(Chancerty Clk has div, pro, deeds from 1836)

Monroe	B4	1821	34	1820-80	Chickasaw Cession 1821 ..... Aberdeen
Montgomery	B3	1871	13	1880	Carroll, Choctaw .... Winona
Neshoba	C3	1833	21	1840-80	Choctaw Cession 1830 ... Philadelphia

(Chancery Clk has div, pro rec from 1890; Clk of Cir Ct has m rec from 1912)

Newton	D3	1836	20	1840-80	Neshoba .... Decatur
Noxubee	C4	1833	17	1840-80	Choctaw Cession 1830 ..... Macon
Oktibbeha	B4	1833	26	1840-80	Choctaw Cession 1830 ..... Starkville
Panola	A2	1836	29	1840-80	Chickasaw Cession 1832 . Batesville, Sardis

(Chancery Clk has div & pro rec 1836; Clk of Cir Ct has m rec 1885, civ ct rec 1836)

| Pearl River | F3 | 1890 | 22 | | Hancock, Marion .... Poplarville |

(Chancery Clk has m, div, pro, civ ct rec from 1890)

| Perry | E3 | 1820 | 9 | 1820-80 | Greene .... New Augusta |

(Chancery & Cir Clk has m, div, pro, civ ct rec from 1878)

| Pike | E2 | 1815 | 35 | 1820-80 | Marion .... Magnolia |

(Chancery Clk has m, div, pro, civ ct rec from 1882)

| Pontotoc | A3 | 1836 | 17 | 1840-80 | Chickasaw Cession of 1832 ... Pontotoc |

(Chancery Clk has div rec from 1912, pro rec from 1850, land rec from 1836)

Prentiss	A4	1870	13	1870-80	Tishomingo .... Booneville
Quitman	A2	1877	21	1880	Panola, Coahoma .... Marks
Rankin	D2	1828	34	1830-80	Hinds .... Brandon
Scott	D3	1833	21	1840-80	Choctaw Cession 1832 ...... Forest
Sharkey	C2	1876	11	1880	Warren, Washington,
					Issaquena .... Rolling Fork
Simpson	D2	1824	20	1830-80	Choctaw Cession of 1820 ... Mendenhall
Smith	D3	1833	14	1840-80	Choctaw Cession of 1820 ..... Raleigh
Stone	F3	1916	7		Harrison .... Wiggins
Sunflower	B2	1844	46	1850-80	Bolivar .... Indianola
Tallahatchie	B2	1833	24	1840-80	Choctaw Cession of
					1820 .... Charleston & Sumner

(Chancery Clk has div, pro, civ ct, deeds 1909; Clk of Cir Ct has m rec 1909)

Tate	A2	1873	13	1880	Marshall, Tunica, DeSoto ... Senatobia
Tippah	A3	1836	15	1840-80	Chickasaw Cession of 1832 ..... Ripley
Tishomingo	A4	1836	14	1840-80	Chickasaw Cession of 1832 ..... Iuka

(Chancery Clk has m, div, pro, civ ct rec from 1887)

Tunica	A2	1836	17	1840-80	Chickasaw Cession of 1832 .... Tunica
Union	A3	1870	19	1880	Pontotoc, Tippah .... New Albany
Walthall	E2	1914	14		Marion, Pike .... Tylertown
Warren	D2	1809	42	1820-80	Natchez District .... Vicksburg
Washington	C1	1827	79	1820-80	Warren, Yazoo .... Greenville
Wayne	E4	1809	16	1820-80	Washington .... Waynesboro
Webster	B3	1871	11		Montgomery Chickasaw, Choctaw,
					Oktibbeha .... Walthall

(Originally Summer, name changed 1882)

Wilkinson	E1	1802	13	1820-80	Adams .... Woodville
Winston	C3	1833	19	1840-80	Choctaw Cession of 1830 ... Louisville
Yalobusha	B3	1833	13	1840-80	Choctaw Cession
					1830 ... Coffeyville & Water Valley
Yazoo	C2	1823	32	1830-80	Hinds .... Yazoo City

(M rec date from 1820)

Genealogists' Check List of the Historical Records Survey, Miss. (see page VIII)

Fed Cts (start 1798); Inv of Co Arch -   mar, Pearl River, Tippah, Tunica, Wal-
Amite, Forrest, Grenada, Humphreys, La-   thall; Trans of Pub Arch, Adams Co, l.

Min of Ct of General Quarter Sessions of the Peace 1799-1801, 2. Min of the Co Ct 1802-1804; Guide to Vital Stat Rec, Vol 1. Pub Arch, Vol 2. Church Arch; See Louisiana for navigation casualties; Inv of the Chr & Syn Arch of Miss - Jewish Congregations and Org - Protestant Episcopal Chr, Diocese of Miss.

A preliminary Check List of Miss Newspaper Files Available in the Miss Dept of Arch & Hist 1805-1940; A Preliminary Union List of Miss Newspaper Files Available in Co Arch, Offices of Publs, Libraries and Private Collection in Miss; Sargent's Code - A Collection of the Orig Laws of the Miss Terr Enacted 1799-1800 by Gov. Winthrop Sargent and the Terr Judges; State and Co Boundaries of Miss; Index to Naturalization Rec Miss Cts; Depo of unpubl Mat, Dept of Arch & Hist, Jackson Miss.

Missouri

Capital Jefferson City - Territory 1812
State 1821 - (24th)

The Mississippi, five hundred miles of which is the eastern border of Missouri, was first seen by a white man in 1541 when the Spanish explorer Hernando or Fernando De Soto saw that mighty river. It was 132 years later that two French explorers, Marquette and Joilet, were the first to see the Missouri river. Only nine years later, in 1682, another French explorer, Robert Cavelier de La Salle, took possession of the section as part of Louisiana and claimed it for France. A Catholic mission was established on the present site of St. Louis about 1700. The first permanent Missouri settlement was established about 1750 by the French. It was located along the Mississippi about 50 miles south of St. Louis and was called Sainte Genevieve.

The first actual American settlement in Missouri was in 1787 when one John Dodge extablished himeslf in Ste. Genevieve County. He was followed there by Israel Dodge in 1790, and three years later by Dr. Jesse Bryan. A John Moore is said to have made his home in 1790 in what since then has become Perry County which borders Ste. Genevieve County on the southeast. In 1795 American settlements were established on Femme Osage creek in what is now St. Charles County, north of St. Louis. It was then called Upper Louisiana or New Spain. Authority for these statements comes from Pioneer Families of Missouri," published in 1876 by Wm. S. Bryan and Robert Rose, and reprinted in 1935 with an introduction by W. W. Elwang.

From 1682 until 1803 control over the Missouri section was passed back and forth between France and Spain. In the Louisiana Purchase consumated in 1803 ownership passed into the hands of the United States.

In 1805 Missouri became part of the Territory of Louisiana and remained so until 1812 when it became a Territory in its own name. At that time it claimed a population of 20,000. Most of its early settlers came from Kentucky and Virginia, and some for North and South Carolina, Maryland, Pennsylvania, and Tennessee. In those early days, indian tribes, enticed by the British, constantly scourged the Missouri settlers in severe plundering raids. It was not until about 1815 that these raids were halted through peace treaties with the various Indian tribes within the territory.

Missouri became a state in 1821. Then it had about 56,000 white settlers. She became the twenty-fourth state in the Union. At present she has 114 counties and one independent city, St. Louis.

For many decades after 1830 a steady stream of European immigrants came into the state, as a result of which St. Louis has a distinct German flavor. Many Irish, English, Polish, Swiss, Bohemian and Italian natives settled in various parts of the state. In his "Creoles of St. Louis," (1893), Paul Beckwith does full justice to the early French immigration, the so called Creoles, the Chouteaus, Gratiots, Cabannes, Papins, Pauls, etc.

Throughout the Civil War, numerous skirmishes and bloody battles were fought in Missouri which was one of the important battle grounds of the conflict, keeping the population in constant excitement and fear.

Birth and death dates after June 1, 1907 are obtainable at the State Bureau of Vital Statistics, Jefferson City, Missouri. Births and deaths from 1883 to 1891 may be obtained from the clerk of the respective counties. Information on some marriages from 1825 to date may be had at the office of the Recorder of Deeds in each county. In those offices are also the records of deeds. Wills are in the Probate Courts. Tax payer lists are in the offices of the county assessors. War service records are under the care of the Adjutant General at Jefferson City, Mo. A law originating in 1863 makes it permissible for the Recorder of Deeds in each county to file birth information on request. The first death recording began in St. Louis in 1841.

Many of the county court houses in Missouri have been lost through fire. With them were lost at the same time many old records.

Among organizations and institutions able to give much genealogical information are the Nancy Hunter Chapter, Daughters of the American Revolution, Cape Giardeau Mo., Ann Haynes Chapter, DAR, Kirksville Mo., the Missouri Historical Society, St. Louis, Mo., the Missouri Valley Historical Society Kansas City, Mo.

The following libraries may also be of great assistance:

Columbia, (Boone), University of Missouri Library, (Western Americana, books and manuscripts); Jefferson City, (Cole), State Library, State Office Bldg.; Kansas City, (Jackson), City Public Library, 311 E 12th St., (local and western history, benealogy); St. Louis, Missouri Historical Society Library, Jefferson Memorial Bldg.; County Library, 6814 Natural Bridge Rd.; St. Louis Public Library, Olive, 13th & 14th Sts., (genealogy and local history); Springfield, (Green), Public Library, Central & Jefferson Sts.

From the secretary of State Historical Society of Missouri, corner Hitt and Lowry Streets, Columbia, Mo., comes this information.

"No official compilation of the vital statistics of Missouri has been issued and for the most part, such records as are still existant are to be found in the archives of the several counties. Registration of births, marriages and deaths began in 1909 and are on file in the Bureau of Vital Statistics of the Missouri State Board of Health at Jefferson City.

"The biographical sections of a number of the general histories of Missouri and those in the histories of Missouri counties contain information of value to persons undertaking genealogical research. And of course, numbers of separate volumes on individual families of the state have been published.

"The greater number of Missouri county histories are now out of print and can only be bought through second-hand book sellers. There are several dealers from whom some of these volumes might be obtained.

"The MISSOURI HISTORICAL REVIEW is a quarterly magazine exclusively to Missouri history and biography. Biographical and genealogical information is frequently included in the articles on various phases of the state's history published in the Review, but we do not maintain a genealogical department or publish genealogical queries in the magazine. In certain early volumes of the Review a few articles of a genealogical nature were published, such as "Monmuental Inscriptions in Missouri Cemeteries" (Volumes 5, 6, 7 and 8), early marriage records of Carroll county, 1833-1852 (Volume 9, No. 2) and Pike County marriage records, 1818-1837 (Vol. 9, No. 3), The Review was first published in October, 1906 and complete unbound sets are available.

"Our Society has an excellent collection of general genealogical books and periodicals which is made available to anyone visting our library. Unfortunately, because of the large number of requests we receive and the amount of time required for work of this kind, we find it impossible to undertake genealogical research even for our members.

"For anyone interested in enrolling as a member of the Society, the annual dues are $1. which includes a free subscription to the MISSOURI HISTORICAL REVIEW".

Missouri County Histories

(Population figures to nearest thousand – 1960 Census)
Prepared and published through the courtesy of
MISS NANON L. CARR
6102 the Paseo, Kansas City 10, Missouri

Name	Map Index	Date Formed	Pop. By M	Census Reports Available	Parent County	County Seat
Adair	C1	1841	20	1850-80	Macon	Kirksville

(Co Clk has b rec ca 1880 to 1903)

Andrew   E1 1841   11 1850–80 Platte Purchase . . . . Savannah
(Co Clk has b & d rec from 1884 to 1892)
Arkansas   1813   New Madrid . . . .
(abolished 1819 when Territory of Arkansas was formed)
Atchison   E1 1845   9 1850–80 Holt . . . . Rockport
(Part of Platte Purchase; attached to Holt Co until 1854; lost 10-mile strip to
Iowa, 1848)
Audrain   C2 1836   26 1840–80 Monroe . . . . Mexico
(Created in 1831, but remained attached to Callaway, Monroe, and Ralls Cos
until 1836. In 1842 gained an additional 31 sq. miles from Monroe Co)

Barry   D5 1835   19 1840–80 Greene . . . . Cassville
(Error in survey, rectified in 1876, established the western line 2 1/2 miles east
of previous boundary. In 1872 many rec in cir clks office were destroyed by fire)
Barton   D4 1855   11 1860–80 Jasper . . . . Lamar
(Courthouse burned in 1860; no mention of fate of records)
Bates   D3 1841   16 1850–80 Jackson . . . . Butler
(Feb 22, 1855, the three southern tiers of townships in Cass Co were added to
Bates; courthouse burned in 1861; some rec prior to 1861)
Benton   D3 1835   9 1840–80 Pettis, St. Clair . . . . Warsaw
(Remained unorganized until Jan 1837; in 1845, 24 sq miles of n w part of Benton
became parts of Pettis, and Hickory Co was created, reducing Benton to its
present size)
Bollinger A4 1851   9 1860–80 Cape Girardeau, Stoddard,
                                   Wayne . . . . Marble Hill
(In 1866, courthouse destroyed by fire and with it some of the rec; in 1884,
courthouse burned while occupied only by the co clks office)
Boone   C2 1820   55 1830–80 Howard . . . . Columbia
Buchanan   E2 1839   91 1840–80 Platte Purchase . . . . Saint Joseph
Butler   B5 1849   35 1850–80 Wayne . . . . Poplar Bluff

Caldwell   D2 1836   9 1840–80 Ray . . . . Kingston
(April 19, 1860, courthouse destroyed by fire, together with all recs except those
of the pro ct; Nov 28, 1896, courthouse destroyed by fire)
Callaway   C3 1820   24 1830–80 Montgomery . . . . Fulton
(Co Clk has b, d, bur rec from 1910)
Camden   C3 1841   9 1850–80 Benton, Pulaski . . . . Camdenton
(Organized as Kinderhook, renamed Feb 23, 1843; line between Camden and
Miller changed in 1845)
Cape Girardeau A4 1812 42 1830–80 Original District . . . . Jackson
(Present size since Mar 5, 1849; in 1870 courthouse burned; Co Clk has b rec
1883 to 1893; Co Rec has m rec from 1805; Clk of Cir Ct has div & civ ct rec
from 1815; Pro Clk has pro rec from 1805)
Carroll   D2 1833   14 1840–80 Ray . . . . Carrollton
Carter   B4 1859   4 1860–80 Ripley, Shannon . . . . Van Buren

Cass   D3 1835   30 1850–80 Jackson . . . . Harrisonville
(Organized as Van Buren renamed Feb 19, 1849; three southern tiers of town-
ships relinquished to Bates Co Feb 22, 1855; Co Clk has partial b rec 1883 to 1890)
Cedar   D4 1845   9 1850–80 Dade, St. Clair . . . . Stockton
Chariton   C2 1820   13 1830–80 Howard . . . . Keytesville
(Courthouse burned Sept 20, 1864; only a few rec lost; Co Clk has b rec 1883 to 1887)
Christian D4 1859   12 1860–80 Greene, Taney, Webster . . . . . . Ozark
(Sources differ on date organized, some say Mar 8, 1859, others Mar 8, 1860;
county seat, Ozark selected May 1859; courthouse burned in 1865; no mention
of fate of records)
Clark (old)   1818   Arkansas . . . .
(Never organized; abolished in 1819 when Terr of Arkansas was created)
Clark   C1 1836   9 1840–80 Lewis . . . . Kahoka
Clay   D2 1822   87 1830–80 Ray . . . . Liberty
Clinton   D2 1833   12 1840–80 Clay . . . . Plattsburg
Cole   C3 1820   41 1830–80 Cooper . . . . Jefferson City
Cooper   C3 1818   15 1830–80 Howard . . . . Boonville

Crawford   B3   1829   13   1830-80   Gasconade . . . .   Steelville
(1829-1835 Co Ct rec lost; courthouse burned Feb 15, 1873; courthouse burned
Jan 5 1884; no mention of fate of rec)
Dade   D4   1841   8   1850-80   Greene . . . .   Greenfield
(Lost 10-mile strip on northern boundary to Cedar Co, and 9-mile strip on
southern boundar to Lawrence Co, reducing it to its present limits, Mar 28,
1845; courthouse burned in 1863, but rec had been removed to safety; Co Clk has
m & div rec from 1867)
Dallas   D4   1844   9   1850-80   Polk . . . .   Buffalo
(Organized 1842 as Niangua Co; in 1844 boundaries slightly changed and name
changed to Dallas; courthouse burned Oct 18, 1863; second courthouse burned Jul
30, 1864, and rec destroyed; the replaced rec were burned Sept 3, 1867)
Daviess   D1   1836   10   1840-80   Ray . . . .   Gallatin
DeKalb   D2   1845   7   1850-80   Clinton . . . .   Maysville
(In 1878 courthouse burned, many rec being destroyed, but rec of cir clks office
were preserved along with a few papers of other offices; Co Clk has b rec 1880
to 1892)
Dent   B4   1851   10   1860-80   Crawford, Shannon . . . .   Salem
(Courthouse burned in 1864, destroying some of the ct rec)
Dodge   1851   1850   Putnam . . . .
(Discontinued in 1853; had lost territory when Iowa boundary was established,
bringing its area below the constitutional limit of 400 sq miles; its territory
was added to Putnam Co)
Douglas   C4   1857   10   1860-80   Ozark, Taney . . . .   Ava
(Terr increased in 1864 by addition of portions of Taney and Webster Cos)
Dunklin   A5   1845   1850-80   Stoddard . . . .   Kennett
(In 1853 a strip one mile wide was taken from Stoddard and added to northern
boundary; courthouse burned during Civil War; in 1872 a newly-completed
courthouse burned with all the records; all records prior to 1872 are lost)
Franklin   B3   1818   45   1830-80   St. Louis . . . .   Union
(Boundaries not accurately defined until 1845; Co Clk has b rec from 1883 to
1892, d rec from 1883 to 1885)
Gasconade   B3   1820   12   1830-80   Franklin . . . .   Hermann
(In 1869 relinquished   36 sq miles to Crawford Co; Co Clk has b rec 1883 to
1896, m rec from 1850)
Gentry   D1   1841   9   1850-80   Clinton . . . .   Albany
(Organization completed 1843; Mar 6, 1885 courthouse burned with all Co rec)
Greene   D4   1833   126   1840-80   Crawford . . . .   Springfield
(Courthouse burned in 1861; no mention of fate of records)
Grundy   D1   1841   12   1850-80   Livingston . . . .   Trenton
(Co Clk has incom b rec from 1870 to 1891)
Harrison   D1   1845   12   1850-80   Daviess . . . .   Bethany
(Jan 7, 1874, courthouse destroyed by fire; land books, ct recs, pro recs and
most of the Co rec were saved; tax books were destroyed; Co Clk has b rec 1883
to 1893; Clk Cir Ct has m & div rec 1858; civ ct rec from 1845; Pro Clk has
pro rec from 1853)
Hempstead   1818   Arkansas . . . .
(Abolished 1819 when Territory of Arkansas was created)
Henry   D3   1834   19   1850-80   Lafayette . . . .   Clinton
(Originally Rives Co; name changed Oct 15, 1841)
Hickory   D3   1845   5   1850-80   Benton, Polk . . . .   Hermitage
(Courthouses burned 1852 and 1881; many rec destroyed; Co Clk has b rec 1883
to 1898; Clk of Cir Ct has m rec 1872, div rec 1858 civ ct rec 1858; Pro Judge
has pro rec from 1845)
Holt   E1   1841   8   1850-80   Platte Purchase . . . .   Oregon
(Co Clk has b & d rec 1883 to 1893; Co Recorder has incom m rec from 1899;
Clk Cir Ct has div & civ ct rec from 1841; Pro Clk has pro rec from 1849)
Howard   C2   1816   11   1830-80   St. Charles, St. Louis . . . . .   Fayette
(Courthouse burned 1887; records were saved and some date to 1816)
Howell   C5   1857   22   1860-80   Oregon, Ozark . . . .   West Plains
(Courthouse destroyed during CW no mention of fate of rec; Co Clk has b rec
1883 to 1895)

Iron   B4   1857   8   1860-80 Dent, Madison, Reynolds, St. Francis,
                                        Washington, Wayne . . . . Ironton
Jackson   D2   1826 623   1830-80 Lafayette . . . . Independence
   (Nearly all its terr was acquired from Osage & Kansas Indians, June 2, 1825)
Jasper   D4   1841   79   1850-80 Newton . . . . Carthage
   (Courthouse destroyed in 1863; records had been removed and were returned in
   1865; courthouse burned in 1883; no mention of fate of records)
Jefferson   B3   1818   66   1830-80 Ste. Genevieve, St. Louis . . . . Hillsboro
Johnson   D3   1834   29   1840-80 Lafayette . . . . Warrensburg
Kinderhook   1841   Benton, Pulaski . . . .
   (Renamed Camden Feb 23, 1843)
Knox   C1   1845   7   1850-80 Scotland . . . . Edina
Laclede   C4   1849   19   1850-80 Camden, Pulaski, Wright . . . . Lebanon
Lafayette   D2   1820   25   1830-80 Cooper . . . . Lexington
   (Originally called Lillard; changed Feb 16, 1825)
Lawrence (old)   1815   New Madrid . . . .
   (Abolished 1818)
Lawrence   D4   1845   23   1850-80 Barry, Dade . . . . Mount Vernon
Lewis   C1   1833   11   1840-80 Marion . . . . Monticello
Lillard   1820   Cooper . . . .
   (Changed to Lafayette, Feb 16, 1825)
Lincoln   B2   1818   15   1830-80 St. Charles . . . . Troy
   (Co Recorder has m rec from 1825; Pro Judge has pro rec from 1823)
Linn   C2   1837   17   1840-80 Chariton . . . . Linneus
Livingston   D2   1837   16   1840-80 Carroll . . . . Chillicothe
McDonald   D5   1849   12   1850-80 Newton . . . . Pineville
   (In 1876 an error in survey was corrected, establishing a new eastern line which
   annexed a 2 1/2 mile strip previously included in Barry Co.; in 1863 courthouse
   and rec were burned)
Macon   C2   1837   16   1840-80 Randolph . . . . Macon
   (Co Clk has b rec from 1883 to 1893)
Madison   B4   1818   9   1830-80 Cape Girardeau, Ste.
                                        Genevieve . . . . Fredericktown
Maries   C3   1855   7   1860-80 Osage, Pulaski . . . . Vienna
   (In 1859 and 1868, small tracts of land were exchanged with Phelps Co; Nov 6,
   1868 courthouse burned with nearly all the records)
Marion   C2   1826   30   1830-80 Ralls . . . . Palmyra
   (Co Clk has m, div, pro, civ ct rec from 1827)
Mercer   D1   1845   6   1850-80 Grundy . . . . Princeton
   (March 24, 1898, courthouse burned; nearly all rec of the cir clk and recorder,
   treas, and sheriff were destroyed or badly damaged; rec in office of pro judge
   and Co clk were saved, but many were badly damaged)
Miller   C3   1837   14   1840-80 Cole . . . . Tuscumbia
   (Line between Camden and Miller changed 1845; terr from Morgan annexed 1860;
   minor changes in 1868; Co Clk has b rec from 1884 to 1891)
Mississippi   A4   1845   21   1850-80 Scott . . . . Charleston
Moniteau   C3   1845   11   1850-80 Cole, Morgan . . . . California
Monroe   C2   1831   11   1840-80 Ralls . . . . Paris
Montgomery   B3   1818   11   1830-80 St. Charles . . . . Montgomery City
   (Co rec burned 1864)
Morgan   C3   1833   9   1840-80 Cooper . . . . Versailles
   (Courthouse burned 1887; records were saved)
New Madrid   A5   1812   31   1830-80 Original district . . . . New Madrid
Newton   D4   1838   30   1840-80 Barry . . . . Neosho
   (In 1846 a strip two miles wide was detached from Newton and attached to
   Jasper; courthouse burned 1862; no mention of fate of records)
Niangua   1842   Polk . . . .
   (Boundaries slightly changed and name changed to Dallas, Dec 10, 1844)
Nodaway   D1   1845   22   1850-80 Andrew . . . . Maryville
Oregon   B5   1845   10   1850-80 Ripley . . . . Alton
   (Courthouse burned during Civil War; rec were removed and most of them saved)

Osage   C3 1841   11 1850–80 Gasconade .... Linn
   (Mar 1, 1855 boundaries between Osage and Pulaski defined Nov 15, 1880,
   courthouse burned; fireproof vaults saved records)
Ozark   C5 1841   7 1850–80 Taney .... Gainesville
Pemiscot   A5 1851   38 1860–80 New Madrid .... Caruthersville
   (Courthouse and contents burned 1883)
Perry   A4 1820   15 1830–80 Ste. Genevieve .... Perryville
Pettis   D3 1833   35 1840–80 Cooper, Saline .... Sedalia
Phelps   C4 1857   35 1860–80 Crawford, Pulaski, Maries .... Rolla
Pike   B2 1818   17 1830–80 St. Charles .... Bowling Green
   (Courthouse burned 1864; no mention of fate of records)
Platte   E2 1838   23 1840–80 Platte Purchase .... Platte City
   (Attached to Clay for civil and military purpose from Dec 1836 to Dec 31, 1838)
Polk   D4 1835   14 1840–80 Greene .... Bolivar
Pulaski (old)   1818   Franklin ....
   (Organization not perfected and much of its terr became Gasconade in 1820;
   abolished 1819 when Terr of Arkansas was created)

County Map of Missouri

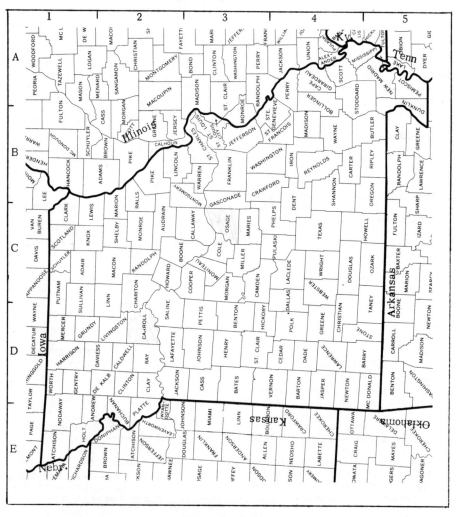

Pulaski   C4   1833   47 1840-80 Crawford . . . . Waynesville
(Co Clk has m, div, pro, civ ct rec from 1903)
Putnam   C1   1845   7 1850-80 Linn . . . . Unionville
(When Iowa boundary was established, the areas of both Putnam and Dodge were
below the constitutional limit; Dodge disorganized in 1853 and its terr was
regained by Putnam)
Ralls   B2   1820   8 1830-80 Pike . . . . New London
Randolph   C2   1829   22 1830-80 Chariton . . . . Huntsville
(a few rec lost when courthouse burned 1880)
Ray   D2   1820   16 1830-80 Howard . . . . Richmond
Reynolds   B4   1845   5 1850-80 Shannon . . . . Centerville
(Courthouse burned during CW; no mention of damage to records)
Ripley   B5   1823   9 1840-80 Wayne . . . . Doniphan
Rives   1834   1840   Lafayette . . . .
(Name changed to Henry Oct 15, 1841)
St. Charles B3   1812   53 1830-80 Original district . . . . St. Charles
St. Clair   D3   1841   8 1850-80 Rives (later Henry) . . . . Osceola
Ste. Genevieve B4 1812   12 1830-80 Original district . . . . . Ste. Genevieve
(Co Clk has b rec from 1883 to 1893)
St. Francois B4   1821   37 1830-80 Jefferson, Ste. Genevieve,
                                       Washington . . . . Farmington
St. Louis   B3   1812   704 1830-80 Original district . . . . Clayton
(Co Clk has b rec from 1877 to 1910)
St. Louis City B3 1764   750 1830-80 . . . . St. Louis
Saline   D2   1820   25 1830-80 Cooper, Howard . . . . Marshall
(Courthouse burned 186? but records were saved)
Schuyler   C1   1845   5 1850-80 Adair . . . . Lancaster
(Co Clk has few b & d rec from 1883 to 1893)

Scotland   C1   1841   6 1850-80 Lewis . . . . Memphis
Scott   A4   1821   33 1830-80 New Madrid . . . . Benton
Shannon   B4   1841   7 1850-80 Ripley, Washington . . . . Eminence
(Courthouse destroyed during CW; no mention of fate of records)
Shelby   C2   1835   9 1840-80 Marion . . . . Shelbyville
Stoddard   A4   1835   29 1840-80 Cape Girardeau . . . . Bloomfield
(Courthouse burned 1864, but rec had been removed to safety)
Stone   D5   1851   8 1860-80 Taney . . . . Galena
Sullivan   C1   1845   9 1850-80 Linn . . . . Milan
Taney   D5   1837   10 1840-80 Greene . . . . Forsyth
(County rec destroyed by fire 1885)
Texas   C4   1845   18 1850-80 Shannon, Wright . . . . Houston
(Co Clk has b & d rec from 1881 to 1889)
Van Buren   1835   1840   Jackson . . . .
(Name changed to Cass Feb 19, 1849)
Vernon   D4   1855   21 1860-80 Bates . . . . Nevada
(Created Feb 15, 1851, but act was declared unconstitutional since its terr was
exactly that of Bates; legally created Feb 27, 1855; reorganized Oct 17, 1865
after total suspension of civil order during CW; courthouse destroyed during
that period but clk had taken the rec with him when he joined the army and all
rec were later recovered except one deed book; Co Clk has m rec from 1912, div
rec from 1885, pro rec from 1855)
Warren   B3   1833   9 1840-80 Montgomery . . . . Warrenton
Washington   B3   1813   14 1830-80 Ste. Genevieve . . . . Potosi
Wayne   B4   1818   9 1830-80 Cape Girardeau . . . . Greenville
(Courthouse burned with all the rec 1854)
Webster   C4   1855   14 1860-80 Greene, Wright . . . . Marshfield
(Courthouse burned 1863 but rec were saved with the exception of tax rolls and
election returns)
Worth   D1   1861   4 1870-80 Gentry . . . . Grant City
Wright   C4   1841   14 1850-80 Pulaski . . . . Hartville
(1864 courthouse burned, destroying many rec; 1897 courthouse destroyed with
all its records)

Genealogists' Check List of the Historical Records Survey, Missouri (see page VIII)

Fed Cts (start 1805); Inv of Co Arch - Cass, Cole, Dallas, Henry (2 Vol), Johnson, Linn, McDonald, Macon, Marion (3 Vol), Jasper, Pettis, Pike, Reynolds, Ripley, Shelby; St Louis - Tran of Min of the Bd of Trustees 1808-1809; Guide to Pub Vit Stat Rec; Guide to Chr Vit Stat Rec.

Inv of the Chr Arch of Mo: Bap Bodies, No. 1 Tebo Bap Assn; Tran Bethel Chr Bk Min of the Proceedings of the Bethel Chr 1806-1867; Bethel Chr Min (Reprint from Rec of Proceedings of the Bethel Chr.)

Guide to Depo of Ms Col in Mo; Info Concerning the Ms Depo Col of the Mo Bap Hist Soc, Liberty, Mo (Reprinted with Additions from "Guide to Depo of Ms Col in the US: Mo"); Preliminary Check List of Mo Imprints 1808-1850; Early Hist of Mo; Early Mo Arch (3 Vol); County Ct Rec of St Charles Co; The Organization of Mo Co. Depo of unpubl mat, Univ of Mo, Columbia, Mo.

BIBLIOGRAPHY

Conard, Howard L. **Encyclopedia of the History of Missouri**, 6 vols. New York: 1901
Missouri: A Guide to the "Show Me" State: American Guide Series. New York: 1941
Violette, Eugene Morrow. **A History of Missouri**. 1918 (Reprint, Cape Girardeau: 1951)
Williams, Walter. **A History of Northwest Missouri**. 3 vols. Chicago: 1915.

Montana

Capital Helena - Territory 1864 - State 1889 -(41st)

At least sixteen tribes of Indians roamed over Montana when white explorers first came into the section. Traders from France, Scotland and England were the first whites to visit there.

The eastern part of Montana was part of the Louisiana Purchase in 1803. Members of the Lewis and Clark Expedition crossed the state in 1805 en route west and on the return trip in 1806.

The western part of Montana was included in the section that came to the United States in 1846 through the Oregon Treaty.

The first influx of people really attracted to Montana was in 1862 when gold was discovered in what is now Madison county, southeast of Butte. About twenty years later, copper and silver were found in the Butte region. To work the resulting mines, many workers were shipped in from Ireland, Germany, Austria, Poland, and Czechoslovakia.

In 1864 Montana became an organized Territory. Prior to this, various parts of the section had belonged at sundry times to surrounding Territories, including those of Missouri, Nebraska, Oregon, Washington, and Idaho.

The state has 56 counties. Of the original counties, nine were formed in 1864 and two in 1865. Eleven counties have census reports available from 1860 on.

Birth and death records from June 1907 to the present are at the office of the State Registrar, State Board of Health, Helena, Montana. No birth and death records are available before 1907, with the exception of Bozeman, Great Falls, and Helena at the office of the county clerk. Butte and Missoula have some records in the office of the city health department.

Marriage license information is at the office of the county clerks, where records of wills, probate matters, deeds and land records also are available.

Library facilities in Montana are in keeping with its population. Libraries are established in about seventy-five cities. Among the larger libraries, most of which have fine historical collections, are the Historical Society of Montana at Helena, the public libraries at Billings, Butte, Missoula, and Great Falls, and the Montana State University Library at Missoula.

Montana County Histories
(Population figures to nearest thousand - 1960 Census)

Name	Map Index	Date Formed	Pop. By M	Census Reports Available	Parent County	County Seat
Beaverhead	E4	1864	7	1860-80	Original county	Dillon
Big Horn	B4	1913	10	1860-80	Rosebud, Yellowstone	Hardin
Blaine	C2	1912	8		Chouteau, Hill	Chinook

Broadwater   D3   1897   3   Jefferson, Meagher .... Townsend
  (Co Clk has b & d rec from 1907)
Carbon   C4   1895   8   Park, Yellowstone .... Red Lodge
  (Co Clk has b & d rec from 1882, pro rec from 1895)
Carter   A4   1917   2   Custer .... Ekalaka
  (Co Clk has b, d, bur rec from 1917)
Cascade   D2   1887   73   Chouteau, Meagher .... Great Falls
  (Co Clk & Recorder have b, d, bur, pro rec from 1887)
Chouteau   D2   1865   7 1860-80 Original county .... Fort Benton
  (Co Clk has b & d rec from 1895, m rec from 1887, div, pro, civ ct rec 1879)
Custer   A3   1865   13 1880   Original county .... Miles City
  (Co Clk has b rec from 1900, d rec from 1907)
Daniels   A1   1920   4   Valley .... Scobey
Dawson   A2   1865   12 1860-80 Original county .... Glendive
Deer Lodge   E3   1864   19 1860-80 Original county .... Anaconda
Fallon   A3   1913   4   Custer .... Baker
Fergus   C2   1885   14   Meagher .... Lewistown
Flathead   E1   1893   33   Missoula .... Kalispell
  (Co Clk has b rec from 1885, m rec from 1893, d rec from 1897)
Gallatin   D3   1864   26 1860-80 Original county .... Bozeman
  (Co Clk has b & d rec from 1907)
Garfield   B2   1919   2   Valley, McCone .... Jordan
  (Co Clk has b rec from 1919)
Glacier   E1   1919   12   Teton .... Cut Bank
  (Co Clk has b & d rec from 1919)
Golden Valley C3 1920   1   Musselshell .... Ryegate
Granite   E3   1893   3   Deer Lodge .... Philipsburg
Hill   D1   1912   19   Chouteau .... Havre
Jefferson   E3   1864   4 1860-80 Original county .... Boulder
  (Co Clk has incom b & d rec from 1903)
Judith Basin D2   1920   3   Fergus, Cascade .... Stanford
  (Co Clk has b rec from 1900, m & d rec from 1920)
Lake   E2   1923   13   Flathead, Missoula .... Polson
Lewis & Clark E2 1864   28 1860-80 Original county .... Helena
Liberty   D2   1920   3   Chouteau .... Chester
Lincoln   F1   1909   13   Flathead .... Libby
  (Co Clk has incom b & d rec from 1898)
McCone   A2   1919   3   Dawson, Richland .... Circle
  (Co Clk has b, m, d, bur, div, pro, civ ct rec from 1919)
Madison   E4   1864   5 1860-80 Original county .... Virginia City
Meagher   D3   1867   3 1860-80 Original county ... White Sulpher Springs
  (Co Clk has b, d, bur rec from 1905, deeds & mtgs from 1867)
Mineral   F2   1914   3   Missoula .... Superior
  (Co Clk has b rec from 1914)
Missoula   E2   1864   45 1860-80 Original county .... Missoula
Musselshell C3   1911   5   Fergus, Meagher .... Roundup
Park   D4   1887   13   Gallatin .... Livingston
  (Co Clk has b & d rec from 1907)
Petroleum   C2   1925   .9   Fergus, Garfield .... Winnett
  (Director of Rec has b, m, d, bur rec from 1925)
Phillips   B2   1915   6   Valley .... Malta
  (Co Clk has b, d, bur rec from 1915)
Pondera   E2   1919   8   Yellowstone .... Conrad
  (Co Clk has m, div, pro, civ ct rec from 1919)
Powder River A4   1919   2   Custer .... Broadus
  (Co Clk has b, d, bur rec 1919; Clk of Ct has m, div, pro, civ ct rec 1919)
Powell   E2   1901   7   Missoula .... Deer Lodge
Prarie   A3   1915   2   Custer .... Terry
  (Co Clk has b & d rec from 1915)
Ravalli   F3   1893   12   Missoula .... Hamilton
  (Co Clk has b, d, bur rec from 1911)
Richland   A2   1914   11   Dawson .... Sidney

Roosevelt	A2	1919	12		Valley, Richland	....	Wolf Point
Rosebud	B3	1901	6		Dawson	....	Forsyth
(Co Clk has b & d rec from 1900)							
Sanders	F2	1906	7		Missoula	....	Thompson Falls
Sheridan	A1	1911	6		Custer	....	Plentywood

County Map of Montana

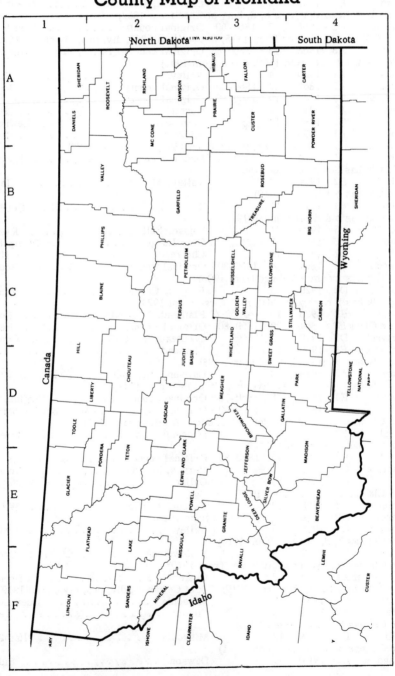

Silver Bow	E3	1881	46	Deer Lodge	Butte
Stillwater	C4	1913	6	Sweet Grass, Yellowstone	
				Carbon	Columbus
(Co Clk has b & d rec from 1913)					
Sweet Grass	D3	1895	3	Meagher, Park, Yellowstone ..	Big Timber
Teton	E2	1893	7	Chouteau	Choteau
(Co Clk has b & d rec from 1919)					
Toole	D1	1914	8	Teton	Shelby
Treasure	B3	1919	1	Big Horn	Hysham
Valley	B2	1893	17	Dawson	Glasgow
Wheatland	D3	1917	3	Meagher, Sweet Grass	Harlowton
Wibaux	A3	1914	2	Dawson	Wibaux
(Co Clk has b, d, bur rec from 1914)					
Yellowstone	C3	1893	79	Gallatin, Meagher, Custer	Billings

Genealogists' Check List of the Historical Records Survey, Montana (see page VIII)

Fed Cts; Inv of Co Arch - Beaverhead, Carbon, Flathead, Galatin, Lake, Lincoln, Madison, Mineral,Missoula, Park, Ravalli, Sanders, Silver Bow, Stillwater, Sweet Grass, Toole; Guide to Pub Vit Stat Rec; Inv of Vit Stat Rec of Chrs & Rel Org; Dir of Chrs and Rel Org in Mont; Ms Publ- Bibliography of Graduate Theses in the U of Mont; Depo of unpbl mat, State College, Bozeman, Mont.

Nebraska
Capital Lincoln
Part of Mo. Terr. 1812 - State 1867 - (37th)

Nebraska was long a choice spot for several rather belligerent Indian Tribes. The first settlers were stragglers of the California Gold Rush days and the Oregon migration. Others unused to mountain terrain returned to the level lands of Nebraska which had formed a delightful picture in their memory as they were westward bound.

The first settlement was established in 1823. It was called Bellevue, and is situated less than ten miles below Omaha on the Missouri.

Nebraska was part of the Missouri Territory before 1820. In 1834 it was carved into three sections and placed under the supervision of Arkansas, Michigan and the state of Missouri. Twenty years later it became a Territory in its own name, including sections of Colorado, Montana, North and South Dakota, and Wyoming.

All during the 1850's many Germans settled in Nebraska. Twenty years later a large contingent of Germans came out of Russia and settled Lancaster and nearby counties. Many Scandinavians established homes there after the adoption of the Homestead Act of 1862.

In 1867 Nebraska was admitted to the union - the thirty-seventh state. Many Civil War veterans secured cheap land after the close of that struggle.

Most Nebraskans of today are of German, Czech, Swedish or Russian descent.

Birth and death records since 1904 and marriage records since 1909 are at the Bureau of Vital Statistics, State Department of Health, Lincoln, Nebraska. Prior to those dates, the birth, death and marriage records are available at the offices of the county clerks, where wills and probate matters are recorded.

Land records, such as deeds, mortgages and all land titles are recorded in the office of the Register of Deeds in the various county seats.

The earliest census record of any Nebraska county is that of 1860.

Nebarska Libraries -- Lincoln, (Lancaster), Nebraska State Historical Library, 1500 R St., Lincoln, (local manuscripts, newspapers of state, midwest lore); University of Nebraska, Don L. Love Memorial Library, (history of Great Plains region); Omaha, (Douglas), Public Library, Harney & 19th Sts.

Genealogists' Check List of the Historical Records Survey, Nebraska (see page VIII)

Fed Cts; Inv of Co Arch - Gosper, Greeley, Howard, Loup, Merrick, Seward, Webster; Guide to Pub Vit Stat Rec; Guide to Depo of Ms Col in Nebr; A Check List of Nebr Non-Documentary Imprints 1847- 1876; Depo of unpubl mat, State Hist Soc, Lincoln, Nebr.

Nebraska County Histories

(Population figures to nearest thousand – 1960 Census)

Name	Map Index	Date Formed	Pop. By M	Census Reports Available	Parent County	County Seat
Adams	C3	1870	29	1870–80	Clay	Hastings
Antelope	B2	1875	10	1880	Pierce	Neligh
Arthur	E2	1888	.7		Unorganized Territory	Arthur
Banner	F2	1888	1		Cheyenne	Harrisburg

(Co Clk has m, div, pro, civ ct rec from 1888)

Blaine	D2	1885	1		Custer	Brewster
Blackbird				1870		
Boone	B2	1871	9	1880	Platte	Albion
Box Butte	F2	1886	12		Unorganized Territory	Alliance

(Co Clk has b rec from 1919, d rec from 1924, m, div, pro, civ ct rec from 1887)

Boyd	C1	1890	5		Holt	Butte
Brown	D2	1883	4		Unorganized Territory	Ainsworth

(Co Judge has m & civ ct rec from 1883; Clk of Dist Ct has div rec from 1883; Attached to Holt Co. Nebr. prior to 1883)

Buffalo	C3	1857	26	1860–80	Original county	Kearney
Burt	A2	1855	10	1860–80	Original county	Tekamah
Butler	B3	1857	10	1860–80	Unorganized Territory	David City
Calhoun				1860		
Cass	A3	1854	18	1860–80	Original county	Plattsmouth
Cedar	B1	1855	13	1860–80	Original county	Hartington
Chase	E3	1873	4	1880	Unorganized Territory	Imperial

(Co Clk has div rec from 1890)

Cherry	E2	1883	8		Unorganized Territory	Valentine
Cheyenne	F3	1867	15	1870–80	Unorganized Territory	Sidney
Clay	B3	1857	9	1860–80	Original county	Clay Center
Colfax	B2	1865	10	1870–80	Dodge	Schuyler
Cuming	B2	1858	12	1860–80	Burt '	Westpoint

(Co Judge has m & pro rec from 1858; Clk Dist Ct has div rec from 1858)

Custer	D3	1875	17	1880	Unorganized Territory	Broken Bow

(Co Judge has m rec from 1878, pro rec from 1887, civ ct rec from 1880; Clk of Dist Ct has div rec from 1881)

Dakota	A2	1854	12	1860–80	Original county	Dakota City
Dawes	F1	1885	10		Sioux	Chadron
Dawson	D3	1860	19	1860–80	Buffalo	Lexington
Deuel	E3	1888	3		Cheyenne	Chappell
Dixon	B2	1853	8	1860–80	Original county	Ponca
Dodge	B2	1855	32	1860–80	Original county	Fremont
Douglas	A3	1854	343	1860–80	Original county	Omaha
Dundy	E4	1873	4	1880	Unorganized Territory	Benkelman
Fillmore	B3	1856	9	1860–80	Unorganized Territory	Geneva
Franklin	C4	1867	5	1870–80	Kearney Org. 1871	Franklin
Frontier	D3	1872	4	1880	Unorganized Territory	Stockville
Furnas	D4	1877	8	1880	Unorganized Territory	Beaver City
Gage	A4	1855	27	1860–80	Original county	Beatrice
Garden	E2	1887	3		Unorganized Territory	Oshkosh
Garfield	C2	1884	3		Wheeler	Burwell
Gosper	D4	1877	2		Unorganized Territory	Elwood
Grant	E2	1887	1		Unorganized Territory	Hyannis

(Co Clk has div & civ ct rec from 1890)

Greeley	C2	1875	5	1880	Boone	Greeley
Green				1860		
Hall	C3	1855	36	1860–80	Original county	Grand Island

(Co Judge has m & pro rec from 1860; Clk of Dist Ct has div rec from 1860)

Hamilton	B3	1870	9	1870–80	York	Aurora
Harlan	C4	1871	5	1880	Unorganized Territory	Alma

(Co Clk has m, div, pro, civ ct rec, deeds from 1870's)

Hayes	D3	1873	2	1880	Unorganized Territory	...	Hayes Center
Hitchcock	D4	1873	5	1880	Unorganized Territory	......	Trenton
Holt	C2	1876	14	1880	Knox	....	O'Neill
Hooker	E2	1889	1		Unorganized Territory	......	Mullen

(Co Clk has b & d rec from 1919)

| Howard | C3 | 1871 | 7 | 1880 | Hall | .... | Saint Paul |

(Co Judge has m, pro, civ ct rec from 1871; Co Clk has div rec from 1871)

Jackson   1870

County Map of Nebraska

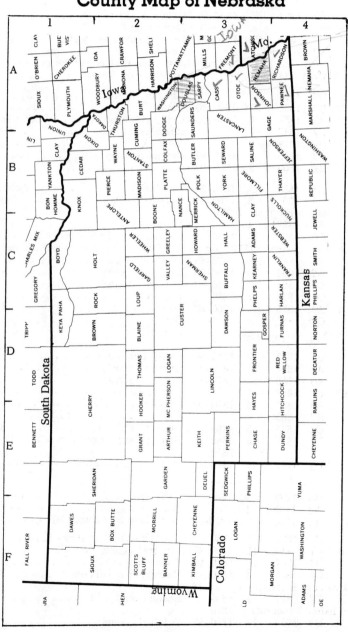

Jefferson	B4	1865	12	1870-80	Gage	Fairbury
Johnson	A3	1854	6	1860-80	Original county	Tecumseh
Jones				1860		
Kearney	C3	1860	7	1860-80	Original county	Minden
(Co Clk has div, pro, civ ct rec from 1872)						
Keith	E3	1873	8	1880	Lincoln	Ogallala
Keya Paha	D1	1884	2		Brown, Rock	Springview
Kimball	F3	1888	8		Cheyenne	Kimball
Knox	B1	1854	13	1880	Formerly L'Eau Qui Court	Center
Lancaster	A3	1854	155	1860-80	Original county	Lincoln
L'Eau Qui Court				1860-70	(see Knox)	
Lincoln	D3	1867	28	1870-80	Unorganized Territory	North Platte
Logan	D2	1885	1		Custer	Stapleton
(Co Judge has m & civ ct rec from 1885; Co Clk has div rec from 1885)						
Loup	C2	1883	1		Unorganized Territory	Taylor
McPherson	D2	1887	.7		Lincoln, Keith	Tryon
Madison	B2	1856	25	1860-80	Platte	Madison
Merrick	B3	1854	8	1860-80	Original county	Central City
Morrill	F2	1887	7		Cheyenne	Bridgeport
Nance	B3	1879	6	1880	Merrick	Fullerton
Nemaha	A3	1855	9	1860-80	Original county	Auburn
Nuckolls	B4	1860	8	1860-80	Clay	Nelson
Otoe	A3	1854	17	1860-80	Original county	Nebraska City
Pawnee	A4	1854	5	1860-80	Original county	Pawnee City
(Co Judge has m rec from 1870)						
Perkins	E3	1887	4		Keith	Grant
Phelps	C3	1873	10	1880	Unorganized Territory	Holdrege
(Co Clk has m rec 1877, pro rec 1895; Clk of Dist Ct has div rec 1880)						
Pierce	B2	1867	9	1870-80	Madison	Pierce
Platte	B2	1854	24	1860-80	Original county	Columbus
Polk	B3	1854	7	1860-80	Original county	Osceola
Red Willow	D4	1873	13	1880	Frontier	McCook
Richardson	A4	1855	14	1860-80	Original county	Falls City
Rock	C2	1888	3		Brown	Bassett
(Co Clk has m, div, pro, civ ct rec from 1889)						
Saline	B3	1855	13	1860-80	Gage, Lancaster	Wilber
Sarpy	A3	1854	31	1860-80	Original county	Papillion
Saunders	A3	1865	17	1870-80	Sarpy, Douglas	Wahoo
Scotts Bluff	F2	1888	34		Cheyenee	Gering
Seward	B3	1867	14	1870-80	Lancaster	Seward
Sheridan	E2	1885	9		Sioux	Rushville
Sherman	C3	1873	5	1880	Buffalo	Loup City
Sioux	F2	1877	3	1880	Unorganized Territory	Harrison
Shorter				1860		
Stanton	B2	1865	6	1870-80	Dodge	Stanton
Taylor				1870		
Thayer	B4	1872	9	1880	Jefferson	Hebron
Thomas	D2	1887	1		Blaine	Thedford
Thurston	A2	1865	7	1870-80	Burt (see Blackbird Co).	Pender
Valley	C2	1871	7	1880	Unorganized Territory	Ord
Washington	A2	1854	12	1860-80	Original county	Blair
Wayne	B2	1867	10	1870-80	Thurston	Wayne
Webster	C4	1871	6	1880	Unorganized Territory	Red Cloud
(Co Clk has div & civ ct rec from 1871)						
Wheeler	C2	1877	1	1880	Boone	Bartlett
Winnebago Indian Reservation				1870		
York	B3	1854	14	1860-80	Original county	York

Nevada

Capital Carson City - Territory 1861 - State 1864 - (36th)

Twelve years after the Mormon Pioneers had reached the Great Salt Lake, gold and silver were found in the Comstock Mine in Virginia City, Nevada, midway -twenty or twenty-five miles -between Reno and Carson City. The strike was rich enough to turn California gold seekers eastward. Almost overnight, the Nevada population, which up to that time had stood around a thousand, doubled over and over again. Among Europeans attracted by the rich mineral discovery were people from all sections of Britain, Italy, Scandinavia, Germany, and France. Many Mexicans came also.

Nevada became a territory in 1861 and three years later was admitted into the union as the thirty-sixth state.

Birth and death records from 1887 to June 30, 1911, marriage records from 1864 to date, deeds and land records from 1864 to date are all in the office of the Recorder of each county.

Birth and death files from July 1, 1911 to date are at the Nevada State Department of Health, Division of Vital Statistics, Carson City, Nevada.

Marriage bans are not filed.

Wills from 1864 to date are in the office of the clerk of each county.

The records of the state Census of 1872 are in the custody of the Secretary of State, Carson City, Nevada.

Tax payers lists from 1864 are at the office of the Assessor of each county.

Library - Reno, (Washoe), University of Nevada Library.

Genealogists' Check List of the Historical Records Survey, Nevada (see page VIII)

Fed Cts; Inv of Co Arch -Douglas, Elko, Eureka, Mineral, Nye, Ormsby, Washoe; Guide to Pub Vit Stat Rec; Inv of the Chr Arch of Nev - Protestant Episcopal Chr - RC Chr; A Check list of Nev Imprints 1859-1890; Depo of unpubl mat, Nevada Hist Soc, Reno, Nev.

Nevada County Histories

(Population figures to nearest thousand - 1960 Census)

Name	Map Index	Date Formed	Pop. By M	Census Reports Available	Parent County	County Seat
Carson				1860	(see Utah) discontinued	
Churchill	C2	1861	8	1870-80	Original county	Fallon
Clark	F4	1909	127		Lincoln	Las Vegas
Douglas	C1	1861	3	1870-80	Original county	Minden
(Co Clk has m, div, pro, civ ct rec from 1870)						
Elko	A4	1869	12	1870-80	Lander	Elko
(Co Clk has m license, div, pro, civ ct rec from 1875; Co Recorder has m rec from 1875, b & d rec from 1875 to 1917)						
Esmeralda	D2	1861	.6	1870-80	Original county	Goldfield
(Co Clk has b rec from 1900, m, d, bur rec from 1898, div rec from 1908, pro, civ ct rec from 1907)						
Eureka	B3	1873	.8	1880	Lander	Eureka
Humboldt	A2	1861	6	1860-80	Original county	Winnemucca
(Co Clk has m rec from 1881, div & civ ct rec from 1863, pro rec from 1900, Naturalization rec from 1864, Inquests 1862) See Utah 1860 cen.						
Lander	B3	1861	2	1870-80	Original county	Austin
Lincoln	D4	1869	2	1870-80	Nye	Pioche
(Co Clk has m, div, pro, civ ct rec from 1873)						
Lyon	C1	1861	6	1870-80	Original county	Yerington
Mineral	D2	1911	6		Esmeralda	Hawthorne
Nye	D3	1864	4	1870-80	Esmeralda	Tonopah
Ormsby	C1	1861	8	1870-80	Original county	Carson City
Pahute				1870	Discontinued	
Pershing	B2	1919	3		Humboldt	Lovelock
(Co Clk has m, div, pro, civ ct rec from 1919)						
Roop				1870	Discontinued	
St. Mary's				1860	Discontinued (see Utah)	
Storey	C1	1861	.6	1870-80	Original county	Virginia City

Washoe   B1 1861   85 1870-80 Original county . . . . Reno
   (Co Clk has m rec from 1871, div, pro, civ ct rec from 1862)
White Pine C4 1864   10 1870-80 Lincoln . . . . Ely

County Map of Nevada

New Hampshire

Capital Concord - State 1788 - (9th)

New Hampshire, in the northeast corner of the United States, is one of the thirteen original colonies. Its history dates back to 1603 when an Englishman, Martin Pring anchored in Piscataqua harbor. The French explorer, Samuel de Champlain discovered the Isles of Shoals in 1605 while sailing along the coast of N.H. In 1614 Captain John Smith landed on its shores. It was settled about 1623 at Rye (Little Harbor), Dover and Portsmouth. This was only three years after the landing of the Pilgrim Fathers in Massachusetts. A little later settlements were made at Exeter and Hampton. These places were on or near the coast, or on a river bank near its mouth. After these first settlements, little effort was put forth to establish new settlements for almost a hundred years. The fear of Indians kept the settlers from moving inland.

New Hampshire became part of the Massachusetts colony in 1641, and continued so, with brief interruptions, for about a hundred years. In 1741 it became a Royal British Province and remained so until the Revolutionary War.

A large part of the early settlers came from Massachusetts and Connecticut. The Connecticut River is the western boundary of the state. Apparently it was much easier to go up the river than to cut long roads through the forests from the eastern shore. Many of the river towns, as a result, are much older than those in the interior. If the ancestry of the early settlers of one of those towns is sought, it will more than likely be found in Connecticut or western Massachusetts.

Of New Hampshire, Archibald F. Bennett, former secetary of the Genealogical Society of Utah, has said: "In the great migration to the west, New Hampshire and Vermont were stopping places for a few years for one or more generations of families now established far from there. Many families from their homelands in Massachusetts and Connecticut seemed to pause here briefly, and then resume their westward trek. Their residence in New Hampshire was often during the pioneer period when records were not kept too regularly. Then they removed so early that almost all trace of their presence in those localities is obliterated. Consequently, many ancestral lines of western families are followed back to New Hampshire or Vermont, and then are hopelessly lost. Yet there are actually many sources which can assist in the solution of such problems."

During the first two hundred years or more of its history, it was mainly people from England who came to New Hampshire. During the next seventy-five years, tens of thousands came into the state from the Scandinavian countries and from Greece, Italy and France.

New Hampshire entered the union in 1788, the ninth state to ratify the constiution. Vital statistics have been kept in the towns since 1640, though they are not complete. Copies of all statistics records since that date have been made. They include town records, church records, cemetery records, and all other available old records. These have all been indexed, and may be searched for a small fee. These records are available at the office of the Registrar of Vital Statistics, State House, Concord, N.H., and at some of the offices of the town clerks. Wills are in the charge of the clerks of the probate courts of the ten counties. The Registrars of deeds are in charge of deeds and land titles. The State Library at Concord has charge of the Census Records. Cemetery records are handled by the cemetery superintendents or selectmen of the towns. Tax payers are handled by the town and city clerks throughout the state.

Almost all towns have town histories. Many of these contain much genealogical information about the early settlers. In the genealogical departments of the public libraries will be found many books with valuable information about the town families. Many records are available at the New Hampshire State Library and the New Hampshire Historical Society, both in Concord. The Census reports from 1800 are available, as well as those of subsequent years.

New Hampshire libraries - Concord, (Merrimac), Public Library, 45 Green St.; New Hampshire Historical Society Library 30 Park St., (local histories of state family and genealogical reocrds, old maps, early newspapers); New Hampshire State Library, 20 Park St.; Manchester, (Hillsboro), City Public Library 405 Pine St., (community articles).

Valuable genealogy records are found in the following books which form only a small part of the many that have been written about this state and its people:

STERNS, EZRA S., *Genealogy and Family History of the State of New Hampshire.*

4 vol. Pub. 1908 Lewis Publishing Co., New York, Chicago.

AYLING, AUGUSTUS D., *Revised Register of the Soldiers and Sailors of N.H. in the War of Rebellion 1861-1866.*. Pub. 1895 by the New Hampshire Legislature.

New Hampshire Towns
Organized Before 1800

BELKNAP COUNTY — Alton, 1770; Barnstead, 1727; Belmont; Center Harbor, 1797. Gilmanton, 1761; Meredith, 1748; New Hampton, 1765; Sanbornton, 1764.

CARROLL COUNTY — Albany, 1766; Bartlett, 1790; Brookfield, 1794; Conway, 1764; Chatham, 1767; Eaton, 1760; Effingham, 1749; Hart's Location, 1773; Jackson, 1778; Madison, 1785; Moultonborough, 1763; Ossipee, 1765; Sandwich, 1763; Tamworth, 1771; Tuftonboro, 1750; Wakefield, 1774; Wolfeboro, 1768.

CHESHIRE COUNTY — Alstead, 1763; Chesterfield, 1761; Dublin, 1752; Fitzwilliam, 1752; Gilsum, 1764; Jaffray, 1752; Keene, 1754; Marlborough, 1752;

County Map of New Hampshire

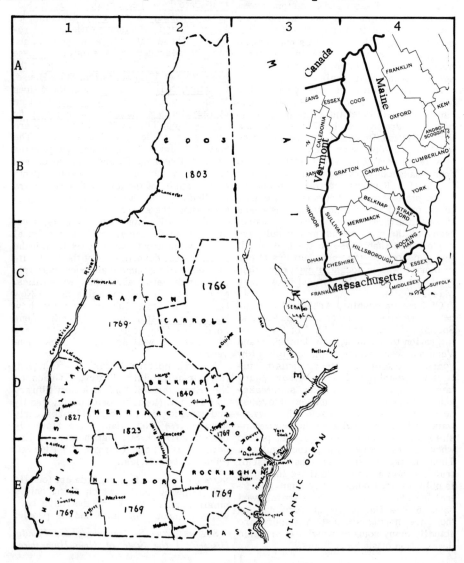

Marlow, 1753; Nelson, 1767; Rindge, 1754; Richmond, 1758; Stoddard, 1769 Sullivan, 1760; Swanzey, 1753; Surry, 1769; Walpole, 1749; Westmoreland, 1741; Winchester, 1732.

COOS COUNTY — Berlin, 1771; Colesbrook, 1762; Columbia, 1762; Cambridge, 1793; Drummer, 1773; Dalton, 1764; Jefferson, 1765; Lancester, 1763; Milan, 1771; Northumberland, 1767; Randolph, 1772; Stark, 1788; Shelburne, 1770; Stratford, 1775.

GRAFTON COUNTY — Alexandria, 1782; Benton, 1764; Bath, 1765; Bethlehem, 1799; Bridgewater, 1788; Canaan, 1761; Compton, 1765; Danbury, 1795; Dorchester, 1761; Enfield, 1761; Ellsworth, 1769; Franconia, 1754; Grafton, 1772; Groton, 1761; Hanover, 1765; Haverhill, 1763; Holderness, 1751; Hebron, 1792; Landaff, 1764; Lebanon, 1761; Lisbon, 1763; Littleton, 1764; Lyme, 1764; Lyman, 1761; Lincoln, 1764; Orange, 1790; Oxford, 1765; Pierpont, 1768; Plymouth, 1764; Rumney, 1705; Thornton, 1770; Warren, 1767; Wentworth, 1766; Woodstock, 1763.

HILLSBOROUGH COUNTY — Amherst, 1760; Antrim, 1744; Bedford, 1736; Brookline, 1769; Deering, 1765; Francestown, 1752; Goffstown, 1733; Greenfield, 1771; Hancock, 1765; Hillsborough, 1735; Hollis, 1731; Hudson, 1722; Litchfield, 1720; Lyndeborough, 1759; Manchester, 1751; Mason, 1768; Merrimack, 1722; Milford, 1740; Nashua, 1673; New Boston, 1735; New Ipswich, 1735; Petersborough, 1749; Pelham, 1745; Sharon, 1791; Temple, 1750; Weare, 1735; Wilton, 1749; Windsor, 1798.

MERRIMACK COUNTY — Allenstown, 1747; Andover, 1761; Boscowan, 1760; Bow, 1727; Bradford, 1771; Canterbury, 1723-50; Chichester, 1727; Concord, 1727; Dunbarton, 1746, Danbury, 1795; Epsom, 1727; Henniker, 1760; Hill, 1768; Hopkinton, 1740; Loudon, 1765; Newbury, 1762; New London, 1758; Northfield, 1760; Pembroke, 1728; Pittsfield, 1782; Salisbury, 1750; Sutton, 1767; Warner, 1773.

ROCKINGHAM COUNTY — Atkinson, 1728; Auburn, 1734; Brentwood, 1742; Candia, 1748; Chester, 1720; Danville, 1738; Deerfield, 1750; E. Kingston, 1738; Epping, 1741; Exeter, 1638; Fremont, 1764; Greenland, 1704; Hempstead, 1728; Hampton, 1635; Hampton Falls, 1726; Kensington, 1737; Kingston, 1694; Londonderry, 1719; Newcastle, 1693; Newington, 1670; Newfields, 1681; Newmarket, 1727; Newton, 1749; North Hampton, 1690; Northwood, 1763; Nottingham, 1722; Plaistow, 1642; Portsmouth, 1623; Raymond, 1764; Rye, 1635; Sandown, 1756; Seabrook, 1758; South Hampton, 1742; Stratham, 1629; Windham, 1741.

STAFFORD COUNTY — Barrington, 1762; Dover, 1623; Durham, 1623; Farmington, 1798; Lee, 1766; Madbury, 1755; Middleton, 1778; Milton, 1760; New Durham, 1749; Rochester, 1722; Somersworth, 1754.

SULLIVAN COUNTY — Acworth, 1767; Charlestown, 1735; Claremont, 1764; Cornish, 1765; Croydon, 1766; Goshen, 1761; Grantham, 1761; Langdon, 1773; Lempster, 1785; Newport, 1765-6; Plainfield, 1765; Springfield, 1772; Unity, 1754; Washington, 1768.

New Hampshire County Histories

(Population figures to nearest thousand - 1960 Census)

Name	Map Index	Date Formed	Pop. By M	Census Reports Available	Parent County	County Seat
Belknap	D2	1840	29	1850–80	Strafford, Merrimac	Laconia
Carroll	C2	1840	16	1850–80	Strafford	Ossipee
Cheshire	E1	1769	43	1790–80	Original county	Keene
Coos	B2	1803	37	1810–80	Grafton	Lancaster
(Clk of Sup Ct has div, pro, civ ct rec from 1887)						
Grafton	C1	1769	49	1790–80	Original county	Woodsville
(1820 census missing)						
Hillsboro	E1	1769	178	1790–80	Original county	Nashua
(Co Clk has div, & pro rec from 1771)						
Merrimack	D1	1823	68	1830–80	Rockingham, Hillsboro	Concord
(Co Clk has div rec from 1840, civ ct rec from 1823)						
Rockingham	E2	1769	99	1790–80	Original county	Exeter
Strafford	D2	1769	60	1790–80	Original county	Dover
Sullivan	D1	1827	28	1830–80	Cheshire	Newport

Genealogists' Check List of the Historical Records Survey, N. H. (see page VIII)

Fed Cts; Inv of Co Arch - Belnap, Carroll, Cheshire, Coos, Grafton, Merrimack; Inv of Mun & Tn Arch - Atkinson, Auburn, Bedford, Candia, Canterbury, Chester, Exeter, Greenland, New Hampton, Sandbornton, Guide to Pub Vit Stat Rec; Guide to Chr Vit Stat Rec; Inv of the Chr Arch of N H - Prot Episcopal Chr - RC Chr; Guide to Depo of Ms Col in N H; Preliminary Check List of Am Portraits, 1620-1860, found in N H; Depo of unpubl mat, Univ of N H, Manchester, N H.

New Jersey

Capital Trenton - State 1787 - (3rd)

French explorers sailed along the New Jersey coast as early as 1524. In the service of Holland, Henry Hudson sailed up the Hudson River in 1609. Nine yeas later the Dutch had settlers opposite the present upper New York City. Commissioned by their King, Swedish adventurers established a colony in the Delaware Valley, shortly after the Dutch came to the area.

With the experience gained in colonizing southern sections of America, two English court favorites, Lord Berkeley and Sir George Carteret induced the Duke of York to grant them the area between the Hudson and the Delaware rivers. They named the colony New Jersey after the English Channel home of Carteret. Throwing the territory open to land-seekers in 1664, the promoters made tempting offers to those willing to come. To the small Dutch communities along the Hudson came folks from every section of Britain. Puritans came down from Connecticut and established Newark. Scotch-Irish Presbyterians poured into the eastern counties, and English Quakers came into the fertile regions of the Delaware.

While differing strongly in their religious convictions, the settlers were solidly united against the tax and monetary ideas of the Crown and the proprietors. Disgusted with the lack of financial returns in the venture, the proprietors sold out to William Penn and his Quaker Friends.

In the intervening years, difficulties were erased and more unity ensued. In the early part of the eighteenth century, New Jersey and New York had the same royal governor, but this ended in 1738. During the next 49 years New Jersey had a governor and a legislature of its own.

She became the third state to ratify the constitution of the United States in 1778 Three years later, the first U. S. Census gave New Jersey a population of 184,139. The majority of these were English from the Old World as well as from New England. The Dutch and the Swedes were also represented by large numbers. In the west part of the state were many French and Scotch.

Before William Penn acquired Pennsylvainia, he and a company of Quakers settled West Jersey. The early Swedish and Dutch settlers continued to live there. Hence, a New Jersey pedigree may trace back to the English Quakers, the Puritans from New England, the Swedes who waged war on the early English settlers, the Dutch settlers who came from New Amsterdam (New York) and the Huguenots who fled from France in search of religious liberty and peace.

Research conditions are not so favorable in New Jersey as in some other states. Since they were not required by law to keep a record of births and deaths the family Bible was about the only place where these things were recorded. And yet, researchers willing to dig into available records can find a wealth of information.

The office of the State Registrar of Vital Statistics, State Department of Health, Trenton 7, New Jersey, has birth records from 1848 to 1929 and death records from 1878 to 1929. Marriage information from 1848 to 1929 is also available there, although some are incomplete.

Only in Hudson County does the county clerk issue marriage licenses. In all other counties such licenses are handled by the town or city clerks, the township assessor or the local registrar of vital statistics.

Early marriage records which were kept by the Secretary of State are printed in the Archives.

Divorce records are kept in the Superior Court, Chancery Divison, at the State House in Trenton.

The federal circuit and district courts and the State Supreme court, all in Trenton and the county circuit courts have records of naturalization proceedings. Records of Deeds in N. J. may be found as follows: From 1664 to 1703 in New Jersey Archives, Vol. XXI; From 1664 to 1790 in Secretary of State's Office; From 1790 to the present in the County Clerk's Offices (A few of earlier date are included); In Gloucester County deeds recorded before 1786 were destroyed by fire, deeds recorded after that date (even tho dated earlier) are extant.

Most of the churches in the state have records of their respecitve memberships for many years back.

The originals of wills and probate matters, together with early guardianship and orphans' court proceedings are in the custody of the Secretary of State in Trenton. Copies of Wills and administrations of estates beginning in 1804 are at the county court houses. Wills and administrations of estates from 1682 to 1805 have been digested and published in the State Archives. There are ten volumes, each completely indexed. The state also published an index of New Jersey Wills, three volumes. These wills extend to a much later date than those given in the Archives. Many libraries, including the Cache County Library in Logan, Utah, have a complete set of the Archives of New Jersey.

County Map of New Jersey

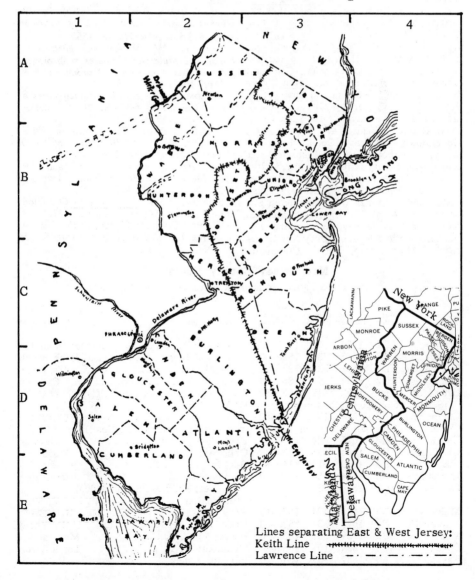

Lines separating East & West Jersey:
Keith Line
Lawrence Line

Although thirteen of the twenty-one counties in New Jersey were established before 1790, no federal census schedules are available until the 1830 census. All of the New Jersey schedules for 1790, 1800, 1810, and 1820 are missing. The available schedules are enumerated in the New Jersey County Histories in this section.

The New Jersey State Library has custody of the state census records taken every ten years since 1855.

More than 275 libraries serve the people of New Jersey. Many of these have valuable genealogical and historical books on their shelves.

Among the libraries are the following: Atlantic City, (Atlantic), Free Public Library, Illinois and Pacific Aves., (genealogical material on N.J., N.Y., and Pa., limited number of family histories and family Bible records); Camden, (Camden), (across the Delaware River from Philadelphia), County Free Public Library; City Public Library; Jersey City, (Hudson), (across the river from New York City), Free Public Library, 472 Jersey Ave.; Morristown, (Morris), County Free Library, Courthouse, (local histories and genealogies); City Public Library, Miller Road and South St., (family histories and genealogical publications); Newark, (Essex), Public Library, 5 Washington St., (state and local history); Genealogical Society of New Jersey, 33 Lombardy St., (genealogies and local history); New Brunswick, (Middlessex), Rutger University

Library, (old newspapers and local histories); Paterson, (Passaic), Free Public Library; Princeton, (Mercer), Princeton University Library, (American History, especially Southern States); Trenton, Free Public Library, 120 Academy St.; New Jersey State Teachers College Library.

Many books have been printed over the years concerning the history of the various communities and families of New Jersey. The following are only a mere mention of a half a dozen available in libraries or book stores:

BARBER, JOHN W. *Historical Collections of New Jersey, Past and Present*, biographies, the State Census of all the towns in 1865. 543 pp. New Haven, 1868.

CLAYTON, W. WOODFORD. *History of Union and Middlesex Counties*, with biographies of many pioneers and prominent men. 885 pp. Philadelphia, 1882.

FOLSOM, JOSEPH S. *The Municipalities of Essex County, 1666-1924*. Four volumes. New York, 1925.

HATFIELD, EDWIN F. *History of Elizabeth, including the Early History of Union County*. 701 pp. New York, 1868.

LEE, FRANCIS B. *Genealogical and Personal Memorial of Mercer County*. Two volumes. New York, 1907.

STEWART, FRANK H. *Notes on Old Gloucester County*. 342 pp. Camden, 1917.

WICKES, STEPHEN. *History of the Oranges in Essex County, from 1666 to 1806*. 334 pp. Newark, 1892.

New Jersey County Histories
(Population figures to nearest thousand - 1960 Census)

Name	Map Index	Date Formed	Pop. By M	Census Reports Available	Parent County	County Seat
Atlantic	D2	1837	161	1840-80	Gloucester	Mays Landing
Bergen	A3	1675	780	1830-80	Prov East Jersey	Hackensack
Burlington	D2	1681	224	1830-80	Original county	Mt. Holly
Camden	D2	1844	392	1850-80	Glouc.	Camden
Cape May	E2	1692	49	1830-80	Cumberland	Cape May C. H.
(Settled 1682; Co Clk has m rec from 1795 to 1826)						
Cumberland	E2	1748	107	1830-80	Salem	Bridgeton
(Co Clk has naturalization papers from 1885; newspaper files from 1840)						
Essex	B3	1675	924	1830-80	Prov East Jersey	Newark
Gloucester	D2	1686	135	1830-80	Original county	Woodbury
Hudson	E3	1840	611	1840-80	Bergen	Jersey City
Hunterdon	B2	1714	54	1830-80	Burlington	Flemington
Mercer	C2	1838	226	1840-80	Somerset, Middlesex, Hunterdon, Burlington	Trenton
Middlesex	B3	1675	434	1830-80	Prov. East Jersey . . .	New Brunswick
Monmouth	C3	1675	334	1830-80	Prov. East Jersey	Freehold
Morris	B2	1739	362	1830-80	Hunterdon	Morristown
Ocean	C3	1850	108	1850-80	Monmouth	Toms River
Passaic	A3	1837	407	1840-80	Bergen, Essex	Paterson

Salem	D1	1681	59	1830-80	Original county	Salem

(Co Clk has civ ct rec from 1850)

Somerset	B2	1688	144	1830-80	Middlesex	Somerville
Sussex	A2	1753	49	1830-80	Morris	Newton

(Co Clk has m rec from 1795 to 1878, civ ct rec from 1760)

Union	B3	1857	504	1860-80	Essex	Elizabeth
Warren	B2	1824	63	1830-80	Sussex	Belvidere

Genealogists' Check List of the Historical Records Survey, N. J. (see page VIII)

Fed Cts (listed with Del); Inv of Co Arch-Bergen, Morris, Ocean, Passaic, Sussex; Inv of Mun & Tn Arch - Belmar, Denville, East Newark, Orange, Wharton; Guide to Vit Stat Rec - Vol 1 Public Arch, Vol 2 Chr Arch; Guide to Naturalization Rec; Transcriptions: 1. Glouster Co Rev War Doc - 2, Slave Doc.

Inv of the Chr Arch of N J: Baha'i Assemblies; Bap Bodies; Bap Bodies (Seventh Day Bap Sup); Christian Reformed; Congregational Christian; Evangelical Chr; Presbyterian Chrs; Prot Episcopal Chr - Diocese of N J and Diocese of Newark; Salvation Army - Jersey City; Soc of Friends; Unitarian Chr; Tran Colporteur Reports to the Am Tract Soc, 1841-1846; Trans John Brainerd's Jour 1761-1762, Presbyterian.

Dir of the Chrs in N J: Vol 1 Atlantic Co; 2 Bergen Co; 3 Burlington Co; 4 Camden Co; 5 Cape May Co; 6 Cumberland Co; 8 Essex Co; 9 Hudson Co; 10 Hunterdon Co; 11 Mercer Co; 12 Middlesex Co; 13 Monmouth Co; 14 Morris Co; 15 Ocean Co; 16 Passaic Co; 17 Salem Co; 18 Somerset Co; 19 Sussex Co; 20 Union Co; 21 Warren Co.

Guide to Ms Depo in N J: Cal of the N J State Lib Mx Col in the Cataloguing Rm State Lib, Trenton, N J; Cal of the Stevens Family Papers, Lieb Memorial Lib, Stevens Institute of Tech., Hoboken, N J (Preliminary Vol - Vol 1, 1664-1750 - Vol 2 1751-1777); Check List of N J Imprints 1784-1800; Am Portrait Inv - 1440 Early Am Portrait Artists 1663-1860; Manual of N J Recording Acts, Series I, Co Requirements; Index of the Official Reg of the Officers and Men of N J in the Rev War.

N J microfilms; (Filmed by N J Hist Rec Survey showing location of orig rec) Films in possession of Am Documentation Institute, Washington, D.C.: Min of the Council of Proprietors of the Eastern Div of NJ, (ABI) 1685-1705, 32 Ft, Surveyor General's Off, City Hall, Perth Amboy N J; Min of the Council of Proprietors of the Eastern Div of N J 1725-1764, 36 ft, Surveyors General's Off, City Hall, Perth Amboy, N J; Min of the Council of Pro-prietors of the Eastern Div of N J 1764-1794, No. "B" 34 ft, Surveyor General's Off, City Hall, Perth Amboy, J N; Min of the Council of the Council of the Propri-etors of the Eastern Div of N J 1794-1866 30 ft, Surveyor General's Off, City Hall, Perth Amboy, N J; Min of the Supreme Ct 1681-1709 ("The Burlington Ct Bk") 20 ft, Supreme Ct Clerk's Off, State House Annex, Trenton, N J; Min of the Supreme Ct 1760-1764, 25 ft, Supreme Ct Clerk's Off, State House Annex, Trenton, N J; Min of the Supreme Ct 1761-1765, 30 ft, Supreme Ct Clerk's Off, State House Annex, Trenton N J; Min of the Supreme Ct 1767-1768, 30 ft, Supreme Ct Clerk's Office, State House Annex, Trenton, N J; A Bill in the Chancery on N J (Hand printed by James Parker in N Y 1747) 15 ft; Ct of Common Rights of Chancery 1684 (D-2 Liber 2) 35 ft, Sec of State's Vault, State House, Trenton, N J; Early Index to Burlington Ct Min 1681-1709, 25 ft, Supreme Ct Clerk's Vlt, State House Annex, Trenton, N J; Burlington Supreme Ct Docket 1731-1737 Feb Term, 1 Vol, 30 ft, Supreme Ct Clerk's Safe, State House Annex, Trenton, N J; Burlington Supreme Ct Docket May Term 1742, 14 ft, Supreme Ct Clerk's Safe, State House Annex, Trenton, N J; Lib A For Judgments 1755-1758, 10 ft, Supreme Ct Clerk's Off, State House Annex, Trenton, N J; Min of the Ct of Sessions and Common Pleas Ct 1700-1713, 1713-1731, 1730-1739, 30 ft, Gloucester Co Hist Soc, Gloucester Co Build, Woodbury, N J; Supreme Ct Docket-May Term 1738-Nov 1741 Vol 2, 30 ft - May Term 1742-45, 15 ft - Nov 1745-1748 No. 4, 22 ft, - Supreme Ct Clerk's Vault, State House Annex, Trenton, N J; Min and Rules of the Supreme Ct - 1704-1715, 10 ft - 1716-1731, 14 ft - 1772-1776, 5 ft - 1775-1776, 5 ft - Supreme Ct Clerk's Off, State House Annex, Trenton, N J; Supreme Ct Min Memoranda 1782-1783, 5 ft, Supreme Ct Clerk's Off, State House Annex, Trenton, N J; Liber AAA of Deeds 1680, 30 ft, Sec of State's Vault, State House, Trenton, N J; Deeds-Patents, Liber I, 1666-1682, 30 ft, Sec of State, State House, Trenton, N J; Min of Gloucester Co Free-holders 1700-1812, 2 Vol, 45 ft, Gloucester Co Hist Soc, Gloucester Co Building,

Woodbury, N J; Old Road Book 1745-1775, 30 ft, County Clerk's Off, County Ct House, Somerville, N J; Bd of Chosen Freeholders of Somerset Co Min No. 1 1772-1810, 25 ft, Treasurer's Vault, Co Ct House, Somerville, N J; Min of Piscataway Township Feb 1, 1682 to July 1933, Township Clerk, Township Hall, New Market, N J; Woodbridge Township Freeholders Book, Liber A 1668-1757, 28 ft, Clerk's Vault, Woodbridge City Hall, Woodbridge, N J; Votes and Proceedings of the Common Council of the City of Burlington, 25 ft, 104 Vault, Burlington City Hall, Burlington, N J; Chester Township's "Ponsoking" 1692-1823, 15 ft, David L. Libbincott, 1 East Oak St., Moorestown, N J; Burlington Town Book 1693-1780, 30 ft, Masonic Home Vault, Masonic Home, Burlington, N J; Burlington Rec 1680-1717, 27 ft, Sec of State's Vault, State House, Trenton, N J; Road Book A Essex Co 3 Dec 1698-30 Mar 1804, 30 ft, Rm 228, Co Clerk's Vault, Hall of Rec, Newark, N J; Commissions - Acts of Assembly & C, 1682-1898, 40 ft, Sec of State's Vault (Locker No. 12), State House, Trenton, N J; Commissions AAA 1703-1774, 30 ft, Sec of State's Vault, State House, Trenton, N J; Declarations of Intentions of Aliens, Feb 1852, 10 ft, Supreme Ct Clerk's Off, State House Annex, Trenton, N J; Rec of Naturalization - Minors, 1851, Book No. 1, 5 ft, Supreme Ct Clerk's Off, State House Annex, Trenton, N J; Rec of Naturalization - Minors 1851-1873, Bk 2, 10 ft, Supreme Ct Clerk's Off, State House Annex, Trenton, N J; Min Bk of Gov Carteret 1665 (Deeds Liber 3), 30 ft, Sec of State's Vault (Locker 12, State House, Trenton, N J; The Treas of Eastern Div of N J to the Commissioner of Loan Office of Co of Morris, 27 May 1776-30 Apr 1838, 10 ft, Surrogate's Off Vault, Hall of Rec, Morristown, N J; Proceedings of Justice and Freeholders, Co of Morris 10 May 1786-1 Dec 1823, 10 ft, Surrogate's Off Vault, Hall of Rec, Morristown, N J; Documentary Evidence, Old Kings Highway, 3 Vol, 45 ft, Gloucester Co Hist Soc, Gloucester Co Bldg, Woodbury, N J; Historic Houses of Woodbury, Gloucester Co, 2 Vol, 30 ft, Gloucester Co Hist Soc, Gloucester Co Bldg, Woodbury, N J.

Depo of unpubl mat, Columbia Univ Lib, New York, N Y (Atlas of Congressional Roll Calls, Presidential Messages, & Papers and Executive Orders) - (All other materials) State Lib, Trenton, NJ.

New Mexico

Capital Santa Fe - Territory 1850 - State 1912 -(47th)

Until 1821 when the 780-mile Santa Fe Trail was opened from Independence, Mo., to Santa Fe, N.M., few Americans or Europeans had made their homes in New Mexico. For years, the region had belonged to Mexico and was inhabited mainly by Indians and Spanish-Americans. Its main city, Santa Fe, had been the capital of the Mexican territory since 1609. At that early date and for the next 150 years or more, its connections were more with Mexico than the United States. Indians and Spanish-Americans were its only inhabitants until the first part of 1800.

New Mexico became part of the United States in 1848. In 1850 when it was created a territory, it included most of its present domain, plus Arizona and Colorado. The Gadsden Purchase in 1854 included within its boundaries the Gila Valley in Catron and Grant counties.

The Colorado section was taken from New Mexico in 1861 and made into a separate territory. Two years later, Arizona was also withdrawn and created into a separate territory.

After operating for 62 years under territorial laws, New Miexico became a state in 1912, when it was made the forty-seventh state in the union.

Birth and death records from 1919 are at the office of the State Health Department, Santa Fe, N.M. They are not complete.

The County Clerk in each county seat has marriage records, wills, property deeds, and administration of estates.

Land grants are at the office of the State Land Office in Santa Fe, N.M.

Tax payers lists are at the office of the County Assessors, war service records at the office of the Adjutant General, cemetery records with the cemetery boards, and guardianship proceedings with the district courts.

Valuable genealogical information is contained in hundreds of volumes in the Stephen Watts Kearney Chapter of the Daughters of the American Revolution in Santa Fe and the New Mexico Historical Society, Santa Fe, N.M.. Other libraries in the larger cities have also much genealogical information. Albuquerque, (Bernalillo), Public Library, 423 E. Central American publications and history, Southwest lore); University of New Mexico Library, (Mexican and South Ave., (Southwest lore); University of New west lore); Santa Fe, (Santa Fe), New Mexico State Library Commission, 301 Don Gaspar, (Southwestern lore).

Genealogists' Check List of the Historical Records Survey, N. Mex. (see page VIII)

Fed Cts; Inv of Co Arch – Bernalillo, Colfax, Dona Ana, Eddy, Grant, Hidalgo, Luna, Mora, Otero, Sandoval, San Miguel, Sierra, Torrance, Union, Valencia; Guide to Pub Vit Stat Rec; Dir of Chrs & Rel Org in N Mex; Check List of N Mex Im- prints and Publication, 1784–1876; Index to Final Report on investigations Among the Indians of the Southwestern U S - Carried on Mainly in the years 1880–1885 by A.F. Bandelier; Depo of unpubl mat, State Museum, Santa Fe, N Mex.

County Map of New Mexico

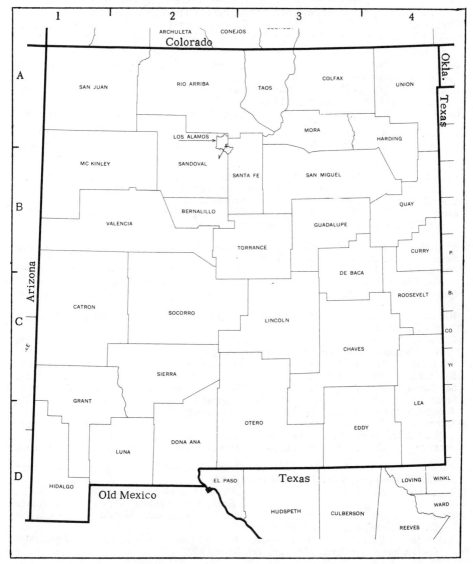

New Mexico County Histories

(Population figures to nearest thousand – 1960 Census)

Name	Map Index	Date Formed	Pop. By M	Census Reports Available	Parent County	County Seat
Bernalillo	B2	1852	262	1850–80	Original county	Albuquerque
Catron	C1	1921	3		Socorro	Reserve
(Co Clk has m & pro rec from 1921)						
Chaves	C3	1887	58		Lincoln	Roswell
(Co Clk has m & pro rec from 1891)						
Colfax	A3	1869	14	1870–80	Mora	Raton
Curry	B4	1909	33		Quay, Roosevelt...........	Clovis
(Co Clk has b, m, d, pro rec from 1909)						
De Baca	C3	1917	3		Chaves, Guadalupe, Roosevelt .	Fort Sumner
(Co Clk has b, m, d, bur, div, pro, civ ct, real estate, deeds & Mtgs from 1917)						
Dona Ana	D2	1852	60	1860–80	Original county	Las Cruces
(Co Clk has b & m rec 1816, d rec 1907, pro, deeds, leins 1850, mtg from 1860, discharge rec 1943)						
Eddy	D4	1887	51		Lincoln	Carlsbad
(Co Clk has m rec from 1887)						
Grant	D1	1868	19	1870–80	Socorro	Silver City
(Co Clk has m & pro rec from 1900)						
Guadalupe	B3	1905	6		Lincoln, San Miguel	Santa Rosa
Harding	A4	1921	2		Mora, Union	Mosquero
Hidalgo	D1	1920	5		Grant	Lordsburg
Lea	D4	1917	53		Chaves, Eddy	Lovington
Lincoln	C3	1869	8	1870	Socorro	Carrizozo
(Co Clk has m rec from 1882, pro rec from 1880, newspapers from 1890)						
Los Alamos	B2	1949	13		Sandoval, Santa Fe	Los Alamos
Luna	D2	1901	10		Dona Ana, Grant	Deming
(Co Clk has m, div, pro, civ ct, newspapers from 1901)						
McKinley	B1	1899	37		Bernalillo, Valencia, San Juan ...	Gallup
Mora	A3	1859	6	1860–80	San Miguel	Mora
Otero	D3	1899	37		Dona Ana, Lincoln, Socorro .	Alamogordo
(Co Clk has b rec from 1908, m rec 1899, d & bur rec 1907, pro rec 1901)						
Quay	B4	1903	12		Chaves	Tucumcari
Rio Arriba	A2	1852	24	1850–80	Original county	Tierra Amarilla
(Co Clk has m & pro rec from 1852)						
Roosevelt	C4	1903	16		Chaves	Portales
(Co Clk has m, div, pro, civ ct rec from 1903)						
Sandoval	B2	1903	14		Rio Arriba	Bernalillo
San Juan	A1	1887	53		Rio Arriba	Aztec
San Miguel	B3	1852	23	1850–80	Original county	Las Vegas
Santa Fe	B3	1852	45	1860–80	Original county	Santa Fe
(Co Clk has m rec from 1863, pro rec from 1862)						
Sierra	C2	1884	6		Socorro	Truth or Consequences
(Co Clk has m rec from 1884, pro rec from 1913)						
Socorro	C2	1852	10	1860–80	Original county	Socorro
Taos	A3	1852	16	1850–80	Original county	Taos
(Co Clk has b, m, d, bur, pro rec from 1846)						
Torrance	B3	1903	6		Lincoln, San Miguel, Socorro, Santa Fe, Valencia	Estancia
Union	A4	1894	6		Colfax, Mora, San Miguel ...	Clayton
(Co Clk has m, div, pro rec from 1894)						
Valencia	B1	1852	39	1850–80	Original county	Los Lunas
(Co Clk has m rec from 1865, pro rec from 1900)						

New York
Capital Albany - State 1788 - (11th)

The Dutch settled New York in 1624 when they established a colony at Albany, then called Fort Orange. The next year other settlers from Holland came to New York City, then New Amsterdam. Previously, at least two explorers, Hudson and Champlain, had looked over the territory.

In the next few years the Dutch induced individuals from Scandinavia, Great Britain, and Germany to come with them to the New World.

Many Puritan families in Massachusetts and Connecticut drifted south into New York around 1640. Some sixty years later German families came into the Mohawk Valley looking for places in which to build their homes. About the same time French settlers were straggling into the new section from Canada. Other French families, together with some Spaniards and Portuguese, disturbed by the uprisings in the West Indies, where they had been for some time, sought refuge in New York.

The total population of the colony in 1740 was established at only 50,000. About that time many former Connecticut dwellers went across the sound and settled in Long Island. Others came into Dutchess, Westchester and Orange counties. A population check previous to the outbreak of the Revolutionary War would find settlers on Long Island, on the banks of the Hudson River, a few Palatine Germans along the Mohawk River and some New Englanders in the extreme south-eastern part of the state.

In 1776 New York broke with the Mother Country, and joined the other colonies in their fight for freedom. This struggle continued until 1781. Seven years later New York became the eleventh state in the Union by ratifying the constitution.

New York is described as a land of many tongues, not less than sixty languages being heard. The predominating nationalities are Italian, Russian, German, Polish, Irish, Austrian, English, Hungarian, Swedish, Norwegian, Czech, Greek, French, Finish and Danish.

The researcher interested in New York records should first of all, before undertaking any search whatsoever, spend a day or two or more carefully reading Rosalie Fellows Bailey's "Guide to Genealogical Sources for New York City, 1783-1898." The Guide "is in its field one of the most important, perhaps the most important, in the United States." This most worthy appraisal comes from one of the foremost present day genealogists, an individual who has devoted much thought and energy to the science of genealogy. Carefully adhearing to Miss Bailey's suggestions in her valuable treatise "will give reasonable hope that any problem within its limit of time and place may be solved."

Births, Deaths, and Marriages, from 1880 to present, for the entire state exclusive of all New York City records and certain records of Albany, Buffalo and Yonkers, noted below, are in the charge of the Director, Office of Vital Statistics, State Department of Health, Alfred E. Smith State Office Building, Albany. The records of Albany, Buffalo and Yonkers not on file in the Health Department but available in the registrars' office of the cities concerned are: Births and deaths prior to Jan. 1, 1914; marriages prior to Jan 1, 1908. The central office for New York City vital records is Board of Health, 125 Worth St., New York City. Registration was not very complete until about 1900. For data on records prior to 1880, when the Department of Health became the central depository for the state, see Historical records survey, New York State, "Guide to Public Vital Statistics in New York State," 1942, 3v. wherein the status of the vital records of each community is given.

Marriage Bonds, from 1752 to 1784, originally 40v., are in charge of Associate Librarian, Manuscripts and History Section, New York State Library, Albany. These and other licenses, some as early as 1641 which are contained in other series filed in the State Library, are indexed in Secretary of State, "Names of Persons for Whom Marriage Licenses were Issued by the Secretary of the Province of New York Previous to 1784." 1860. See also "Supplementary List of Marriage Licenses," (State Library Bulletin, History No. 1, April 1898) for list of bonds for years 1752-53, 1755-56, and 1758, formerly bound as v.41 of Marriage Bonds.

Wills - usually in county surrogates' office. For other wills see Berthold Fernow ed., "Calendar of Wills on File and Recorded in the Offices of the Clerk of the Court of Appeals, of the County Clerk at Albany, and of the Secretary of State, 1626-1836," 1896. For abstracts of wills on file in the Surrogate's office, City of New York, 1665-1800, see New York Historical Society, "Collections." v.25-41. Included therein are wills for the southern district of New York State. Care should be exercized in the use of the abstracts as many errors have been found – get the original when ever possible.

In the Manuscripts and History Section, New York State Library are wills, 1823–1940, of non-resident property owners.

Deeds and Land Grants – deeds are usually on file in the county clerk's offices.

The following are state records:

Patents, land papers, deeds 1630–64 (Dutch) in New York Colonial Manuscripts, v.GG and HH in custody of Associate Librarian, Manuscripts and History section, New York State Library, Albany.

New York Colonial Manuscripts indorsed Land Papers, 1643–1803. Same custody as preceding.

Deeds, including mortgages and releases to state, 1642 to present, in custody of Secretary, Land Board, Department of State, 164 State St., Albany.

Letters – Patent of Lands, 1664–1878. Custody same as preceding.

Census Records – All schedules of the Federal Census from 1790 to and including 1940 are at Bureau of the Census, Washington, D. C.

From the State Librarian, New York State Library, Albany, N.Y., may be obtained "An Inventory of New York State and Federal Census Records." 1942, showing the available schedules from each county. From one to 14 different schedules are on hand at the office of the County Clerk of each county. In addition to those noted therein, the Manuscripts and History Section, New York State Library has microfilm of the 1800, 1810, and 1830 Federal Censuses for New York State. Originals are on file in the National Archives, Washington, D. C.

Tax Payers Lists – The New York State Library, Manuscripts and History Section, Albany, has some assessment rolls in its collection, both public and private. No inventory of them is available.

Local divisions of government – county, town, etc. – frequently have such records of file.

Church or Parish Records Transferred to State – In custody of the Associate Librarian, Manuscripts and History Section, New York State Library, Albany, is a large collection of Church records, originals and copies. See Historical Records survey, New York State, "Guide to Vital Statistics Records of Churches in New York State," 1942 2 v. for information concerning those on file in the State Library and elsewhere.

An invaluable source of basic information has been found in the collections of the Dept. of History and Archives of Montgomery Co. at the old Court House at Fonds, N.Y. Either original or copied church records of baptisms, marriages and deaths from old churches of the entire county have been preserved and catalogued there.

War Service Records – Colonial and Revolutionary war service records for New York State are in the custody of the Associate Librarian, Manuscripts and History Section, New York State Library, Albany. War of 1812, 1860–65, Spanish-American, World War I and World War II records for this state are in the office of the Adjutant General, Bureau of War Records, 112 State St., Albany.

Cemetery Records – The Manuscripts and History Section, New York State Library, Albany, has a large collection of New York State cemetery records.

Guardianship and Orphan Court Proceedings – In custody of county surrogate's offices.

New York Libraries – Albany, (Albany), New York State Libary (state and local histories and genealogy). Binghampton, (Broome), Public Library, 78 Exchange St. Brooklyn, (Kings), Public Library, Grand Army Plaza, (Civil War Records); Long Island Historical Society, Library, 128 Pierrepont St. (local and personal histories); St. Johns University Library, 75 Lewis Ave. (Irish History). Buffalo, (Erie), Public Library, 120 W. Eagle St.; The Grosvenor Library, Edward and Franklin Sts., (genealogy and local history). Cooperstown, (Otsego), New York State Association Library, (community and personal histories). Ithaca, (Tompkins), Cornell University Library, (collections on Iceland, history of the states, Civil War). New York City, (N.Y.), American Irish Historical Society Library, 991 Fifth Ave., (Irish in colonial America and later, genealogy, personal histories); Columbia University Libraries, 535 W. 114th St., School of Journalism, (newspaper files); Editor and Publisher Library, 1475 Broadway, (newspaper files); Fordham University. Duane Library, (early American collections); The Holland Society of New York Library, 90 West St., (genealogical collections); National Lutheran Council Library, 50 Madison Ave., (history of Lutheran Church in America); New York Genealogical and Biographical Society Library, 122 E. 58th St.; New York Herald Tribune Library, 230 W. 41st St. (newspaper collection); The New York Historical Library, 170 Central Park West, (genealogy, newspapers, local histories of N.Y. Complete file of N. Y. City directories from 1786 to date); The New York Public Library, Fifth Ave. and 42nd St., (Irish History, Local History, British and American genealogies manuscript personal histories); New York Times Library, 229 W. 43rd St., (more than a million biographical files); Sons of the Revolution Library, 54 Pearl St.; James T. White & Co. Library, 101 Fifth Ave., (state, county and persoanl histories) Rochester, (Monroe), Public Library, 115 South Ave., (Rochester Historical Society collection); University of Rochester Library, (Western New York history collection). Syracuse, (Onondaga). Public Library, 335 Montgomery St., (local histories and genealogies).

Thousands upon thousands of volumes have been written about New York people and communities and every library in the nation have some of them on its shelves. Just to make a mere mention, consider these, some of which are very valuable:

BARBER, JOHN W. AND HOWE, HENRY. *Historical Collections of the State of New York.* 608 pp. New York, 1841.

Census of New York, 1790, First Federal Census. 308 pp. Washington, D. C., 1908.

New York Genealogical and Biographical Record, a quarterly magazine. Eighty seven volumes. 1870-1956.

New York Historical Society Collections. Sixty six volumes. 1868-1923.

O'CALLAGHAN, E. B. *The Documentary History of the State of New York.* Vol. I, 536 pp. A roll of names and surnames of 1689; N. Y. Army List of 1700; 1702, 1714 and 1720 Census of Orange, Dutches and Albany counties; 1703 Census of N. Y. City; inhabitants of Hempstead in 1673; roll of those taking oath of allegiance in N. Y. in 1687; inhabitants in 1698. Vol. II, 1676 Assessment Rolls; 711 pp.. Vol. III, Early Immigrants to New Netherlands, 1657-1664, and where they came from; restoration of N. Y. to the English; state of religion in province; names of some residents in 1737; papers relating to the Palatines and the first settlement of Newburgh, Orange Co.; Ulster County Freeholders in 1728; Quakers and Moravians; state of Anglo-American Church, 748 pp. Vol 4, Journal of New Netherland, 1647; a description of New Netherland in 1644; 1663 massacre of Wildwyck, now Kingston; assessment rolls of the five Dutch towns of Kings Co., L. I. in 1675; census of Flat Bush, Flatt Lands, Gravesend, New Utrecht, Brockland, Bushwyck, Suffolk County, Dutchess County, and soldier lists, all of 1738; 674 pp. Weed, Parsons and Company, Albany, N. Y., 1850.

New York County Histories

(Population figures to nearest thousand – 1960 Census)

Name	Map Index	Date Formed	Pop. By M	Census Reports Available	Parent County	County Seat
Albany	B3	1683	273	1790-80	Original county	Albany
Allegany	D2	1806	44	1810-80	Genesee	Belmont
Bronx	B4	1914	1425		New York	Bronx
(Co Clk has m, div, sup civ ct rec from 1914)						
Broome	C3	1806	213	1810-80	Tioga	Binghamton
(Co Clk has m rec from 1908, div, civ ct rec from 1806)						
Cattaraugus	E2	1808	80	1810-80	Genesee	Little Valley
(Co Clk has m rec from 1908, div ct rec from 1880, civ ct rec from 1850)						
Cayuga	C2	1799	74	1800-80	Onondaga	Auburn
Charlotte		1772			Albany (renamed Washington 1784)	
Chautauqua	E2	1808	145	1810-80	Genesee	Mayville
(Co Clk has m rec from 1908)						
Chemung	D2	1836	99	1840-80	Tioga	Elmira
Chenango	C2	1798	43	1800-80	Herkimer, Tioga	Norwich
(Co Clk has m rec from 1908 to 1935, div ct rec from 1847, civ ct rec from 1850)						
Clinton	A1	1788	73	1790-80	Washington	Plattsburg
Columbia	B3	1786	47	1790-80	Albany	Hudson
(Co Clk has m rec 1908 to 1935, div & civ ct rec 1882, deeds & mtgs 1800)						
Cortland	C2	1808	41	1820-80	Onondaga	Cortland
Delaware	B3	1797	44	1800-80	Ulster, Otsego	Delhi
Dutchess	B3	1683	176	1790-80	Original county	Poughkeepsie
(Co Clk has m rec 1908 to 1935, div rec from 1850, div ct rec from 1850; collection of misc ancient documents indexed by name 1714 to 1800)						
Erie	D2	1821	1065	1830-80	Niagara	Buffalo
(Co Clk has m rec 1830 to 1935, div, civ ct rec from 1821)						

Essex   A2 1799   35 1800–80 Clinton . . . . Elizabethtown
  (Co Clk has m rec 1908 to 1936, div, pro, civ ct rec from 1799)
Franklin   A1 1808   45 1810–80 Clinton . . . . Malone
Fulton   B2 1838   51 1840–80 Montgomery . . . . Johnstown
  (Co Clk has m rec from 1900 to 1926)
Genesee   D1 1802   54 1810–80 Ontario . . . . Batavia
  (Co Clk has m rec 1908 to 1932, div rec from 1802, civ ct rec from 1848)
Greene   B3 1800   31 1800–80 Ulster, Albany . . . . Catskill
Hamilton   B2 1816   4 1820–80 Montgomery . . . . Lake Pleasant
Herkimer   B2 1791   66 1800–80 Montgomery . . . . Herkimer
Jefferson B1 1805   88 1810–80 Oneida . . . . Watertown
  (Co Clk has m rec 1908 to 1933, civ ct rec from 1847, deeds Oneida 1795,
  Jefferson 1805, many other rec & censuses)
Kings   B4 1683 2627 1790–80 Original county . . . . Brooklyn
Lewis   B1 1805   23 1810–80 Chenango . . . . Lowville
  (Co Clk has b, d, m rec 1848 to 1850, div rec from 1847, civ ct rec from 1907,
  real estate rec from 1805)

County Map of New York

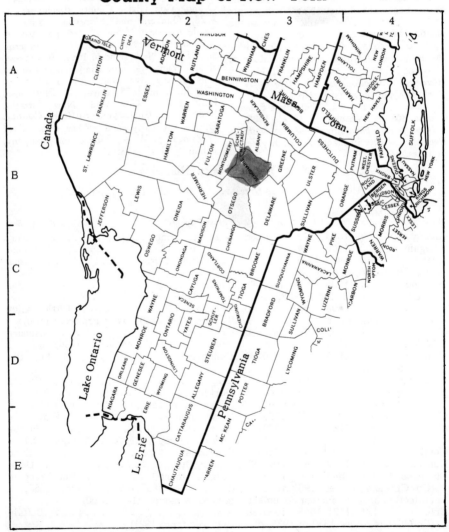

Livingston D2 1821 44 1830-80 Genesee, Ontario .... Geneseo
  (Co Clk has m rec 1908 to 1929, div & civ ct rec from 1878)
Madison C2 1806 55 1810-80 Chenango .... Wampsville
  (Co Clk has m rec 1908 to 1935, div & civ ct rec from 1889, deeds from 1806)
Monroe D1 1821 586 1830-80 Genesee, Ontario .... Rochester
  (Co Clk has m rec from 1808 to 1935, div & civ ct rec from 1860)
Montgomery B2 1772 57 1790-80 Albany (as Tryon to 1784) ..... Fonda
Nassau B4 1899 1300 Queens .... Mineola
  (Co Clk has m rec 1907 to 1935, div & pro rec from 1899)
New York B4 1683 1698 1790-80 Original county .... New York
Niagara D1 1808 242 1810-80 Genesee .... Lockport
Oneida B2 1798 264 1800-80 Herkimer (See Jefferson) .... Utica
Onondaga C2 1794 423 1800-80 Herkimer .... Syracuse
Ontario D2 1789 68 1790-80 Montgomery .... Canandaigua
Orange B4 1683 184 1790-80 Original county .... Goshen
Orleans D1 1824 34 1830-80 Genesee .... Albion
Oswego C2 1816 86 1820-80 Oneida, Onondaga .... Oswego, Pulaski
  (Co Clk has m rec 1907 to 1935)
Otsego B2 1791 52 1800-80 Montgomery .... Cooperstown
  (Co Clk has m rec 1908 to 1936, div rec from 1900, civ ct rec from 1791)
Putnam B4 1812 32 1820-80 Dutchess .... Carmel
Queens B4 1683 1810 1790-80 Original county .... Jamaica
Rensselaer A3 1791 143 1800-80 Albany .... Troy
Richmond B4 1683 222 1790-80 Original county .... St. George
Rockland B4 1798 137 1800-80 Orange .... New City
St. Lawrence B1 1802 111 1810-80 Clinton, Herkimer, Montgomery . Canton
Saratoga A2 1791 89 1800-80 Albany .... Ballston Spa
Schenectady B2 1809 153 1810-80 Albany .... Schenectady
  (Co Clk has m rec 1908 to 1935, div & civ ct rec from 1809)
Schoharie B3 1795 23 1800-80 Albany, Ostego .... Schoharie
  (Co Clk has m rec 1908 to 1935, div & civ ct rec 1898, deeds & mtgs 1797)
Schuyler D2 1854 15 1860-80 Tompkins, Steuben, Chemung . Watkins Glen
  (Co Clk has m rec 1908 to 1943, div, civ ct 1885)
Seneca C2 1804 32 1810-80 Cayuga .... Ovid, Waterloo
Steuben D2 1796 98 1800-80 Ontario .... Bath
  (Co Clk has m rec 1908 to 1936, div rec from 1900)
Suffolk B4 1683 667 1790-80 Original county .... Riverhead
Sullivan B3 1809 45 1810-80 Ulster .... Monticello
Tioga C3 1791 38 1800-80 Montgomery .... Owego
Tompkins C2 1817 66 1820-80 Cayuga, Seneca .... Ithaca
Tryon 1772 Albany (renamed Montgomery 1784)
Ulster B3 1683 119 1790-80 Original county .... Kingston
Warren A2 1813 44 1820-80 Washington .... Lake George
  (Co Clk has m rec 1908 to 1934, div & civ ct rec from 1813)
Washington A2 1772 48 1790-80 Albany (see Charlotte) ... Hudson Falls
Wayne C2 1823 68 1830-80 Ontario, Seneca .... Lyons
Westchester B4 1683 809 1790-80 Original county .... White Plains
  (Co Clk has m rec 1908 to 1935, div & civ ct rec from 1847)
Wyoming D2 1841 35 1850-80 Genesee .... Warsaw
  (Co Clk has m rec 1908 to 1933, div, civ ct, deeds from 1841, town, co, village
  maps from 1861, CW muster rolls from 1861)
Yates D2 1823 19 1830-80 Ontario, Steuben .... Penn Yan

Genealogists' Check List of the Historical Records Survey, New York (see page VIII)

Fed Cts; Inv of Co Arch - Albany Broome, Cattaraugus, Chautauqua, Chemung, New York City (Bronx, Kings, Richmond Borough & Co), Ulster; Inv of Mun and Tn Arch - New York City (Bronx, Richmond).
  Trans of Pub Arch; NYC (Newtown); Trans of Early Tn Rec, Tn Min of Newtown,

Queens Co Vol 1, 1656-1688, Vol 2, 1653-1734 Part 1 & 2 (Index in Pt 2); Tn Cts 1656-1690; NYC (Staten Island) Earliest Vol of Rec 1678-1813; Ulster Co -1 Min of the Bd of Supervisors 1710/1 to 1730/1 - 2, Records of the Road Commissioners Vol 1, 1722-1769 - Vol 2, 1769-1795.
  Guide to Pub Vit Rec (Inclusive of

NYC) Vol 1, Birth Rec - Vol 2, Mar Rec - Vol 3 Death Rec; Guide to Vit Stat Rec of Chrs (Exclusive of NYC) Vol 1, & Vol 2; Guide to Vit Stat Rec of Chrs in NYC, 1, Borough of Bronx, 2, Borough of Queens, 3, Borough of Richmond, 4, Borough of Manhattan, 5, Borough of Brooklyn.

Inv of the Chr Arch of N Y State; Prot Episcopal Chr, Diocese of Western N Y: Diocese of Rochester; Inv of the Chr Arch of NYC - Eastern Orthodox Chrs and the Armenian Apostolic Chr in Am - Lutheran Chr - Methodist Chr - Presbyterian Chr in the US - Protestant Episcopal Chr Diocese of Long Island, Vol 2 Brooklyn & Queens; Diocese of NY, Vol 2 the Bronx, Manhattan & Richmond; RC Chr Archdiocese of NY, Vol 2 The Bronx, Manhattan and Richmond; Society of Friends.

Guide to Ms Depo in NYC; Guide to Depo of Ms Col in NY State; Guide to Ten Major Depo of Ms Col in NY State; Cal of the Gerrit Smith Papers in the Syracuse Univ Lib Vol 1, 1819-1846, Vol 2, 1846-1854; Check List of Imprints of Sag Harbor,

Long Island 1791-1820; Check List of Am Imprints of Batavia, N Y 1819-1876; Check List of Utica N Y Imprints 1799-1830; A Bibliography of Bks and Pamphlets Printed at Canadaigua, N Y 1799-1850 (Being Vol 21, No. 4 of Grosvenor Lib Bulletin, 62-107 p. printed 1939); Inv of Maps (Partial) Located in Various State, Co, Mun and other Pub Off in N Y State.

Microfilm: (Filmed by NYC Hist Rec Survey) Am Loyalists Transcripts 1783-1790, NY Pub Lib, NYC, Subject Cards of US Hist in NY, Pub Lib Card Cat.

Depo of unpubl mat: NYC Hist Soc, (List & index of Early Am Portrait Painters & Am Slavery Imprints); Columbia U Lib (George D White Papers); Cooper Union for the Advancement of Society & Art (Cal of Cooper-Hewitt Papers); Am-Jewish Hist Soc (Dir of Jewish Cong USA & Yiddish Anthology); Modern Art Film Lib (Film Index); NY Pub Lib (Negros of NY); NYC Dept of Health, Div of Vit Stat (Pub Vit Stat); Mun Ref Lib, NYC (all other mat on NYC); State Lib, Albany, N Y (all other N Y State mat.)

North Carolina
Capital Raleigh - State 1789 - (12th)

The first permanent settlement in North Carolina territory was established in 1653 when groups of settlers came south from Virginia to occupy the section north of the Albermarle Sound. The influx of new settlers was so limited that in an eighty year period the population had increased only to about 14,000.

For several years prior to the Revolution, Highland Scotch immigrants were arriving frequently in the North Carolina section. Most of them established themselves in the southeast section. So rapidly did they arrive that in a few years there were more than 20,000 of them in that territory.

When large groups of Scotch-Irish departed from Pennsylvania down the Shenandoah Valley to settle in Virginia, many continued on into North Carolina. For religious reasons they had been banished from Scotland, where their strong Protestant views irked the religious leaders. Thousands of them were transplanted into Ireland, where they remained long enough to get an opportunity to come to the New World. Many of them established homes in the western section of the state, around the present region of Iredell county. Many Germans came into North Carolina

in the early days. In 1760 there were about 15,000 in Forsyth and Guilford counties. A colony of English speaking Quakers from Virginia, Pennsylvania, and Nantucket, Mass., settled in Rockingham, Guilford, and Chatham counties. Disliking slavery, they later moved to Ohio and Indiana. However, some of them remained and their descandants are still in North Carolina.

Before the Revolution, the Church of England was in "power" in North Carolina as in Virginia. Only the ordained ministers of that church were permitted to perform marriage ceremonies. Those who wished to marry could have their "banns" published or announced from the pulpit or they could buy a license. Those married by license had to furnish a fifty pound bond. Those old marriage bonds, many of which are still in the county court houses, are full of genealogical information. In the parish registers kept by the priests were records of births, deaths and marriages. Some of the old parish records are in the office of the State Historical Commission, though some are still in the offices of the County Clerk or the County Register of Deeds.

The National Archives have the Census schedules for all of the North Carolina counties. Almost half of the hundred counties were represented in the 1790 Federal Census.

North Carolina libraries - Charlotte, (Mecklenburg), Public Library 310 N. Tryon St.; Durham, (Durham), Duke University Library, (Southern history, lore, and newspapers); Raleigh, (Wake), North Carolina State Library, Morgan St., (South history and genealogy); Winston-Salem, (Forsyth). Carnegie Public Library.

Books on North Carolina:

ALLEN, W. C. *The Annals of Haywood County, N. C.*, historical, sociological, biographical, and genealogical. 632 pp. 1935.

CRITTENDEN, CHARLES CHRISTOPHER AND LACY, DAN. *The Historical Records of North Carolina*. Vol. I, 491 pp. County Records of Alamance through Columbus Counties. Vol. II. 568 pp. Craven through Moore Counties. Vol III, 760 pp. Nash through Yancey Counties. North Carolina Historical Commission, Raleigh, 1939.

GRIFFEN, CLARENCE W. *History of Old Tryon and Rutherford Counties*, N. C., 1730-1936. 640 pp. The Miller Printing Co., Asheville, N. C. 1937.

GRIMES, J. BRYAN. *North Carolina Wills and Inventories*, 587 pp. *Abstract of Wills*, 1690-1760. 670 pp. Edwards & Broughton Printing Co., Raleigh, 1912.

Genealogists' Check List of the Historical Records Survey, N. C.

(see page VIII)

Fed Cts; Inv of Co Arch - Vol 1 Almace thru Columbus, Vol 2 Craven thru Moore, Vol 3 Nash thru Yancey; Guide to Vit Stat Rec Vol 1; Inv of State Arch -NC Hist Commission; Inv of the Chr Arch of NC Southern Bap Convention - Allegany Assn, Brunswick Assn, Central Assn, Flat River Assn, Raleigh Assn, Stanley Assn, Yancey Assn.

Guide to Deop of Ms Col in NC; Guide to the Ms Col in the Arch of the NC Hist Commission; Guide to the Ms Col in Duke Univ Lib; Guide to the Ms in the Arch of the Moravian Chr in Am, Southern Prov, Winston-Salem, N C; Guide to the Ms in the Southern Hist Col of the Univ of N C; A Cal of the Bartlett Yancey Papers in the Southern Hist Col of the Univ of N C; List of the Papeles Procedentes De Cuba (Cuban Papers) in the Arch in the NC Hist Commission; Depo of unpubl mat, Hist Commission, Raleigh, N C.

County Map of North Carolina

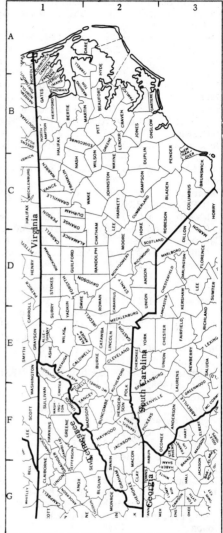

North Carolina County Histories

(Population figures to nearest thousand - 1960 Census)

Name	Map Index	Date Formed	Pop. By M	Census Reports Available	Parent County	County Seat
Alamance	D1	1849	86	1850-80	Orange	Graham
(Clk of Sup Ct has div, pro, civ ct rec from 1849)						
Albemarle		1663			1 of 3 original cos. discontinued in 1751	
Alexander	E1	1847	16	1850-80	Iredell, Caldwell & Wilkes ... Taylorsville	

Alleghany   E1   1859   8   1860–80   Ashe . . . .   Sparta
(Clk of Sup Ct has div, pro, civ ct rec from 1863)
Anson   D2   1750   25   1790–80   Bladen . . . .   Wadesboro
(CH burned 1868)
Ashe   E1   1799   20   1800–80   Wilkes . . . .   Jefferson
Archdale   1705   Changed to Beaufort 1712)
Avery   E1   1911   12   Caldwell, Mitchell & Watauga .. Newland
Bath   1696   Discontinued in 1739
Beaufort   B2   1712   36   1790–80   Bath (Formerly Archdale) .. Washington
Bertie   B1   1722   24   1790–80   Chowan, Bath . . . .   Windsor
Bladen   C3   1734   29   1790–80   New Hanover, Bath . . . . .   Elizabethtown
(Clk of Sup Ct has wills from 1734; CH burned 1800–1893)
Brunswick   C3   1764   20   1790–80   New Hanover, Bladen . . . . . .   Southport
Buncombe   F2   1791 130   1800–80   Burke, Rutherford . . . .   Asheville
(CH burned 1830–1835)
Burke   E2   1777   53   1790–80   Rowan . . . .   Morganton
Bute   1764   Discontinued in 1779
Cabarrus   D2   1792   68   1800–80   Mecklenburg . . . .   Concord
(CH burned 1874)
Caldwell   E1   1841   50   1850–80   Burke, Wilkes . . . .   Lenoir
(Clk of Sup Ct has div, pro, civ ct rec from 1841)
Camden   A1   1777   6   1790–80   Pasquotank . . . .   Camden
(Clk of Sup Ct has div & civ ct rec from 1896, pro rec from 1912)
Carteret   B2   1722   31   1790–80   Bath . . . .   Beaufort
Caswell   D1   1777   20   1800–80   Orange . . . .   Yanceyville
Catawba   E2   1842   73   1850–80   Lincoln . . . .   Newton
Chatham   D2   1771   27   1790–80   Orange . . . .   Pittsboro
(Register of Deeds has b & d rec from 1913, m rec from 1771)
Cherokee   G2   1839   16   1840–80   Macon . . . .   Murphy
Chowan   B1   1670   12   1790–80   Prec. Albermarle . . . .   Edenton
Clay   G2   1861   6   1870–80   Cherokee . . . . Brasstown & Hayesville
Cleveland   E2   1841   66   1850–80   Rutherford, Lincoln . . . .   Shelby
(Register of Deeds has b & d rec 1913, m rec 1841; Clk of Sup Ct has div & civ
ct rec 1868, pro rec 1841)
Columbus   C3   1808   49   1810–80   Bladen, Brunswick . . . .   Whiteville
Craven   B2   1712   59   1790–80   Prec. Bath Co. . . . .   New Bern
(1810 census missing)
Cumberland   C2   1754 149   1790–80   Bladen . . . .   Fayetteville
Currituck   A1   1670   7   1790–80   Albemarle . . . .   Currituck
(1820 census missing; CH burned 1842)
Dare   A2   1870   6   1870–80   Currituck, Tyrell . . . .   Manteo
Davidson   D2   1822   79   1830–80   Rowan . . . .   Lexington
Davie   D1   1836   17   1840–80   Rowan . . . .   Mocksville
(Register of Deeds has b rec from 1913, m & d rec from 1837; Clk of Sup Ct has
div, pro, civ ct rec from 1837)
Dobbs   1758   Johnston, discontinued 1791
Duplin   C2   1750   40   1790–80   New Hanover . . . .   Kenansville
Durham   C1   1881 112   Orange, Wake . . . .   Durham
(Clk of Sup Ct has div & civ ct rec from 1881)
Edgecombe   B1   1741   54   1790–80   Bertie . . . .   Tarboro
Forsyth   D1   1849 189   1850–80   Stokes . . . .   Winston–Salem
Franklin   C1   1779   29   1800–80   Bute . . . .   Louisburg
(1820 census missing)
Gaston   E2   1846 127   1850–80   Lincoln . . . .   Gastonia
(Clk of Sup Ct has div, pro, civ ct rec from 1846)
Gates   B1   1779   9   1790–80   Chowan, Hertford . . . .   Gatesville
Glasgow   1791   Discontinued 1799
Graham   G2   1872   6   1880   Cherokee . . . .   Robbinsville
(Register of Deeds has b & d rec from 1913, m rec from 1872; Clk of Sup Ct has
div, pro, civ ct, wills from 1872)
Granville   C1   1746   33   1800–80   Edgecombe, Orig. Glasgow . . . . .   Oxford

Greene   B2   1791   17   1800-80   Dobbs or Glasgow .... Snow Hill
(CH burned 1876)
Guilford   D1   1771 247   1790-80   Rowan, Orange .... Greensboro
(CH burned 1872, many older records still available)
Halifax   B1   1758   59   1790-80   Edgecombe .... Halifax
Harnett   C2   1855   48   1860-80   Cumberland .... Lillington
Haywood   F2   1808   40   1810-80   Buncombe .... Waynesville
Henderson   F2   1838   36   1840-80   Buncombe .... Hendersonville
Hertford   B1   1759   23   1790-80   Bertie, Chowan, Northampton .. Winton
(Register of Deeds has b, d, bur rec 1913, m rec 1884; CH burned 1832-1862)
Hoke   C2   1911   16   Cumberland, Robeson .... Raeford
(Register of Deeds has b, m, d, bur rec from 1911; Clk of Sup Ct has div, pro,
civ ct rec from 1911)
Hyde   A2   1712   6   1790-80   Wickham, Prec. Bath Co. ... Swanquarter
Iredell   E2   1788   63   1790-80   Rowan .... Statesville
(CH burned 1854)
Jackson   F2   1851   18   1860-80   Haywood, Macon .... Sylva
Johnston   C2   1746   63   1790-80   Craven .... Smithfield
Jones   B2   1778   11   1790-80   Craven .... Trenton
(CH burned 1862)
Lee   C2   1907   27   Chatham, Harnett, Moore ..... Sanford
Lenoir   B2   1791   55   1800-80   Dobbs .... Kinston
(Clk of Sup Ct has div, pro, civ ct rec from 1880; CH burned 1878)
Lincoln   E2   1779   29   1790-80   Tryon .... Lincolnton
Macon   F2   1828   15   1830-80   Haywood .... Franklin
Madison   F2   1851   17   1860-80   Buncombe, Yancey .... Marshall
Martin   B2   1774   27   1790-80   Halifax, Tyrrell .... Willamston
(Clk of Sup Ct has div & civ ct rec 1885, wills 1774; CH burned 1884; 1820 census
missing)
McDowell   F2   1842   27   1850-80   Burke, Rutherford .... Marion
Mecklenburg   E2   1762 272   1790-80   Anson .... Charlotte
Mitchell   F1   1861   14   1870-80   Burke, Caldwell, McDowell,
                                         Watauga .... Bakersville
Montgomery   D2   1779   18   1790-80   Anson .... Troy
(CH burned 1835; 1820 census missing)
Moore   D2   1784   37   1790-80   Cumberland, Hoke .... Carthage
(CH burned 1889)
Nash   C1   1777   61   1790-80   Edgecombe .... Nashville
New Hanover   C3   1729   72   1790-80   Preceding Bath .... Wilmington
(CH burned 1798-1819; 1810 census missing)
Northampton   B1   1741   27   1790-80   Bertie .... Jackson
(Clk of Sup Ct has div rec from 1800, pro rec & civ ct rec from 1761)
Onslow   B2   1734   83   1790-80   Preceding Bath .... Jacksonville
Orange   C1   1752   43   1800-80   Bladen, Granville, Johnston ... Hillsboro
(CH burned 1789)
Pamlico   B2   1872   10   1880   Beaufort, Craven .... Bayboro
(Register of Deeds has b & d rec from 1913, m rec from 1872; Clk of Sup Ct has
div, pro, civ ct rec from 1872)
Pasquotank   B1   1670   26   1790-80   Prec. Albemarle .... Elizabeth City
(CH burned 1862)
Pender   B3   1875   19   1880   New Hanover .... Burgaw
Perquimans   B1   1670   9   1790-80   Prec. Albermarle .... Hertford
Person   C1   1791   26   1800-80   Caswell .... Roxboro
Pitt   B2   1760   70   1790-80   Beaufort .... Greenville
(CH burned 1857)
Polk   F2   1855   11   1860-80   Henderson, Rutherford .... Columbus
Randolph   D2   1779   61   1790-80   Guilford .... Asheboro
(1820 census missing)
Richmond   D2   1779   39   1790-80   Anson .... Rockingham
Robeson   C3   1787   89   1790-80   Bladen .... Lumberton
(Co Clk has b & d rec from 1913, m rec from 1868, div & civ ct rec from 1870)

Rockingham D1 1785ʹ 70 1790-80 Guilford .... Wentworth
(CH burned 1906)
Rowan   D2 1753 83 1790-80 Anson .... Salisbury
Rutherford E2 1779 45 1790-80 Burke, Tyron .... Rutherfordton
(Clk of Sup Ct has wills from 1790; CH burned 1857)
Sampson   C2 1784 48 1790-80 Duplin, New Hanover .... Clinton
(CH burned 1921)
Scotland   D2 1899 25   Richmond .... Laurinburg
(Register of Deeds has b rec from 1913, m, d, bur rec from 1899; Clk of Sup Ct
has div, pro, civ ct rec from 1899)
Stanly   D2 1841 41 1850-80 Montgomery .... Albemarle
Stokes   D1 1798 22 1800-80 Surry .... Danbury
Surry   E1 1771 48 1790-80 Rowan .... Dobson
Swain   G2 1871   8 1880   Jackson, Macon .... Bryson City
(Register of Deeds has b & d rec 1913, m rec 1907; Clk of Sup Ct has div, civ
ct rec from 1900)
Transylvania F2 1861 16 1870-80 Henderson, Jackson .... Brevard
Tryon   1768   Discontinued 1779. See Lincoln)
Tyrrell   A1 1729   5 1790-80 Prec. Albemarle .... Columbia
(Register of Deeds has b & d rec from 1914, m rec from 1868)
Union   D2 1842 45 1850-80 Anson Mecklenburg .... Monroe
Vance   C1 1881 32   Franklin, Granville, Warren .. Henderson
Wake   C2 1771 169 1790-80 Cumberland, Johnston, Orange .. Raleigh
(1810 and 1820 census missing)
Warren   C1 1779 20 1790-80 Bute, Discontinued 1779 ... Warrenton
(Clk of Sup Ct has pro rec from 1776, civ ct rec from 1864)
Washington B2 1779 13 1790-80 Tyrrell .... Plymouth
(CH burned 1862-1869-1873)
Watauga   E1 1849 18 1850-80 Ashe, Caldwell, Wilkes, Yancey .. Boone
(Register of Deeds has b & d rec from 1914, m rec from 1872; Clk of Sup Ct has
div, pro, civ ct rec from 1872)
Wayne   C2 1779 82 1790-80 Craven, Dobbs .... Goldsboro
Wilkes   E1 1777 45 1790-80 Burke, Surry .... Wilkesboro
Wilson   C2 1855 58 1860-80 Edgecombe, Johnston, Nash, Wayne . Wilson
Yadkin   E1 1850 23 1860-80 Surry .... Yadkinville
Yancey   F2 1833 14 1840-80 Buncombe, Burke .... Burnsville
(Register of Deeds has b & d rec from 1913, m rec from 1833; Clk of Sup Ct has
div, pro, civ ct rec from 1833)

North Dakota

Capital Bismarck - Territory 1861 - State 1889 - (39th)

Many Indian tribes roamed the Dakota plains when the white man began to build the mid-section of the American continent. Although explorers had visited the section off and on since the early 1700s, it was not until 1851 that the region was thrown open for settlement.

The first settlers were attracted there by the highly productive Red River district soil. That river is the boundary line between North Dakota and Minnesota. Some hardy Scotch pioneers arrived as early as 1812 in Pembina. Farm folks from the northern European countries, especially from Norway, came there in large numbers in the mid 1800s. In the early days of the section, bloody skirmishes between the Redmen and the settlers were common place occurances.

The Dakota Territory was organized in 1861. It embraced the two Dakotas and Montana and Wyoming. In 1864 the Wyoming and Montana parts of the territory were formed into a separate section as the Montana Territory. The remaining Dakota Territory was divided about equally, north and south, into North Dakota and South Dakota about 1873. In 1889 North Dakota became the thirty-ninth state in the Union.

It was the vision of homes and fertile acres, big barns and cattle, that drew the poor peasants of northern and middle Europe to North Dakota. From Norway they came in the largest numbers, scattering all over the state. They were accompanied by large groups of Swedes, Danes and Icelanders, while numbers of Czechs, Poles and Dutch also came at that time. Previously

French-Canadians came down from the north following the Red River. Many Germans and other Europeans settled around Bismarck and the south-central counties indicated by the many German place names in that area, like Leipzig, Strassburg, and Danzig.

Genealogical records are difficult to obtain in North Dakota. Some birth and death records are obtainable from the county offices. But in general they must come from the office of the State Registrar of Vital Statistics, Bismarck, N. D. Marriage records are also on file there, but may also be secured from the Judge of the county in which the ceremony was performed, or from the Clerks of the District Courts who have charge of Civil Court, divorce and Probate matters and may also have the above mentioned birth and death records.

The Register of deeds has charge of deeds and land titles.

North Dakota Libraries - Bismarck, (Burleigh), State Library, (North Dakota lore); Fargo, (Cass, Public Library; North Dakota Agricultural College Library; Grand Forks, (Grand Forks), University of North Dakota Library, (North Dakota and Scandinavian lore); Minot, (Ward), Public Library; North Dakota State Teachers College Library.

North Dakota County Histories

(Population figures to nearest thousand. 1950 Census)

Name	Map Index	Date Formed	Pop. By M	Census Reports Available	Parent County	County Seat
Adams	C2	1907	4		Hettinger	Hettinger
Barnes	B4	1875	17	1880	Cass	Valley City
Benson	B4	1883	9		Ramsey	Minnewaukan
Billings	B1	1879	2	1880	Unorganized Territory	Medora
Bottineau	A3	1873	11	1884	Unorganized Territory	Bottineau
Bowman	C1	1883	4		Billings	Bowman
Buffalo				1880	Disorganized 1873	

(See Burleigh, Kidder, Logan, McHenry, Rolette, & Sheridan.)

Name	Map Index	Date Formed	Pop. By M	Census Reports Available	Parent County	County Seat
Burke	A2	1910	6		Ward	Bowbells
Burleigh	B3	1873	34	1880	Buffalo – discontinued	Bismarck
Cass	B5	1873	67	1880	Original county	Fargo
Cavalier	A4	1873	10		Pembina	Langdon

(Clk of Ct has m, pro, civ ct rec from 1881, div rec from 1888)

County Map of North Dakota

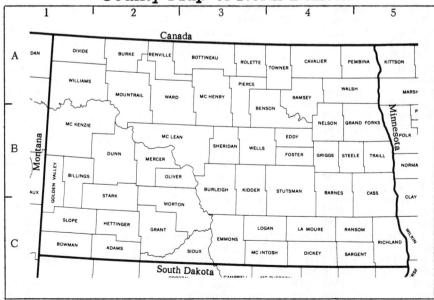

Dickey	C4	1881	8		Lamoure .... Ellendale
Divide	A1	1910	6		Williams .... Crosby

(Clk of Dist Ct has m, div, pro, civ ct rec from 1910)

Dunn	B2	1883	6		Howard – discontinued ..... Manning
Eddy	B4	1885	5		Foster .... New Rockford
Emmons	C3	1879	8	1880	Unorganized Territory .... Linton
Foster	B4	1873	5	1880	Pembina .... Carrington

(Clk of Ct has b, d, bur rec from 1900, m, div, pro, civ ct rec from 1884)

Golden Valley	B1	1912	3		Billings .... Beach
Grand Forks	B5	1873	49	1880	Pembina .... Grand Forks

(Clk of Dist Ct has b & d rec from 1908, div & civ ct rec from 1878; Co Judge has m rec from 1887, pro rec from 1880)

Grant	C2	1916	6		Morton .... Carson
Griggs	B4	1881	5		Foster .... Cooperstown

(Clk of Dist Ct has b rec from 1881, d rec from 1904, div & civ ct rec from 1887)

Hettinger	C2	1883	6		Stark .... Mott
Kidder	B3	1873	5	1880	Buffalo .... Steele
LaMoure	C4	1873	9	1880	Pembina .... La Moure
Logan	C4	1873	5		Buffalo .... Napoleon
McHenry	A3	1873	11		Buffalo .... Towner
McIntosh	C4	1883	7		Logan .... Ashley
McKenzie	B1	1883	7		Howard .... Watford City
McLean	B2	1883	14		Stevens .... Washburn
Mercer	B2	1875	7		Original county .... Stanton

(Clk of Dist Ct has m, div, pro, civ ct rec from 1908)

Morton	C2	1878	21	1880	Original county .... Mandan

(Clk of Dist Ct has div & civ ct rec 1880, pro rec 1890; Co Judge has m rec 1890)

Mountrail	A2	1909	10	1880	Ward .... Stanley

(Old Mountrail formed 1873, annexed to Ward in 1891)

Nelson	B4	1883	7		Foster, Grand Forks .... Lakota
Oliver	A2	1885	3		Mercer .... Center
Pembina	A5	1867	13	1880	Indian Lands .... Cavalier

(Clk of Ct has b rec from 1893, m rec from 1872, d rec from 1903, div rec from 1889, pro rec from 1875, civ ct rec from 1883)

Pierce	A3	1887	7		De Smet .... Rugby
Ramsey	A4	1873	13	1880	Pembina .... Devils Lake
Ransom	C5	1873	8	1880	Pembina .... Lisbon

(Clk of Dist Ct has b rec from 1893, m rec from 1882, d rec from 1883, div rec from 1885, pro rec from 1881, civ ct rec from 1891)

Renville	A2	1873	5		Deuel, Pembina .... Mohall

(Co Judge has m & pro rec from 1910; Clk of Dist Ct has div & civ ct rec from 1910) (Co Clk says it was formed from Ward 1910)

Richland	C5	1873	19	1880	Original county .... Wahpeton
Rolette	A3	1873	11		Buffalo .... Rolla
Sargent	C5	1883	7		Ransom .... Forman

(Co Judge has m rec 1887, pro rec 1901; Clk of Dist Ct has div & civ ct rec 1901)

Sheridan	B3	1873	4		Buffalo .... McClusky

(Co Clk has b, m, d, bur, div, pro, civ ct rec from 1909)

Sioux	C3	1914	4		Standing Rock Reservation ... Fort Yates
Slope	C1	1915	2		Billings .... Amidon
Stark	B2	1879	18		Unorganized Territory ...... Dickinson
Steele	B5	1883	5		Grand Forks .... Finley

(Clk of Dist Ct has b & d rec 1894 to 1896, 1900 to 1901, div & civ ct rec 1886; Co Judge has m rec from 1883, pro rec from 1886)

Stutsman	B4	1873	25	1880	Pembina .... Jamestown
Towner	A4	1885	6		Rolette .... Cando

(Co Clk has m rec from 1885, div rec from 1890, pro & civ ct rec from 1888)

Traill	B5	1875	11	1880	Grand Forks .... Hillsboro

(Clk of Dist Ct has b rec from 1910, m rec from 1887, d rec from 1907, bur rec from 1915, div rec from 1890, pro rec from 1882)

Walsh	A4	1881	18		Grand Forks .... Grafton
Ward	A2	1885	47		Renville .... Minot

| Wells | B3 | 1881 | 9 | Sheridan | . . . . | Fessenden |
| Williams | A1 | 1890 | 22 | Mountrail | . . . . | Williston |

Genealogists' Check List of the Historical Records Survey, N. Dak. (see page VIII)
Fed Cts; Inv of Co Arch - Golden Valley, raphy of Theses Prepared at the Univ of
Mercer, Williams; Guide to Pub Vit Stat N D; Abstract and Check List of Statutory
Rec; Guide to Chr Vita Stat Rec; Bibliog- Req for Co Rec; Depo of unpubl mat, State
Lib Commission, Bismark, So Dak.

Ohio

Capital Columbus - State 1803 - (17th)

Prior to the mid-1700s the established American communities were located east of the Alleghenies along the Atlantic Coast. The constantly increasing population was ever on the alert for the best available land at the lowest possible cost. The presence of numerous Indian tribes prevented the land-longing immigrants from going too far away from the colonies established along the Atlantic sea coast.

For a long time the French and the British had quarrelled over the ownership between the Ohio River and Canada. After France had rescinded all claims to the territory and had transferred jurisdiction of the area to Britain, the United States claimed possession by virtue of its victory over the British in the Revolutionary War.

The idea then prevailed for a time that the boundary lines of the original colonies would be extended westward to include the newly acquired territory. After the creation of the Northwest Territory in 1787 that idea was discarded. Instead the central government decided the land should be used as bounty for the soldiers in the Revolutionary War and it was opened for settlement through the Ordinance of 1787 establishing the Northwest Territory.

Within sixty-one years five full states and part of a sixth had been created and admitted into the union from the Northwest Territory.

Massachusetts and Connecticut not-too-ardent Puritans formed the Ohio Company which purchased about a million acres of land for two-thirds of a dollar per acre, including what afterwards became Washington, Noble, Morgan, Athens, Meigs, and Gallia counties.

Known as the Viriginia Military Bounty, about four and a quarter million acres were set aside between the Scioto and the Little Miami Rivers for settlement by Virginians and Kentuckians about 1800.

The Chillicote section in Ross county attracted many impatient and unrestrained Kentuckians and Tennesians.

Sometime later two other districts were thrown open to settlers. The first of these movements brought large groups of Scotch-Irish, Germans and Quakers from the neighboring Pennsylvania, across the Ohio to the section from which later were created Columbiana, Carroll, Jefferson, Harrison, Belmont, and Monroe counties.

The second of these migrations brought settlers from New Jersey floating down the Ohio and settling the area between the two Miami Rivers, the Little and the Big. They and some Scotch-Irish and Dutch began the cultivation of some 300,000 acres in that southwestern corner of Ohio. Cincinnati became an important part of that colonization.

After General Anthony Wayne and his United States' forces had driven the hostile Indian tribes westward from the Lake Erie section in 1794, another four million acre tract, known as the Western Reserve, was opened for settlement in the northeast corner of Ohio, along Lake Erie. It was settled mainly by former Connecticut residents. Closely allied with that project was the settlement of the half-a-million acres in what became the Erie and the Huron county just south of Lake Erie. The settlers of that tract were also former Connecticut residents whose holdings had been burned out by the British during the Revolutionary War. For that reason that section was often referred to as "the Fire Lands."

The "Refugee Tract" was set aside by congress for Canadians who had aided the American cause of the Revolution and had lost their lands in Canada. It was a tract 4 1/2 miles wide (N & S) and extended eastward from the Scioto River to near the Muskingum River. It was in the proximity of Franklin, Licking and Perry counties. It was created 1801, effective 1802.

After 1815 the large north-western section of the state was thrown open to settlers who flocked there from east and south. The opening of the Erie Canal in 1825 brought more settlers along that route from the north-eastern states.

In 1799 Ohio was organized as a territory included in which was the Indiana Section. The very next year, Indiana was organized as a Territory, and in 1803 Ohio became a state, the seventeenth in the Union.

Birth and death records before 1909 are in the custody of the Clerks of the Probate Court in the respective counties and in the offices of the City Board of Health. From 1909 to the present the records are in the charge of the Department of Health, Columbus, Ohio.

Marriage records and licenses are on file in each county office of the Clerk of the Probate Court, where are also records of wills and real estate matters.

Each County Recorder has charge of land records within the county.

Much genealogical information is obtainable in the following libraries:

Akron, (Summit); Public Library, 11 Summit St.; Canton, (Stark), Public Library Association, 326 Third St., S. W.; Cincinnati, (Hamilton), Chamber of Commerce Library, (historical collections); Public Library, 8th and Vine Streets,

(Ohio Valley history and genealogy); Circleville, (Pickaway), Pickaway County District Public Library, Main St., (Ohio history and genealogical collections); Cleveland, (Cuyahoga), City Public Library, 325 Superior Ave., (Ohio lore); County Public Library, 1150 W. Third St.; Western Reserve Historical Society Library, 10825 East Blvd.; Columbus, (Franklin), Public Library, 96 Grant Ave.; Ohioana Library; Ohio State Archaeological & Historical Society Library; State Library, State Office Bldg.; Dayton, (Montgomery), Public Library, 215 E. Third St., (Dayton and Miama Valley collections); Delaware, (Delaware), Ohio Wesleyan University, (Ohio Methodists Historical Society); Oxford, (Butler, Miami University Library, (Ohio Valley history); Portsmouth, (Scioto), Public Library. (old Northwest Territory collections); Toledo, (Lucus), Public Library, 325 Michigan St., (Northwester Ohio history and genealogy); University of Toledo Library, 2801 West Bancroft St., (American biographies and histories); Youngstown (Mahoning), City and County Library, 305 Wick Ave., (local history and genealogy).

Ohio County Histories

(Population figures to nearest thousand - 1960 Census)

Name	Map Index	Date Formed	Pop. By M	Census Reports Available	Parent County	County Seat
Adams	D2	1797	20	1820-80	1 of 4 Original counties . . .	West Union
Allen	B1	1820	104	1830-80	Mercer, Indian Terr.	Lima
(Pro Ct has b & d rec 1867, m rec 1831; Clk of Cts has div & civ ct rec 1831)
Ashland	B3	1846	39	1850-80	Wayne, Richland, Huron , Lorain .	Ashland
Ashtabula	A4	1807	93	1820-80	Trumbull, Geauga	Jefferson
Athens	C3	1805	47	1820-80	Washington	Athens
Auglaize	B1	1848	36	1850-80	Allen, Logan, Darke, Shelby, Mercer, Van Wert	Wapakoneta
(Clk of Cts has div, pro, civ ct rec from 1848)
Belmont	C4	1801	84	1820-80	Jefferson, Washington . . .	St. Clairsville
Brown	D2	1817	25	1820-80	Adams, Clermont	Georgetown
Butler	C1	1803	199	1820-80	Hamilton	Hamilton
Carroll	B4	1832	21	1840-80	Columbiana, Stark, Harrison, Jefferson, Tuscarawas . . .	Carrollton
Champaign	C2	1805	30	1820-80	Greene, Franklin	Urbana
Clark	C2	1817	131	1820-80	Champaign, Madison, Greene ..	Springfield
Clermont	D2	1800	81	1820-80	Original county . . . . , .	Batavia
Clinton	C2	1810	30	1820-80	Highland	Wilmington
Columbiana	B4	1803	107	1820-80	Jefferson, Washington	Lisbon
Coshocton	B3	1811	32	1820-80	Muskingum	Coshocton
Crawford	B2	1820	47	1830-80	Old Indian Territory	Bucyrus
Cuyahoga	A3	1810	1648	1820-80	Geauga	Cleveland
Darke	C1	1809	46	1820-80	Miami	Greenville
Defiance	A1	1845	32	1850-80	Williams, Henry, Paulding . .	Defiance
(Clk of Cts has div & civ ct rec from 1845; General Health Dist has d & bur rec; Pro Ct has b & m rec from 1845)

Delaware   B2   1808   36   1820–80   Franklin . . . .   Delaware
(Chancery Ct has div and civ ct rec from 1825)
Erie   A3   1838   68   1840–80   Huron, Sandusky . . . .   Sandusky
Fairfield   C3   1800   64   1820–80   Franklin . . . .   Lancaster
(Clk of Cts has civ ct rec from 1813)
Fayette   C2   1810   25   1820–80   Ross, Highland . . . . . .   Washington C. H.
Franklin   C2   1803 683   1830–80   Ross . . . .   Columbus
(Clk of Cts has div rec from 1803)
Fulton   A2   1850   29   1850–80   Lucas, Henry, Williams . . . . .   Wauseon
Gallia   D3   1803   26   1820–80   Washington . . . .   Gallipolis
Geauga   A3   1805   48   1820–80   Trumbull . . . .   Chardon
(Clk of Cts has div, civ ct rec from 1806, naturalization rec from 1908)
Greene   C2   1803   95   1820–80   Hamilton, Ross . . . .   Xenia
(Pro Ct has b rec 1869 to 1908, pro & m rec 1803; Clk of Cts has div, civ ct,
criminal rec 1802; Recorder has deeds & plat maps 1803; Auditor has tax rec 1803)
Guernsey   C3   1810   39   1820–80   Belmont . . . .   Cambridge
(Clk of Cts has div rec from 1850, civ ct rec from 1810)
Hamilton   D1   1790 864   1820–80   1 of 4 Original counties . . . .   Cincinnati
Hancock   B2   1818   54   1830–80   Wood, Indian Lands . . . .   Findlay
Hardin   B2   1820   30   1820–80   Indian Lands . . . .   Kenton
Harrison   B4   1814   18   1820–80   Jefferson, Tuscarawas . . . .   Cadiz
Henry   A2   1820   25   1830–80   Wood . . . .   Napoleon
Highland   D2   1805   30   1820–80   Ross, Adams, Clermont . . . . .   Hillsboro
Hocking   C3   1818   20   1820–80   Athens, Ross, Fairfield . . . . . .   Logan
Holmes   B3   1824   22   1830–80   Coshocton, Wayne,
                                        Tuscarawas . . . .   Millersburg
Huron   B3   1809   47   1820–80   Indian Lands (Firelands) . . . .   Norwalk
Jackson   D3   1816   29   1820–80   Pike . . . .   Jackson
Jefferson   B4   1797   99   1820–80   Original county . . . .   Steubenville

County Map of Ohio

Knox	B3	1808	39	1820-80	Fairfield . . . . Mt. Vernon

(Clk of Cts has div & civ ct rec from 1808)

Lake	A3	1840	149	1840-80	Geauga, Cuyahoga . . . . . . Painesville
Lawrence	D3	1816	55	1820-80	Gallia . . . . Ironton
Licking	C3	1808	90	1820-80	Fairfield . . . . Newark
Logan	B2	1817	35	1820-80	Champaign . . . . Bellefontaine

(Pro Ct has b & div rec from 1865; Co Recorder has deeds & mtgs from 1818; Histories, Logan Co Dist Library)

Lorain	A3	1822	218	1830-80	Huron, Cuyahoga, Medina . . . . . Elyria
Lucas	A2	1835	457	1840-80	Wood . . . . Toledo
Madison	C2	1810	26	1820-80	Fayette . . . . London
Mahoning	B4	1846	300	1850-80	Columbiana, Trumbull . . . . Youngstown
Marion	B2	1824	60	1830-80	Crawford . . . . Marion
Medina	B3	1812	65	1820-80	Portage . . . . Medina
Meigs	D3	1819	22	1820-80	Gallia, Athens . . . . Pomeroy
Mercer	B1	1820	33	1820-80	Darke . . . . Celina

(Pro Ct has b & d rec 1867 to 1908, m rec from 1830, pro rec from 1829; Clk of Cts has div & civ ct rec from 1824)

Miami	C1	1807	73	1820-80	Montgomery . . . . Troy

(Clk of Cts has div & civ ct rec from 1807)

Monroe	B4	1813	15	1820-80	Belmont, Wash., Guernsey . . Woodsfield
Montgomery	C1	1803	527	1820-80	Hamilton, Ross . . . . Dayton
Morgan	C3	1818	13	1820-80	Washington . . . . McConnelsville
Morrow	B2	1848	19	1850-80	Knox, Marion, Delaware, Richland . . . . Mt. Gilead
Muskingum	C3	1804	79	1820-80	Washington, Fairfield . . . . Zanesville

(Clk of Co Commissioners has div & civ ct rec from 1847)

Noble	C3	1851	11	1860-80	Monroe, Washington, Morgan, Guernsey . . . . Caldwell
Ottawa	A2	1840	35	1840-80	Erie, Sandusky, Lucas . . . . Port Clinton
Paulding	B1	1820	17	1830-80	Indian Lands . . . . Paulding
Perry	C3	1817	28	1820-80	Washington, Fairfield, Muskingum . . . . New Lexington
Pickaway	C2	1810	36	1820-80	Ross, Fairfield, Franklin . . . Circleville
Pike	D2	1815	19	1820-80	Ross, Highland, Scioto, Adams .. Waverly
Portage	B3	1807	92	1820-80	Trumbull . . . . Ravenna

(Clk of Cts has div & civ ct rec from 1820)

Preble	C1	1808	32	1820-80	Montgomery, Butler . . . . Eaton
Putnam	B1	1820	28	1830-80	Old Indian Territory . . . . Ottawa
Richland	B3	1813	118	1820-80	Knox . . . . Mansfield
Ross	C2	1798	61	1820-80	6th Co. from N.W. Terr. . . . Chillicothe
Sandusky	A2	1820	56	1820-80	Huron . . . . Fremont
Scioto	D2	1803	84	1820-80	Adams, Washington . . . . . . Portsmouth
Seneca	B2	1824	59	1830-80	Wayne, Franklin, Delaware . . . . Tiffin
Shelby	B1	1819	34	1820-80	Miami . . . . Sidney

(Clk of Cts has civ ct rec from 1819)

Stark	B3	1809	340	1820-80	Old Indian Lands . . . . Canton
Summit	B3	1840	514	1840-80	Portage, Medina, Stark . . . . . . Akron
Trumbull	A4	1800	209	1820-80	Jefferson, Western Reserve . . . Warren
Tuscarawas	B3	1808	77	1820-80	Jefferson, Muskingum . . New Philadelphia
Union	B2	1820	23	1820-80	Franklin, Madison, Logan, Delaware . . . . Marysville
Van Wert	B1	1820	29	1830-80	Indian Territory . . . . Van Wert
Vinton	C3	1850	10	1850-80	Gallia, Athens, Ross, Jackson, Hocking . . . . McArthur
Warren	C1	1803	66	1820-80	Hamilton . . . . Lebanon
Washington	C3	1788	52	1820-80	Original county . . . . Marietta

(Clk of Cts has div & civ ct rec from 1795)

Wayne	B3	1796	75	1820-80	Original county . . . . Wooster
Williams	A1	1820	30	1830-80	Henry . . . . Bryan
Wood	A2	1820	73	1830-80	Indian Lands . . . . Bowling Green
Wyandot	B2	1845	22	1850-80	Marion, Crawford, Hardin, Hancock . . . . Upper Sandusky

Genealogists' Check List of the Historical Records Survey, Ohio (see page VIII)

Fed Cts; Inv of Co Arch – Adams, Allen, Ashland, Athens, Belmont, Brown, Columbiana, Cuyahoga, Fayette, Franklin, Geauga, Hamilton, Hancock, Jackson, Knox, Lake, Lorain, Lucas, Madison, Montgomery, Pike, Ross, Scioto, Seneca, Stark, Summit, Trumbull, Washington; Inv of Mun & Tn Arch – Cleveland, Also Rec of Cuyahoga Co Mun other than Cleveland.

RC Chr Par of the Diocese of Cleveland; Inv of the Chr Arch of W Va – Preliminary Bibliograph of Mat Relating to Chrs in W Va, Va, Ky and Southern Ohio.

Cal of the Joshua Reed Giddings Mss in the Lib of the Ohio State Archaeological and Hist Soc, Columbus, Ohio; A Check List of Ohio Imprints Prior to 1820; Hist Sites of Cleveland Hotels and Taverns; Depo of unpubl mat – Western Reserve Hist Soc, Cleveland, Ohio (Historic sites material); Hayes Memorial Lib, Freemont, Ohio (Bibliographical mat); Ohio State Archaelogical & Hist Soc, Columbus, Ohio (All other mat.)

Oklahoma
Capital Oklahoma City
Territory 1890 - State 1907 - (46th)

"Westward" for the red man ended with Oklahoma when it became the last gathering place of the displaced Indian. Here the Indian gave up the nomadic existance of his forefathers and accepted the white man's mode of living.

Little significance attaches to the fact that Spanish and French explorers, in search of the proverbial pot of gold at the end of the rainbow, traversed the Oklahoma section time and again from 1590.

While the territory was still dedicated for the use of the Indians, white settlers came there in such hordes to secure land that eventually they had to be driven away by United States soldiers. The clamor for more land became so vociferous that the government purchased from the Indians about two million acres in the section adjacent to Logan and Oklahoma counties.

During the influx of new settlers, Illinois Iowa and Kansas farmers seemed to favor the western and the northwestern sections of the state, while those from Arkansas, Missouri and Texas preferred the southern and the eastern parts of the state.

After Oklahoma became part of the United States with the Louisiana Purchase in 1803, it was included in the Indiana Territory. In 1812 it was combined with the Missouri Territory, and in 1819 with the Arkansas Territory. For several years, most of Oklahoma was included in what was called the Indian Territory, which continued until about 1893 when the section was divided into the Indian Territory and the Oklahoma Territory, the latter being thrown open to white settlements.

In 1890 the Territorial Government was established with Guthrie as its first capital. 1891 saw two new counties formed and in 1892 six more were formed. The Chero-

kee Outlet in the northwest section of the state, next to the panhandle, was opened for white settlers in 1893. A court decision and an act of congress awarded Greer County to Oklahoma in 1896. Prior to that time it had been claimed by both Oklahoma and Texas. In 1906 Congress passed the enabling act. Oklahoma became the forty-sixth state to enter the Union when it was admitted November 16, 1907. The capital was moved from Guthrie to Oklahoma City in 1910.

The first seven counties of the Oklahoma Territory were designated First, Second, Third, Fourth, Fifth, Sixth and Seventh, thereafter as other counties were added they were named after the letters of the alphabet. Later on by vote of the people they were given their present names. The original seven counties took the following names when this change was accomplished: Logan, Cleveland, Oklahoma, Canadian, Kingfisher, Payne and Beaver.

Birth and death records since 1908 are obtainable at the Department of Health, Division of Vital Statistics, Oklahoma City, Okla.

Marriage records may be obtained from the respective County Court Clerks, who also have supervision of all court and land records.

Books which might help you:

Johnson, Roy M., "Oklahoma South of the Canadian." Historical and biographical. Published by S. J. Clarke Publishing Co., Chicago, 1925. Three Vols.

Oklahoma libraries – Muskogee, (Muskogee) Public Library; Oklahoma, (Oklahoma), City Public Library, NW at Robinson; Oklahoma Historical Society Library, Historical Bldg., (historical and genealogical collections); State Library, 109 State Capital, (biography, genealogy); Tulsa, (Tulsa), Public Library, 220 South Cheyenne Ave., (Tulsa and Okla. histories).

We are indebted to Mrs. Merlyn Houck, Rt. 2, Stillwater, Okla. for information on the organization of counties of Oklahoma. In checking it with the information found in the 1953 Handy Book for Genealogists we noted considerable discord. A further check was made with other sources and these sometimes confirmed either one or the other and in some cases gave still different data. In the Oklahoma County Histories which follow you will find printed in parenthesis the data furnished by Mrs. Houck which does not coincide with that found in the 1953 Handy Book for Genealogists. In each case the information from Mrs. Houck is under the data in question.

Some additional light on the information of counties in Oklahoma has been forwarded by Sam M. Myers, Box 306, Stillwater, Okla., who writes as follows:

"All of Oklahoma except the extreme southwestern tip (Greer County) and No Man's Land and possibly the Unassigned Lands were Indian Territory until April 22, 1889. On this date the Unassigned Lands were thrown open for settlement in 'Run of 89'. Out of this 2,000,000 acres were formed Logan, Oklahoma, Cleveland, Canadian, Kingfisher and Payne counties by Act of May 2, 1890 when Oklahoma Territory was authorized and at the same time Beaver County (No Man's Land) was made a part of it.

"The Iowa, Sac, Fox, and Pottawatomie, Shawnee Reservations were opened to form Lincoln and Pottawatomie Counties in the 'Run of 1891.'

"In 1892 the Cheyenne & Arapho Lands were opened and Day, Roger Mills, Beckham, Dewey, Custer, Washita and Blain Counties were Organized out of it.

"The 'Strip' (Cherokee Outlet) opened in the 'Run of 1893,' to form Woodward,

Woods, Grant, Garfield, Kay, Noble and Pawnee Counties. In 1901 the Whichita-Caddo and Comanche, Kiowa and Apache Lands were opened and formed the Counties of Caddo, Kiowa and Comanche.

"Generally this is the way things remained until 1907 when Oklahoma was admitted as the 46th state. When this happened there were some readjustments of county bounderies or new counties were added by carving them out of existing counties. In the case of Day County it no longer existed after statehood. A part of it and a part of Woodward County formed the new Ellis County. Roger Mills was formed out of a part of Beckham (and perhaps a part of Day). Woodward and Woods were reduced in area to form Harper, Alfalfa and Major. Out of a part of Comanche, Cotton County was formed also the Jackson County was formed out of Greer (In 1908 or 1909 Harmon County was also formed out of Greer).

In that part of Oklahoma which had been as Indian Territory, before statehood called the 'Indian Nations,' only the Osage and Seminole Nations were designated single counties of the same name. The other four Indian Nations were carved into the following counties:

CHEROKEE NATION: Washington, Rogers, Nowata, Craig, Mayes, Cherokee, Sequoyah, Adair, Delaware and part of Ottawa.

CREEK NATION: Creek, Okfuskee, Hughes, McIntosh, Okmulgee, Muskogie, Wagoner and Tulsa.

CHOCTAW NATION: Bryan, Atoka, Coal, Pittsburg, Haskell, Leflore, Latimer, Pushmataha, Choctaw and McCurtain.

CHICKASAW NATION: Grady, McClain, Pontotoc, Stephens, Murray, Johnston, Marshall, Love, Jefferson and Carter.

In 1908 as previously stated Harmon County was created out of Greer and Jackson and thus were formed the 77 counties of Oklahoma as they exist today."

Oklahoma County Histories

(Population figures to nearest thousand – 1960 Census)

Name	Map Index	Date Formed	Pop. By M	Census Reports Available	Parent County	County Seat
Adair	A2	1907	13		Cherokee Lands	Stilwell
Alfalfa	D1	1907	8		Woods	Cherokee
Atoka	B3	1907	10		Choctaw Lands	Atoka
Beaver	E1	1890	7		Original county (Public Lands) ..	Beaver
Beckham	E3	1907	18		Roger Mills	Sayre
Blaine	D2	1892	12		Original county	Watonga
					(Cheyenne-Arapaho Lands)	

(Ct Clk has m, div, pro, civ ct rec from 1892)

| Bryan | B4 | 1907 | 24 | | Choctaw Lands . . . . | Durant |

Caddo	D3	1901	29	Original Lands .... (Wichita-Caddo Lands)	Anadarko

(Co Ct Clk has m, div, pro, civ ct rec from 1902)

Canadian	C2	1889	25	Original county	El Reno

(Co Ct Clk has m rec from 1890, div, pro, civ ct rec from 1900, voting rec 1909)

Carter	C4	1907	39	Chickasaw Lands	Ardmore
Cherokee	A2	1907	18	Cherokee Lands	Tahlequah
Choctaw	B4	1907	16	Choctaw Lands	Hugo
Cimarron	G1	1907	4	Beaver	Boise City
Cleveland	C3	1889	48	Unassigned Lands	Norman
Coal	B3	1907	6	Choctaw Lands	Coalgate
Comanche	D3	1901	91	Kiowa, Comanche, Apache Lands .	Lawton

(Co Ct Clk has m, div, pro, civ ct rec from 1901)

Cotton	D4	1912	8	Comanche	Walters

(Co Ct Clk has m, div, pro, civ ct rec from 1912)

Craig	B1	1907	16	Cherokee Lands	Vinita
Creek	B2	1900	40	Creek Lands	Sapulpa
Custer	D2	1892-08	21	Cheyenne, Arapaho Lands	Arapaho

(Co Clk has real-estate, deeds, mtgs & releases, Army and U. S. Service rec from 1892)

Day		1892		Cheyenne-Arapaho Lands Discontinued 1906	
Delaware	A1	1907	13	Cherokee	Jay
Dewey	D2	1892	6	Original county .... (Cheyenne-Arapaho Lands)	Taloga
Ellis	E2	1907	5	Day, Woodward	Arnett

(Co Ct Clk has m, div, pro, civ ct rec from 1910, deeds & patents from 1898)

Garfield	C2	1893	53	Originally "O" changed to Garfield 1901 (Cherokee Outlet) ...	Enid

(Co Clk has deeds & mtgs, Chattels from 1893, All service men's discharges from Spanish American War to present)

Garvin	C3	1907	28	Chickasaw Lands	Pauls Valley
Grady	C3	1907	30	Caddo, Comanche .... (Chickasaw Lands)	Chickasha
Grant	C1	1893	8	Original county .... (Cherokee Outlet)	Medford
Greer	E3	1890	9	Org. by Texas, to Okla. by court decision	Mangum

(Organized as Greer Co., Texas in 1886. An act of Congress on May 4, 1896 declared it Greer Co., Okla. A fire in 1901 destroyed the county records. Co Ct has m, div, pro, civ ct rec from 1901)

Harmon	E3	1909	6	Greer, Jackson	Hollis
Harper	E1	1907	6	Indian Lands .... (Woods County)	Buffalo
Haskell	A3	1908	9	Choctaw Lands	Stigler
Hughes	B3	1907	15	Creek Lands .... (Creek and Choctaw Lands)	Holdenville

(Co Ct Clk has m, div, pro, civ ct rec from 1907)

Jackson	E3	1907	30	Greer	Altus
Jefferson	C4	1907	8	Comanche .... (Chickasaw)	Waureka
Johnston	C3	1907	9	Chickasaw Lands	Tishomingo
Kay	C1	1895	51	Original county .... (Cherokee Outlet)	Newkirk
Kingfisher	C2	1890	11	Original county	Kingfisher
Kiowa	D3	1901	15	Original county .... (Kiowa-Comanche-Apache Lands)	Hobart
Latimer	A3	1902	8	Choctaw Lands	Wilburton
Le Flore	A3	1907	29	Choctaw Lands	Poteau
Lincoln	C2	1891	19	Original county .... (Iowa-Kickapoo-Sac-Fox Lands)	Chandler
Logan	C2	1890	19	Original county	Guthrie
Love	C4	1907	6	Chickasaw Lands	Marietta

| McClain | C3 | 1908 | 13 | Chickasaw Lands | .... | Purcell |
| McCurtain | A4 | 1907 | 32 | Choctaw Lands | .... | Ibabel |

(Co Ct Clk has m, div, pro, civ ct rec from 1907)

County Map of Oklahoma

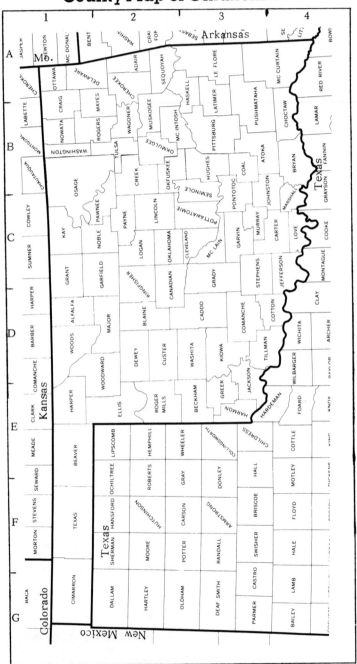

McIntosh	B2	1907	12	Indian Lands	Eufaula
				(Creek Lands)	

(Co Clk has b rec from 1911 to 1948, d rec 1911 to 1918)

Major	D2	1907	8	Woods	Fairview
Marshall	C4	1907	7	Chickasaw Lands	Madill
Mayes	B2	1907	20	Indian Lands	Pryor
				(Cherokee Lands)	
Murray	C3	1907	11	Chickasaw Lands	Sulphur
Muskogee	B2	1898	62	Creek	Muskogee
Noble	C2	1893	10	Cherokee Outlet	Perry
Nowata	B1	1907	11	Cherokee Lands	Nowata
Okfuskee	B2	1907	12	Creek Lands	Okemah
Oklahoma	C2	1890	440	Original county	Oklahoma City
Okmulgee	B2	1907	37	Creek Lands	Okmulgee
Osage	B1	1907	32	Osage Indian Lands	Pawkuska
Ottawa	A1	1907	28	Cherokee Nation	Miami
Pawnee	C2	1893	11	Cherokee Outlet	Pawnee
Payne	C2	1890	44	Original county	Stillwater
Pittsburg	B3	1907	34	Choctaw Lands	McAlester
Pontotoc	C3	1907	28	Chickasaw Lands	Ada
Pottawatomie	C3	1891	41	Original county	Shawnee
				(Pottawatomie-Shawnee Lands)	
Pushmataha	B3	1908	9	Choctaw Lands	Antlers
Roger Mills	E2	1892	5	Cheyenne-Arapaho Lands . . .	Cheyenne
Rogers	B2	1907	21	Cherokee Nation	Claremore
				(Coo-wee-Scoowee Dist)	
Seminole	B3	1907	28	Seminole Indian Lands	Wewoka
Sequoyah	A2	1907	18	Cherokee Indian Lands	Sallisaw
Stephens	C3	1907	38	Comanche County	Duncan
Texas	F1	1907	14	Beaver	Guymon
Tillman	D3	1907	15	Comanche Indian Lands	Frederick
Tulsa	B2	1905	346	Creek Lands	Tulsa
Wagoner	B2	1908	16	Creek Lands	Wagoner
Washington	B1	1897	42	Cherokee Lands	Bartlesville
Washita	D3	1900	18	Cheyenne-Arapaho Lands	Cordell
Woods	D1	1900	12	Cherokee Outlet	Alva
Woodward	D2	1893	14	Cherokee Outlet	Woodward

Genealogists' Check List of the Historical Records Survey, Oklahoma (see page VIII)

Fed Cts; Inv of Co Arch - Atoka, Beckham, Cherokee, Cimarron, Haskell, Lincoln, McIntosh, Mayes, Muskogee, Pittsburg, Pushmataha; Guide to Pub Vit Stat Rec; Inv of the Chur Arch of Okla - No. 7 Bryan Co; Preliminary List of Chrs & Rel Org in Okla; Check List of Var Rec Required by Law in Okla; Depo of unpubl mat, State Lib, Okla City, Okla.

Oregon

Capital Salem - Territory 1848 - State 1859 - (33rd)

Arguments over prior right of Spain, Russia, Great Britain, and the United States kept things in a turmoil in the Oregon country while the western section of our nation was in preparation to receive the restless, moving hordes always headed for places where opportunity beckoned the tireless, willing workers.

Simultaneously as the Mormon Pioneers were headed for the then uninviting Utah Valleys as a refuge from religious persecutions, and the gold-seekers were rushing toward California, thousands of sturdy tillers of the soil who already had broken virgin soil in three or four different states were trekking toward the northwest with the same enthusiasm as those participating in the other movements. A steady stream of these prairie schooners headed toward the Oregon country for several years was attracted by a generous offer. In 1850 the Territorial Legislature of Oregon guaranteed settlers ownership of considerable tracts of land if for four years they would live on and cultivate those farm lands. At the time there were in Oregon slightly more than 13,000 people. The attractiveness of the free land offer is evident in the four-fold increase in population during the following ten-year period. Not only did people from many sections of the United States change their residence to Oregon, but people came there from all parts of the world. Among Europeans countries whose people came there in large numbers are, in order of their numerical contributions to its citizenry, Germany, Sweden, England, Norway, Russia, Finland, Italy, Denmark, Ireland, Austria, Greece, and Czechoslovakia.

Oregon became a territory in 1848, when it also embraced all of the present Washington and Idaho. It remained so for eleven years and then in 1859 became the thirty-third state in the Union. At that time it had been shrunk to its present size.

The State Registrar, State Board of Health, 1400 SW 5th Ave., Portland, Oreg., has birth and death records since 1903 and marriage records since 1907. The County Clerks in the respective counties have marriage records since creation of county in some instances. The County Clerk also has custody of the records of wills and the administration of estates, deeds, and matters pertaining to real estate ownership.

Oregon Libraries - Eugene, (Lane), Public Library, 115 Willamette St.; University of Oregon Library, (Oregoniana and manuscripts of the Pacific Northwest); Portland, (Multnomah), Library Association of Portland, 801 SW 10th Ave.; Oregon Historical Society Library, 235 SW Market St., (newspapers and manuscripts, Pacific Northwest lore); Salem, (Marion), The Oregon State Library, State Library Bldg., (genealogy, Northwest history, Oregoniana); Oregon State Archives, (will answer requests for information on Oregonians free, based on indexes).

Oregon County Histories

(Population figures to nearest thousand - 1960 Census)

Name	Map Index	Date Formed	Pop. By M	Census Reports Available	Parent County	County Seat
Baker	A2	1862	17	1870–80	Unorganized Terr., Wasco	Baker
(Co Clk has m, div, pro, civ ct rec from 1862)						
Benton	E2	1847	39	1850–80	Polk	Corvallis
(Co Clk has m & div rec from 1850)						
Champoeg		1843			Orig. Co., (Name changed to Marion)	
Clackamas	D1	1843	113	1850–80	Original county	Oregon City
(Co Clk has m rec from 1853, div & civ ct rec from 1850, pro rec from 1844, deeds & mtgs from 1850, terr. from 1842)						
Clark		1850				
Clatsop	E1	1844	27	1850–80	Twality	Astoria
Columbia	E1	1854	22	1860–80	Washington	St. Helens
(Co Clk has m, div, pro, civ ct rec from 1854)						
Coos	F3	1853	55	1860–80	Umpqua, Jackson	Coquille
(Co Clk has m rec from 1864, div, pro, civ ct rec from 1853)						
Crook	C2	1882	9		Wasco	Prineville
Curry	F4	1855	14	1860–80	Coos	Gold Beach
Deschutes	D3	1916	23		Crook	Bend
Douglas	E3	1852	68	1860–80	Umpqua 1852 & 1862	Roseburg
(Co Clk has m, div, pro, civ ct rec from 1852)						
Gilliam	C1	1885	3		Wasco, Morrow	Condon
Grant	B2	1864	8	1870	Wasco, Umatilla	Canyon City
(Co Clk has m, bur, div, pro, civ ct rec from 1864)						
Harney	B3	1889	7		Grant	Burns
(Co Clk has m, div, pro, cir ct rec from 1889)						
Hood River	D1	1908	13		Wasco	Hood River
(Co Clk hasm, div, pro, civ ct rec from 1908)						
Jackson	E4	1852	74	1860–80	Umpqua	Medford
(Co Clk has m rec from 1855, div & civ ct rec from 1861, pro rec from 1874, deeds, mtgs, mining rec from 1854)						
Jefferson	D2	1914	7		Crook	Madras
(Co Clk has m, div, pro, civ ct rec from 1915)						
Josephine	E4	1856	30	1860–80	Jackson	Grants Pass
(Co Clk has m, civ ct, crim ct rec from 1867, div & pro rec from 1868)						

Klamath   D4   1882   47   West part of Lake Co. ... Klamath Falls
Lake   C4   1874   7   1880   Jackson, Wasco .... Lakeview
  (Co Clk has m, div, pro, civ ct rec from 1874)
Lane   E3   1851 163 1860-80 Linn, Umpqua .... Eugene
Lewis   1850
Lincoln   E2   1893   25   Benton, Polk .... Newport
  (Co Clk has m, div, pro, civ ct rec from 1893)
Linn   E2   1847   59   1850-80 Champoeg .... Albany
  (Co Clk has m rec from 1850, div, pro, civ ct rec from 1854)
Malheur   A3   1887   23   Baker .... Vale
  (Co Clk has m, div, pro, civ ct rec from 1887)
Marion   E2   1843 121 1850-80 Orig. Co. Name changed from
  (Co Clk has m rec from 1847)   Champoeg .... Salem

County Map of Oregon

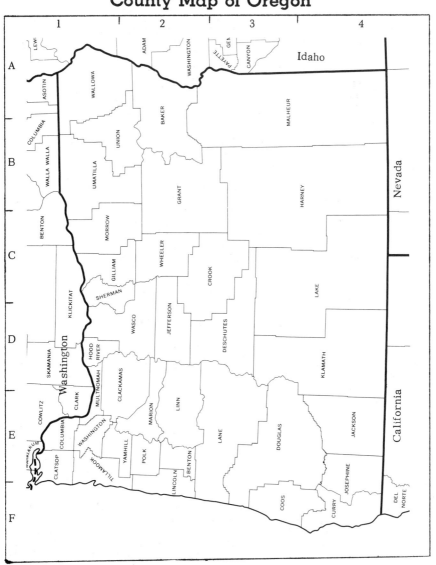

Morrow   D1   1865   5   1870-80   Umatilla, Wasco . . . . Heppner
(Co Clk has m, div, civ ct rec from 1885)
Multnomah   E1   1854   523 1860-80   Washington, Clackamas . . . . Portland
Polk   E2   1845   27 1850-80   Yamhill . . . . Dallas
(Co Clk has m rec from 1850, div & pro rec from 1898)
Sherman   C1   1889   2   Wasco . . . . Moro
(Co Clk has b, m, d, div, pro, civ ct rec from 1889)
Tillamook   E1   1853   19 1860-80   Clatsop, Polk, Yamhill . . . . . Tillamock
(Co Clk has m rec from 1862, div , pro, civ ct rec from 1860)
Twality   Changed to Washington 1849
Umatilla   B1   1862   44 1870-80   Wasco . . . . Pendleton
(Co Clk has m, div, pro, civ ct rec from 1862)
Umpqua   1851   1860   Benton (absorbed by Douglas 1862)
Union   B1   1864   18 1870-80   Baker . . . . La Grande
(Co Clk has m, div, pro, civ ct rec from 1864)
Wallowa   A1   1887   7   Union . . . . Enterprise
Wasco   D2   1854   20 1860-80   Clackamas, Linn, Marion, Lane . The Dalles
Washington E1   1843   92 1850-80   Orig Co formerly Twality . . . Hillsboro
(Co Clk has m rec from 1852, div & civ ct rec from 1893, pro rec from 1874)
Wheeler   C2   1899   3   Crook, Gilliam, Grant . . . . Fossil
(Co Clk has m, div, pro, civ ct rec from 1899)
Yamhill   E2   1843   33 1850-80   Original county . . . . McMinnville
(Co Clk has m, div, pro rec from 1857)

Genealogists' Check List of the Historical Records Survey, Oregon (see page VIII)

Fed Cts; Inv of Co Arch - Benton, Clatsop, Coos, Hood River, Josephine, Klamath, Linn, Morrow, Multnomah, Tillamock, Umatilla. Wasco, Washington; Guide to Pub Vit Stat Rec; Dir of Chr & Rel Org of Ore; Guides to Depo of Ms Col in US - Ore & Washington; Guide to Ms Col of the Ore Hist Soc; Diary of Basil N Longsworth, Ore Pioneer; The Diary of Eli Sheldon Glover, Oct - Dec 1875; Abstract of Willamette Valley and Cascade Mountain Road Co 1864-1911; Corvallis to Cresent City, Calif in 1874; Daily Sales of an Auburn Store in 1868; Letter from Lukiamute Valley in 1846.

Description of Co Offices in Ore and Check List of their Rec; Guide to the Angelus Studio Col of Hist Photos; Rec of Married Women's Separate Property in Baker Co; Transportation Items from the Weekly Oregonian 1852-1862; Ship Reg & Enrollments of Marshfield, Ore 1873-1941; Ship Reg and Enrollments of Portland, Ore 1867-1941; Depo of unpubl mat, Univ of Ore, Eugene, Ore.

Pennsylvania
Capital Harrisburg - State 1787 - (2nd)

Give me your tired, your poor,
Your huddled masses yearning to
   breathe free,
The wretched refuse of your teeming
   shore.
Send these, the homeless, tempest-tost
   to me.
I lift my lamp beside the golden door.

Long before the Statue of Liberty had been comtemplated or Emma Lazarus had written these immortal lines for its pedestal, William Penn extended an invitation to Europe's religiously persecuted and exiled to come to Pennsylvania where he had established a haven of religious freedom and liberty.

Responding to the earnest solictation the Society of Friends, or Quakers, came from England, Scotland, Ireland and Wales; the severely persecuted Palatines came from the Rhine section; the Anabaptists, or Mennonites, arrived from Germany and Switzerland; the Church of the Brethren, or Dunkards, so called from their belief in triple baptism, came from Germany in 1721; the Roman Catholics from England came there in 1732; the Moravians, or Czech followers of John Huss, came for Moravia and Bohemia to Pennsylvania via Georgia in 1740 and the so-called Dutch, who were Germans, not Hollanders.

With the rapidly advancing mineral and business developments in the early 1800s tens of thousands of workers came from Europe in the following numerical strength, according to Bureau of Census figures: Italians, Poles, Russians, Austrians, Germans, Czechs, English, Irish, Hungarians, Swedes, Greeks, French, Norwegians, Danes, and Finns.

The Pennsylvania Historical & Museum Commission of Harrisburg has been microfilming early wills, orphans' court, deed and tax records of Pa. counties. The Division of Public Records holds copies of these records but they have no staff to search them. Microfilm readers are available, however, for those wishing to do their own research. If certified copies of the records are desired you will have to get them from the county which holds the original record as the films are classed as unofficial.

On the north bank of the Susquehanna River for a distance of 20 miles is the three mile wide Wyoming Valley. Here is the highly industrialized city of Wilkes-Barre and numerous rich anthracite coal mines. In 1778 this section was an incorporated county in the colony of Connecticut. More than 200 settlers were killed that year in the Pennamite-Yankee War fought between the colonists of Conn. and Pa. The dispute was finally settled by Congress in 1782 in what is known as the Decree of Trenton. Researchers looking for material from the Wyoming Valley prior to 1782 must search for it in Hartford, Conn.

Marriage licenses were first issued in Pennsylvania about 1883. Birth and death records have been kept since 1892. Until 1906 these records were kept in their respective counties, since then they have been under the direction of the Bureau of Vital Statistics at Harrisburg, Pa. The marriage licenses are kept at the office of the clerks of the respective counties. From 1852 to 1856 birth and death records were also recorded in the counties. The birth records give the names of other children in the family.

Pennsylvania libraries - Harrisburg, (Dauphin), State Library (genealogical Department); Lancaster, (Lancaster), Franklin and Marshall College, Fackenthal Library, (state history and biography); Philadelphia (Philadelphia), American Swedish Historical Foundation Library, 19th St. and Pattison Ave., (biographies of Swedish-American); The Free Library of Philadelphia, Logan Square, (Western manuscripts); The Historical Society of Pennsylvania. 1300 Locust St., (biographies and genealogies); Pittsburgh, (Allegheny), Carnegie Free Public Library of Allegheny Federal & Ohio Sts., (histories of Pittsburgh and Pennsylvania); Carnegie Library of Pittsburgh, 4400 Forbes St., (histories and biographies, Pittsburgh newspapers from 1768); Reading (Berks), Public Library, Fifth and Franklin Sts., (material on Pennsylvania Dutch); State College, (Centre), The Pennsylvania State Library, (histories and genealogies); Wilkes-Barre, (Luzerne), Osterhout Free Public Library, 71 S. Franklin St., (local history); York, (York) Martin Memorial Public & York County Library, 159 E. Market St.

Pennsylvania County Histories

(Population figures to nearest thousand - 1960 Census)

Name	Map Index	Date Formed	Pop. By M	Census Reports Available	Parent County	County Seat
Adams	C3	1800	52	1800-80	York	Gettysburg
Allegheny	C1	1788	1629	1790-80	Westmoreland, Washington ...	Pittsburgh
Armstrong	B1	1800	80	1800-80	Allegheny, Indiana, Clarion, Butler Jefferson, Westmoreland ...	Kittanning

(Co Clk has div, pro, civ ct, naturalization rec from 1800)

Beaver	B1	1800	207	1800-80	Allegheny, Washington	Beaver

(Co Clk has b rec 1893 to 1907, m rec 1885, d rec 1834, bur rec 1852 to 1855 & 1893 to 1907, div rec 1805, pro rec 1800, civ ct rec 1797)

Bedford	C2	1771	42	1790-80	Cumberland	Bedford

(Clk of Cts has b & d rec 1893 to 1906, m rec 1885, div rec 1804, pro rec 1772, Civ ct rec 1771)

Berks	B4	1752	275	1790-80	Bucks, Chester, Lancaster, Philadelphia	Reading

(Co Clk has b rec 1893 to 1906, d rec from 1906, div rec from 1800)

Blair	C2	1846	137	1850-80	Huntingdon, Bedford	Hollidaysburg

(Co Clk has b rec 1893 to 1905, m rec 1885, div rec 1846, civ ct rec 1846)

Bradford	A3	1810	55	1820-80	Luzerne, Lycoming	Towanda

(Originally Ontario, changed 1812)

Bucks   B4   1682   309   1790-80   Original county . . . . Doylestown
(Orphans Ct has. b & d rec 1893 to 1906, m rec 1885; Prothontary has div rec
1878, civ ct rec 1682; Register of Wills has pro rec 1684)
Butler   B1   1800   115   1800-80   Allegheny . . . . Butler
(Chief Co Clk has b rec from 1893 to 1906, m rec 1885, div, pro, civ ct rec 1800)
Cambria   B2   1804   210   1810-80   Somerset, Bedford, Huntingdon . Ebensburg
Cameron   A2   1860   8   1870-80   Clinton, Elk, McKean, Potter . . Emporium
Carbon   B4   1843   53   1850-80   Northampton, Monroe . . . .   Jim Thorpe
(Chief Co Clk has m rec from 1883, div, pro, civ ct rec from 1843)
Centre   B2   1800   79   1800-80   Lycoming, Mifflin, Northumberland,
                                         Huntingdon . . . . Bellefonte
(Co Clk has b & bur rec 1893 to 1906, m rec from 1885, d rec 1885 to 1906, div,
pro, civ ct rec from 1800)
Chester   C4   1682   211   1790-80   Original county . . . . W. Chester
Clarion   B1   1839   37   1850-80   Venango, Armstrong . . . . Clarion
Clearfield   B2   1804   82   1810-80   Huntingdon, Lycoming . . . . . . Clearfield
Clinton   B2   1839   38   1840-80   Lycoming, Centre . . . . Lock Haven
Columbia   B3   1813   53   1820-80   Northumberland . . . . Bloomsburg
(Co Clk has b rec 1893 to 1905, m rec from 1885, div & civ ct rec from 1813)
Crawford   A1   1800   78   1800-80   Allegheny . . . . Meadville
Cumberland   C3   1750   125   1790-80   Lancaster . . . . Carlisle
Dauphin   C3   1785   220   1790-80   Lancaster . . . . Harrisburg
Delaware   C4   1789   553   1790-80   Chester . . . . Media
Elk   A2   1843   37   1850-80   Jefferson, McKean, Clearfield . . Ridgway
(Clk of Orphans Ct has b rec 1893 to 1906, m rec from 1895)
Erie   A1   1800   251   1800-80   Allegheny . . . . Erie
Fayette   C1   1783   169   1790-80   Westmoreland . . . . Uniontown
Forest   A1   1848   4   1860-80   Jefferson, Venango . . . . Tionesta
Franklin   C2   1784   88   1790-80   Cumberland . . . . Chambersburg
(Co Clk has b rec 1893 to 1906, d rec 1894 to 1906, m & div rec 1885, pro rec
1784, civ ct rec 1784, deeds 1784)
Fulton   C2   1850   11   1850-80   Bedford . . . . McConnellsburg
(Clk of Orphans Ct has b & d rec 1895 to 1905, m rec 1885; Prothonotary has
div & civ ct rec 1850; Register of Wills has pro rec 1850; Recorder of Deeds has
deeds from 1850)
Greene   C1   1796   39   1800-80   Washington . . . . Waynesburg
(Clk of Cts has b & d rec 1893 to 1915, m rec 1885, Prothonotary has div & civ
ct rec 1797; Register has pro rec 1797)
Huntingdon   C2   1787   39   1790-80   Bedford . . . . Huntingdon
(Co Clk has b rec 1894 to 1906, m rec 1885, d rec 1894 to 1905, div, pro, civ ct
rec 1787)
Indiana   B2   1803   75   1810-80   Westmoreland, Lycoming . . . . Indiana
(Clk of the Orphans Ct has b rec 1893 to 1906, m rec 1884, d rec 1852 to 1856,
pro rec 1805)
Jefferson   B2   1804   47   1810-80   Lycoming . . . . Brookville
Juniata   B3   1831   16   1840-80   Mifflin . . . . Mifflintown
Lackawanna   A4   1878   235   1880   Luzerne . . . . Scranton
(Co Commissioners Office has m, div, pro, civ ct rec from 1878)
Lancaster   C3   1729   278   1790-80   Chester . . . . Lancaster
Lawrence   B1   1849   113   1850-80   Beaver, Mercer . . . . New Castle
Lebanon   C3   1813   91   1820-80   Dauphin, Lancaster . . . . Lebanon
Lehigh   B4   1812   228   1820-80   Northampton . . . . Allentown
Luzerne   B3   1786   347   1790-80   Northumberland . . . . Wilkes-Barre
Lycoming   B3   1795   109   1800-80   Northumberland . . . . Williamsport
McKean   A2   1804   55   1810-80   Lycoming . . . . Smethport
Mercer   B1   1800   128   1800-80   Allegheny . . . . Mercer
Mifflin   B2   1789   44   1790-80   Cumberland, Northumberland . Lewistown
Monroe   B4   1836   40   1840-80   Pike, Northampton . . . . Stroudsburg
(Co Clk has m rec from 1885, div rec from 1844, pro & civ ct rec from 1836)
Montgomery   C4   1784   517   1790-80   Philadelphia . . . . Norristown
Montour   B3   1850   17   1850-80   Columbia . . . . Danville
(Prothonotary has b & d rec 1893 to 1905, m rec 1885, div rec 1865, civ ct rec 1850)

Northampton B4 1752 201 1790-80 Bucks . . . . Easton
Northumber-
   land   B3 1772 104 1790-80 Lancaster, Bedford, Berks,
                                        Northampton . . . . Sunbury
Ontario (see Bradford)
Perry   C3 1820 27 1820-80 Cumberland . . . . New Bloomfield
Philadelphia C4 1682 2003 1790-80 Original county . . . . Philadelphia
Pike   A4 1814   9 1820-80 Northampton . . . . Milford
   (Clk of Commissioners has b & d rec 1892 to 1905, m, pro, civ ct rec from 1814)
Potter   A2 1804 16 1810-80 Lycoming . . . . Coudersport
   (Prothonotary has b rec 1893 to 1906, div & civ ct rec from 1804; Register of
   Wills has pro rec from 1804)
Schuylkill B3 1811 173 1820-80 Berks, Northampton . . . . Pottsville
Snyder   B3 1855 26 1860-80 Union . . . . Middleburg
   (Co Clk has b rec 1892 to 1905)
Somerset C2 1795 77 1800-80 Bedford . . . . Somerset
   (Co Clk has b & d rec 1893 to 1906, m rec from 1885, pro rec from 1795)
Sullivan   A3 1847   6 1850-80 Lycoming . . . . Laporte
   (Clk of Orphans Ct has b & d rec 1893 to 1905, m rec from 1885; Prothonotary
   has div rec from 1847, civ ct rec from 1847; Register of wills has pro rec 1847)
Susquehanna A4 1810 33 1820-80 Luzerne . . . . Montrose
   (Co Clk has div and civ ct rec from 1812)
Tioga   A3 1804 37 1810-80 Lycoming . . . . Wellsboro
Union   B3 1813 26 1820-80 Northumberland . . . . Lewisburg
   (Co Clk has b & d rec 1893 to 1905, m rec from 1885, div & civ ct rec from 1813)
Venango   B1 1800 65 1800-80 Allegheny, Lycoming . . . . Franklin
   (Co Clk has b & d rec 1893, m rec 1885, div rec 1802, civ ct rec 1800)
Warren   A1 1800 46 1800-80 Allegheny, Lycoming . . . . Warren
Washington C1 1781 217 1790-80 Westmoreland . . . . Washington
Wayne   A4 1798 28 1800-80 Northampton . . . . Honesdale
Westmoreland C1 1773 353 1790-80 Bedford . . . . Greensburg
Wyoming   A3 1842 17 1850-80 Luzerne . . . . Tunkhannock
   (Co Clk has b & d rec 1893 to 1906, m rec from 1885)
York   C3 1749 238 1790-80 Lancaster . . . . York

County Map of Pennsylvania

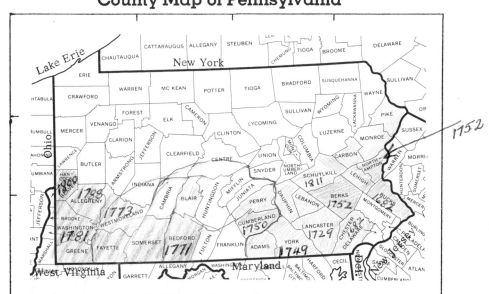

Genealogists' Check List of the Historical Records Survey, Penn. (see page VIII)

Fed Cts; Inv of Co Arch - Adams, Beaver, Berks, Blair, Bradford (printed 1942 & 1946,) Cambria, Delaware (Rev Ed Oct 1941,) Erie, Fayette, Forest, Greene, Lancaster, Lawrence, Lehigh, Luzerne, Warren, Washington, Wayne, Westmoreland; Inv of the Chr & Syn Arch of Pa - Society of Friends; Ship Reg of Port of Philadelphia Vol 1 A to D.

Guide to Depo of Ms Col in Pa; Guide to Ms Col in Hist Soc of Pa; Descriptive Cat of the Du Simitiere Papers in the Lib Company of Philadelphia; Papers of Colonel Henry Bouquet - Series 21631 - 21632 - 21634 - 21643 - 21644 Parts 1 & 2 - 21645 - 21646 - 21647 - 21648 Parts 1 & 2 - 21649 Parts 1 & 2 - 21650 - 21652 - 21653 - 21654 - 21654A - 21654B; Wilderness Chronicles of N W Pa; Cal of the Joel R. Poinsett Papers in the Henry D. Gilpin Col; Jour of Choussegros de Lery; The Expedition of Baron de Longueuil; The Venango Trail.

Check List of Philadelphia Newspapers Available in Philadelphia (2 Editions) ; Check List of Pa Newspapers Vol 1 Philadelphia Co; Manual for Newspaper Trans; Check List of Maps Pertaining to Pa up to 1900; Reprint with Supplement to Check List of Maps to Pa up to 1900.

Pa microfilm: (Filmed by N J Hist Rec Survey showing location of original rec) Ct of Common Pleas of Bucks Co, Hiram H. Keller, Pres. Judge, Doylestown, Pa; Min Bk Common Pleas & Quarter Sessions, Buck Co Pa 1684-1730, Clerk of Quarter Sessions Office, Bucks Co Ct Hs, Doylestown, Pa.; Sessions Docket 1715-1753 Bucks Co, Pa, Clerk of Quarter Sessions Office, Bucks Co Ct House, Doylestown, Pa.; Rules, Forms & Fees of Ct from 1770 to 1890, Bucks Co, Pa, Office of the Clerk of Quarter Sessions, Bucks Co Ct House, Doylestown, Pa.

Depo of unpubl mat, Historical Commission, Harrisburg, Pa.

Rhode Island

Capital Providence - State 1790 - (13th)

Giovanni de Verazzano, a 44-year-old Florentine navigator, in 1524 visited Block Island and the site of the present Newport on Aquidneck Island, both part of today's Rhode Island. He was then a privateer in the French service.

In 1636 Roger Williams, a 30-year-old Welshman, and some of his followers established the first Rhode Island settlement at Providence. His religious pronouncements, too advanced for the clergy to accept, led to his banishment from Massachusetts. An uncompromising advocate of freedom, he held that difference of opinion is not a bar to friendship. All land he settled or tiled was purchased from the Indians.

The banishment of Williams from Massachusetts was soon followed by others including Anne Marbury Hutchinson, John Clarke, and William Coddington. They established a colony at Portsmouth in 1638. Later Clarke and Coddington settled Newport, after their attempt to establish a government based on the Jewish nation had failed. A fourth colony was established at Warwick in 1642.

Many Quakers found a haven in Rhode Island in the early days. The large majority of the people who came into Rhode Island were former residents of Massachusetts.

New England researchers have an abundance of material at their command. Both the state and the cities have large genealogical libraries or genealogical sections in their public libraries. The Rhode Island Historical Society has a wonderful assortment of books at 52 Power Street, Providence 6, R. I. The Society has one of the largest genealogical collections in New England, probably the third largest. Many people from various sections, searching for the progenitors among Rhode Island families have attained splendid results in the library of the Rhode Island Historical Society.

Among its large numbers of industrial workers are members of almost every nationality. Those with the largest numbers are the Italians, English, Irish, Polish, Russians, Swedes, Germans and Austrians.

All vital statistics are in the custody of the town or city clerks. Birth and death records since 1853 are in the office of the Registrar of Vital Statistics, Providence R. I.

Rhode Island libraries - Newport, (Newport), The Peoples Public Library; Providence, (Providence), Brown University Library, (R.I. history); Providence Public Library, 229 Washington St. Zone 3; Rhode Island Historical Society Library, 52

Power St.; Rhode Island State Library, State House, (historical, R.W. records).

Rhode Island Towns
Organized Before 1800

BRISTOL COUNTY—Barrington, 1717; Bristol, 1681; Warren, 1746-7.

KENT COUNTY — Coventry, 1741; East Greenwich, 1677; Warwick, 1642-3; West Greenwich, 1741.

NEWPORT COUNTY — Jamestown 1678; Little Compton, 1746-7; Middleton, 1743; Newport, 1639; New Shoreman, 1672; Portsmouth, 1638; Tiverton, 1746-7.

PROVIDENCE COUNTY — Cranston, 1754; Cumberland, 1746-7; Foster ,1781; Glocester, 1730-1; Johnston, 1759; North Providence, Providence, 1636; Scituate, 1730-1; Smithfield, 1730-1.

WASHINGTON COUNTY — Charlestown, 1738; Exeter, 1742-3; Hopkinton, 1757; North Kingston, 1641; Richmond, 1747; South Kingston, 1657-8; Westerly, 1669.

Genealogists' Check List of the Historical Records Survey, R. I. (see page VIII)

Fed Cts; Inv of Mun & Tn Arch - North Providence, West Greenwich; Summary of Legislation Concerning Vit Stat Rec; Guide to Pub Vit Stat Rec in RI & Providence Plantations; Guide to Chr Vit Stat Rec in R I & Providence Plantations; Ship Reg & Enrollments of Providence, R I, 2 Vol 1773-1939; Ship Reg & Enrollments of Bristol-Warren, R I 1773-1939; Ship Reg & Enrollments of Newport, RI 1790-

County Map of Rhode Island

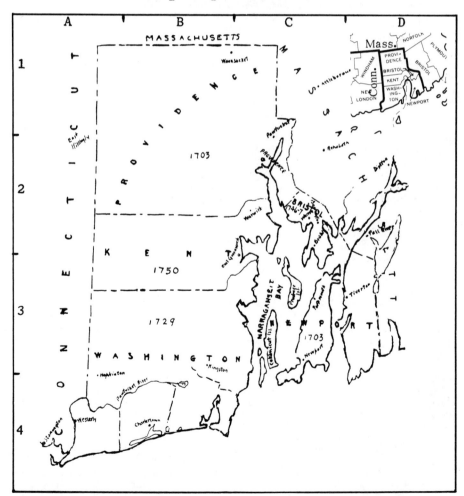

1939 2 Vol; Inv of the Chr Arch of R I - of Am Portraits 1620-1825 found in R I; Bap Chrs - Society of Friends; Dir of Chrs Depo of unpubl mat, State Lib, Providence, & Rel Org of R I; Preliminary Check List Rhode Island.

Rhode Island County Histories

(Population figures to nearest thousand - 1960 Census)

Name	Map Index	Date Formed	Pop. By M	Census Reports Available	Parent County	County Seat
Bristol	C2	1747	37	1790-80	Newport	Bristol
Kent	B3	1750	113	1790-80	Providence, Newport	E. Greenwich
Newport	D3	1703	82	1790-80	Original county	Newport
Providence	B1	1703	569	1790-80	Original county	Providence
Washington	B4	1729	59	1790-80	Newport (For. Naragannset) . .	W. Kingston

South Carolina

Capital Columbia - State 1788 - (8th)

Several attempts by the Spaniards and the French to establish settlements in what is now South Carolina between 1526 and 1664 failed.

The first colony was established on the Ashley River in the southeastern part of the state in 1671. The settlers were a group of English people direct from the Old World, and another group, the members of which had been living on the Barbados Island, the south-easternmost island in the West Indies group. They called their settlement Charles Town. A few months later some Dutch families, who had left New York after the English had taken over there established themselves along the Ashley River. They were later joined by many families direct from Holland.

In 1675 a group of Quakers came into the Territory. In 1680 about 45 families of Huguenots also established homes there. Quite a colony of dissenters from the Episcopal Church came in 1683 from Somersetshire to the present site of Charleston. In that year came also an Irish colony and settled along the Ashley River. In 1684 ten families of Scotch Presbyterians established themselves at Port Royal.

Immigrants continued to come in large streams until by 1730 there were gathered "on the banks of the Santee, the Edisto, and the Combahee some of the best elements of the European nations. The Huguenot, the Scotch Presbyterian, the English Dissenter, the loyalist and High Churchman, the Irish adventurer, and the Dutch mechanic composed the powerful material out of which soon grew the beauty and renown of the Palmetto State." (Ridpath's History of the United States.)

From 1732 until 1736 quite a number of families from England, Scotland, Ireland, Wales, Switzerland, and Germany came into the central section of South Carolina. Some of the first settlements in the so-called "Up Country," the western half of the state, were created from 1745 to 1760 by immigrants from the Rhine section of Germany, the northern American colonies, and the Ulster section of Ireland. After the Indian Wars, Scotch-Irish immigrants came about 1761.

In 1790 the capital of the state, was moved from Charleston to Columbia. From 1845 to 1850 many Irish settled in the state because of the potato famine in their own country. The political struggle in Germany in 1848 brought thousands of the expatriates to the United States, many of them coming to South Carolina.

South Carolina was the eighth state to enter the Union, 1788. More than a hundred years before, 1683, the first three counties Berkley, Colleton, and Craven, were established. All were discontinued and the present Berkeley county is not the original.

By an Act ratified in 1769 the province of South Carolina was divided into seven judicial districts: Charleston, Georgetown, Beaufort, Orangeburg, Ninety-Six, Camden and Cheraws. The first six of these were given the names of the principal towns within their borders and those towns were made the seats of their respective districts. Cheraws District derived its name from the fact that the Cheraw Indians had formerly occupied a considerable portion of the land within its borders and after they had gone elsewhere and white settlers moved in, the section was at first called "the Cheraws' lands", soon simplified into "The Cheraws".

In 1795 Pinckney and Washington Districts were established. Pinckney embraced the present counties of Union and York and a part of Cherokee. Washington embraced the present counties of Greenville, Pickens, Oconee and Anderson.

In 1798 the nine districts then existing were divided up into twenty-four. From Ninety-Six District, Abbeville, Edgefield, Newberry, Laurens, and Spartanburg Districts were formed; from Washington District, Pendleton and Greenville Districts were formed; from Pinckney District, Union and York Districts were formed; from Camden District, Chester, Lancaster, Fairfield, Kershaw and Sumter Districts were formed; from Cheraws District, Chesterfield, Darlington and Marlborough Districts were formed; Ninety-Six, Washington, Pinckney, Camden and Cheraw were discarded as district names; Georgetown District was divided into Georgetown and Marion Districts; Charleston into Charleston and Colleton; and Orangeburg into Orangeburg and Barnwell.

In 1799 Richland District was formed from Kershaw. In 1802 Horry and Williamsburg Districts were formed from parts of Georgetown. In 1804 Lexington was formed from Orangeburg. In 1826 Pendleton District was formed into Pickens and Anderson Districts and the name Pendleton discarded as a district name. In 1855 Clarendon District was formed from a part of Sumter.

From the settlement of South Carolina in 1671 until 1783 all vital statistics and property records were recorded at Charleston where they are still available at the office of the Judge of Probate. Since the Episcopal Church held full sway in the early days of the colony, in 1706 an act was passed making the parishes its legislative units. Regardless of church affilations, all persons were required to register their vital statistics with the church officers. In 1783 offices of Register of Mesne (legal) Conveyance were authorized in all counties.

Archibald F. Bennett, former secretary of the Genealogical Society of Utah, who some years ago made a personal inspection of all record deposits in South Carolina, says that the Judge of Probates office in Charleston has records of wills and estates back to 1692. They are recorded in chronological volumes, with indexes.

Records of deeds and other estate matters are available from 1719 in Charleston. Those prior to 1719 are in the office of the Historical Commission of South Carolina in Columbia.

What few marriage bonds are available from those early days have been printed in the 'South Carolina Historical and Genealogical Magazine." Between 1778 and 1911 no marriage bonds or licenses were required in South Carolina, and only for brief intervals were such records kept.

"Records of land grants earlier than 1695 are in the office of the Historical Commission of South Carolina in Columbia," says Mr. Bennett. "The Secretary of State in Columbia has records of land grants from 1695 to the present time, and a plat to land grants from 1688, warrants for entry and surveys made and certified before the corresponding final grants or patents were issued. The plat records and grant records in the Secretary of State's office are in separate books. There are sets of index books for plats and index books for grants.

'In our Genealogical Library in Salt Lake City, Utah, we have a series of seven printed volumes containing copies of the Stub Entries to Indents for Revolutionary Claims. These contain valuable items for information on the service of soldiers who were paid or received bounty for service."

Birth and death records from 1915 to the present are in the office of the State Health Department, Columbia, S. C. Marriage records from July 1, 1950 to the present are also at that office. Marriages from July 1, 1911 to the present are at the office of the Probate Judge, County Court House, in respective county seats.

Birth records kept at the city of Charleston are available since 1877 at the City Health Department, where also are available deaths from 1821 to the present.

The Clerk of the Court in the various counties has charge of wills, deeds, and land grants. Dates will vary with the different counties.

War service records are in the custody of Adjutant General in Columbia, S. C.

Available census records are listed in the "South Carolina County Histories" herewith.

The South Carolina Historical and Genealogical Magazine, a quarterly, has been published regularly since 1900. It contains much valuable information. Many libraries have bound volumes of this magazine.

All schedules of the U.S. Census for 1790 of South Carolina are available, but are not necessarily listed in the names of the present counties, since most of them, with the probably exception of three, have all been formed after the 1790 census.

South Carolina district were formed as follows. Abbeville, 1798; Anderson 1826; Barnwell, 1798; Beaufort, 1769; Berkeley, 1683; Camden, 1769; Cartaret, 1683; Charleston, 1769, Cheraws, 1769; Chester, 1798; Chesterfield, 1798; Clarendon, 1785; Colleton 1798; Darlington, 1798; Dorchester, 1785; Edgefield 1798; Fairfield, 1798; Georgetown, 1769; Granville, 1700; Greenville, 1798; Horry, 1802; Kershaw, 1798; Lancaster, 1798; Laurens, 1798; Lexington, 1804; Marion, 1798; Marlboro, 1798; Newberry, 1798; Ninety-Six 1796; Orangeburg, 1769; Pendleton 1798; Pickens, 1826; Pickney 1795; Richland, 1799; Spartanburg, 1798; Sumter, 1798; Union, 1798; Washington, 1798; Williamsburg, 1802, and York 1798.

South Carolina libraries - Charleston, (Charleston), Charleston Free Library, 94 Rutledge Ave.; Columbia, (Richland) Richland County Public Library, 1400 Sumter St. (South Carolina); South Carolana State Library; Spartanburg, (Spartanburg). Spartanburg Public Library, 224 Magnolia Street.

The 1868 Constitution changed 30 districts to counties. And even after 1868 some recorders continued to use "dis-trict" as they felt it has been a "yankee' imposition. Those marked below with an asterisk (*) are those so changed.

South Carolina books:

ERVIN, SARA SULLIVAN, *South Carolinians in the Revolution*, 186 pp. (Index separate) Pub. 1949, DAR.

Heads of Families at the First Census of the U. S. 1790, South Carolina, Government Printing Office, 1908.

REVILL, JANIE, *Copy of the Original Index Book Showing the Revolutionary Claims Filed in South Carolina between August 20, 1783 and August 31, 1786*. Kept by James McCall, Auditor General.

SALLY, A. S. JR., *Warrants for Lands in South Carolina 1672-1679*. Published by the Historical Commission of South Carolina, 1910.

South Carolina Historical & Genealogical Magazine. Published since 1900 — 57 Vol.

YOUNG, MISS PAULINE, *A Collection of South Carolina Wills and Records*. 2 Vols. (Vol. 1 printed, vol. 2 mimeographed)

South Carolina County Histories

(Population figures to nearest thousand - 1960 Census)

Name	Map Index	Date Formed	Pop. By M	Census Reports Available	Parent County	County Seat
Abbeville*	B1	1785	21	1800-80	District 96	Abbeville
Aiken	B2	1871	81	1880	Edgefield, Orangeburg, Barnwell Lexington	Aiken
Allendale	C3	1919	11		Barnwell, Hampton	Allendale
Anderson*	A1	1826	98	1830-80	Pendleton District	Anderson
Bamberg	B3	1897	16		Barnwell	Bamberg
Barnwell*	B2	1798	18	1800-80	Orangeburg	Barnwell
Berkley		1683	(Discontinued)		Original Co not present Berkley Co	
Berkeley	B4	1882	38		Charleston	Moncks Corner
(Co Clk has civ ct rec from 1884)						
Beufort*	C3	1764	44	1790-80	Original county	Beaufort
(Co Clk has b, d, rec from 1915)						
Calhoun	B3	1908	12		Lexington, Orangeburg . . .	St. Matthews
(Co Health Dept has b & d rec from 1915; Judge of Pro has m rec 1911, pro rec 1908; Clk of Ct has civ ct rec 1908, land, Bible, cemetery and gen col from 1735)						
Charleston*	C4	1769	216	1800-80	Original District	Charleston
Cherokee	A2	1897	35		Union, York, Spartanburg . . .	Gaffney
Chester*	A2	1798	31	1800-80	Camden District	Chester
Chesterfield*	A3	1798	34	1800-80	Cheraws District	Chesterfield
Claremont				1800-10		
Clarendon*	B3	1855	29	1800-80	Sumter District	Manning
(Census schedules missing for 1820, 1830, 1840, 1850)						
Colleton*	C3	1798	28	1800-80	Charleston District	Walterboro
Darlington*	A3	1798	53	1800-80	Cheraws District	Darlington
Dillon	A4	1910	31		Marion	Dillon
(Clk of Cts has civ ct rec, deeds, real estate, mtgs from 1910)						
Dorchester	B3	1897	24		Berkeley, Colleton	St. George
(Co Clk has b rec from 1915)						
Edgefield*	B2	1785	16	1800-80	District 96	Edgefield
(Co Clk has b, d, bur rec from 1915)						

Fairfield*   A2   1785   21   1800-80   Camden District ....   Winnsboro
(Co Clk has civ ct rec, deeds, releases, sale of slaves rec from 1785)
Florence   A3   1888   84   Marion, Darlington, Clarendon
                                             Williamsburg ....   Florence
Georgetown*   B4   1769   35   1790-80   Original District ....   Georgetown
Greenville*   A1   1798   210   1800-80   Washington ....   Greenville
Greenwood   B2   1897   44   Abbeville, Edgefield ....   Greenwood
Hampton   C3   1878   17   1880   Beaufort ....   Hampton
(Clk of Cts has b rec 1915 to 1957, civ ct rec 1878; Judge of Pro Ct has m rec 1911)
Horry*   A4   1802   68   1810-80   Georgetown ....   Conway
Jasper   C3   1912   12   Beaufort, Hampton ....   Ridgeland
(Co Clk has b & d rec from 1915, civ ct, deeds, mtgs, judgments, wills from 1912)
Kershaw*   A3   1798   34   1800-80   Camden District ....   Camden
Lancaster*   A3   1798   39   1800-80   Camden District ....   Lancaster
(Co Clk has b & d rec from 1915, civ ct rec from 1866)
Laurens*   A2   1785   48   1800-80   District 96 ....   Laurens
Lee   A3   1902   22   Darlington, Sumter, Kershaw ..   Bishopville
(Co Clk has b, d, civ ct rec from 1902)
Lexington*   B2   1804   61   1800-80   Orangeburg ....   Lexington
Liberty   1800
McCormick   B2   1916   9   Greenwood, Abbeville .....   McCormick
Marion*   A4   1798   32   1800-80   Georgetown ....   Marion
Marlboro*   A3   1798   29   1800-80   Cheraws District ....   Bennettsville
Newberry*   B2   1785   29   1800-80   District 96 ....   Newberry
Oconee   A1   1868   40   1870-80   Pickens ....   Wahalla
(Pro Judge has m rec from 1912, Pro rec 1868, Co Clk has civ ct rec from 1868)
Orange   1800
Orangeburg*   B3   1769   69   1800-80   Original district ....   Orangeburg
Pendleton   1800-20
Pickens*   A1   1826   46   1830-80   Pendleton ....   Pickens
Richland*   B3   1799   200   1810-80   Kershaw ....   Columbia
(Census schedules missing for 1800)
Salem   1800-10
Saluda   B2   1895   15   Edgefield ....   Saluda

County Map of South Carolina

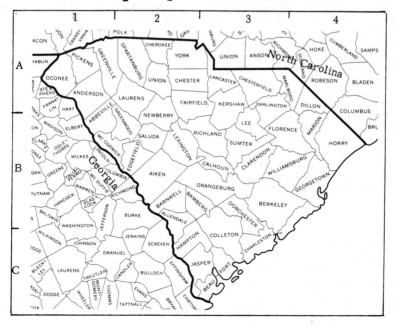

Spartanburg* A2 1785 157 1800-80 District 96 .... Spartanburg
  (Pro Judge has m rec from 1911, pro rec 1700; Clk of Ct has civ ct rec 1785)
Sumter*   B3 1798   75 1800-80 Camden District .... Sumter
Union*   A2 1798   30 1800-80 District 96 .... Union
  (Clk of Ct has civ ct rec from 1785)
Winyaw   1800
Williamsburg* B4 1802   41 1800-80 Georgetown .... Kingstree
York*   A2 1798   79 1800-80 Pinckney .... York
                          * See page 152

Genealogists' Check List of the Historical Records Survey, S. C. (see page VIII)

Inv of Co Arch - Abbeville, Aiken, Allen- ence, Jasper, Lee, McCormick, Oconee,
dale, Anderson, Cherokee, Dillon, Flor- Pickens, Richland, Saluda.

South Dakota

Capital Pierre - Territory 1861 - State 1889 - (40th)

Part of the Louisiana Purchase in 1803, the Dakotas were wedded to numerous Territories before finally becoming states. Until 1820 they were part of the Missouri Territory. At intervals, the eastern half was tied to the Territories of Minnesota, Iowa, Wisconsin, and Michigan. During those periods, the western parts of the Dakotas belonged to the Nebraska Territory. The Dakotas were formed into a Territory by itself in 1861. In 1887 it was divided into two Territories, North and South Dakota.

Attracted by the rich soil between the Big Sioux and the Missouri Rivers, farm families from adjoining states established homes there as early as 1857. Several communities were established, most of them along the Missouri, but two or three along the Big Sioux. The real influx of settlers came about 1863, after the passing of the first Homestead Act in the U. S.

South Dakota became the fortieth state to enter the Union. This was in 1889. All of her 68 counties, with the exception of three were already organized at that time.

The predominating nationality in South Dakota is the Norwegian. Other nationalities represented among its citizenry, in the order of their predominance, are the German, Russian, Swedish, Danish, Czechoslovakian, English, Austrian, Irish, Finnish, Polish, Greek and Italian.

Records of births, marriages, divorces and deaths from 1905 to the present are on file at the office of the State Public Health Department, Pierre, S.D.

Wills and probate matters are in the offices of the Clerk of the Court in each county who also have a record of marriages since 1905.

All land records are at the office of the Register of Deeds in the county of filing. Land grants are at the office of the Commissioner of School and Public Lands. Pierre, S. D.

The state census records from 1890 to the present are in charge of the Will Robinson Division, Department of History, Pierre, S. D.

Taxpayers lists are at the offices of the County Treasurer of each county.

The war service records are under the direction of the Register of Deeds of each county. The Sexton of each cemetery is supervising the records of the respective cemeteries.

KINGSBURY, GEO. W., *History of Dakota Territory. Its History and Its People.* Vols. four and five, biographical. S. J. Clarke Publishing Co., Chicago, 1915.

Libraries: Aberdeen, (Brown), Alexander Mitchell Public Library, 21 6th Ave., SE; Pierre, (Hughs), South Dakota Free Public Library Commission; Sioux Falls, (Minnehaha), Carnegie Free Public Library, Tenth & Dakota Sts.

South Dakota County Histories

(Population figures to nearest thousand - 1960 Census)

Name	Map Index	Date Formed	Pop. By M	Census Reports Available	Parent County	County Seat
Armstrong	C2	1883	.05	1880	Merged with Dewey	
Aurora	B4	1879	5	1880	Brule	Plankinton
Beadle	B4	1873	22	1880	Spink, Clark	Huron

Bennett   C2   1909   3   Indian Lands . . . . Martin
(Attached to Fall River Co until 1911)
BonHomme   C4   1862   9   1860-80   Charles Mix . . . . Tyndall
Brookings   B5   1868   20   1860-80   Unorganized Territory . . . . . Brookings
Brown   A4   1879   34   1880   Beadle . . . . Aberdeen
(Co Auditor has b & d rec from 1905, m rec 1880, div, pro, civ ct rec 1882)
Brule   B4   1879   6   1880   Old Buffalo (disc.) . . . . . . Chamberlain
(Clk of Cts has b & d rec from 1905, m rec 1882, div rec 1885, pro & civ ct 1882)
Buffalo   B3   1872   2   1880   Territorial County . . . . . . Gannvalley
Butte   B1   1883   9   Harding . . . . Belle Fourche
Campbell   A3   1873   4   1880   Buffalo . . . . Mound City
(Clk of Cts has b & d rec from 1905, m rec 1888, pro rec 1885, div & civ ct 1890)
Charles Mix   C4   1865   12   1860-80   Original District . . . . Lake Andes
(Clk of Cts has b, m, d rec from 1905, div, pro, civ ct rec from 1890)
Clark   B4   1873   7   1880   Hanson . . . . Clark
(Clk of Cts has b & d rec from 1905, m rec 1886, div rec 1900, pro rec 1885)
Clay   C5   1862   11   1860-80   . . . . Vermillion
(Clk of Cts has b, d, div rec from 1905, m rec 1870, pro rec 1875, civ ct rec 1866)
Codington   B5   1878   20   1880   Indian Lands . . . . Watertown
Corson   A2   1909   6   Boreman, Dewey . . . . McIntosh
(Clk of Cts has b, m, d, div, pro, civ ct rec from 1909)
Custer   C1   1877   5   1880   Indian Lands . . . . Custer
(Clk of Cts has b & d rec from 1905, m rec 1877, div, pro, civ ct rec 1880)
Davison   B4   1875   17   1880   Hanson . . . . Mitchell
Day   A4   1879   11   1880   Clark . . . . Webster
Deuel   B5   1878   7   1880   Brookings . . . . Clear Lake
(Clk of Cts has b & d rec from 1905, m rec 1887, div & pro rec 1885, civ ct rec
1883) (Duel Co Dakota has 1860-70 Federal Census)
Dewey   A3   1910   5   Indian Res., Armstrong . . . Timber Lake
Douglas   C4   1873   5   1880   Charles Mix . . . . Armour
(Clk of Cts has b & d rec from 1905, m rec from 1884)
Edmunds   A3   1873   6   Buffalo . . . . Ipswich
(Clk of Cts has b & d rec from 1905, m & div rec 1887, pro & civ ct rec 1884)
Fall River   C1   1883   11   Custer . . . . Hot Springs
(Clk of Cts has b & d rec from 1905, m & pro rec from 1889, div & civ rec 1884)

County Map of South Dakota

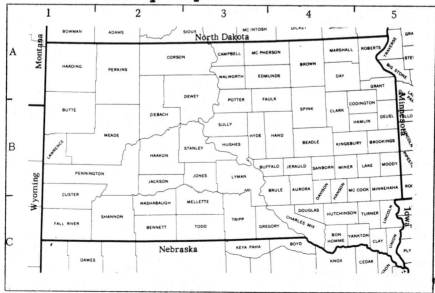

Faulk   A4   1873   4   1880   . . . .   Faulkton
(Clk of Cts has b rec from 1886, m rec from 1885, d rec from 1905, div rec from 1887, pro rec from 1884, civ ct rec from 1890)
Grant   A5   1873   10   1880   Codington, Deuel . . . .   Milbank
(Clk of Cts has b & d rec from 1905, m rec from 1890, div rec from 1897, pro & civ ct rec from 1888, newspapers from 1880)
Gregory   C3   1889   7   Yankton . . . .   Burke
(Clk of Cts has b, m, d, div, pro, civ ct rec from 1905)
Haakon   B2   3   . . . .   Philip
(Clk of Cts has b, m, d, div, pro rec from 1915)
Hamlin   B5   1878   6   1880   Deuel . . . .   Hayti
(Clk of Cts has b & d rec from 1905, m rec from 1879, div rec from 1885, pro rec from 1893, civ ct rec from 1885)
Hand   B4   1873   7   1880   Buffalo . . . .   Miller
Hanson   B4   1872   5   1880   Buffalo, Deuel . . . .   Alexandria
Harding   A1   1881   2   Unorganized Territory . . . .   Buffalo
(Clk of Cts has b, m, d, bur, div, pro, civ ct rec from 1909)
Hughes   B3   1874   13   1880   Buffalo . . . .   Pierre
Hutchinson   C4   1871   11   1860-80 Unorganized Territory . . . .   Olivet
(Clk of Cts has b & d rec from 1905, m rec from 1887, bur rec from 1895, pro rec from 1885, civ ct rec from 1876)
Hyde   B3   1873   3   Buffalo . . . .   Highmore
(Clk of Cts has b & d rec from 1905, m rec 1890, pro rec 1892, civ ct rec 1888)
Jackson   B2   1915   2   Stanley . . . .   Kadoka
Jerauld   B4   1883   4   Aurora . . . .   Wessington Springs
(Clk of Cts has b rec from 1905, m & pro rec from 1890, div & d rec from 1900)
Jones   B3   1917   2   Lyman . . . .   Murdo
Kingsbury   B4   1879   9   Hanson . . . .   De Smet
Lake   B5   1873   12   1880   Brookings, Hanson . . . .   Madison
Lawrence   B1   1875   17   1880   Unorganized Territory . . . .   Deadwood
(Clk of Cts has b, d, bur rec from 1905, m rec 1890, div, pro, civ ct rec 1879)
Lincoln   C5   1871   12   1860-80 Minnehaha . . . .   Canton
(Clk of Cts has b & d rec from 1905, m & pro rec from 1890)
Lyman   B3   1873   4   1880   Unorganized Territory . . . . . .   Kennebec
McCook   B5   1873   8   1880   Hanson . . . .   Salem
(Clk of Cts has b & d rec from 1905, m rec from 1882, bur rec from 1895, div rec from 1887, pro rec from 1881, civ ct rec from 1880)
McPherson   A3   1873   6   Buffalo . . . .   Leola
(Clk of Cts has b & d rec from 1905, m rec 1887, div, pro, civ ct rec 1893)
Marshall   A4   1885   7   Day . . . .   Britton
(Clk of Cts has b & d rec from 1905, m rec 1887, div & civ ct rec 1888, pro rec 1901)
Meade   B2   1889   12   Lawrence . . . .   Sturgis
Mellette   C3   1909   3   Lyman . . . .   White River
Miner   B4   1873   5   1880   Hanson . . . .   Howard
(Clk of Cts has b & d rec from 1905, m, div, pro, civ ct rec from 1886)
Minnehaha   B5   1865   87   1860-80 Territorial County . . . .   Sioux Falls
(Clk of Cts has b & d rec from 1905, m, div, pro, civ ct rec from 1876)
Moody   B5   1873   9   1880   Brookings, Minnehaha . . . . .   Flandreau
(Clk of Cts has b & d rec from 1905, m rec 1873, div rec 1883, pro & civ ct 1881)
Pennington   B1   1877   58   1880   Unorganized Territory . . .   Rapid City
(Clk of Cts has b & d rec from 1905, m rec 1887, div & civ ct rec 1877, pro rec 1884)
Perkins   A2   1909   6   Harding, Butte . . . .   Bison
(Clk of Cts has b, m, d, bur, div, pro, civ ct rec from 1909)
Potter   A3   1875   5   Buffalo . . . .   Gettysburg
Roberts   A5   1883   13   Grant . . . .   Sisseton
(Clk of Cts has b & d rec from 1905, m, div, pro rec from 1890, civ ct rec from 1889)
Sanborn   B4   1883   5   Miner . . . .   Woonsocket
(Clk of Cts has b, m, d, bur, div, pro, civ ct rec from 1905)
Shannon   C2   1875   6   1880   Terr. Co. - Attached to Fall River County.
Spink   B4   1879   12   1880   Hanson, Walworth . . . .   Redfield
(Clk of Cts has b & d rec from 1905, m rec 1887, bur & pro rec 1880, civ ct rec 1882)
Stanley   B3   1873   4   1880   Unorganized Territory . . . . . .   Ft. Pierre

Sully	B3	1873	3	1880	Potter . . . . Onida
Todd	C3	1871	5	1860-80	Indian Lands-Attached to Tripp County
Tripp	C3	1873	9		Unorganized Territory . . . . . . Winner

(Clk of Cts has b, m, div, pro, civ ct rec from 1909, d rec from 1910)

| Turner | C5 | 1871 | 11 | 1880 | Lincoln . . . . Parker |

(Clk of Cts has b & d rec from 1905, m rec from 1872, div rec from 1907, pro rec from 1886, civ ct rec from 1900)

| Union | C5 | 1864 | 10 | 1880 | Unorganized Territory . . . . . Elk Point |
| Walworth | A3 | 1868 | 8 | 1880 | Territorial County . . . . Shelby |

(Clk of Cts has b rec from 1905, m, d, bur, div, civ ct rec 1889, pro rec 1892)

| Washabaugh | C2 | 1883 | | | Indian Lands-Attached to Jackson Co. |
| Yankton | C5 | 1884 | 18 | 1860-80 | Unorganized Territory . . . . . . Yankton |

(Clk of Cts has b & d rec from 1905, m, div, pro, civ ct rec from 1900)

| Ziebach | B2 | 1869 | 2 | | Pennington . . . . Dupree |

Genealogists' Check List of the Historical Records Survey, S. Dak. (see page VIII)

Fed Cts; Inv of Co Arch - Bennett, Buffalo, Clark, Faulk, Haakon, Jackson, Mellette, Miner, Washabaugh; Guide to Pub Vit Stat Rec; Depo of unpubl mat, Univ of South Dakota, Vermillion, So Dak.

Tennessee

Capital Nashville - State 1796 - (16th)

Four or five hostile Indian tribes inhabited Tennessee up to as late as 1800. Explorers, representing Spain, France, and England, visited the territory intermittently from about 1540 until the early part of the seventeen hundreds.

White settlers moved into what later became Sullivan and Hawkins counties in the northeast corner of the state and established settlements as early as 1772.

The Blue Ridge Mountains, which form the boundary between North Carolina and Tennessee, are barriers to travel. They were so more in the early days than now. For that reason it was easier to come into Tennessee from the north than from the east. Many of the settlers therefore came into Tennessee from Virginia. It was in fact thought by some that it was part of that state.

In those early days came several families into the northeast corner of Tennessee from the Uplands of North Carolina. They banded together as the Watauga Association and spread over the eastern part of the section. North Carolina shortly accepted the district as Washington County which eventually embraced all of the present Tennessee. To secure federal protection for that territory, North Carolina handed it to the national government as a present. But apparently no one in Washington became enthusiastic about the gift, refusing even to acknowledge it. After it had been ignored for four of five years some of the settlers retaliated by organizaing the territory into a new state, Franklin. But even that action received cold treatment from Washington, and eventually vanished into the air.

Most of the early settlers in Tennessee came from North Carolina. Almost equal numbers came from South Carolina and Virginia. Many of the Tennessee counties were settled by Scotch-Irish immigrants coming into the state via the Shenandoah Valley. Many German families settled in several of the counties west of Chattanooga where still live many of their descendants.

Many present Tennessee counties were settled years before they were formed into counties. Some of those sections and the dates of their earliest settlement are as follows: Johnson, 1770; Washington, 1772; Robertson 1776; Greene, 1778; Sumner, 1779; Hawkins, Hamilton, Davidson, Montgomery, 1780; Hamblen, Jefferson, Cooke, Jackson, 1783; Grainger, Williamson, 1784; Blount, 1786; Smith, 1787; Cheatham, 1790; Dickson, Stewart, 1793; Claiborne, 1794; Hancock, 1795; Campbell, 1796; De Kalb, Wilson, 1797; Houston, Trousdale, 1798; Anderson, Franklin, Humphreys, Moore, Van Buren, 1800; Lincoln, 1806; Morgan, Lewis, Marshall, Maury, 1807; Lawrence, Henderson, 1815; Marion, Meiga, Benton, 1817; McMinn, Gibson, Hardeman, Hardin, Henry, Madison, McNairy, Obion, Shelby, Weakley, 1819; Carroll, Decatur, Lauderdale, 1820; Haywood, 1821; Fayette, 1822; Crockett, 1823; Lake, 1825; Polk 1836

In 1790, perhaps earlier, Tennessee had seven counties, each one embracing the following present counties: SULLIVAN - Johnson and Sullivan; WASHINGTON - Washington, Carter and Unicoi; HAWKINS -

Hawkins, Hamblen, Grainger, Hancock, Claiborne, Campbell, Union, Anderson, Jefferson, Knox, Roane, Rhea, and Hamilton; GREENE - Greene, Cocke, corner of

County Map of Tennessee

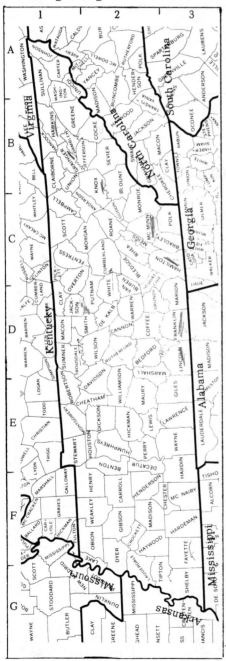

Jefferson, Blount, Loudon, south-west corner of Roane, Monroe, M'Minn, Polk, Meigs, Bradley, James, south-east corner of Hamilton; SUMNER - eastern third of Robertson, Sumner, Macon, Clay, Pickett, western half of Fentress, Overton, Jackson, Smith, Trousdale, Wilson, DeKalb, western two-thirds of White, Warren, northwest half of Coffee, and Cannon; DAVIDSON - Bedford, Marshall, Maury, Williamson, Rutherford, Davidson, Cheatham, and about middle third of Robertson; TENNESSEE - Stewart, Houston, Humphreys, Hickman, Dickson, Montgomery, and western third of Robertson. The rest of the territory was included in the Indian Country.

It should be noted that the counties to be settled first were in the East and the Middle Tennessee districts, the East district rather leading the Middle. The West Tennessee district was the last to be settled.

"The Colonial and State Records of North Carolina," found in many genealogical libraries, contains many records with much history of the early counties of Tennessee prior to 1790. The State Library at Nashville has one of the largest genealogical sections in the South.

Official registration of births and deaths began in Tennessee in 1914. Official registration of marriages and divorces began in 1945. These records may be had from the Division of Vital Statistics, State Dept. of Public Health, Nashville 3, Tenn. In the larger cities of Tennessee birth and death records are available for many years back. Check with the office of the City Health Dept. in the particular city in which your ancestors lived as you are ready to conduct your search.

The counties maintain marriage license records and records of wills, deeds, taxpayers lists, guardianship and other court proceedings in the respective county court houses. Some of these records have been transcribed and are in the State Library.

The early land grants are recorded in the Land Grant Office of the State Division of Archives, although these records are far from complete. Although limited in number, there are in the State Library some Church or Parish records, as well as cemetery records. There is no full collection of such records in the state.

The most complete collection of war service records in the state is held by the office of the Adjutant General, Employment Security Bldg., Nashville, Tenn. There may not be many records of the early wars. There are records of Tennesseans who served in the Union Forces during the

Civil War but not those serving in the Confederate Army. Available are also records of the National Guard, Tennesseans who served in the Spanish-American War and World War I. The State Library has a considerable card index of Tennesseans who served in the earlier wars and in the Confederate Army, but they are not complete and not official. They merely indicate the sources from which the information may be obtained.

All of the 1790 census were lost, and all but one county of the 1810 census. Tax lists help fill the gaps.

A letter from the Tennessee State Librarian and Archivist, Mr. Dan M. Robinson, in 1942 says, "It is my understanding that all the Tennessee records we have and many we do not have were microfilmed back in the 1930's by the Genealogical Society of Utah, the Joseph F. Smith Memorial Building, 80 North Main St., Salt Lake City, Utah. You will probably find there the most complete Tennessee records available in any one place."

Four books which may help you in your Tennessee research are:

AKLEN, JEANNETTE TILLOTSON AND ASSITANTS, *Tennessee Bible Records and Marriage Bonds*. Published by Cullom and Ghertner, Nashville, 1933. 2 Vols.

RAY, WORTH S., *Tennessee Cousins*, A history of Tennessee people. Published by the author, Austin, Texas, 1950.

TEMPLE, O. P., *Notable Men of Tennessee, 1833-1875*, published 1912

WPA. Bibliography of Research Projects Reports. Check list of Historical Records Survey Publication, published 1940.

Libraries: Chattanooga, (Hamilton), Chattanooga Public Library, McCallis Ave.; Knoxville, (Knox), Lawson McGhee Public Library, 217 Market St. (Tennessee History and Genealogy); Memphis, (Shelby), Cossitt Public Library, Front & Monroe Sts.; Nashville, (Davidson), Nashville Public Library, 222 8th Ave.

Tennessee County Histories

(Population figures to nearest thousand - 1960 Census)

Name	Map Index	Date Formed	Pop. By M	Census Reports Available	Parent County	County Seat
Anderson	C2	1801	60	1830-80	Knox	Clinton
Bedford	D2	1807-8	23	1820-80	Rutherford	Shelbyville
Benton	E2	1835	11	1840-80	Henry, Humphreys	Camden
Bledsoe	C2	1807	8	1830-80	Roane	Pikeville
(Co Clk has m & pro rec from 1908)						
Blount	B2	1795	58	1830-80	Knox	Maryville
Bradley	C3	1835	38	1840-80	Indian Lands	Cleveland
(Co Clk has m, pro, wills from 1864)						
Campbell	C1	1806	28	1830-80	Anderson, Claiborne	Jacksboro
(Co Clk has m rec from 1838)						
Cannon	D2	1836	9	1840-80	Coffee, Warren, Wilson	Woodbury
Carroll	F2	1821	23	1830-80	Western District	Huntingdon
Carter	A1	1796	42	1830-80	Washington	Elizabethton
Cheatham	E2	1856	9	1860-80	Davidson, Dickson, Montgomery	Ashland City
Chester	F3	1875	10	1880	Hardeman, Madison, Henderson	Henderson
Claiborne	B1	1801	19	1830-80	Grainger, Hawkins	Tazewell
Clay	D1	1870	7	1880	Jackson, Overton	Celina
Cocke	B2	1797	23	1830-80	Jefferson	Newport
(CH burned 1875 most records lost)						
Coffee	D2	1836	29	1840-80	Franklin, Warren, Bedford	Manchester
Crockett	F2	1845	15	1880	Dyer, Madison, Gibson, Haywood	Alamo
(Many early census rec of residents of Crockett Co may be found in surrounding counties)						
Cumberland	C2	1856	19	1860-80	Bledsoe, Morgan, Roane	Crossville
(Co Clk has m & pro rec from 1905)						
Davidson	E2	1783	400	1820-80	Washington	Nashville
Decatur	E2	1845	8	1850-80	Perry	Decaturville
(Co Clk has m & pro rec from 1869)						
DeKalb	D2	1837-8	11	1840-80	Cannon, Warren, White	Smithville
Dickson	E2	1803	19	1820-80	Montgomery, Robertson	Charlotte
Dyer	F2	1823	30	1830-80	Western District	Dyersburg
Fayette	F3	1824	25	1830-80	Shelby, Hardeman	Somerville

Fentress	C1	1823	13	1830–80	Morgan, Overton	Jamestown
Franklin	D3	1807	26	1820–80	Bedford, Warren	Winchester
Gibson	F2	1823	45	1830–80	Western District	Trenton
Giles	E3	1809	22	1820–80	Maury	Pulaski
Grainger	B1	1796	13	1830–80	Hawkins, Knox	Rutledge
Greene	B1	1783	42	1830–80	Washington	Greenville
Grundy	D2	1844	12	1850–80	Coffee, Warren	Altamont
Hamblen	B1	1870	33	1880	Grainger, Hawkins	Morristown
Hamilton	C3	1819	238	1830–80	Rhea	Chattanooga
Hancock	B1	1844	8	1850–80	Claiborne, Hawkins	Sneedville
Hardeman	F3	1823	22	1830–80	Western District	Bolivar
Hardin	E3	1819	17	1820–80	Western District	Savannah
Hawkins	B1	1786	30	1830–80	Sullivan	Rogersville

(Co Clk has m rec from 1865, pro rec from 1800)

Haywood	F2	1823	23	1830–80	Western District	Brownsville
Henderson	F2	1821	16	1830–80	Western District	Lexington

(Ct house burned 1863 & 1895 some rec saved)

Henry	F2	1821	22	1830–80	Western District	Paris
Hickman	E2	1807	12	1820–80	Dickson	Centerville
Houston	E2	1871	5	1880	Dickson, Stewart	Erin
Humphreys	E2	1809	12	1820–80	Stewart, Smith	Waverly
Jackson	D1	1801	9	1820–80	Smith	Gainesboro

(Co Clk has m & pro rec from 1870)

Jefferson	B2	1792	21	1830–80	Green, Hawkins	Dandridge
Johnson	A1	1836	11	1840–80	Carter	Mountain City
Knox	B2	1792	251	1830–80	Greene, Hawkins	Knoxville
Lake	F2	1870	10	1870–80	Obion	Tiptonville
Lauderdale	G2	1835	22	1840–80	Dyer, Tipton	Ripley
Lawrence	E3	1817	28	1820–80	Hickman, Maury	Lawrenceburg
Lewis	E2	1843	6	1850–80	Hickman, Maury, Wayne, Lawrence	Hohenwald
Lincoln	D3	1809	24	1820–80	Bedford	Fayetteville
Loudon	C2	1871	24	1880	Blount, Monroe, Roane	Loudon
McNairy	F3	1823	18	1830–80	Hardin	Selmer
McMinn	C2	1819	34	1830–80	Indian Lands	Athens
Macon	D1	1842	12	1850–80	Smith, Sumner	Lafayette
Madison	F2	1821	61	1830–80	Western District	Jackson
Marion	D3	1817	21	1830–80	Indian Lands	Jasper
Marshall	D2	1836	17	1840–80	Bedford, Lincoln, Giles, Maury .	Lewisburg

(Co Clk has m & pro rec from 1836)

Maury	D2	1807	42	1820–80	Williamson	Columbia
Meigs	C2	1836	5	1840–80	Hamilton, McMinn, Rhea	Decatur
Monroe	C2	1819	23	1830–80	Roane	Madisonville

(Co Clk has m rec from 1838, pro rec 1853, wills 1833, co ct rec 1868)

Montgomery	E1	1796	56	1820–80	Tennessee	Clarksville
Moore	D3	1871	3	1880	Bedford, Franklin	Lynchburg
Morgan	C2	1817	14	1830–80	Roane	Wartburg
Obion	F2	1823	27	1830–80	Western District	Union City
Overton	C1	1806	15	1820–80	Jackson	Livingston
Perry	E2	1818	5	1820–80	Hickman	Linden
Pickett	C1	1879	4		Fentress, Overton	Byrdstown
Polk	C3	1839	12	1840–80	Bradley, McMinn	Benton
Putnam	D2	1842	29	1860–80	Smith, White, DeKalb	Cookeville
Rhea	C2	1807	16	1830–80	Roane	Dayton

(Co Clk has m rec from 1808)

Roane	C2	1801	39	1830–80	Knox, Blount	Kingston

(Co Clk has m & pro rec from 1801)

Robertson	E1	1796	27	1820–80	Tennessee	Springfield
Rutherford	D2	1803	52	1810–80	Davidson	Murfreesboro

(Co Ct clk has m & pro rec from 1804)

Scott	C1	1849	15	1850–80	Fentress, Morgan, Anderson ..	Huntsville
Sequatchie	C2	1857	6	1860–80	Hamilton	Dunlap
Sevier	B2	1794	24	1830–80	Jefferson	Sevierville

(Co Clk has m rec from 1856, wills from 1850)

Shelby	G3	1819	627	1820–80	Hardin	. . . .	Memphis

(Co Ct Clk has m rec from 1820)

Smith	D2	1799	12	1820–80	Sumner	. . . .	Carthage
Stewart	E1	1803	8	1820–80	Montgomery	. . . .	Dover
Sullivan	A1	1779	114	1830–80	Washington	. . . .	Blountville

(Co Clk has m & pro rec from 1863)

Sumner	D1	1786	36	1820–80	Davidson	. . . .	Gallatin
Tennessee		1788			Co. surrendered name when state		

became Tennessee 1796

Tipton	G3	1823	29	1830–80	Western District	. . . .	Covington

(Co Clk has m rec from 1823)

Trousdale	D1	1870	5	1880	Macon, Smith, Wilson	. . . .	Hartsville
Unicoi	A1	1875	15	1880	Carter, Washington	. . . .	Erwin
Union	B1	1850	8	1860–80	Anderson, Campbell	. . . . . .	Maynardville
Van Buren	D2	1840	4	1850–80	Bledsoe, Warren, White	. . . .	Spencer
Warren	D2	1807	23	1820–80	White	. . . .	McMinnville
Washington	A1	1777	65	1830–80	Covered present state. Many counties		

from section . . . . Jonesboro

(This County also embraced parts of present N. C. Counties)

Wayne		1785	Abolished 1788

(This Wayne Co created under the State of Franklin. Included present Carter Co and part of Johnson Co.)

Wayne	E1	1819	12	1820–80	Hickman	. . . .	Waynesboro
Weakley	F2	1823	24	1830–80	Western District	. . . .	Dresden
White	C2	1806	16	1820–80	Smith	. . . .	Sparta
Williamson	E2	1799	25	1820–80	Davidson	. . . .	Franklin

(Co Clk has m rec from 1800, tax, wills, minutes, deeds from 1799)

Wilson	D2	1799	28	1820–80	Sumner	. . . .	Lebanon

(Co Clk has m, pro, wills from 1800)

Genealogists' Check List of the Historical Records Survey, Tenn. (see page VIII)

Fed Cts; Inv of Co Arch - Anderson, Bedford, Blount, Bradley, Cheatham, Crockett, Hamilton, Haywood, Loudon, Rutherford, Sullivan, Tipton, Wilson; Tran of Pub Arch - Min of Shelby Co Ct 1820-1824, Min of Knox Co Ct 1792-1795; Guide to Pub Vit Stat Rec; Guide to Chr Vit Stat Rec; Inv of the Chr & Syn Arch of Tenn - Tenn Bap Convention (Nashville Bap Assn) - Ocoee Bap Assn - Jewish Congregations - Outline of Development of Methodism in Tenn; Dir of Chr, Missions and Rel Institutions of Tenn - Davidson Co - Hamilton Co - Knox Co - Shelby Co - Washington Co; Guide to Depo of Ms Col in Tenn; Guide to Col of Mss in Tenn; Check List of Tenn Imprints 1793-1840 in Tenn Lib; Check List of Tenn Imprints 1841-1850; Check List of Tenn Imprints 1793-1840; Check List of Rec Required or Permitted by Law in Tenn; Instructions for using Co Rec as Source Mat; Dir of Lib in Tenn; History and Org of the Shelby Co Judiciary; Summary of Gen Highway Legislation in Tenn 1881-1909; Summary of Special Legislation Relating to Gov of Sullivan Co; Check List of Acts and Codes of the State of Tenn 1792-1939; Depo of unpubl mat, State Planning Commission, Nashville, Tenn.

Texas

Capital Austin - State 1845 - (28th)

Texas has been under the jurisdiction of six separate governments since 1685, those of France, Spain, Mexico, the Republic of Texas, the Confederacy, and the United States.

In 1820 the white settlers of Texas could be counted in four digits. Shortly afterwards former residents of Alabama, Louisiana, Mississippi, and Tennessee were brought into the section under the leadership of Moses Austin and his son, Stephen.

By 1830 more than 20,000 Americans had become tillers of Texas soil.

Austin has been the capital of Texas since statehood. Other cities which have been the capitals of Texas are Sen Felip de Austin, Washington-on-the-Brazos, Harrisburg, Galveston, Velasco and Columbia during the Revolution, 1835, 1836; Houston, 1837-1839; Austin, 1839; Houston, Washington-on-the-Brazos, 1842-1845; Austin since 1845.

The State Historical Society in Austin has many records of value to the genealogist. Among the public libraries with genealogical sections are those in San Antonio, Dallas, Houston, and Fort Worth. There are collections of material in the museum libraries of the Daughters of the Republic of Texas, and the United Daughters of the Confederacy, both of which are in the Old Land Office Building, Austin 11, Texas. The Archives section of the Texas State Library, State Capital, Austin 11, Texas, is a relatively large proportion of the library's holdings. The Museum Library of San Jacinto Monument has a collection of earlier and colonial period publications. The Cody Memorial Library, Southwestern University, Georgetown, Texas, and the Rosenberg Library in Galveston also cater to researchers. Several Genealogical Societies have sprung up in recent years to assist ancestor searchers. Among the more prominent are:

West Texas Genealogical Society, 3418 Woodridge Dr., Abilene, Texas.

Local History and Genealogical Society, 3209 Mockingbird Lane, Dallas 5, Texas.

Fort Worth Genealogical Society, Box 864, Fort Worth, Texas.

San Antonio Genealogical and Historical Society, P. O. Box 6383, San Antonio 9, Texas.

Texas State Genealogical Society, 1404 South Lake Street, Fort Worth 4, Texas.

Central Texas Genealogical Society, 3828 North 22nd St., Waco, Texas.

Other Texas Libraries – Amarillo, (Potter), Amarillo Public Library, City Auditorium; Austin, (Travis), Austin Public Library, 401 W. 9th St.; Texas State Library & Historical Commission, State Capital; The University of Texas, Mirabeau B. Lamar Library, (Texas History); Beaumont, (Jefferson), Tyrrell Public Library, Pearl and Forsythe; Dallas, (Dallas), Dallas Historical Society Library, Hall of Records; Dallas Public Library, Commerce and Harwood Sts.; El Paso, (El Paso), El Paso Public Library, (Southwest); Fort Worth, (Tarrant), Fort Worth Public Library, Ninth & Throckmorton Sts. (Southwestern History); Galveston, (Galveston), Rosenberg Public Library, 823 Tremont; Houston (Harris), Harris County Public Library, 1223 Elder St.; Houston Public Library, 500 McKinney Ave.; San Antonio, (Bexar), San Antonio Public Library, 210 W. Market St.; Waco, (McLennan), Baylor University Library, (Texas History); Waco, Public Library.

The Bureau of Vital Statistics, Texas State Department of Health, Austin, Texas, has birth and death records from 1903 to the present, and delayed birth records from about 1850 to 1951, including voluntary registrations made during and since 1929 for births not registered at time of events. The City Clerk of the city, or the County Clerk of the county may have birth or death records prior to 1903.

The County Clerk of each county is custodian of other material of interest to the genealogical researcher.

Johnson, Sid S. "Texans Who Wore the Gray.' Names and deeds of the men who fought for the South in the war between the states.

Texas County Histories

(Population figures to nearest thousand – 1960 Census)

Name	Map Index	Date Formed	Pop. By M	Census Reports Available	Parent County	County Seat
Anderson	B2	1846	28	1850-80	Houston	Palestine
Andrews	E2	1875	13		Bexar	Andrews
Angelina	A2	1846	40	1850-80	Nacogdoches	Lufkin
Aransas	B4	1871	7	1880	Refugio	Rockport
Archer	C1	1858	6	1880	Fannin	Archer City
Armstrong	F1	1876	2	1880	Bexar	Claude
Atascosa	C4	1856	19	1860-80	Bexar	Jourdanton
Austin	B3	1837	14	1850-80	Old Mexican Municipality . . .	Bellville
Bailey	E1	1876	9		Bexar	Muleshoe
Bandera	C3	1856	4	1860-80	Uvalde, Bexter	Bandera

(Co Clk has m, div, pro, civ ct, cattle brands from 1856, b & d rec from 1904)

Name	Map Index	Date Formed	Pop. By M	Census Reports Available	Parent County	County Seat
Bastrop	B3	1836	17	1850-80	Old Mexican Municipality	Bastrop
Baylor	C1	1858	6	1880	Fannin	Seymour
Bee	B4	1857	24	1860-80	Goliad, Refugio, Live Oak, San Patricio	Beeville

(Co Clk has b & d rec from 1903, civ ct rec from 1876)

Name	Map Index	Date Formed	Pop. By M	Census Reports Available	Parent County	County Seat
Bell	B2	1850	94	1860-80	Milam	Belton
Bexar	C3	1836	687	1850-80	Old Mexican Municipality . . .	San Antonio

Blanco   C3   1858   4   1870-80   Gillespie, Comal, Burnet,
                                         Hays . . . . Johnson City
Borden   D2   1876   1   1880   Bexar . . . . Gail
Bosque   C2   1854   11   1860-80   McLennan, Milam Dist. . . . . . Meridian
Bowie   A1   1840   60   1850-80   Red River . . . . Texarkana
Brazoria   A3   1836   76   1850-80   Old Mexican Municipality . . . . Angelton
     (Co Clk has b rec from 1900, m rec from 1841, d rec from 1903)
Brazos   B3   1841   45   1850-80   Washington, Robertson . . . . Bryan
     (Originally Navasota Co.- changed to Brazos 1842; Co Clk has m rec from 1841)
Brewster   E3   1887   6   Presidio . . . . Alpine
     (Co Clk has b & d rec from 1903, m, div, pro, civ ct rec from 1887)
Briscoe   F2   1876   4   1880   Bexar . . . . Silverton
Brooks   F4   1911   9   Starr, Zapata, Hidalgo . . . . . Falfurrias
     (Co Clk has b, m, d, pro, civ ct rec from 1911)
Brown   C2   1856   25   1860-80   Travis, Comanche . . . . Brownwood
     (Co Clk has b, d rec from 1903, m, pro, civ ct rec from 1880)
Buchanan   1860   Discontinued
Burleson   B3   1846   11   1850-80   Milam, Washington . . . . Caldwell
     (Co Clk has b & d rec from 1903, m rec 1845, pro rec 1846, civ ct & deeds 1845)
Burnet   C3   1852   9   1860-80   Travis, Bell, Williamson . . . . Burnet
     (Co Clk has b & d rec from 1903, m, pro, civ ct rec from 1852)
Caldwell   B3   1848   17   1850-80   Gonzales . . . . Lockhart
Calhoun   B4   1846   17   1850-80   Victoria, Matagorda, Jackson . Port Lavaca
     (Co Clk has b & d rec from 1903, m & deeds from 1846, pro rec from 1849, civ
     ct rec from 1850, criminal rec from 1909, discharge rec from 1919)
Callahan   C2   1858   8   1880   Bexar, Travis, Bosque . . . . Baird
Cameron   E4   1848 151   1850-80   Nueces . . . . Brownsville
Camp   A1   1874   8   1880   Upshur . . . . Pittsburg
Carson   F1   1876   8   Bexar . . . . Panhandle
Cass   A1   1846   23   1850-80   Bowie . . . . Linden
     (Name changed to Davis in 1861 - renamed Cass in 1871)
Castro   F2   1876   9   Bexar . . . . Dimmitt
Chambers   A3   1858   10   1860-80   Jefferson, Liberty . . . . Anahuac
     (Co Clk has b rec from 1903, m rec 1877, d & bur rec 1908, div rec 1910)
Cherokee   A2   1846   33   1850-80   Nacogdoches . . . . Rusk
     (Co Clk has b & d rec from 1903, m, pro, civ ct rec from 1846)
Childress   E2   1876   8   1880   Bexar, Youngland Dist. . . . . . . Childress
     (Co Clk has b & d rec from 1903, m rec from 1891, pro rec from 1892)
Clay   C1   1857   8   1860-80   Cooke . . . . Henrietta
     (Co Clk has b & d rec from 1903, m rec 1874, pro rec 1873, civ ct rec 1876)
Cochran   E1   1876   6   Bexar . . . . Morton
     (Co Clk has b, m, d, div, pro, civ ct rec from 1924)
Coke   D2   1889   4   Tom Green . . . . Robert Lee
     (Co Clk has b rec from 1903, m rec 1890, div, pro, civ ct rec 1890, d rec 1906)
Coleman   C2   1858   12   1870-80   Travis, Brown . . . . Coleman
Collin   B1   1846   41   1850-80   Fannin . . . . McKinney
Collingsworth E1   1876   6   1880   Bexar, Youngland Dist. . . . . Wellington
Colorado   B3   1836   18   1850-80   Old Mexican Municipality . . . . Columbus
Comal   C3   1846   20   1850-80   Bexar, Gonzales, Travis . . New Braunfels
     (Co Clk has b & d rec from 1903, m rec from 1846)
Comanche   C2   1856   12   1860-80   Bosque, Coryell . . . . Comanche
Concho   C2   1858   4   1880   Bexar . . . . Paint Rock
Cooke   B1   1848   23   1850-80   Fannin . . . . Gainesville
Coryell   C2   1854   24   1860-80   Bell . . . . Gatesville
Cottle   D1   1876   4   1880   Fannin . . . . Paducah
Crane   E2   1887   5   Tom Green . . . . Crane
Crockett   D3   1875   4   1880   Bexar . . . . Ozona
     (Co Clk has b, d, bur rec from 1903, div, pro, civ ct rec from 1892)
Crosby   D1   1876   10   1880   Bexar Dist. (Org 1886) . . . . Crosbyton
Culberson   E2   1911   3   El Paso . . . . Van Horn
Dallam   F1   1876   6   Bexar . . . . Dalhart
     (Co Clk has b, d, pro rec from 1903, m rec 1891, div & civ ct rec 1892)
Dallas   B2   1846 952   1850-80   Nacogdoches, Robertson . . . . Dallas

Name	Map Index	Date Formed	Pop. By M	Census Reports Available	Parent County	County Seat
Davis				1870	Discontinued	
Dawson	D2	1876–58	19	1860–80	Bexar (Org. 1905)	Lamesa
Deaf Smith	F1	1876	13	1880	Bexar	Hereford
Delta	B1	1870	6	1880	Hopkins, Lamar	Cooper

(Co Clk has b, pro, civ ct rec from 1903, m rec 1870, d & bur rec 1916)

Name	Map Index	Date Formed	Pop. By M	Census Reports Available	Parent County	County Seat
Denton	B1	1846	47	1850–80	Fannin	Denton
DeWitt	B3	1846	21	1850–80	Goliad, Gonzales, Victoria	Cuero
Dickens	D1	1876	5	1880	Bexar	Dickens
Dimmit	C4	1858	10	1880	Uvalde, Bexar, Maverick Webb	Carrizo Springs

(Co Clk has b & d rec from 1903, m & civ ct rec 1881, pro rec 1882)

Name	Map Index	Date Formed	Pop. By M	Census Reports Available	Parent County	County Seat
Donley	E1	1876	4	1880	Jack, Bexar	Clarendon

(Co Clk has b, m, d, div, pro, civ ct rec from 1876)

Name	Map Index	Date Formed	Pop. By M	Census Reports Available	Parent County	County Seat
Duval	F4	1858	13	1870–80	Live Oak, Starr, Neuces	San Diego
Eastland	C2	1858	20	1860–80	Bosque, Coryell, Travis	Eastland
Ector	E2	1887	91		Tom Green	Odessa
Edwards	D3	1858	2	1880	Bexar	Rocksprings
Ellis	B2	1849	43	1850–80	Navarro	Waxahachie
El Paso	F2	1850	314	1860–80	Bexar	El Paso
Encinal				1860–70	Discontinued	
Erath	C2	1856	16	1860–80	Bosque, Coryell	Stephenville

(Co Clk has b & d rec from 1903, m rec 1869, pro & civ ct rec 1890)

Name	Map Index	Date Formed	Pop. By M	Census Reports Available	Parent County	County Seat
Falls	B2	1850	21	1860–80	Limestone, Milam	Marlin

(Co Clk has b & d rec from 1903, m & pro rec from 1854)

Name	Map Index	Date Formed	Pop. By M	Census Reports Available	Parent County	County Seat
Fannin	B1	1837	24	1850–80	Red River	Bonham

(Co Clk has b & d rec from 1903, m rec from 1836, pro rec from 1850)

Name	Map Index	Date Formed	Pop. By M	Census Reports Available	Parent County	County Seat
Fayette	B3	1837	20	1850–80	Bastrop, Colorado	La Grange

(Co Clk has b & d rec from 1903, m, pro, civ ct rec from 1838)

Name	Map Index	Date Formed	Pop. By M	Census Reports Available	Parent County	County Seat
Fisher	D2	1876	8	1880	Bexar	Roby

(Co Clk has b, m, d, rec from 1903, pro & civ ct rec from 1886)

Name	Map Index	Date Formed	Pop. By M	Census Reports Available	Parent County	County Seat
Floyd	D1	1876	12	1880	Bexar (Org. 1890)	Floydada
Foard	C1	1891	3		Hardman, Knox, King, Cottle ..	Crowell
Fort Bend	B3	1837	41	1850–80	Austin	Richmond

(Co Clk has b & d rec from 1903, m & pro rec from 1837)

Name	Map Index	Date Formed	Pop. By M	Census Reports Available	Parent County	County Seat
Franklin	A1	1875	5	1880	Titus	Mt. Vernon

(Co Clk has b & d rec from 1903, m, pro, civ ct rec from 1875)

Name	Map Index	Date Formed	Pop. By M	Census Reports Available	Parent County	County Seat
Freestone	B2	1850	13	1860–80	Limestone	Fairfield

(Co Clk has b & d rec from 1903, m & pro rec from 1851)

Name	Map Index	Date Formed	Pop. By M	Census Reports Available	Parent County	County Seat
Frio	C4	1871	10	1860–80	Atascosa, Bexar, Uvalde	Pearsall
Gaines	E2	1876	12	1880	Bexar	Seminole

(Co Clk has b, m, d, bur, pro, civ ct rec from 1905)

Name	Map Index	Date Formed	Pop. By M	Census Reports Available	Parent County	County Seat
Galveston	A3	1838	140	1850–80	Brazoria	Galveston
Garza	D1	1876	7	1880	Bexar	Post
Gillespie	C3	1848	10	1850–80	Bexar, Travis	Fredericksburg
Glasscock	D2	1887	1		Tom Green	Garden City

(Co Clk has b, m, d, bur, div, pro, civ ct rec from 1893)

Name	Map Index	Date Formed	Pop. By M	Census Reports Available	Parent County	County Seat
Goliad	B4	1836	5	1850–80	Old Mexican Municipality	Goliad
Gonzales	B3	1837	18	1850–80	Old Mexican Municipality	Gonzales

(Co Clk has b & d rec from 1903, m rec from 1829)

Name	Map Index	Date Formed	Pop. By M	Census Reports Available	Parent County	County Seat
Gray	E1	1876	32	1880	Bexar	Pampa
Grayson	B1	1846	73	1850–80	Fannin	Sherman
Gregg	A2	1873	69	1880	Rusk, Upshur	Longview

(Co Clk has b, m, d, pro rec from 1873)

Name	Map Index	Date Formed	Pop. By M	Census Reports Available	Parent County	County Seat
Grimes	B3	1846	13	1850–80	Montgomery	Anderson
Guadalupe	C3	1846	29	1850–80	Bexar, Gonzales	Seguin

(Co Clk has b, d, bur rec from 1935, m & pro rec from 1838)

Name	Map Index	Date Formed	Pop. By M	Census Reports Available	Parent County	County Seat
Hale	D1	1876	37		Bexar	Plainview

(Co Clk has pro rec from 1908, civ ct rec from 1900)

Name	Map Index	Date Formed	Pop. By M	Census Reports Available	Parent County	County Seat
Hall	E2	1876	7	1880	Bexar, Young	Memphis

(Co Clk has b & d rec from 1903, m, pro, civ ct, deeds from 1890)

Hamilton   C2   1842   8   1860-80   Bosque, Comanche, Lampasas,
                                         Coryell .... Hamilton
(Co Clk has b & d rec from 1903, m rec from 1880)
Hansford   F1   1876   6   1880   Bexar, Young .... Spearman
Hardeman   C1   1858   8   1880   Fannin .... Quanah
Hardin   A3   1858   25   1860-80   Jefferson, Liberty .... Kountze
Harris   A3   1836 1243   1850-80   Formerly Harrisburg Municipality
                                         (Original county) .... Houston
Harrison   A2   1839   46   1850-80   Shelby .... Marshall
(Co Clk has b & d rec from 1903, m & pro rec 1840, Co civ ct rec 1900)
Hartley   F1   1876   2   1880   Bexar, Young .... Channing
(Co Clk has b rec from 1903, m, d, div, pro, civ ct rec from 1891)
Haskell   C1   1858   11   1880   Fannin, Milam .... Haskell
(Co Clk has b & d rec from 1903, m rec from 1885)
Hays   C3   1848   20   1850-80   Travis .... San Marcos
Hemphill   E1   1876   3   1880   Bexar, Young .... Canadian
(Co Clk has b rec from 1896)
Henderson   B2   1846   2? 1850-80   Houston, Nacogdoches .... Athens
(Co Clk has b & d rec from 1903, m & pro rec1860, Voters from 1867 to 1872,
Cattle brands 1846)
Hidalgo   F4   1852   181   1860-80   Cameron .... Edinburg
Hill   B2   1853   24   1860-80   Navarro .... Hillsboro
Hockley   E1   1876   22   Bexar, Young (Org. 1921) .... Levelland
(Co Clk has b, m, civ ct rec from 1921, d & pro rec 1922; attached to Lubbock
from 1891 to 1921)
Hood   C2   1866   5   1870-80   Johnson .... Granbury
Hopkins   B1   1846   19   1850-80   Lamar, Nacogdoches ... Sulphur Springs
Houston   A2   1837   19   1850-80   Nacogdoches .... Crockett
(Co Clk has b & d rec from 1903, m & pro rec from 1882)
Howard   D2   1876   40   1880   Bexar, Young .... Big Spring
Hudspeth   F2   1917   3   El Paso .... Sierra Blanca
Hunt   B1   1846   39   1850-80   Fannin, Nacogdoches .... Greenville
(Co Clk has b & d rec from 1903, m rec 1858, pro rec 1896, deeds 1846)
Hutchinson   F1   1876   34   Bexar Dist. .... Stinnett
Irion   D2   1889   1   Tom Green .... Mertzon
(Co Clk has b, d, bur, div, pro, civ ct rec from 1903, m rec from 1889)
Jack   C1   1856   7   1860-80   Cooke .... Jacksboro
Jackson   B4   1835   14   1850-80   Old Mexican Municipality ...... Edna
Jasper   A2   1836   22   1850-80   Old Mexican Municipality ...... Jasper
Jeff Davis   E3   1887   2   Presidio .... Fort Davis
Jefferson   A3   1836   246   1850-80   Old Mexican Municipality ... Beaumont
(Co Clk has b & d rec from 1903, m, pro, civ ct rec from 1836)
Jim Hogg   F4   1913   5   Brooks, Duval .... Hebbronville
Jim Wells   E4   1911   35   Nueces .... Alice
Jones   C2 1858-61 19   1880   Bexar, Bosque (Org. 1881) ..... Anson
(Co Clk has b & d rec from 1903, m, pro, civ ct rec from 1882)
Johnson   B2   1854   35   1860-80   Ellis, Hill, Navarro .... Cleburne
Karnes   B4   1854   15   1860-80   Bexar .... Karnes City
Kaufman   B2   1848   30   1850-80   Henderson .... Kaufman
(Co Clk has b & d rec from 1903, m & pro rec from 1850)
Kendall   C3   1862   6   1870-80   Kerr, Blanco .... Boerne
Kenedy   E4   1921   .9   Willacy, Hidalgo, Cameron ...... Sarita
Kent   D1   1876   2   Bexar, Young .... Jayton
(Co Clk has b & m rec from 1893)
Kerr   C3   1856   17   1860-80   Bexar .... Kerrville
Kimble   C3   1858   4   1870-80   Bexar .... Junction
King   D1   1876   .6   1880   Bexar .... Guthrie
Kinney   D3   1850   2   1860-80   Bexar .... Brackettville
(Co Clk has b, m, d, div, pro, civ ct rec from 1873)
Kleberg   E4   1913   30   Nueces .... Kingsville
Knox   C1   1858   8   1880   Young, Bexar .... Benjamin
Lamar   B1   1840   34   1850-80   Red River .... Paris
(Co Clk has b & d rec from 1903, pro rec 1840, civ ct rec 1826)

Name	Map Index	Date Formed	Pop. By M	Census Reports Available	Parent County	County Seat
Lamb	E1	1876	22		Bexar	Littlefield
Lampasas	C2	1856	9	1860-80	Bell, Travis	Lampasas
La Salle	C4	1858	6	1870-80	Bexar	Cotulla
Lavaca	B3	1846	20	1850-80	Colorado, Victoria, Jackson Gonzales	Hallettsville
Lee	B3	1874	9	1880	Bastrop, Burleston, Washington Fayette	Giddings
Leon	B2	1846	10	1850-80	Robertson	Centerville

(Co Clk has b & d rec from 1903, m rec from 1885, pro rec from 1846)

Name	Map Index	Date Formed	Pop. By M	Census Reports Available	Parent County	County Seat
Liberty	A3	1836	32	1850-80	Old Spanish Municipality	Liberty
Limestone	B2	1846	20	1850-80	Robertson	Groesbeck

(Co Clk has b & d rec from 1903, m, pro, civ ct rec from 1872)

Name	Map Index	Date Formed	Pop. By M	Census Reports Available	Parent County	County Seat
Lipscomb	E1	1876	3	1880	Bexar	Lipscomb

(Co Clk has b, m, d, bur, div, pro, civ ct rec from 1887)

Name	Map Index	Date Formed	Pop. By M	Census Reports Available	Parent County	County Seat
Live Oak	C4	1856	8	1860-80	Nueces, San Patricio	George West

(Co Clk has b & d rec from 1903, m rec from 1856, pro rec from 1857)

Name	Map Index	Date Formed	Pop. By M	Census Reports Available	Parent County	County Seat
Llano	C3	1856	5	1860-80	Bexar	Llano
Loving	E2	1887	.2		Tom Green	Mentone
Lubbock	D1	1876	156	1880	Bexar, Crosby	Lubbock

(Co Clk has b & d rec from 1903, m rec from 1891, pro & civ ct rec from 1904; At one time attached to Crosby)

Name	Map Index	Date Formed	Pop. By M	Census Reports Available	Parent County	County Seat
Lynn	D1	1876	11	1880	Bexar	Tahoka

(Co Clk has b, m, civ ct rec from 1903, d rec from 1904, pro rec from 1905)

Name	Map Index	Date Formed	Pop. By M	Census Reports Available	Parent County	County Seat
McCulloch	C2	1856	9	1870-80	Bexar	Brady
McLennan	B2	1850	150	1860-80	Milam	Waco
McMullen	C4	1858	1	1870-80	Bexar, Live Oak, Atascosa	Tilden
Madison	B2	1853	7	1860-80	Leon, Grimes, Walker	Madisonville
Marion	A1	1860	8	1860-80	Cass	Jefferson
Martin	D2	1876	5	1880	Bexar	Stanton

(Co Clk has b rec from 1903, m & civ ct rec 1885, div rec 1895, pro rec 1888)

Name	Map Index	Date Formed	Pop. By M	Census Reports Available	Parent County	County Seat
Mason	C3	1858	4	1860-80	Gillespie	Mason

(Co Clk has b & d rec from 1903, m, bur, div, civ ct rec from 1877)

Name	Map Index	Date Formed	Pop. By M	Census Reports Available	Parent County	County Seat
Matagorda	B4	1836	26	1850-80	Old Mexican Municipality	Bay City
Maverick	D4	1856	15	1860-80	Kenedy	Eagle Pass
Medina	C3	1848	19	1850-80	Bexar	Hondo

(Co Clk has b & d rec from 1912, m & pro rec from 1848)

Name	Map Index	Date Formed	Pop. By M	Census Reports Available	Parent County	County Seat
Menard	C3	1858	3	1870-80	Bexar	Menard
Midland	D2	1885	68		Tom Green	Midland

(Co Clk has b rec from 1917, m rec from 1885)

Name	Map Index	Date Formed	Pop. By M	Census Reports Available	Parent County	County Seat
Milam	C3	1836	22	1850-80	Old Mexican Municipality	Cameron
Mills	C2	1887	4		Comanche, Brown, Hamilton, Lampasas	Goldthwaite

(Co Clk has b & d rec from 1903, m, div, pro, civ ct rec from 1887)

Name	Map Index	Date Formed	Pop. By M	Census Reports Available	Parent County	County Seat
Mitchell	D2	1876	11	1880	Bexar	Colorado City
Montague	C1	1857	15	1860-80	Cooke	Montague

(Co Clk has b & d rec from 1903, m, pro, civ ct rec from 1873)

Name	Map Index	Date Formed	Pop. By M	Census Reports Available	Parent County	County Seat
Montgomery	B3	1837	27	1850-80	Washington	Conroe

(Co Clk has b rec from 1903, m & pro rec from 1838)

Name	Map Index	Date Formed	Pop. By M	Census Reports Available	Parent County	County Seat
Moore	F1	1876	15		Bexar	Dumas
Morris	A1	1875	13	1880	Titus	Daingerfield

(Co Clk has b & d rec from 1903, m & pro rec from 1875)

Name	Map Index	Date Formed	Pop. By M	Census Reports Available	Parent County	County Seat
Motley	D1	1876	3	1880	Bexar (Org. 1891)	Matador

(Co Clk has b & d rec from 1903, m, div, pro, civ ct rec from 1891)

Name	Map Index	Date Formed	Pop. By M	Census Reports Available	Parent County	County Seat
Nacogdoches	A2	1836	28	1850-80	Old Mexican Municipality ...	Nacogdoches

(Co Clk has b & d rec from 1903, m, pro, civ ct rec from 1837)

Name	Map Index	Date Formed	Pop. By M	Census Reports Available	Parent County	County Seat
Navarro	B2	1846	34	1850-80	Robertson	Corsicana

Navasota (Name changed to Brazos in 1842)

Name	Map Index	Date Formed	Pop. By M	Census Reports Available	Parent County	County Seat
Newton	A2	1846	10	1850-80	Jasper	Newton
Nolan	D2	1876	19	1880	Young, Bexar	Sweetwater

(Co Clk has b & d rec from 1903, m rec from 1881)

Nueces   E4   1846   222 1850-80 San Patricio .... Corpus Christi
Ochiltree   E1   1876   9   Bexar .... Perryton
  (Co Clk has b rec from 1903, m, div, civ ct rec 1889, d rec 1904, pro rec 1894)
Oldham   F1   1865   2   1880   Bexar (Org. 1880) .... Vega
Orange   A3   1852   60   1860-80 Jefferson .... Orange
  (Co Clk has b & d rec from 1903, m, pro, civ ct rec from 1852)
Palo Pinto   C2   1856   21   1860-80 Navarro, Bosque .... Palo Pinto
Panola   A2   1846   17   1850-80 Harrison, Shelby .... Carthage
Parker   C2   1855   23   1860-80 Bosque, Navarro .... Weatherford
Parmer   F2   1876   10   Bexar .... Farwell
Pecos   E3   1871   12   1880   Presidio .... Fort Stockton
Polk   A3   1846   14   1850-80 Liberty .... Livingston
Potter   F1   1876 116   1880   Bexar .... Amarillo
  (Co Clk has b & d rec incom from 1903, m & pro rec from 1888, civ ct rec 1899)
Presidio   E3   1850   5   1860-80 Bexar .... Marfa
Rains   B1   1870   3   1880   Hopkins, Hunt, Wood .... Emory
Randall   F1   1876   34   Bexar .... Canyon
Reagan   D2   1903   4   Tom Green .... Big Lake
  (Co Clk has b, m, d, div, pro, civ ct rec from 1903)
Real   C3   1913   2   Bandera, Kerr, Edwards ..... Leakey
  (Co Clk has b, m, d, div, pro, civ ct rec from 1913)
Red River   A1   1836   16   1850-80 Old Mexican Municipality ... Clarksville
Reeves   E2   1883   18   Pecos .... Pecos
  (Co Clk has b & d rec from 1903, m, pro, co civ ct rec from-1885)
Refugio   B4   1836   11   1850-80 Old Mexican Municipality .... Refugio
  (Co Clk has b & d rec from 1903, m rec 1851, pro rec 1840, co civ ct rec 1881)
Roberts   E1   1876   1   Bexar .... Miami
  (Co Clk has b & d rec from 1903, m, div, pro, civ ct rec from 1889)
Robertson   B2   1837   16   1850-80 Milam .... Franklin
Rockwall   B1   1873   6   1880   Kaufman .... Rockwall
  (Co Clk has b, m, d, pro, civ ct rec some from as far back as 1873)
Runnells   C2   1858   15   1880   Bexar, Travis (Org. 1880) ... Ballinger
Rusk   A2   1843   36   1850-80 Nacogdoches .... Henderson
Sabine   A2   1836   7   1850-80 Old Mexican Municipality .... Hemphill
San Augustine A2   1836   8   1850-80 Old Mexican Municipality .. San Augustine
San Jacinto   A3   1869   6   1880   Liberty, Polk, Montgomery,
                                        Walker .... Coldspring
San Patricio B4   1836   45   1850-80 Old Mexican Municipality ... Sinton
  (Co Clk has b rec from 1903, m rec 1858, d rec 1910, pro rec 1847)
San Saba   C2   1856   6   1860-80 Bexar .... San Saba
Schleicher   D3   1887   3   Crockett .... Eldorado
Scurry   D2   1876   20   1880   Bexar .... Snyder
  (Co Clk has b & d rec from 1903, m, pro, civ ct rec from 1884)
Shackelford   C2   1858   4   1860-80 Bosque .... Albany
  (Co Clk has b & d rec from 1903, m rec 1886, div, pro, civ ct rec 1887)
Shelby   A2   1836   20   1850-80 Old Mexican Municipality ..... Center
Sherman   F1   1876   3   Bexar .... Stratford
Smith   A2   1846   86   1850-80 Nacogdoches .... Tyler
Somervell   C2   1875   3   1880   Hood, Johnson .... Glen Rose
Starr   F4   1848   17   1850-80 Nueces .... Rio Grande City
  (Co Clk has b & d rec from 1903, m rec 1858, pro rec 1870, civ ct rec 1885)
Stephens   C2   1858   9   1870-80 Bosque .... Breckenridge
  (Co Clk has b rec from 1903, m rec 1876, pro rec 1886, civ ct rec 1881; Orig.
  Buchanan, name changed in 1861)
Sterling   D2   1891   1   Tom Green .... Sterling City
  (Co Clk has b & d rec from 1909, m, pro, civ ct rec 1891, div rec 1892)
Stonewall   D1   1876   3   Bexar .... Aspermont
Sutton   D3   1887   4   Crockett .... Sonora
Swisher   F2   1876   11   Bexar, Young .... Tulia
  (Co Clk has b, d, div, pro rec from 1903, m & civ ct rec from 1890)
Tarrant   B2   1849 538   1850-80 Navarro (1860 census missing) . Fort Worth
Taylor   C2   1858 101   1880   Bexar, Travis .... Abilene
Terrell   D3   1905   3   Pecos .... Sanderson

Terry   E1 1876   16   Martin, Bexar . . . . Brownfield
Throckmorton C1 1858   3 1860–80   Fannin (1870 cen missing). Throckmorton
     (Co Clk has b & d rec from 1903, m, div, pro, civ ct rec from 1879)
Titus   A1 1846   17 1850–80   Red River, Bowie . . . . . . Mt. Pleasant
Tom Green   D2 1874   65 1880   Bexar . . . . San Angelo
     (Co Clk has b & d rec from 1903, m, pro, civ ct rec, deeds, mgts from 1875)

County Map of Texas

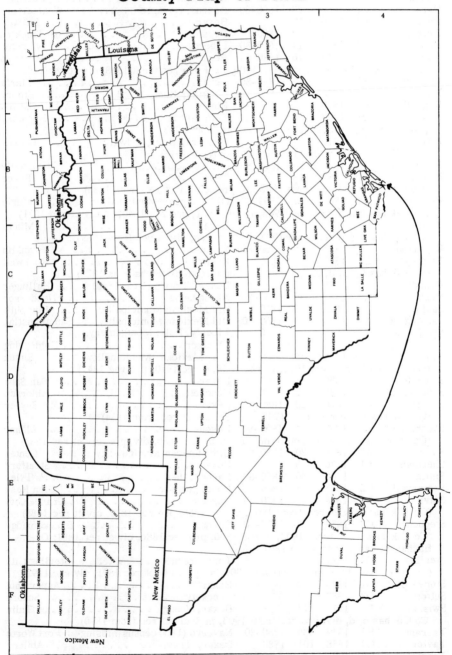

Name	Map Index	Date Formed	Pop. By M	Census Reports Available	Parent County	County Seat
Travis	B3	1840	212	1850-80	Bastrop	Austin
Trinity	A2	1850	8	1860-80	Houston	Groveton
Tyler	A3	1846	11	1850-80	Liberty	Woodville
·Upshur	A2	1846	20	1850-80	Harrison, Nacogdoches	Gilmer

(Co Clk has b & d rec from 1903, m rec 1873, pro rec 1881, civ ct rec 1876)

Upton	D2	1867	6		Tom Green (Org. 1910)	Rankin

(Co Clk has b, m, d, div, civ ct rec from 1910, pro rec from 1910)

Uvalde	C3	1850	17	1860-80	Bexar	Uvalde

(Co Clk has b & d rec from 1903, m rec 1856, pro rec 1857, civ ct rec 1876)

Val Verde	D3	1885	24		Crockett, Kinney, Pecos	Del Rio
Van Zandt	B2	1848	19	1850-80	Henderson	Canton

(Co Clk has b rec from 1903, m, d, div, pro, civ ct rec from 1848)

Victoria	B4	1836	46	1850-80	Old Mexican Municipality	Victoria

(Co Clk has b & d rec from 1903, m, pro, civ ct rec from 1838)

Walker	B3	1846	21	1850-80	Montgomery	Huntsville
Waller	B3	1873	12	1880	Austin, Grimes	Hempstead

(Co Clk has b & d rec from 1903, m, pro, civ ct rec from 1873)

Ward	E2	1887	15		Tom Green	Monohans

(Co Clk has b & d rec from 1903, m rec from 1893, pro rec from 1895)

Washington	B3	1836	19	1850-80	Texas Municipality	Brenham
Webb	F4	1848	65	1850-80	Bexar	Laredo

(Co Clk has b rec from ca 1856, m & d rec ca 1850)

Wharton	B3	1846	38	1850-80	Matagorda, Jackson	Wharton
Wheeler	E1	1876	8	1880	Bexar, Young	Wheeler
Wichita	C1	1858	124	1880	Youngland Dist.	Wichita Falls
Wilbarger	C1	1858	18	1880	Bexar (Org. 1881)	Vernon

(Co Clk has b, m, d, rec from 1903, civ ct rec from 1890)

Willacy	E4	1911	20		Hidalgo, Cameron	Raymondville
Williamson	B3	1848	35	1850-80	Milam	Georgetown

(Co Clk has b & d rec from 1903, m, pro, civ ct rec from 1848)

Wilson	C3	1860	13	1870-80	Bexar, Karnes	Floresville
Winkler	E2	1887	14		Tom Green	Kermit
Wise	C1	1856	17	1860-80	Cooke	Decatur
Wood	B2	1850	18	1860-80	Van Zandt	Quitman
Yoakum	E1	1876	8		Bexar	Plains
Young	C1	1856	17	1860-80	Bosque, Fannin	Graham
Zapata	F4	1858	4	1860-80	Starr, Webb	Zapata
Zavala	C4	1858	13	1860-80	Uvalde, Maverick	Crystal City

Genealogists' Check List of the Historical Records Survey, Texas (see page VIII)

Fed Cts; Inv of Co Arch - Bandera, Bastrop, Brown, Caldwell, Calhoun, Denton, DeWitt, Fayette, Gillespie, Gregg, Guadalupe, Hays, Hood, Jackson, Marion, Milam, Mills, Orange, Robertson, Rockwall, Sabine, Somervell, Uvalde, Wilson; Inv of Mun & Tn Arch - Brazoria; Guide to Pub Vit Stat Rec; Index to Probate Cases Filed in Texas Counties - #7 Atascosa - #19 Bowie, #20 Brazoria - #21 Brazos - #25 Brown - #32 Camp - #36 Chambers - #42 Coleman - #60 Delta - #80 Franklin, #92 Gregg - #94 Guadalupe - #100 Hardin - #105 Hays - #146 Liberty - #155 Marion - #172 Morris - #176 Newton - #177 Nolan - of Rec Required or Permitted by Law in Texas; A Check List of Texas Imprints 1848-1860; A Check List of Texas Imprints 1861-1876; Texas Newspapers 1813-1839 - A Union List of Newspaper Files Available in Offices of Publishers, Lib and a number of Private Collections; See Lousiana for Navigation Casualties; Depo of unpubl mat, Univ of Texas, Austin Texas.

#181 Orange - #198 Robertson - #200 Runnels - #206 San Saba - #210 Shelby - #225 Titus - #228 Trinity - #237 Waller - #246 Williamson - #250 Wood.

Tran & Translation of San Antonio Spanish Min Bk 1 & 2 1815-1835; Jour A Rec of City of San Antonio 1837-1840; Check List

Utah

Capital Salt Lake City

Territory 1850 - State 1896 - (45th)

As the Puritans, the Pilgrims, the Quakers, the Huguenots, and many other religious devotees came to the American shore for the opportunity to worship Almighty God according to their conscience, so the members of the Church of Jesus Christ of Latter-day Saints, or the so-called "Mormons," came to the then arid forbidding valleys of Utah. When they came the land was barren and desolate, nothing but the bluish gray of the sagebrush and greasewood covered the land. Not a sign of human life, except here and there, scattered along the shores of a small lake or the banks of a tiny mountain stream, a few Indian Wigwams. Not even the hoof-prints of the horses that carried Father Escalante and Father Dominguez on a hurried journey through part of the state seventy-one years earlier were anywhere to be found.

It was on July 24, 1847, that the colonization of the Great Salt Lake Basin began with the arrival on the site of the present Salt Lake City of the first Pioneer group 148 - 143 men, three women, and two boys. New groups arrived several times each month. In three years, 1850, there were 11,380.

Most of the early settlers of Utah came from New England, Ohio, Illinois, Missouri, and Canada, and since then from almost every state in the Union. Most of the Europeans who have come in order of their numerical strength, are English, Germans, Danes, Swedes, Norwegians, Swiss, Hollanders, Welsh, and Scotch, with a sprinkling of Piedmont Italians, and a few Czechs. Many Austrians, Greeks, Mexicans and Italians, not affected by church affiliation, have come to work in the mining and smelting operations of the state. Only about two per cent of the population are Negroes.

The Division of Vital Statistics, State Board of Health, Capital Bldg., Salt Lake City, Utah, has records of births since 1890 and deaths since 1848. Marriage records are at the offices of the County Clerks.

The prinicpal sources of genealogical information are the LDS Church records which have been carefully kept and preserved since 1830. Besides that, records have been gathered for years from all over the world and brought to Salt Lake City by the Genealogical Society of the Church of Jesus Christ of Latter-day Saints.

The growth of this society has been astounding. It is now recognized as one of the foremost genealogical libraries in the world, and continues to accelerate its growth by expanding a long time activity of microfilming original records around the world and gathering all types of printed and other records whereever they may be found.

About 95 miles north of Salt Lake City is located the beautiful Cache Valley with its principal city, Logan. A block east of its business section is the Cache County Library. One of the important departments of that Library is the genealogical section, not large, but choice. It is good enough to elicit from a stranger who has visited most of the important libraries on a leisurely auto trip across the nation the remark, "This is the best Genealogical Library I have seen between the Mississippi and the Pacific, with the exception of course, of your large library in Salt Lake City."

Any community with an enthusiastic genealogists can do for his or her library what has been done here. Several years ago the late Walter M. Everton, the founder of the GENEALOGICAL HELPER and the HANDY BOOK FOR GENEALOGISTS, opened the genealogical section of the Cache County Library. He brought with him to the library one genealogical book he had purchased some time previously. He appealed for books from those interested, money from those who had no books. He solicited the merchants of Logan for donations and collected about $7,000.00 all of which was spent for books. It is mainly through his efforts and the cooperation of the Board of Directors of the library that there are now about 8,000 genealogical books on the shelves of the department.

Genealogists' Check List of the Historical Records Survey, Utah (see page VIII)

Fed Cts; Inv of Co Arch - Box Elder, Carbon, Daggett, Emery, Grand, Morgan, Sanpete, Tooele, Uintah, Utah, Wasatch, Weber; Inv of Mun & Tn Arch - A Hist of

Ogden; Census of Weber Co (Exclusive of Green River Precinct) Provisional State of Deseret; Guide to Pub Vit Stat Rec; Inv of the Chr Arch of Utah – Vol 1 Hist & Bibliography of Religion – Vol 2 Bap Chr – Vol 3 Smaller Denominations; Dir of Chrs & Rel Org in Utah – except L D S: Check List of Newspapers & Magazines Pub in Ogden; Co Gov of the Provisional State of Deseret; Rec Required of Co Officers, State of Deseret 15 Mar 1849 to 5 Apr 1851; Depo of unpubl mat, State Historical Soc, Salt Lake City, Utah.

County Map of Utah

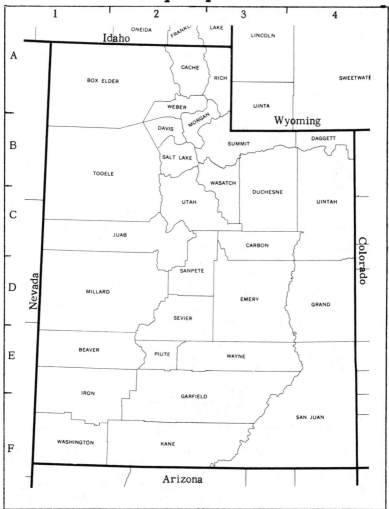

Utah County Histories

(Population figures to nearest thousand – 1960 Census)

Name	Map Index	Date Formed	Pop. By M	Census Reports Available	Parent County	County Seat
Beaver	E1	1856	4	1860–80	Iron, Millard	Beaver
Box Elder	A1	1856	25	1860–80	Unorganized Territory . . .	Brigham City
Cache	A2	1856	36	1860–80	Unorganized Territory	Logan
Carbon	C3	1894	21		Sanpete	Price

| Daggett | B4 | 1917 | 1 | | Uintah | . . . . | Manila |
| Davis | B2 | 1850 | 65 | 1850-80 | Salt Lake | . . . . | Farmington |

(Co Clk has b & d rec from 1898 to 1905)

| Duchesne | C3 | 1914 | 7 | | Wasatch | . . . . | Duchesne |
| Emery | D3 | 1880 | 6 | 1880 | Sanpete, Sevier | . . . . | Castle Dale |

(Co Clk has div rec from 1900, civ ct rec from 1890)

| Garfield | F3 | 1864 | 4 | | Iron, Sevier, Kane | . . . . | Panguitch |

(Co Clk has m rec from 1887, div, pro, civ ct rec from 1888)

| Grand | D4 | 1892 | 6 | | Emery, Uintah | . . . . | Moab |

(Co Clk has m, div, pro, civ ct rec from 1890)

| Iron | F1 | 1852 | 11 | 1850-80 | Unorganized Territory | . . . . | Parowan |

(Co Clk has m rec from 1880, div, pro, civ ct rec from 1860)

Juab	C1	1849	5	1860-80	Original county	. . . .	Nephi
Kane	F2	1864	3	1870-80	Washington, Unorganized Terr.	. .	Kanab
Millard	D1	1852	8	1860-80	Juab	. . . .	Fillmore

(Co Clk has m rec from 1887, div, pro, civ ct rec from 1896)

Morgan	B2	1862	3	1870-80	Davis, Summit	. . . .	Morgan
Piute	E2	1866	1	1870-80	Sevier	. . . .	Junction
Rich	A3	1864	2	1870-80	Formerly Richland	. . . .	Randolph

(Co Clk has m, div, pro, civ ct rec from 1888)

| Salt Lake | B2 | 1849 | 383 | 1850-80 | Orig. Co. (Great S. L.) | . . . | Salt Lake City |

(Co Clk has m rec from 1887, div, pro, civ ct rec from 1896)

| San Juan | F4 | 1880 | 9 | 1880 | Kane | . . . . | Monticello |

(Co Clk has m rec from 1889, div rec 1890, pro rec 1888, civ ct rec 1891)

| Sanpete | D3 | 1849 | 11 | 1850-80 | Original county | . . . . | Manti |
| Sevier | D2 | 1864 | 11 | 1870-80 | Sanpete | . . . . | Richfield |

(Co Clk has m rec from 1888, div, pro, civ ct rec from 1896)

| Summit | B3 | 1854 | 6 | 1860-80 | Salt Lake | . . . . | Coalville |
| Tooele | B1 | 1849 | 18 | 1850-80 | Original county | . . . . | Tooele |

(Co Clk has b & d rec 1899 to 1904, m rec 1887, div, pro, civ ct rec 1897)

| Uintah | C4 | 1880 | 12 | 1880 | Wasatch | . . . . | Vernal |
| Utah | C2 | 1849 | 107 | 1850-80 | Original county | . . . . | Provo |

(Co Clk has b & d rec from 1906, div rec 1887, pro rec 1859, civ ct rec 1870)

| Wasatch | B3 | 1862 | 5 | 1870-80 | Summit | . . . . | Heber |

(Co Clk has b & d rec 1897 to 1905, m rec 1862, div, pro, civ ct rec 1897)

| Washington | F1 | 1852 | 10 | 1860-80 | Unorganized Territory | . . . . . | St. George |
| Wayne | E3 | 1864 | 2 | | Piute | . . . . | Loa |

(Co Clk hs b rec from 1898, d rec 1899, m, div, pro, civ ct rec 1892)

| Weber | A2 | 1849 | 111 | 1850-80 | Original county | . . . . | Ogden |

(Co Clk has m rec from 1887, div & civ ct rec from 1878, pro rec from 1892)

Vermont

Capital Montpelier - State 1791 - (14th)

Vermont was late in getting settled as compared with other states in New England. One reason was the hostility of the French and Indians in the Quebec district north of Vermont. As soon as the French released all claims on the sections within the American colonies, security was established and settlers felt free to go into the distant and lonely Vermont sections. As early as 1724 English people living along the New England coastline became interested in Vermont.

Massachusetts and Connecticut played the biggest role in the settling of Vermont, although people moved from several of the other states to settle the communities established in Vermont from 1714 on, but mostly between 1740 and 1800. As mentioned, Connecticut and Massachusetts furnished settlers for almost every early community in Vermont, but settlers also came from Canada, New Hampshire, New York, Rhode Island, Maine, and New Jersey.

French Canadians came into the northern counties as late as the 1900s. They were preceded by several years by the Irish. Into the Markham Mountain region in southwestern Windsor county and the Equinox Mountain section of northern Bennington County came many farmers from Finland. Welsh came to work in the slate quarries in the midwest section of Rutland

County. Scotch and Italian stone cutters came to the quarries southeast of Montpelier, Russians, Poles, Czechs, Austrians and Swedes came to the granite quarries of Rutland County. About half of the foreign born population of Vermont came from Canada.

Birth, marriage, and death records from approximately 1760 until the present time are on file in the office of the Secretary of State, Division of Vital Records, State House, Montpelier, Vermont. Each month this office recieves a group of vital records from the town and the county officers. These records are generally about six months in arrear. It may be well to try the City or Town Clerk if the Secretary of State does not have the record.

Wills are recorded in the twenty probate districts of the state, with each county having one or more probate district. For information write the Registrar, Probate Court, County Seat. Deeds are recorded in 246 Town and fourteen County Clerks offices. Land grants are on file in the offices of the Town Clerk. Census records are available at the State Library in Montpelier. Tax payers lists are with the Town Clerks. War service records are on file in the office of the Adjutant General in Montpelier. Cemetery records are with the church records of the sextons.

CARLETON, HIRAM, *Genealogical & Family History of the State of Vermont*, 2 vols., Lewis Publishing Co., New York, Chicago, 1903.

CLARK, BYRON N., *A List of Pensioners of the War of* 1812, pub. 1904.

DODGE, PRENTISS CUTLER, *Encyclopedia, Vermont Biography*, pub., 1912.

First Census of the United States, 1790, Vermont, Government Printing Office, 1907.

GOODRICH, JOHN E., *Vermont Rolls of the Soldiers in the Revolutionary War*, Published by authority of the Legislature, The Tuttle Co., Rutland, Vt., 1904.

Heads of Families, Second Census of the United States, 1800, State of Vermont, Published by Vermont Historical Society, Montpelier, Vt., 1938.

WPA, *Bibliography of Research Projects Reports, Check List of Historical Records Survey Publications*, 1940.

Vermont Libraries: Burlington (Chittenden), University of Vermont and State (Agricultural) College Libraries, Billings Library, (Vermont), (Civil War); Montpelier, (Washington), Vermont Free Public Library Commission, State Library Bldg.; Vermont Historical Society Library, State House, (History, Vermontiana).

Vermont Towns Organized Before 1800

ADDISON, organized 1785. Addison, 1783; Bridport, 1786; Cornwall, 1774; Ferrisburgh, 1769; Leicester, 1774; Lincoln, 1790; Middlebury, 1766; Monktown, 1774; New Haven, 1769; Orwell, 1775; Panton, 1764; Ripton, 1781; Salisbury, 1774; Shoreham, 1766; Starksborough, 1788; Vergennes, 1764; Waltham, S. bef. Rev.; Weybridge, 1775; Whiting, 1773.

BENNINGTON, organized 1779 Arlington, 1763; Bennington, 1761; Dorset, 1768; Glastenbury, 1661; Landgrove, 1761; Manchester, 1764; Peru abt. 1773; Pownal, 1762; Rupert, 1767; Sandgate, 1771; Shaftsbury, 1763; Sunderland, 1766; Winhall, 1761.

CALEDONIA, Organized 1796. Barnet, 1770; Burke, 1790; Cabot, 1785; Danville, 1785; Groton, 1787; Hardwick, 1790; Kirby, 1799; Lyndon, 1788; Peacham, 1775; Ryegate, 1774; Sheffield, 1792; St. Johnsbury, 1786; Sutton, 1791; Walden, 1789; Waterford, 1797; Wheelock, 1785.

CHITTENDEN, Organized 1787. Bolton, 1763; Burlington, 1773; Charlotte, 1776; Colchester, 1772; Essex, 1783; Hinesburg ,1774; Huntington, 1786; Jericho, 1774; Milton, 1783; Richmond, 1775; Shelburne, 1768; St. George, 1784; Underhill, 1786; Willistown, 1774.

ESSEX, Organized 1797. Bloomfield, 1762; Brunswick, 1780; Canaan, 1791; Concord, 1783; Guildhall, 1764; Lunenburg, 1770; Maidstone, 1772; Victory, 1781.

FRANKLIN, Organized 1796. Bakersfield, 1799; Berkshire, 1780; Enosburgh, 1797; Fairfax, 1783; Fairfield, 1788; Fletcher, 1781; Franklin ,1789; Georgia, 1784-5; Highgate, 1763; Montgomery, 1780; Richford, 1797; Sheldon, 1790; Swantown, 1787; St. Albans, 1775.

GRAND ISLE, Organized 1802. Alburgh, 1782; Grand Isle, 1783; Isle la Mott, 1785; North Hero 1783; South Hero, 1779.

LAMOILLE, Organized 1835. Cambridge, 1783; Elmore, 1790; Hyde Park, 1787; Johnson, 1784; Morristown, 1790; Sterling, 1799; Stowe, 1793; Waterville, 1789; Wolcott, 1781.

ORANGE, Organized 1781. Bradford, S. 1765; Braintree, S. 1783; Brookfield, S. 1771; Chelsea, S. 1784; Corinth. O. 1777; Fairlee, S. 1766; Newbury, S. 1763; Orange, O. 1793; Randolph, O. 1781; Stratford, S. 1768; Thetford, S. 1764; Topsham, S. 1781; Turnbridge, S. 1776; Vershire, O. 1780; Washington, O. 1785; W. Fairlee, 1761; Williamtown, 1784.

ORLEANS, Organized 1797. Barton,

1789; Craftsbury, 1788; Derby, 1795; Glover, 1797; Greensborough, 1789; Holland, 1800; Jay, S. bef. Rev.; Salem, 1798; Westfield, 1790.

RUTLAND, Organized 1781. Benson, 1783; Brandon, 1772; Castleton, 1767; Chittenden aft. Rev.; Clarendon, 1768; Danby, 1765; Fairhaven, 1779; Hubbardton, 1775; Ira, 1779; Mendon, 1781; Middletown, 1774; Mt. Holly, 1787; Mt. Tabor, 1761; Pawlet, 1761; Pittsford, 1767; Poultney, 1777; Rutland, 1769; Sherburn, 1785; Shrewsbury, 1763; Sudbury, bef. Rev.; Tinsmith, 1770; Wallingsford, 1773; Wells, 1768; West Haven, 1770.

WASHINGTON, Organized 1810. Barre, 1780; Berlin 1785; Calais, 1787; Duxbury, 1786; Payston, 1798; Marshfield, 1782; Middlesex, 1787; Montpelier, 1786; Moretown, 1790; Northfield, 1785; Plainsfield, 1794; Roxbury, 1789; Waitsfield,

1789; Warren, 1797; Waterbury, 1784; Worcester, 1797.

WINDHAM, 1781. Athens, 1780; Brattleboro, 1724; Brookline, 1777; Dover, 1780; Grafton, 1768; Guilford, 1761; Halifax, 1761; Jamacia, 1780; Londonderry, 1773; **Marlborough, 1763; Newfane, 1766; Putney, 1744; Rockingham, 1753; Townsend, 1761; Woodborough, 1780; Westminister, 1741; Whitington, 1771; Wilmington S. bef. Rev.; Windham, 1773.**

WINDSOR, Organized before Statehood. **Andover, 1776; Baltimore, 1794; Barnard, 1774; Bethel, 1779; Bridgewater, 1779; Cavendish, 1769; Chester, 1764; Hartford, 1763; Hartland, 1763; Ludlow, 1714; Norwich, 1762; Plymouth, 1777; Pomfret, 1770; Reading, 1772; Royalton, 1771; Sharon, 1764; Springfield, 1761; Stockbridge, 1784; Weathersfield, 1761; Weston, 1790; Windsor, 1764; Woodstock, 1768.**

Vermont County Histories

(Population figures to nearest thousand - 1960 Census)

Name	Map Index	Date Formed	Pop. By M	Census Reports Available	Parent County	County Seat
Addison	B1	1785	20	1790-80	Rutland	Middlebury
Bennington	D1	1779	25	1790-80	Original county	Bennington
Caledonia	B3	1792	23	1800-80	Newly Organized Terr.	St. Johnsbury
(Co Clk has div, civ ct, chancery ct rec from 1797)						
Chittenden	B1	1787	74	1790-80	Original county	Burlington
Essex	A3	1792	6	1800-80	Unorganized Territory	Guildhall
(Co Clk has b, m, d rec from 1885, div & civ ct rec from 1800)						
Franklin	A1	1792	29	1800-80	Chittenden	St. Albans
(Co Clk has div rec from 1900)						
Grand Isle	A1	1802	3	1810-80	Franklin	North Hero
Lamoille	A2	1835	11	1840-80	Chittenden	Hyde Park
Orange	B2	1781	16	1790-80	Original county	Chelsea
(Co Clk has div & civ ct rec from 1781, pro rec 1793, land rec 1771)						
Orleans	A2	1792	20	1800-80	Original county	Newport
Rutland	C1	1781	47	1790-80	Original county	Rutland
Washington	B2	1810	43	1820-80	Addison, Orange	Montpelier
(Co Clk has div, pro, civ ct rec from 1791)						
Windham	D2	1779	30	1790-80	Bennington	Newfane & Marlboro
Windsor	C2	1781	44	1790-80	Original county	N. Hartland & Woodstock
(Co Clk has div & civ ct rec from 1782)						

Genealogists' Check List of the Historical Records Survey, Vermont (see page VIII)

Fed Cts; Inv of Co Arch - Lamoille; Inv of Mun & Tn Arch - Albany, Alburgh Village, Belvidere, Benson, Bolton, Bridport, Brookline, Cambridge, Charlotte, Castleton, Cavendish, Clarendon, Coventry, Dandy, Derby (also supplement), Derby Line, Eden, Elmore, Essex, Fairfax, Grafton, Grand Isle, Hubbardton, Hyde Park, Isle LaMotte, Jamaica, Johnson, Mansfield, Morristown, Morrisville, Mt Tabor, North Hero, Plymouth, Salem, Shrewsbury, South Hero, Sterling Village, Stowe, Walcott, Wallingford, Waterville, Villages of Derby, Tinmouth, Two Heroes.

Inv of the Chr Arch of Vt - Prot Episcopal, Diocese of Vt - Preprint of Chrs of Hinesburg; Dir of Chrs and Rel Org in Vt; Cal of the Ira Allen Papers in the Wilburn Lib of the Univ of Vt; Index to the Burling-Free Press in the Billings Lib, Univ of Vt-Vol 1 1848-1852, Vol 2 1853-1855, Vol 3 1856-1858, Vol 4 1859-1861, Vol 5 1862-

1863, Vol 6 1864-1865, Vol 7 1866-1867, of unpubl mat, State Hist Soc, Montpelier,
Vol 8 1868, Vol 9 1869, Vol 10 1870; Depo   Vt.

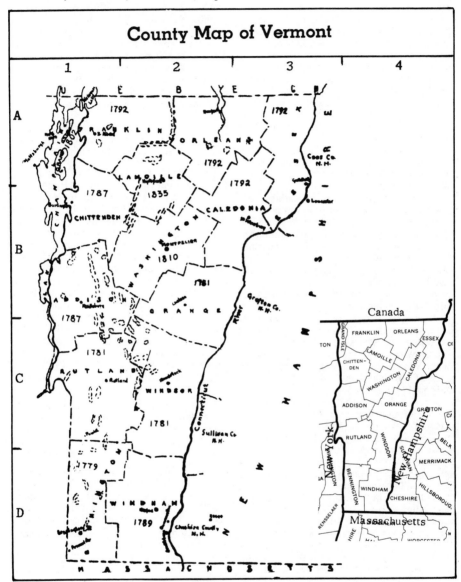

County Map of Vermont

Virginia

Capital Richmond - State 1788 - (10th)

The colonization of the American continent in modern times began with the arrival of three boatloads of English immigrants in May, 1607 on the northeast shore of James River in the present Virginia.

One of the leaders was Captain John Smith, a daring adventurous fellow with an inquisitive mind who had been in many tight situations on the outskirts of civilization. With a score of companions, he sailed into several of the many bays and river openings along the zigzagging east coast, and thus became acquainted with the lay of the land.

Having done nothing to provide food for the winter, more than half of the colony succumbed from illness and lack of nourishing food.

The summer of 1608 brought them new supplies from England and 120 more immigrants.

In the fall of 1608 the colony of 130 or 140 persons was augmented by the arrival of seventy more immigrants in the third expediton to Virginia.

At the beginning of the winter of 1609 the colony consisted of 490 persons. When the spring of 1610 arrived there were only 60 persons left in the colony.

Determined to return to England, the group embarked. The ship was coming out of the mouth of the James River when Virginia bound ships under the command of Lord Delaware came in sight. Against their own judgment, the disgruntled colonists were persuaded to return to their abandoned homes.

Early in 1610 more food and additional colonists arrived from England.

Virgina became a royal colony in 1624. From then until 1776 when it announced its independence, it was in almost constant trouble with the Crown or its representatives. Mainly, the colonists objected to the arbitrary action of the colony officials and their ruthless demands.

Every month in the year, with the exception of the winter months, saw boatloads of new immigrants arriving. More and more settlements were established, some as far north as the Potomac River. By 1700 there were more than 80,000 persons living in the Tidewater region of Virginia. Twenty thousand more had come by 1717. During the next 37 years, the population increased by almost two hundred per cent, reaching 284,000 by 1754.

Even before that time the settlers had scattered over the coastal plain, the Piedmont plateau, and had crossed over the Blue Ridge highlands and settled in the Valley of Virginia, with the Appalachian Plateau at their back. There they had settled along the rivers, hundreds of miles from the coast line.

As early as 1730 there had been a heavy immigration from Pennsylvania into Virginia of Scotch-Irish, Welsh, and Germans, most of whom settled in the upper valleys. Naturally, therefore, it was in that section where flourished the Welsh Baptist Church, the English Quakers, and the Scotch Presbyterians. Methodist churches were established about 1800.

Virginia was well settled by 1775. By 1800 it had upwards of 90 counties and a population of nearly a million.

Nine other states had preceded Virginia into the Union when she entered in June 1788. In the first three U. S. Census reports 1790, 1800, 1810, Virginia registered the highest population in the nation. In 1820 she was second to New York. In 1830 she was surpassed by New York and Pa.

Foreign born residents predominate in the following order in Virginia: Russians, English, Germans, Italians, Greeks, Polish, Czechs, Irish, Austrians and Hungarians.

Until 1686 the Episcopal Church was the state church in Virginia. All children, regardless of religious affiliation, were required to be baptized by the ministers of that church. Dates of their baptism, together with their names, dates of birth, and names of their parents were recorded in the parish registers. The same information was taken of all marriages and burials. All of these church records are preserved, some are printed. They are available in the Virginia State Library in Richmond.

The Quit Rent list is used as a Census Report or Schedule. In 1704 all Virginia landowners, except those in Lancaster, Northumberland, Westmoreland, Richmond and Stafford counties, had to pay the king a Quit Rent of one shilling for each fifty acres bought.

Since the 1790 U. S. Census records were destroyed in a fire, Fothergill and Naugle in "Taxpayers of Virginia" have tried to augment similar lists gathered from other counties by the government.

In the 1790 to 1860 Federal Census schedules for Virginia will be found 50 counties now in West Virginia. These counties withdrew from Virginia in 1861 and in 1863 became our thirty-fifth State.

Excellent service is extended researchers at the Virginia State Library in Richmond, Va. Loan volumes are limited to those books of which they have duplicates. Photostats of original record books may be obtained at a reasonable price. The library has Parish Registers and Vestry Books from 1618 to 1860. Not that all of those records are from that period, but somewhere within that span of time. It also has a collection of State Land Office Records. These records contain patents for land dating from 1623, and a name index has been compiled. However, the nature of the records is such that they give no information as to the date, place of arrival of the patentees in America, or the names of the ships.

The State Bureau of Vital Statistics, Richmond, Va., has birth and death records from 1853 to 1896, and after 1912. Marriage records are available from 1853 to the present. Some marriage bonds are in the State Library, Richmond, Va., others are in the office of the Clerk of the Court or city in which the marriage took place. Several of the so-called independent cities have their own records of birth and deaths. Inquire at the City Board of Health office.

Virginia's independent cities are Alexandria, Bristol, Buena Vista, Charlottesville, Clifton Forge, Colonial Heights, Covington, Danville, Falls Church, Fredericksburg, Galax, Hampton, Harrisonburg, Hopewell, Lynchburg, Martinsville, Newport News, Norfolk, Petersburg, Portsmouth, Radford, Richmond, Roanoke, South Boston, South Norfolk, Staunton, Suffolk, Virginia Beach, Waynesboro, Williamsburg and Winchester.

Virginia libraries - Charlottesville, (Albermarle), University of Virginia, Alderman Library, (Virginiana); Danville, (Pittsylvania), Danville Public Library, 975 Main St.; Fredricksburg, (Spotsylvania), Mary Washington College of the University of Virginia, E. Lee Trinkle Library, (Virginiana, American History); Lexington, (Rockbridge), Virginia Military Institute, Preston Library, (Confederate History); Norfolk, (Norfolk), Norfolk Public Library, 345 W. Freemason St., (local history); Richmond, (Henrico), Richmond Public Library, 101 E. Franklin St.; Union Theological Seminary Library, 3401 Brook Rd., (Presbyterian History); Virginia His-

torical Society, 707 E. Franklin St. (mss. Virginia and Colonial Americans, Confederate state histories); Virginia State Library, Capital St., (Virginia and Southern history. Virginia newspapers and public records); Roanoke, (Roanoke), Roanoke Public Library, 722 S. Jefferson St.; Williamsburg, (James City), College of William and Mary Library, (Virginiana Early Americana).

Some of the more important books on Virginia:

BURGESS, LOUIS A., *Virginia Soldiers of 1776*, 3 Vol., pub. 1927 Richmond Press. Richmond, Va.

Du BELLET, LOUISE PECQUET, *Some Prominent Virginia Families*, 4 Vol. pub 1907 Lynchburg.

GWATHMEY, JOHN H., *Historical Register of Virginia in the Revolution,—Soldiers, Sailors, Marines, 1775-1783.* Pub. 1938, Dietz Press. Richmond, Va.

HAYDEN, REV. HORACE EDWIN, *Virginia Genealogies*, Reprint 1931, The Rare Book Shop, Washington, D. C.

NUGENT, NELL MARION, *Cavaliers and Pioneers*, Abstracts of Land Patents and Grants 1623-1800, 5 Vol. pub. 1934, Deitz Printing Co., Richmond, Va.

SWEM, E. G., *Virginia Historical Index*, 2 Vol. pub. 1934, Stone Printing and Mfg. Co., Roanoke, Va.

Virginia Magazine of History and Biography, Published by the Virginia Historical Society, 707 E. Franklin St., Richmond, Va.

William and Mary Quarterly, (a magazine of early American history, institutions and culture) Published by College of William and Mary, Williamsburg, Va.

Virginia County Histories

(Population figures to nearest thousand - 1960 Census)

Name	Map Index	Date Formed	Pop. By M	Census Reports Available	Parent County	County Seat
Accomack	A2	1663	31	1810-80	Northampton	Accomac
Albemarle	C2	1744	31	1810-80	Goochland, Louisa	Charlottesville
Alexandria		1801		1850-80	Fairfax, became part of Dist. of Columbia	Alexandria

(See Dist. of Columbia for cen rec of 1800-40; 1920 changed to Arlington)

Alleghany	D2	1822	12	1830-80	Bath, Botetourt, Monroe . . .	Covington

(Clk of Cir Ct has div, pro, civ ct rec from 1822)

Amelia	C2	1734	8	1810-80	Brunswick, Prince George	. Amelia C.H.

(Clk of Cir Ct has m, div, pro, civ ct deeds, from 1735)

Amherst	D2	1761	23	1810-80	Albemarle	Amherst
Appomatox	D2	1845	9	1850-80	Buckingham, Campbell, Charlotte, Prince Edward	Appomattox

(Clk of Cir Ct has m, div, pro, civ ct rec from 1892)

Arlington	B1	1801	163		Fairfax	Arlington
Augusta	D2	1738-45	37	1810-80	Orange	Staunton

(Clk of Cir Ct has b rec 1853 to 1896, m rec from 1785, div rec from 1745)

Bath   D2   1790-1   5   1810-80   Augusta, Botetourt,
                                              Greenbrier . . . . Warm Springs
    (Clk of Cir Ct has b rec 1854 to 1880, d rec 1854 to 1870, div, pro, Law &
Chancery rec from 1791)
Bedford   D2   1753-4 31   1810-80   Albemarle , Lunenburg . . . . . Bedford
    (Clk of Cir Ct has b & d rec 1854 to 1897, m, div, pro, civ ct, deeds from 1754)
Bland   E3   1861   6   1870-80   Giles, Tazewell, Wythe . . . . . . Bland
    (Clk of Cir Ct has m, pro, civ ct rec from 1861)
Botetourt   D2   1769-70 17   1810-80   Augusta . . . . Fincastle
    (Clk of Cir Ct has b & d rec 1853 to 1870, m, div, pro, civ ct rec from 1770)
Brunswick   C3   1720-32 18   1810-80   Prince George, Isle of Wight,
                                              Surry . . . . Lawrenceville
    (Clk of Cir Ct has b rec 1800 to 1896, m & pro rec from 1732)
Buchanan   F3   1858   37   1860-80   Russell, Tazewell . . Big Rock & Grundy
    (Clk of Cir Ct has m, div, pro, civ ct rec from 1885; Ct House burned 1885)
Buckingham   C2   1761   11   1810-80   Albemarle, Appomattox . . . Buckingham
    (Clk of Cir Ct has b & d rec 1869 to 1896, m, div, pro rec from 1869)
Campbell   D3   1781-2 33   1810-80   Bedford . . . . Rustburg
Caroline   C2   1727-8 13   1810-80   Essex, King and Queen,
                                              King William . . . . Bowling Green
Carroll   E3   1842   23   1850-80   Grayson, Patrick . . . . Hillsville
Charles City B2   1634   5   1810-80   Original Shire . . . . Charles City
Charles River (See York)
Charlotte   C3   1764-5 13   1810-80   Lunenburg . . . . . Charlotte Court House
Chesterfield C2   1749   71   1810-80   Henrico . . . . Chesterfield
    (Clk of Cir Ct has m rec from 1771)
Clarke   C1   1836   8   1840-80   Frederick, Warren . . . . . . Berryville
Craig   E2   1851   3   1860-80   Botetourt, Giles, Roanoke, Monroe,
                                              Alleghany, Montgomery . . . NewCastle
    (Clk of Cir Ct has b rec 1864 to 1896, m, div, pro, civ ct, deeds from 1851)
Culpeper   C1   1748-9 15   1810-80   Orange . . . . Culpeper
Cumberland   C2   1748-9   6   1810-80   Goochland . . . . Cumberland
    (Clk of Cir Ct has m, div, pro, civ ct rec from 1749)
Dickenson   F3   1880   20   Buchanan, Russell, Wise . . . Clintwood
Dinwiddie   C3   1752   22   1810-80   Prince George . . . . Dinwiddie
    (Clk of Cir Ct has b & d rec 1865 to 1896, m & pro rec 1833, div rec 1870)
Dunmore (See Shenandoah)
Elizabeth City   1634   89   1810-80   Original Shire . . . . Hampton
    (Now Hampton, Independent City)
Essex   B2   1692   7   1810-80   Old Rappahannock . . . . Tappahannock
Fairfax   C1   1742   275   1810-80   Prince William, Loudoun . . . . . Fairfax
Fauquier   C1   1759   24   1810-80   Prince William . . . . Warrenton
Fincastle   1772   Botetourt (Discontinued 1777)
Floyd   E3   1831   10   1840-80   Montgomery, Franklin . . . . . . Floyd
    (Clk of Cir Ct has m, div, pro, civ ct rec from 1831)
Fluvanna   C2   1777   7   1810-80   Albemarle . . . . Palmyra
    (Clk of Cir Ct has b & d rec 1867 to 1896, m, div, pro, civ ct, deeds from 1777)
Franklin   D3   1785-6 26   1810-80   Bedford, Henry, Patrick . . . Rocky Mount
Frederick   C1   1738-43 22   1810-80   Orange, Augusta . . . . Winchester
Giles   E3   1806   17   1810-80   Montgomery, Monroe, Tazewell, Craig,
                                              Mercer, Wythe . . . . Pearisburg
Gloucester   B2   1651   12   1810-80   York . . . . Gloucester
Goochland   C2   1727-8   9   1810-80   Henrico . . . . Goochland
Grayson   E3   1792-3 17   1820-80   Wythe, Patrick . . . . Independence
    (Clk of Cir Ct has b & d rec 1853 to 1870, div rec 1792, deeds 1793, wills 1796)
Greene   C2   1838   5   1840-80   Orange . . . . Stanardsville
    (Clk of Cir Ct has b & d rec 1838 to 1897, m, div, pro, deeds, civ ct rec 1838)
Greensville   C3   1780-1 16   1810-80   Brunswick, Sussex . . . . Emporia
Halifax   D3   1752   34   1820-80   Lunenburg . . . . Halifax
    (Clk of Cir Ct has m, pro, deeds from 1752)
Hanover   C2   1720-1 28   1810-80   New Kent . . . . Hanover
Henrico   C2   1634   117   1810-80   Original Shire . . . . Richmond
    (Clk of Cir Ct has m & pro rec from 1781)

Henry   D3   1776-7 40   1820-80   Pittsylvania, Patrick . . . . . Martinsville
Highland   D2   1847   3   1850-80   Bath, Pendleton . . . . Monterey
Illinois   1778   (Discontinued 1784)
Isle of Wight B3   1634   17   1810-80   Original Shire . . . . . . Isle of Wight
    (Clk of Cir Ct has b rec 1853 to 1876, d rec 1853 to 1874, m rec from 1772,
    div rec from 1853, pro rec from 1647, civ ct rec from 1746)
James City   B2   1634   12   1820-80   Original Shire . . . . Williamsburg
Kentucky   1777   (Discontinued 1780)
King and Queen B2 1691   6   1810-80   New Kent . . . . King & Queen C.H.
    (Clk of Cir Ct has m, div, pro, civ ct rec from 1864)
King George   B2   1720-1 7   1810-80   Richmond, Westmoreland . . King George
    (Clk of Cir Ct has m rec from 1786, div, pro, civ ct rec from 1721)
King William   B2   1701-2 8   1820-80   King and Queen . . . . . King William
    (Clk of Cir Ct has m, div, pro, civ ct rec from 1885; fire 1885 burned most rec)
Lancaster   B2   1651   9   1810-80   Northumberland, York . . . . . Lancaster
Lee   G3   1792-3 26   1810-80   Russell, Scott . . . . Jonesville
    (Clk of Cir Ct has b & d rec 1853 to 1877, m rec 1830, div rec 1832, pro rec
    1800, civ ct rec & deeds from 1793)
Loudoun   C1   1757   25   1810-80   Fairfax . . . . Leesburg
Louisa   C2   1742   13   1820-80   Hanover . . . . Louisa
    (Clk of Cir Ct has b rec 1867 to 1896, m, div, pro rec from 1742)
Lower Norfolk   1637   New Norfolk (See Princess Anne and Norfolk)
Lunenburg   C3   1746   13   1810-80   Brunswick . . . . Lunenburg
    (Clk of Cir Ct has m, div, pro, civ ct rec from 1746)
Madison   C2   1792-3 8   1810-80   Culpeper . . . . Madison
    (Clk of Cir Ct has m, div, pro, civ ct, chancery ct rec from 1793)
Mathews   B2   1790-1 7   1810-80   Gloucester . . . . Mathews
Mecklenburg   C3   1764-5 31   1820-80   Lunenburg . . . . . . Boydton & Radcliffe
Middlesex   B2   1673   6   1820-80   Lancaster . . . . Saluda
    (Clk of Cir Ct has m, div, pro, civ ct rec from 1668)
Montgomery   E3   1776-7 33   1810-80   Fincastle, Botetourt,
                                           Pulaski . . . . Christiansburg
Nansemond   B3   1637   31   1820-80   Upper Norfolk . . . . Suffolk
Nelson   D2   1807-8 13   1810-80   Amherst . . . . Lovingston
    (Clk of Cir Ct has m, div, pro, civ ct rec from 1808)
New Kent   B2   1654   5   1810-80   York (Pt. James City) . . . . New Kent
    (Clk of Cir Ct has b & d rec 1865 to 1888, m, div, pro rec from 1865)
New Norfolk   1636   Elizabeth City
Norfolk   B3   1691   52   1810-80   Lower Norfolk . . . . Portsmouth
Northampton   A2   1634   17   1820-80   Original Shire . . . . Eastville
Northumberland B2 1648   10   1810-80   York . . . . Heathsville
Nottoway   C3   1788-9 15   1810-80   Amelia . . . . Nottoway
    (Clk of Cir Ct has m, div, pro, civ ct rec from 1865)
Orange   C2   1734   13   1820-80   Spotsylvania . . . . Orange
    (Clk of Cir Ct has b rec 1860 to 1895, m rec 1757, pro, civ ct, deeds from 1734)
Page   C1   1831   16   1840-80   Rockingham, Shenandoah . . . . . . Luray
Patrick   E3   1790-1 15   1820-80   Henry . . . . Stuart
    (Clk of Cir Ct has b rec 1853 to 1896, m rec from 1791)
Pittsylvania   D3   1766-7 58   1820-80   Halifax . . . . Chatham
Powhatan   C2   1777   7   1810-80   Cumberland, Chesterfield . . . Powhatan
Prince Edward C3   1753-4 14   1810-80   Amelia . . . . Farmville
    (Clk of Cir Ct has b rec 1853 to 1896, d rec 1853 to 1869, m, div, pro, guardian
    book from 1754)
Prince George B3   1702-3 20   1810-80   Charles City . . . . Prince George
Prince William C1 1730-1 50   1810-80   King George, Stafford . . . . . . Manassas
    (Clk of Cir Ct has m rec from 1859, pro rec from 1734)
Princess Anne B3   1691   76   1810-80   Lower Norfolk . . . . Princess Anne
    (Clk of Cir Ct has b rec 1889 to 1895, m rec 1853, div rec 1814, pro rec 1783,
    civ ct rec 1937, min bks 1691)
Pulaski   E3   1839   27   1840-80   Montgomery, Wythe . . . . Pulaski
    (Clk of Cir Ct has m rec from 1882, div, pro, civ ct rec from 1839)
Rappahannock C1   1833   5   1840-80   Culpeper . . . . Washington

County Map of Virginia

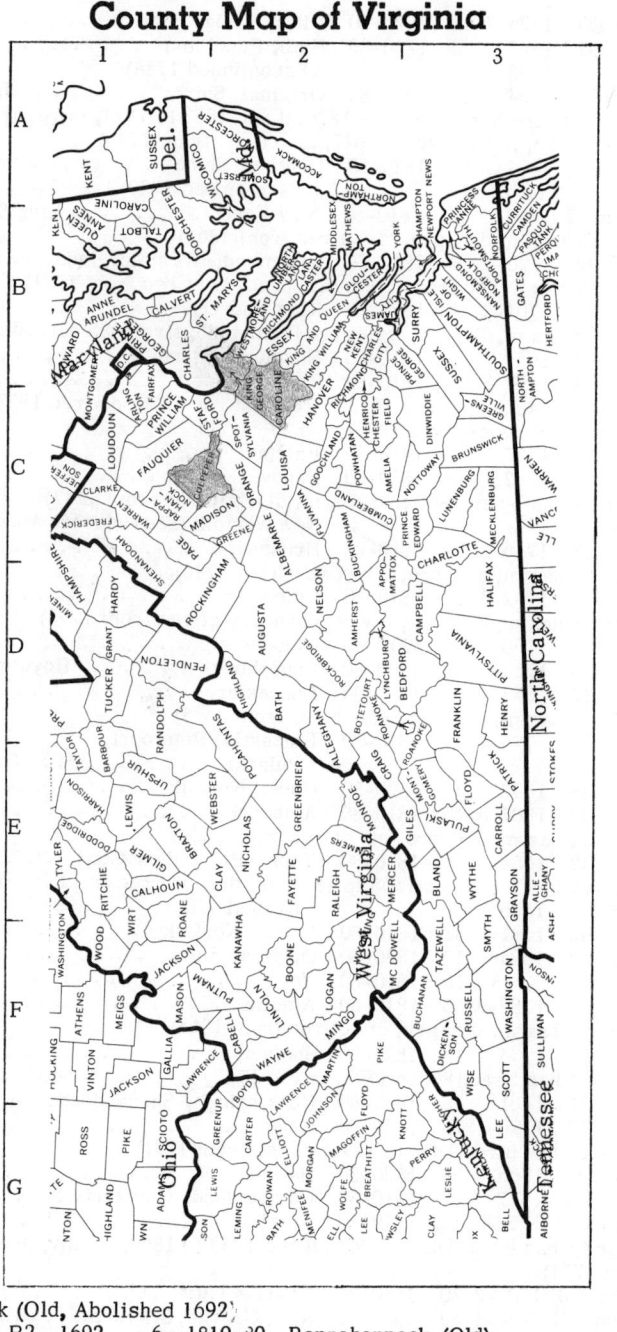

Rappahannock (Old, Abolished 1692)   Lancaster
Richmond   B2   1692   6   1810-80 Rappahannock (Old) . . . . Warsaw
    (Clk of Cir Ct has b & d rec 1853 to 1895, m rec from 1853, div, pro, deeds,
    wills from 1693)
Roanoke   E2   1838   62   1840-80 Botetourt, Montgomery . . . . . . Salem
Rockbridge   D2   1778   24   1810-80 Augusta, Botetourt . . . . Lexington
Rockingham   D1   1778   40   1810-80 Augusta . . . . Harrisonburg
    (Ct House burned in 1864 some rec lost)

Franklin	C3	1883	23		Whitman	. . . .	Pasco
Garfield	C4	1881	3		Columbia	. . . .	Pomeroy
Grant	B3	1909	46		Douglas	. . . .	Ephrata
Gray's Harbor	B1	1885	54		Original county	. . . .	Montesano

(Co Auditor has b, m, d rec from 1891; Co Clk has div, pro, civ ct rec from 1860)

Island	A2	1854	20	1860-80	Original county	. . . .	Coupeville

(Co Clk has div & civ ct rec from 1891, pro rec from 1853)

Jefferson	B1	1854	10	1860-80	Original county	. . . .	Port Townsend

(Co Auditor has b & d rec 1891 to 1907, m rec 1853; Co Clk has div rec 1886, pro rec 1891)

King	B2	1852	935	1860-80	Original county	. . . .	Seattle
Kitsap	B2	1871	84	1860-80	Jefferson	. . . .	Port Orchard
Kittitas	B3	1883	20		Yakima	. . . .	Ellensburg
Klickitat	C2	1858	13	1860-80	Original county	. . . .	Goldendale
Lewis	B2	1855	42	1860-80	Original county	. . . .	Chehalis

(Co Auditor has b & d rec 1891 to 1907, m rec 1850; Co Clk has div, pro, civ ct rec from ca 1870)

Lincoln	B4	1883	11		Spokane	. . . .	Davenport
Mason	B1	1864	16	1870-80	Sawanish	. . . .	Shelton
Okanogan	A3	1883	26		Stevens	. . . .	Okanogan

(Co Clk has div, pro, civ ct, criminal ct rec from 1891)

Pacific	B1	1854	15	1860-80	Original county	. . . .	South Bend
Pend Oreille	A4	1891	7		Stevens	. . . .	Newport
Pierce	B2	1853	322	1860-80	Original county	. . . .	Tacoma
San Juan	A1	1873	3	1870-80	Whatcom	. . . .	Friday Harbor
Sawamish				1860	(See Mason)		
Skagit	A2	1883	51		Whatcom	. . . .	Mount Vernon

(Co Clk has div, pro, civ ct rec from 1883)

Skamania	C2	1854	5	1860-80	Original county	. . . .	Stevenson

(Co Auditor has b rec from 1898, m rec 1856, deeds, mining claims, U. S. Patents from 1856; Co Clk has bur, div, pro, civ ct rec from 1856)

Snohomish	B2	1853	172	1870-80	Original county	. . . .	Everett
Spokane	B4	1858	278	1860-80	Stevens	. . . .	Spokane
Stevens	A4	1854	18	1870-80	Original county	. . . .	Colville

(Co Auditor has b & d rec 1891 to 1907, m rec 1891; Co Clk has div & civ ct rec 1882, pro rec 1887)

Thurston	B1	1853	55	1860-80	Original county	. . . .	Olympia
Wahkiakum	C1	1855	3	1860-80	Original county	. . . .	Cathlamet
Walla Walla	C3	1854	42	1860-80	Original county	. . . .	Walla Walla

(Co Clk has div, pro, civ ct rec from 1860)

Whatcom	A2	1857	70	1860-80	Island	. . . .	Bellingham
Whitman	B4	1871	31	1880	Stevens	. . . .	Colfax
Yakima	C2	1865	145	1870-80	Indian and Unorg. Terr.	. . . . .	Yakima

(Co Clk has div, pro, civ ct rec from 1890)

Genealogists' Check List of the Historical Records Survey, Wash. (see page VIII)

Fed Cts; Inv of Co Arch - Adams, Asotin, Benton, Chelan, Cowlitz, Garfield, King, Lewis, Lincoln, Pend Oreille, Skagit, Snohomish, Spokane, Stevens, Yakima; Guide to Pub Vit Stat Rec; Guide to Chr Vit Stat Rec; Inv of the Chr Arch of Wash - Survey of Everett, Yakima & Wenatchee Chr Arch - Survey of Seattle Chr Arch - Survey of Spokane Chr Arch; Guides to Depo of Ms Col in Ore & Wash; A Check List of Wash Imprints 1853-1876; Depo of unpubl mat, State College, Pullman, Wash.

West Virginia

Capital Charleston - State 1863 - (35th)

West Virginia came into existance as a direct result of the Civil War. That section had always been part of Virginia, even though the two sections never had much in common. One of the main reasons for this, no doubt, is the rugged Allegheny mountain range separating the two sections which made traveling between them rather difficult. When Virginia cast its lot with the Confederacy, the settlers west of the Alleghenies began to murmur. The complaint eventually became so loud and demanding that a separate government for the western section was organized in 1861 under the name of Kanawha. Two years later West Virginia was admitted into the Union as the thirty fifth state with a total of 50 counties. Since then five counties have been added.

The physical features of the section make West Virginia more accessible from Pennsylvania than from Virginia. At least, it was so in the early days. In those days the Indian trails served as roads and much of the travel was in the direction from Pennsylvania to West Virginia. Germans, Welsh, and Irish came as early as 1670. English in 1671, various nationalities in 1715 and 1725. Some of the early settlers merely crossed over from Maryland and made their homes in the present Berkeley and Jefferson counties.

Among different nationalities who have come to West Virginia to man various factories are Italians, Poles, Hungarians, Austrians, English, Germans, Greeks, Russians, and Czechs.

Most of the counties in West Virginia were settled years before they were organized. Here are figures showing the years the respective counties were settled: Brooke 1744; Pendleton, 1747; Randolph, 1753; Monroe, 1760; Monongalia, 1767; Greenbrier and Ohio, 1769; Harrison, Marion, and Preston, 1772; Kanawha 1773; Mason and Tucker 1774; Cabell and Mercer, 1775; Hancock, 1776; Marshall,

1777; Barbour and Wetzel, 1780; Jackson and Wirt, 1796; Wood, 1797; Boone, 1798; Lincoln, 1799; Putnam and Roan, 1800.

The Division of Vital Statistics, State Health Department, State House, Charleston, W. Va., has the records of births and deaths from 1917 to the present, marriages since 1921. Earlier marriages are recorded in the offices of the respective County Clerks.

The Virginia tax lists, published to replace the fire destroyed 1790 Federal Census, give a record of the taxpayers in the West Virginia counties of those days. A number of West Virginia counties have published the 1850 Census, containing the names, ages and dates of birth of all family members. The first Federal Census was taken in W. Va. in 1870. Prior schedules of the original 50 counties are listed under Virginia.

The County Clerk has charge of all court and land records.

Book on West Virginia history and genealogy:

HALE, J. P., *Trans-Allegheny Pioneers*, Pub. 1886.

MYERS, S., *History of West Virginia*, 2 Vols. Pub. 1915.

Sons of the Revolution in the State of West Virginia, published by West Virginia Society, 1941.

West Virginia Libraries: Charleston, (Kanawha), Kanawha County Library, Lee & Dickinson Sts.; West Virginia Dept. of Archives & History Library; Huntington, (Cabell), Huntington Public Library, 900 Fifth Ave.; Morgantown, (Monongalia), West Virginia University Library, (West Virginia).

West Virginia County Histories

(Population figures to nearest thousand - 1960 Census)

Name	Map Index	Date Formed	Pop. By M	Census Reports Available	Parent County	County Seat
Barbour	B3	1843	15	1850-80	Harrison, Lewis, Randolph . . .	Philippi
Berkeley	C4	1772	34	1810-80	Frederick	Martinsburg
(Co Clk has b & d rec from 1865, m rec from 1778, pro rec from 1772)						
Boone	B1	1847	29	1850-80	Kanawha, Cabell, Logan	Madison
(Co Clk has b, m, d rec from 1865, bur rec from 1888)						
Braxton	B2	1836	15	1840-80	Kanawha, Lewis, Nicholas	Sutton
Brooke	A3	1797	29	1810-80	Ohio	Wellsburg
Cabell	A1	1809	108	1820-80	Kanawha	Huntington
(Co Clk has b, m, d, rec from 1809; Clk of Cir Ct has div, pro rec from 1809)						
Calhoun	B2	1856	8	1860-80	Gilmer	Grantsville
(Co Clk has b & d rec from 1855, m rec from 1856)						
Clay	B2	1858	12	1860-80	Braxton, Nicholas	Clay
(Co Clk has b, m, d, pro rec from 1858)						
Doddridge	B3	1845	7	1850-80	Harrison, Tyler, Ritchie, Lewis .	W. Union
(Co Clk has b rec from 1853, m rec from 1850, d rec from 1862)						
Fayette	B2	1831	62	1840-80	Kanawha, Greenbrier, Logan .	Fayetteville

Gilmer   B2   1845   8   1850-80 Lewis, Kanawha .... Glenville
  (Co Clk has b & d rec from 1853, m rec from 1845, pro rec from 1848)
Grant   B3   1866   8   1870-80 Hardy .... Petersburg
  (Co Clk has b, m, d, div, pro, civ ct rec from 1866)
Greenbrier B2   1778   34   1820-80 Montgomery .... Lewisburg
  (Co Clk has b & d rec from 1853, m rec from 1780, pro rec from 1881)
Hampshire   B4   1753   12   1810-80 Frederick .... Romney
  (Co Clk has b & m rec from 1865, d rec 1866, pro rec 1780, chancery ct 1831)
Hancock   A4   1848   40   1850-80 Brooke .... New Cumberland
Hardy   C3   1785   9   1820-80 Hampshire .... Moorefield
Harrison   B3   1784   78   1810-80 Monongalia .... Clarksburg
Jackson   A2   1831   19   1840-80 Kanawha, Mason, Wood .... Ripley
  (Co Clk has b & d rec from 1853, m rec from 1830)
Jefferson   C4   1801   19   1810-80 Berkeley .... Charles Town
  (Co Clk has b & d rec from 1853 except CW years, m & pro rec from 1801)
Kanawha   B2   1789   253   1810-80 Greenbrier, Montgomery ... Charleston
Lewis   B3   1816   20   1820-80 Harrison .... Weston
  (Co Clk has b & d rec from 1853, m & pro rec from 1816)
Lincoln   A1   1867   20   1870-80 Boone, Cabell, Kanawha ...... Hamlin
Logan   B1   1824   62   1830-80 Kanawha, Cabell, Giles .... Logan
  (Co Clk has b, m, d rec from 1872)
McDowell   B1   1858   71   1860-80 Tazewell .... Welch
  (Co Clk has b rec from 1872, m rec 1861, d rec 1894, pro rec 1897)
Marion   B3   1842   64   1850-80 Harrison, Monongalia ...... Fairmont
Marshall   A3   1835   38   1840-80 Ohio .... Moundsville
  (Co Clk has b rec from 1853, m rec 1843, d & deeds 1835, pro rec 1850)
Mason   A2   1804   24   1810-80 Kanawha .... Point Pleasant
Mercer   B1   1837   68   1840-80 Giles, Tazewell .... Princeton
  (Co Clk has b, m, d rec from 1853, pro rec from 1860)
Mineral   B4   1866   22   1870-80 Hampshire .... Keyser
  (Co Clk has b, m, d, pro, land rec, wills, deeds from 1866)
Mingo   B1   1895   40   Logan .... Williamson
Monongalia B3   1776   56   1810-80 Dist of W. Augusta ..... Morgantown

County Map of West Virginia

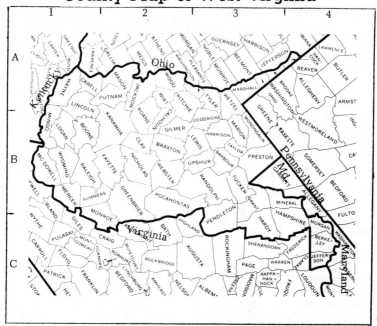

Monroe   B2   1779   12   1810-80   Greenbrier . . . . Union
(Co Clk has b & d rec from 1853, m & pro rec from 1799)
Morgan   C4   1820   8   1830-80   Berkeley, Hampshire . . Berkeley Springs
(Co Clk has b, m, d rec from 1865, pro rec 1820)
Nicholas   B2   1818   25   1820-80   Greenbrier, Kanawha . . . Summersville
Ohio   A3   1777   68   1810-80   Dist. of W. Augusta . . . . Wheeling
Pendleton   C3   1787   8   1810-80   Augusta, Hardy . . . . Franklin
(Co Clk has b & d rec from 1853, m rec from 1800)
Pleasants   A3   1851   7   1860-80   Ritchie, Tyler, Wood . . . . . . St. Marys
Pocahontas B2   1821   10   1830-80   Pendleton, Randolph . . . . Marlinton
Preston   B3   1818   27   1820-80   Monongalia . . . Horse Shoe Run & Kingwood
Putnam   A2   1848   24   1850-80   Kanawha, Mason, Cabell . . . . . Winfield
Raleigh   B1   1850   78   1850-80   Fayette . . . . Beckley
(Co Clk has b, m, d, pro, wills from 1850)
Randolph   B3   1787   26   1810-80   Harrison . . . . Elkins
(Co Clk has b rec from 1856, m, pro, wills from 1787, d rec from 1853)
Ritchie   A2   1843   11   1850-80   Harrison, Lewis, Wood . . . Harrisville
(Co Clk has b & d rec from 1850, m & pro rec from 1843)
Roane   B2   1856   16   1860-80   Kanawha, Jackson, Gilmer . . . . . Spencer
Summers   B1   1871   16   Greenbrier, Monroe, Mercer . . Hinton
Taylor   B3   1844   15   1850-80   Barbour, Harrison, Marion . . . . . Grafton
(Co Clk has b rec from 1853, m, d, pro, land rec from 1844)
Tucker   B3   1856   8   1860-80   Randolph . . . . Parsons
Tyler   A3   1814   10   1820-80   Ohio . . . . Middlebourne
Upshur   B3   1851   18   1860-80   Randolph, Barbour, Lewis . . Buckhannon
Wayne   A1   1842   39   1850-80   Cabell . . . . Wayne
(Co Clk has b & d rec from 1853, m rec from 1854)
Webster   B2   1860   14   1860-80   Braxton, Nicholas . . . . Webster Springs
Wetzel   A3   1846   19   1850-80   Tyler . . . . New Martinsville
Wirt   A2   1848   4   1850-80   Wood, Jackson . . . . Elizabeth
Wood   A2   1798   78   1810-80   Harrison . . . . Parkersburg
(Co Clk has b & d rec from 1850, m rec 1800, land rec 1798)
Wyoming   B1   1850   35   1850-80   Logan . . . . Pineville
(Co Clk has b & d rec from 1853, m rec from 1854, pro rec from 1851)

Genealogists' Check List of the Historical Records Survey, W. Va. (see page VIII)

Fed Cts; Inv of Co Arch - Gilmer, Grant, Lincoln, Marion, Mineral, Monroe, Pendleton, Pocahontas, Putnam, Randolph, Ritchie, Roane, Taylor; Inv of Pub Vit Stat Rec; Guide to Chr Vit Stat Rec; Inv of the Chr Arch of W Va - Presbyterian Chrs - Prot Episcopal Chr - Preliminary Bibliography of Mat Relating to Chrs in W Va, Va, Ky & Southern Ohio; Cal of the Arthur I Boreman Letters in the State Dept of Arch & Hist; Cal of the William E Stevenson Letters in the State Dept of Arch & Hist; Cal of the J J Jacob Letters in W Va Depo; Cal of the Francis Harrison Pierpont Letters and Papers in W Va Depo; Cal of the Governor Henry Mason Matthews Letters & Papers in the State Dept of Arch & Hist; Check List of W Va Imprints 1791-1830; W Va Co Formations and Boundary Changes (2 Editions); Cemetery Readings in W Va, Gideon Magisterial Dist of Cabell Co; Cemetery Readings, Fairmont & Grant Magisterial Dist of Marion Co; Cemetery Readings, Lincoln & Paw Paw Magisterial Dist of Marion Co; Cal of Wills, Upshur Co; Depo of unpubl mat, Dept of Arch & Hist, Charleston, W Va (Historical Materials) - W Va Univ Lib, Morgantown, W. Va (all other mat.)

Wisconsin

Capital Madison - Territory 1836 - State 1848 - (30th)

Settlers established themselves in the Wisconsin area as early as 1766. In 1840, according to the first U. S. Census taken. there were 130,945. The real influx of people came about 1848 when tens of thousands of people, mainly from the north-ern European countries came into the territory. The 1850 Census registered 305,391 and the 1860 Census 775,881.

By far the largest number of these immigrants were Germans.

About 1840 nearly all of the counties

facing Lake Michigan had recieved thousands of settlers. The Rock River Valley in Rock County also had many settlers at that time and earlier.

Wisconsin became a Territory in its own name in 1836. Previously it had been part of several Territories, including Indiana from 1800 to 1809; Illinois, 1809, to 1818; Michigan, 1818 to 1836. In 1848 it became the thirtieth state in the Union.

The leading nationalities represented in Wisconsin, in their numerical order are German (nearly three to one), Polish, Norwegian, Russian, Austrian, Swedish, Czech, Italian, Danish, Hungarian, English, Finnish, Greek, Irish and French.

The Bureau of Vital Statistics, Madison 2, Wisconsin, has birth and death records from 1860 to date.

Marriage Bans - address church where recorded.

Wills, deeds, land grants, tax payers lists - all these records are available in the various county court houses. Address inquiries to the County Clerk.

War Service Records - Adjutant General's Office, State Capital, Madison.

Cemetery Records - a few have been transferred to the various county clerks, but the practice is not at all general. Contact the local sexton.

Guardianship and Orphan Court Proceedings are held by the issuing court and by the Public Welfare Department, State Capital.

The Library of the State Historical Society of Wisconsin includes some 750,000 volumes, nearly one fifth of which deals with genealogy and local history. Books and pamphlets dealing with every state in the union and collective and individual American genealogies are included. Many church histories and records supplement those volumes generally classified as genealogical.

Wisconsin Libraries: Eau Claire, (Eau Claire), Eau Claire Public Library, 217 S. Farwell, (Wisconsin, local history); Kenosha, (Kenosha), Gilbert M. Simmons Public Library, 711 59th Pl.; La Crosse, (La Crosse), La Crosse County Public Library.

Wisconsin County Histories

(Population figures to nearest thousand - 1960 Census)

Name	Map Index	Date Formed	Pop. By M	Census Reports Available	Parent County	County Seat
Adams	D3	1848	8	1850-80	Portage	Friendship
Ashland	A2	1856	17	1860-80	Unorganized Territory	Ashland
Bad Ax				1860	(See Vernon)	
Barron	B1	1868	24	1870-80	Dallas, Polk	Barron
Bayfield	A2	1866	12	1870-80	Ashland, La Pointe	Washburn
Brown	C4	1818	125	1840-80	Territorial county	Green Bay

(Register of Deeds has b rec from 1846, m rec from 1821, d rec from 1834; Clk of Cir Ct has div & civ ct rec 1825; Register of Pro has pro rec 1828; See Mich. for 1820-30 census)

Buffalo	C1	1853	14	1860-80	Trempealeau	Alma
Burnett	B1	1865	9	1860-80	Polk	Grantsburg

(Register of Deeds has b rec from 1861, m & d rec 1880; Co Clk has div, pro civ ct rec from 1888)

Calumet	D4	1836	22	1840-80	Territorial county	Chilton
Chippewa	C2	1845	45	1850-80	Crawford	Chippewa Falls
Clark	C2	1853	32	1860-80	Marathon	Neillsville
Columbia	D3	1846	37	1850-80	Portage	Portage
Crawford	E2	1818	16	1840-80	Territorial county	Prairie du Chien

(Co Clk has b rec from 1866, m rec 1820, d & bur rec 1880, div & civ ct rec 1848, pro rec 1819; See Mich. for 1820-30 census)

Dallas		1859		1860	(Changed to Barron)	
Dane	E2	1838	222	1840-80	Territorial county	Madison

(Co Clk has b rec from 1907, m rec 1850, d rec 1860, div & civ ct rec 1848, pro rec 1839)

Dodge	D3	1836	63	1840-80	Territorial county	Juneau

(Co Clk has b, m, d, div, pro rec from 1887)

Door	C4	1851	21	1860-80	Brown	Sturgeon Bay
Douglas	A1	1854	45	1860-80	Unorganized Territory	Superior

(Register of Deeds has b, m, d rec from 1878; Clk of Cts has div & civ ct rec 1878; Co Ct has pro rec 1878; Co Treas has prop owners rec 1854)

Dunn   C1 1856   26 1860–80 Chippewa . . . . Menomonie
Eau Claire   C2 1856   58 1860–80 Chippewa . . . . Eau Claire
Florence   B3 1882   3   Marinette, Oconto . . . . Florence
Fond du Lac   D3 1836   75 1840–80 Territorial county . . . . . Fond du Lac
Forest   B3 1885   8   Langlade, Oconto . . . . Crandon
   (Co Clk has b, m, d rec from 1885; State census 1875–1905)
Grant   E2 1836   44 1840–80 Territorial county . . . . Lancaster
Green   E2 1836   26 1840–80 Territorial county . . . . Monroe
Green Lake   D3 1859   15 1860–80 Marquette District . . . . . . Green Lake
Iowa   E2 1829   20 1840–80 Territorial county . . . . . Dodgeville
   (Register of Deeds has b, d, bur rec from 1867; Co Clk has m rec from 1899;
   See Mich. for 1830 census)
Iron   A2 1893   8   Ashland, Oneida . . . . Hurley
Jackson   C2 1853   15 1860–80 LaCrosse . . . . Black River Falls
Jefferson   E3 1837   50 1840–80 Milwaukee . . . . Jefferson
Juneau   D2 1856   17 1860–80 Adams . . . . Mauston
Kenosha   D4 1850 101 1850–80 Racine . . . . Kenosha
   (Co Clk has m rec from 1900)
Kewaunee   C4 1852   18 1860–80 Manitowoc . . . . Kewaunee
La Crosse   D2 1851   72 1860–80 Unorganized Territory . . . . . . La Crosse
Lafayette   E2 1846   18 1850–80 Iowa . . . . Darlington
La Pointe   1845   1850–60 (See Bayfield)

County Map of Wisconsin

Langlade	B3	1880	20	1880	Oconto	Antigo
Lincoln	B3	1866	22	1880	Marathon	Merrill
Manitowoc	D4	1836	75	1840-80	Territorial county	Manitowoc
Marathon	C3	1850	89	1850-80	Portage	Wausau
Marinette	B4	1879	35	1880	Oconto	Marinette
Marquette	D3	1836	9	1840-80	Marquette District	Montello

(Register of Deeds has b rec from 1876, m & d rec from 1869; Clk of Ct has
div, pro, civ ct rec from 1870)

Milwaukee	D4	1834	1036	1840-80	Territorial county	Milwaukee

(Co Clk has m rec from 1834)

Monroe	D2	1856	31	1860-80	Unorganized Territory	Sparta
Oconto	C4	1851	25	1860-80	Unorganized Territory	Oconto
Oneida	B3	1885	22		Lincoln	Rhinelander
Outagamie	C3	1851	102	1860-80	Brown	Appleton
Ozaukee	E4	1853	38	1860-80	Milwaukee	Port Washington

(Register of Deeds has b, m, d, bur rec from 1853; Clk of Cts has div rec 1853;
Clk of Co Cts has pro & co ct rec 1853; Co Clk has Election rec 1853; Co
Treas has Tax Rolls 1853)

Pepin	C1	1851	7	1860-80	Chippewa	Durand
Pierce	C1	1853	23	1860-80	St. Croix	Ellsworth
Polk	B1	1853	25	1860-80	St. Croix	Balsam Lake
Portage	C3	1836	37	1840-80	Territorial county	Stevens Point

(Register of Deeds has b rec from 1844, m rec 1848, d rec 1855; Clk of Cts
has div & civ ct rec 1844; Co Judge has pro rec 1890)

Price	B2	1878	14	1880	Chippewa	Phillips
Racine	D4	1836	142	1840-80	Territorial county	Racine
Richland	D2	1842	18	1850-80	Iowa	Richland Center
Rock	E2	1836	114	1840-80	Territorial county	Janesville
Rusk	B2	1902	15		Chippewa	Ladysmith

(Register of Deeds has b, m, d rec from 1902)

St. Croix	C1	1840	29	1840-80	Territorial county	Hudson
Sauk	D2	1840	36	1840-80	Territorial county	Baraboo
Sawyer	B2	1883	9		Ashland, Chippewa	Hayward
Shawano	C3	1856	34	1860-80	Oconto	Shawano
Sheboygan	D4	1836	86	1840-80	Territorial county	Sheboygan
Taylor	B2	1875	18	1880	Clark, Lincoln, Marathon,	
					Chippewa	Medford
Trempealeau	C2	1854	23	1860-80	Crawford, LaCrosse	Whitehall
Vernon	D2	1863	26	1870-80	Richland, Crawford, Bad Ax . . .	Viroqua
Vilas	B3	1893	9		Oneida	Eagle River
Walworth	E2	1836	52	1840-80	Territorial county	Elkhorn
Washburn	B1	1883	10		Burnett	Shell Lake
Washington	E4	1836	46	1840-80	Territorial county	West Bend
Waukesha	E4	1840	158	1850-80	Milwaukee	Waukesha
Waupaca	C3	1851	35	1860-80	. . . .	Waupaca
Waushara	D3	1851	13	1860-80	Marquette	Wautoma
Winnebago	D3	1838	108	1840-80	Territorial county	Oshkosh
Wood	C2	1856	59	1860-80	Portage	Wisconsin Rapids

(Register of Deeds has b, m, d rec from 1875; Clk of Cts has div & civ ct rec
from 1875; Register in Pro has pro rec from 1875)

Genealogists' Check List of the Historical Records Survey, Wisconsin (see page VIII)

Fed Cts; Inv of the Co Arch - Barron, Buffalo, Chippewa, Clark, Douglas, Dunn, Eau Claire, Grant, Jackson, LaCrosse, Marathon, Monroe, Oneida, Pepin, Polk, Rusk, St Croix, Shawano, Sheboygan, Taylor, Trempealeau, Vernon, Waushara; Inv of Mun & Tn Arch - Cudahy, Greendale, Wauwatosa; Tran of Proceedings of the Crawford Co Bd of Supervisors 1821-1850; Tran of the Proceedings of the Iowa Co Bd of Supervisors 1830-1843, Vol 2 1843-1850, Vol 3 Index to Proceedings of the Co Bd of Supervisors 1830-1850; Tran of the Proceedings of the St Croix Co Bd of Supervisors 1840-1849; Guide to Pup Vit Stat Rec; Guide to Chr Vit Stat Rec; Outline of Vit Stat Laws.

Inv of the Chr Arch of Wis: Hist of the Southern Wis Dist of the Evangelical Lutheran Synod of Mo and other States; Prot

Episcopal Chr - Diocese of Eau Clair - Doicese of Fond du Lac; Assemblies of God; Chr of Nazarene; Disciples of Christ; Jewish Congregations; Moravian Chr; RC Chr Diocese of La Crosse; United Brethren in Christ; Dir of Chrs & Rel Org in Wis; Dir of Catholic Chrs in Wis.

Guide to Ms Depo in Wis; Guide to Ms Col in the Wis Hist Soc; A Check List of Wis Imprints - 1833-1849 - 1850-1854 - 1855-1858 - 1859-1863; A Guide to Wis Newspapers - Iowa Co 1837-1940; Abstract & Check List of Statutory Requirements for Co Rec - Supplement to above; Development of Tn Boundaries in Wis - Chippewa Co - Dane Co - Manitowoc Co - Portage Co; Origin and Legislative Hist of County Boundaries in Wis; Depo of Unpubl mat, State Hist Soc, Madison, Wis.

Wyoming

Capital Cheyenne - Territory 1868 - State 1890 -(44th)

When Wyoming was organized as a Territory in 1868 it had only six or seven thousand white inhabitants. The middle west and the southern states provided most of the settlers who came into the state to take advantage of the opportunity to get into the cattle business. Hundreds of thousands of cattle roamed the western hills unherded. The eastern section had good agricultural soil.

In 1940 the foreign born population of Wyoming ranked in this order in numbers: England, Germany, Sweden, Russia, Italy, Austria, Greece, Denmark, Norway, Ireland, Poland, Finland, Czechoslovakia, France and Hungary.

The Wyoming State Library in Cheyenne has a genealogical section.

Birth and death records from 1909 to the present, and marriage records from May 1, 1941 are at the office of the Division of Vital Statistics, Cheyenne, Wyoming.

The County Clerk of each county is custodian of the birth and death records from the beginning of the county until 1909, the marriage records from the beginning of the county until May 1, 1941, the wills, probate matters, and all land records.

Wyoming County Histories

(Population figures to nearest thousand - 1960 Census)

Name	Map Index	Date Formed	Pop. By M	Census Reports Available	Parent County	County Seat
Albany	D4	1868	21	1860-80	Original county	Laramie
(Co Clk has m rec from 1869; for 1860 census see Nebr.)						
Big Horn	A3	1890	12		Fremont, Johnson	Basin
(Co Clk has m rec from 1890)						
Campbell	B4	1911	6		Johnson, Converse	Gillette
Carbon	D3	1868	15	1860-80	Original county	Rawlins
(Co Clk has m rec from 1870; for 1860 census see Nebr.)						
Converse	B4	1888	6		Laramie, Albany	Douglas
Crook	A5	1885	5	1880	Pease	Sundance
(Co Clk has m rec from 1885)						
Fremont	B2	1885	26		Sweetwater	Lander
Goshen	C5	1911	12		Platte, Laramie	Torrington
Hot Springs	B2	1911	6		Fremont	Thermopolis
(Co Clk has m rec from 1913)						
Johnson	B4	1875	5	1880	Pease	Buffalo
Laramie	D5	1868	60	1860-80	Original county	Cheyenne
(Co Clk has m rec from 1868; for 1860 census see Nebr.)						
Lincoln	C1	1913	9		Uinta	Kemmerer
Natrona	C3	1888	50		Carbon	Casper
(Co Clk has m rec from 1890)						
Niobrara	B5	1811	4		Converse	Lusk
(Co Clk has m rec from 1888)						
Park	A2	1909	17		Big Horn	Cody
(Co Clk has m rec from 1911)						
Platte	C5	1913	7		Laramie	Wheatland
(Co Clk has m rec from 1913)						
Sheridan	A3	1888	19		Johnson	Sheridan

Sublette   C2   1921   4   Fremont . . . . Pinedale
  (Co Clk has m rec from 1921; Clk of Cts has div, pro, civ ct rec 1921)
Sweetwater   D2   1868   18   1860-80 Original county . . . . Green River
  (For 1860 census see Nebr.)
Teton   B1   1921   3   Lincoln . . . . Jackson
Uinta   D1   1868   7   1860-80 Original county . . . . Evanston
  (For 1860 census see Nebr.)
Washakie   B3   1911   9   Big Horn, Fremont . . . . Worland
Weston   B5   1890   8   Crook . . . . Newcastle
  (Co Clk has m rec from 1890)

Genealogists' Check List of the Historical Records Survey, Wyoming (see page VIII)

Inv of Co Arch - Goshen, Laramie, Lincoln, Park, Platte, Sweetwater; Guide to Pub Vit Stat Rec; Guide to Chr Vit Stat Rec; Dir of Chrs & Rel Org in Wyo; A Check List of Wyo Imprints 1866-1890; Depo of unpubl mat, State Lib, Cheyenne, Wyo.

County Map of Wyoming

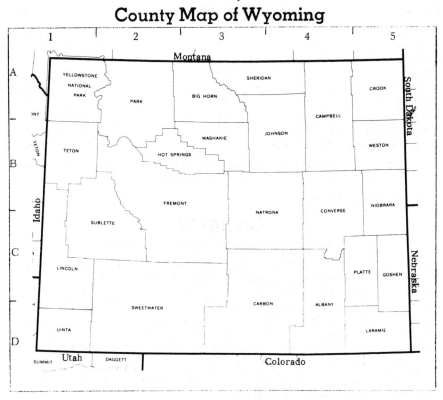

Australia

Captial Canberra - Settled 1788 - Commonwealth 1901

Under the command of Captain Arthur Phillip (first governor) 11 ships with approximately 1500 persons, including nearly 800 prisoners, sailed from England May 13, 1787 and arrived at Botony Bay January 18, 1788. Eight days later the colony was transferred to the site now occupied by Sydney on Port Jackson.

1803 saw the start of other new settlements with the founding of Hobart, Tasmania. Then came Brisbane, Queensland in 1824; Swan River, Western Australia 1829; Melbourne, Victoria 1835; and Adelaide, South Australia 1836. It was not until the discovery of gold in 1851 in the Bathurst District and Victoria that there was any great influx of settlers.

The capital of Australia is Canberra. It is also the capital of the Australian Capital Territory. Other states and territories with their capitals are as follows: New South Wales, Sydney; Victoria, Melbourne; Queensland, Brisbane; South Australia, Adelaide; West-ern Australia, Perth; Tasmania, Hobert; Northern Territory, Darwin.

The Australian Society of Genealogists was founded in 1932. They maintain an office and library at 91A Phillip Street, Sydney. Write to them - G. P. O. Box 860, Sydney, Australia - for information regarding their charges for research.

Belgium
Royaume De Belgique - Koninkrijk Belgie.
Capital, Brussels

Provinces of Belgium

Province	Map Index	Capital
Antwerpen (Antwerp)	D3	Antwerpen (Antwerp)
Brabrant	E3	*Bruxelles (Brussels)
Hainaut	E2	Mons (Bergen)
Liége	E4	Liége (Luik)
Limbourg (Limburg)	D3	Hasselt
Luxembourg	F4	Aarlon (Arlon)
Namur	F3	Namur (Namen)
Oost Vlaanderen (East Flanders)	E2	Gent (Gand or Ghent)
West Vlaanderen (West Flanders	E1	Brugge (Bruges)

The history of Belgium dates from 1831 when the South Netherlands parted from Holland and became an independent kingdom.

FOR MAP SEE PAGE 211

Canada
Capital Ottawa, Dominion 1867

By virtue of discovery and settlement France claimed possession of Canada as early as 1532. By 1642 Acadia, Quebec, and Montreal had been founded. Following the French and Indian Wars extending over a seventy-year period, the Treaty of Paris transferred Canada to British rule in 1763.

After Canada came under British control, many of the early American colonists, unwilling to sever their British citizenship rights, migrated to Canada where they established their homes. The French, who had come there earlier, remained in Canada, later became Canadian citizens, but retained their French language.

Canada is divided into ten provinces, Alberta, British Columbia, Manitoba, New Brunswick, Newfoundland, Nova Scotia, Ontario, Prince Edward Island, Quebec, and Saskatchewan; and two territories, Yukon, created in 1898, and Northwest Territories, which Canada secured in 1870 from Britain and the Hudson's Bay Company.

Ottawa, located in the province of Ontario on the south side of the Ottawa River, is the Dominion Capital.

A wealth of genealogical and historical records is on file at the Public Archives in Ottawa, including a museum, a Library with books and manuscripts dating back to the earliest days. Most of the church records are in the provinces. Researchers should communicate with the Archivists, the Dominion and the Provincial, to ascertain where information may be obtained. Data regarding immigration and naturalization papers may be secured from the Department of Mines and Resources, Citizenship Registration Branch, Ottawa, Canada.

To have the census of Canada searched, write to the Public Archives of Canada, Ottawa, Canada, Census returns since 1871 are not open to the public.

The officers in charge give the following explanation:

"Information available from the census returns are: the family name, the age, the country of birth, the religion, the trade or profession, the kind of house and the property. The census of 1831 and 1842 give the name of the head of the family only. That of 1851, 1861, and 1871 give the names of the father, mother, and the children of each family. Each census is taken by the province, divided into counties, which are subdivided into townships. In order to obtain information from any census return, the township of the place of residence must be given."

If you do not know the township, ask the Archives for the name of a genealogist.

Alberta (D-3)

Edmonton is the provincial capital, with a population of 113,116. Other leading cities are Calgary, 100,044; Lethbridge, 16,522; Medicine Hat, 12,859.

Taken from the Northwest Territories in 1905, Alberta was made a province. The northern half still remains a wilderness. The province is divided into the following counties, Acadia Athabasca, Battle River, Bow River, Calgary East, Calgary West, Camrose, Edmon, Edmonton, Lethbridge, Mac Leod, Medicine Hat, Peace River, Red Deer, Vegerville, and Westaski.

Vital statistics may be secured by inquiring from the Deputy Registrar General, Department of Public Health, Edmonton, Alberta, Canada. Wills are on file at the Court House, Edmonton, Alta, Canada. Deeds are at the Land Titles Office in the same city.

British Columbia (E-3) is the westernmost province in Canada.

Its counties are Cariboo, Comox-Alberni, East Kootenay, Frazer Valley, Nanalmo, Skeena, Vancouver, North West Kootenay, and Yale.

The capital of the province is Victoria, on the south-east tip of Vancouver Island. Victoria has a population of 50,744. Other leading cities in the province are Vancouver, 340,272, and New Westminister, 28,390.

British Columbia is the third largest province both in area and in population. More than 1,165,000 people live in the province. It was organized in 1858. The predominating nationalities in the province are British (almost three-fourths of entire population); Scandinavian, German, French, Russian, Italian, and Dutch.

For vital statistics since 1874, and incomplete records since 1836, write Division of Vital Statistics, Parliament Bldgs., Victoria, B. C. For wills since 1858 contact Registrar of Supreme Court, Victoria, B.C. For Land records and deeds since 1861 write Land Registry Office, Victoria, B. C.

Manitoba (C-3) is the sixth province in area and in population.

Two-thirds of the people of Manitoba are Protestants, belonging to the United Canadian, the Episcopalian, the Lutheran, the Presbyterian, and the Mennonite Church. The other third is Catholic.

Winnipeg is the provincial capital, and about the only large city in the province. It has a population of 350,924, which is very little less than one half of the entire population of the province. The population is mainly English, Scottish, German, Swiss, Polish, and Ukranian. The province was created in 1870 when it was cut out of the Northwestern Territories.

The Manitoba counties are Boniface, Brandon, Dauphin, Lisgar, MacDonald, Marquett, Neepawa, Nelson, which constitutes the northern two-thirds of the provincial area, Portage La Prairie, Provencher, Souris, Springfield, and Winnipeg.

The office of the Registrar General, Vital Statistics Division, Department of Health and Public Welfare, 331 Legislative Bldg., Winnipeg, Canada has vital statistics from 1874, a few scattered perhaps earlier. For wills write the Surrogate Court in the respective district. Some are available from 1891. Land transfers and deeds must also be checked in the district offices of the Registrar of Land Titles.

New Brunswick (A-5) is the eighth largest province in land area and in population. There are a little more than half a million people in the province.

In the days of the American Revolutionary War, English Loyalists moved from the colonies into New Brunswick. Others came over from Yorkshire, England. More recently French Canadians moved south into New Brunswick.

The largest cities are St. John, 51,741, on the south coast; Moncton, in the south - central part of Westmoreland county, 22,763; Fredericton, the provincial capital, in York county, on the St. John River, 10,062.

There are fifteen counties in the province; Albert, Carleton, Charlotte, Gloucester, Kent, Kings, Madawaska, Northumberland, Queens, Restigouche, St. John, Sunbury, Victoria, Westmorland and York.

From 1888 until 1920 all birth, marriage, and death records have been maintained by the County Registrars, since then at the office of the Registrar General, Department of Health and Social Service, Fredericton, N. B. Fredericton is the provincial capital. Records of wills are with the Registrar of Probates of each county. All land titles and real estate transfers are at the office of the Registrar of Deeds of the respective counties.

Newfoundland (A-2) by popular vote, became a province of Canada in 1949.

St. John's the capital, with a population of 52,000, is the only large city in the province. About sixteen other cities have a population between one and six thousand, all others less than a thousand.

The island has been populated since 1750. The English and the French people predominate. The Roman Catholic church is the largest numerically, closely followed by the Episcopalian. The United Canadian Church claims about twenty-five per cent of the population. Other Protestant denominations have smaller memberships.

The vital statistics since 1892 are under the care of the Vital Statistics Division of the Department of Health, St. John's, Newfoundland, Canada. The Registrar of the Supreme Court, St. John's, Newfoundland, is the custodian of wills. The Registry of Deeds and Companies, St. John's, Newfoundland, Canada, is in charge of all land title records

Nova Scotia (A-3) is the next to the smallest in area of the Canadian provinces and the seventh in population. It has more than 640,000 people. Its southern tip is about 250 miles north-northeast from Boston. It changed from French to British rule about 1750.

A little more than half of the population is English and Scottish. There are still some French, also German, Swiss, Dutch and Irish.

Halifax is the capital. It has a population of about 85,000, with Sydney coming next with about 31,000.

Its eighteen counties are: Annapolis, Antigonish, Cape Breton, Colchester, Cumberland, Digby, Guysborough, Halifax, Hants, Inverness, Kings, Lunenburg, Pictou, Queens, Richmond, Shelburne, Victoria, and Yarmouth.

Vital statistics since 1864 are available at the office of the Deputy Registrar General, Department of Public Health, Halifax, N. S., Canada. The Registrar of Probates, in each probate district has the records of the wills. The Registry of Deeds in each probate district is custodian of deeds and land entries.

Ontario (C-4) is the second largest province in land area and the first in population. It has more than four and a half million people living within its boundaries.

Its counties and county seats are as follows: Algoma, Sault Ste. Marie; Brant, Brantford; Bruce, Walkerton; Carleton, Ottawa; Cochrane, Cochrane; Dufferin, Orangeville; Dundas, Morrisburg; Durham; Elgin, St. Thomas; Essex, Windsor; Frontenac, Kingston; Glengarry; Grenville; Gray, Owen Sound; Haldimand, Cayuga; Haliburton, Minden; Halton, Milton West; Hastings, Belleville; Huron, Goderich; Kenora, Kenora; Kent, Chatham; Lambton, Sarnia; Lanark, Perth; Leeds, Brockville; Lennox and Addington, Napanee; Lincoln, St. Catharines; Manitoulin, Gore Bay; Middlesex, London; Muskoka, Bracebridge; Nipissing, North Bay; Norfolk, Simcoe; Northumberland, Cobourg; Ontario, Whitby; Oxford, Woodstock; Parry Sound, Parry Sound; Peel, Brampton; Perth, Stratford; Peterborough, Peterborough; Prescott, L'Orignal; Prince Edward, Picton; Rainy River, Ft. Francis; Renfrew, Pembroke; Russell; Simcoe, Barrie; Stormont, Cornwall; Sudbury, Sudbury; Thunder Bay, Port Arthur; Timiskaming, Haileybury; Victoria, Lindasay; Waterloo, Kitchener; Welland, Welland; Wellington, Guelph; Wentworth, Hamilton; York, Toronto.

Among the cities of Ontario are Toronto, the capital of the province, 670,945; Hamilton, 207,544; Ottawa, the Dominion capital, 198,773; Windsor, 119,-550; London, 94,984.

Birth, marriage, and death records since 1869 may be obtained from the Registrar General, Parliament Bldgs., Toronto, Ontario, Canada. Copies of wills may be secured from the county or district Registrar of the Surrogate Court. Information on deeds and land titles may be had from the county office of the Registrar of Deeds.

Prince Edward Island, (A-3) one of the most productive islands and provinces in Canada, is situated between the Gulf of St. Lawrence and the Northumberland Strait. French colonies were established as early as 1713. The island was made a British colony in 1758. Soon after, colonists from Scotland came to the island. English and Irish settlers followed. There are about 15,000 descendants of the early Acadians.

The island is divided into three districts or counties. The eastern section or county is Kings, with Georgetown as the county seat; the central section or county is Queens, with Charlottetown, the provincial capital also serving as county seat; the West section or county Prince, with Summerside as the county seat. Charlottetown is the largest city on the island with a population of 15,689; Summerside is the next largest with 6,522, and Souris, 1,176.

Vital Statistics records since 1906 are available at the office of the Director of Vital Statistics, Department of Health and Welfare, Charlottetown, P. E. I., Canada. Wills are registered at the office of the Judge of Probate in the

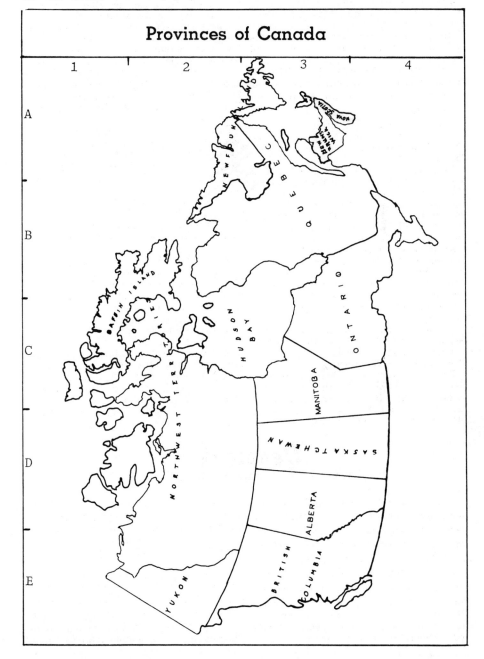

Provinces of Canada

same city. Deeds are recorded with the Registrar of Deeds for King and Queen counties, Charlotteville, P. E. I., Canada, and the Registrar of Deeds for Prince County, Summerside, P. E. I., Canada.

Quebec, (B-3) the largest province in area and the second largest in population, has more than four milion inhabitants.

French settlers came to Quebec in the early sixteen hundreds, and their descendants are now in the majority in the province. More than three-fourths of the population are French and Catholic.

The province has 76 counties, but none of the records in which the genealogical researcher is interested are in any of the county offices.

The most prominent cities are Montreal (Greater) 1,370,044; Quebec, 161,439; Trois-Rivieres (Three Rivers), 45,708

Vital statistics for Quebec Catholics began about 1622; for Protestants about 1887. The Director of the Provincial Bureau of Health, Quebec, Que., Canada, has statistics from 1907. The twenty District Notaries have charge of wills and land transfer records.

Saskatchewan's (D-3) capital is Regina, located in the south-eastern section of the province. It is fifth among the Canadian provinces in area and population, and has more than 800,000 people living mostly in the southern half of the province.

Its largest cities are Regina, 69,928; Saskatoon, 52,732; Moose Jaw, 24,336. Regina is about 700 miles northwest of Minneapolis via Winnipeg.

The Director of Vital Statistics, Dept. of Public Health, Provincial Health Bldg., Regina, Sask., Canada, has charge of the vital statistics of the province. A few records go back to 1888, but most of them from 1905. A record of all grants made in wills is filed with the Registrar of Surrogate Courts, Court House, Regina, Sask., Canada. The wills are filed in the office of the clerk of the Surrogate Court of the respective counties. Land Titles are filed in the Regina Land Titles Office, but applicant must describe land and give the proper Registration District.

The twenty-one counties of Saskatchewan are Assiniboia, Humboldt, Kindersley, Last Mountain, Long Lake, MacKenzie, Maple Creek, Melfort, Melville, Moose Jaw, North Battleford, Prince Albert, Qu Appelle, Regina, Rosetown, Saskatoon, South Battleford, Swift Current, Weyburn,, Willow Bunch, and Yorkton.

Among books dealing with the history and genealogy of Canada are the following:

GRANT, W. L., M. A., *History of Canada,* Authorized by the Minister of Education for Ontario, The Ryerson press, Toronto, 1922.

MC L'AUGHLIN, SARA B., *Canadian Educator,* The Iroquois Press, Toronto, 1920. Gives much on the geography and history of Canada. also many biographies of prominent men.

ROSE, GEO. MACLEAN, *A Cyclopædia of Canadian Biography,* Rose Publishing Co., Toronto, 1888. A collection of persons distinguished in professional and political life; leaders in commerce and industry of Canada and successful pioneers.

Libraries and genealogical societies include: Hamilton Public Library, Hamilton, Ont.; Public Library and Art Museum, Elsie Perrin Williams Mem. Bldg., London, Ont.; Institute Genealogique Drouin, 4148 St. Denis Street, Montreal, Quebec; Vancouver Dist. LDS Gen. Society, 350 East 55th Ave., Vancouver 15, B. C.

Denmark
Capital Copenhagen (Kobenhavn)

Denmark's (Danmark) principal islands and peninsula: 1. Jutland (Jylland); 2. Fyn Island; 3. Zealand (Själland); 4. Falster and Lolland (Laaland) Islands; 5. Bornholm Island.

Jutland (Jylland) Peninsula has the following amter (counties); Aabenraa, Aalborg, Aarhus, Haderslev, Hjöring, Randers, Ribe, Ringköbing (Ringkjobing), Sönderborg (Skanderborg), Thisted, Tönder, Vejle, and Viborg.

Fyn Island has two amter—Odense Amt (County) and Svendborg Amt.

Zealand (Själland) Island is divided as follows: Copenhagen (Köbenhavn), Fredriksborg, Holbäk, Prästo and Sorö amter.

The islands of Lolland (Laaland) and Falster constitute the amt of Maribo. Bornholm Island with Rönne as the administrative center is Bornholm Amt. The Fäeröe (Faeröeren) Islands with Thorshavn as its administrative center

(750 miles west of Norway and 400 miles north of Scotland) have at times been considered as the Fäerõe Amt.

The amter of Denmark in most cases are named after the cities which are their administrative centers. In fact all follow this pattern except Fredriksborg, which has Hilleröd as its administrative center, and Bornholm and Faeroe (mentioned above).

All census records, military levying rolls, civil and government records are gathered into one great central archive at Copenhagen. This is the "Rigsarkivet" or Royal Archive. All church records prior to 1890 are gathered into the three permanent provincial archives located at Copenhagen, Odense, Viborg and the one temporary provincial archive at Aabenraa. These archives are the most important for genealogical research in Denmark. Of the two kinds of archives the provincial archive is the more important to researchers for it is here that the vital statistics are kept for practically everything prior to 1890.

There are other archives and libraries that furnish valuable information for the genealogist. The Royal Library will probably stand first in this respect. Here will be found all printed records in Denmark and also a few manuscript records. This will, of course, save a researcher a great deal of time, if he should find his records already printed then all he needs to do is check-up on the connections. Other archives worthy of mention are the military archive at Copenhagen, the city and county archives and libraries, the Danish-American Archives at Aalborg which may be of great worth to Danish-Americans in establishing their connections with Denmark; also there are the industrial archives, university archives, etc.

In all of these archives thus mentioned all records that are obtainable for the public are from 1890 and back. None are obtainable after that date except by special permission or rights but for those records that are, there is no charge for the use of them in the reading-rooms of the archives.

CHURCH RECORDS. In Denmark most people belong to the same church, the state or Lutheran church. It used to be required of all to belong to this church and to support it by means of a civil tax, but that is a thing of the past now, as far as it being a requirement of every person regardless of desire or personal creed. However, this church still remains the registrar of certain vital statistics. Thus, regardless of what church you may belong to, all births must be registered with the priest of the state church of that particular parish in which you may be residing. All other vital statistics such as marriages, deaths, etc., are either registered here or with the local civil authorities. For this reason the state church records become the most valuable record for the genealogist in Denmark. The number of Danes not belonging to the state church prior to 1890 is practically negligible, thus making this record most valuable for marriages and deaths as well.

The first church record preserved was made by a priest, Jost Poulsen, in Nakskov for the years 1572-90. Another one was kept by a priest of the same place from 1618-1629. The oldest uninterrupted church record in Denmark is that of Holmen's Church in Copenhagen which began in 1617. Several churches began keeping parish records in 1641, and in 1645 all parishes were asked by the government to keep records of all births, marriages, deaths, etc. It was understood at this time that it became the duty of the parish priest to keep such a record and that this record belonged to the parish and not to the priest. Further enforcement was enacted in 1683 and 1685, such that before the end of the seventeenth century, it was definite and practiced by practically all of the priests.

The **birth records** generally consists of two separate lists: the male and the female. The information obtainable is the same for both, and consists of: the name of the child, date of birth, date of christening, name of the parents and their occupation, names of the godmother and the sponsors and possibly some remarks.

The **confirmation record** is also divided into male and female lists. Confirmation generally takes place between fourteen and fifteen years of age. The information obtainable from these records is: name of child, name of parents, date of confirmation, usually the date of either birth or chistening, and character testimonials from the school.

The **marriage record** or list gives the name of the bridegroom and the bride; generally their age or birthdate and the parish they came from, if native of another parish (marriage is performed in the parish which the bride come from), sometimes the names of the fathers are given, the names of the sponsors who are generally fathers or near relatives (male) are always given, date of marriage and possible remarks and banns.

The **removal record** or record of incoming and outgoing members from the parish, is a result of the system of character testimonial employed at one time in Denmark.

The **death record** shows the name of the person deceased, possibly the name of the husband or wife or in the case of a child the name of the father or even both the parents, date of death, date of burial, position or occupation of the deceased, or if a child the posi-

Norway, Sweden, Finland and Denmark

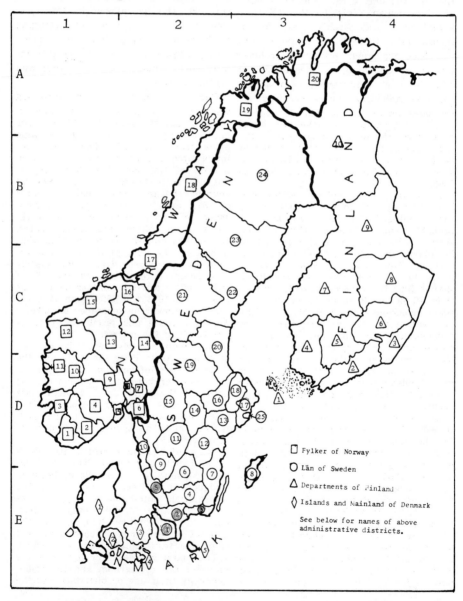

Fylker of Norway

Län of Sweden

Departments of Finland

Islands and Mainland of Denmark

See below for names of above administrative districts.

tion or occupation of the father or mother. The age also is given.

PROBATE RECORDS. Probate records have been in existence since the early part of the sixteenth century in Denmark. In 1874 the old system was done away with entirely. Most of the earliest records have been lost or burnt, however, records from 1574 to 1637 are at the archive. These are mostly for cities since this system began much earlier there. After this period there are many more in existence, and as the end of the sevententh century is approached are found throughout the entire land.

The Royal Archive

The most important records found at this archive are the census records and the military levying rolls. Other records such as tax lists, customs records, commercial records, postal records, pension records and other governmental records are also available.

CENSUS RECORDS. The first complete census record which has not been destroyed is that taken in 1787. Since that date census records have been taken during the following years: 1801, 1834, 1840, 1845, 1850, 1855, 1860, 1870, 1880, 1890, 1901 and thereafter periodically. Of these all up to and including 1890 census are available to the public for their perusal and study at the reading room at the Royal Archive.

These censuses are listed according to parishes, "herreds," and "Amter." The last two mentioned divisions are comparable to county and state within the United States.

MILITARY LEVYING ROLLS. Beginning with 1789 all males born outside of the cities in Denmark were entered upon levying rolls so that they could be used for military training when they reached a certain age. It was required of each male individual to ever have his whereabouts known. Thus if he moved he had to report at his new place of residence, where he came from and the one in charge of the records for the place of his original residence was notified in order that his name could be followed through these records at any time.

EXTRA TAX LISTS. Whenever some extraordinary situation arose in the country wherein more money was needed than that which could be supplied by the government by ordinary means, an extra tax was required of the people. In most cases it just hit the land-owners and other men with rather large capitals or assets. But there were times when it was required from each family. In such cases a list was made out of all the heads of families which were to be taxed,

Royal Library

Genealogical research is greatly aided through the sources found in the Royal Library. Here will be found all the printed records, history, biography, etc. in Denmark. Various types of directories and short biographical sketches of important or more or less outstanding men of Denmark are found here. Very valuable family histories are also located here which many times can save a researcher a great deal of time when his pedigree connects up with one of these.

Military Archives

The military archives at Copenhagen will be of great help to any one searching names on a military line. Accurate records are kept of all officers and sub-officers in the nation's fighting force. Data generally given is mostly that concerning the person's military career.

"Raadstuearkiver"—City Archives

The city archive has several valuable records, but that which is of greatest value to the genealogist is the record of marriage permits issued.

Other Records

Other records of value are wills, deeds, divorces, civil marriages, death registrations at 'Tinghuset," etc. All records pertaining to wills, deeds and divorces in recent years are located at the head office of the Judicial District (Domekontoret) or at least information concerning their whereabouts could be given here. Civil marriages will be with the community government records as well as with the civil confirmations. Deaths are registered at "Tinghuset," so information concerning deaths can also be located here as well as from the church records.

See Scandinavia

(Much of above extracted from an article on Danish research by Henry E. Christensen.)

England

WRITE LETTERS FIRST

You can write letters to find relatives who have genealogy, advertise in newspapers, write to old residents, to postmasters, to city and county officials, to dealers in genealogical books, to names from directories, just the same in England as in America. If you expect to send a number of letters, write to some postmaster and send a money order for some stamps. Because of changing rates we suggest you ask for stamps in denominations for the class of mail you desire your letters to be returned by - air mail or surface mail. You can then send a self-addressed, stamped envelope with your letter to help get a reply. Or for 15 cents you can buy from your postmaster a cupon which can be exchanged in England or any other country for a stamp to pay postage on the answer to your letter.

SEARCHING PARISH REGISTERS

Parish registers, which are the records of the Church of England, are valuable sources of genealogical information. They do not contain the records of Methodists, Quakers, etc. If your ancestors belonged to those religions the records of their churches must be searched for the desired information.

A few parish registers go back as far as 1538, but most of them commence at a later date. Between 1538 and 1 July 1837 they are the principal sources of records of births, deaths and marriages of every class of people in England. ''Burke's Key to the Ancient Parish Registers of England and Wales,'' by Arthur M. Burke, London 1908, lists alphabetically the names of the parishes in England and Wales, giving also the name of the county and the dates of registration. It is not unusual to find gaps in the records - periods when no registrations were made or when they have been lost. Check each register to see if it covers completely the period you are interested in.

If you know the birthplace of your ancestor you can often find his parents and the date of his birth and marriage by searching the parish registers. The record of births or christenings gives only the given name of the mother but by searching the marriage record her surname can often be found. The burial record also gives information that is valuable. There are many thousands of parish registers, only a few of which have been printed.

Parishes may be divided into townships. A small parish may not have a township. A town may have several churches. To be a city in England there must be a cathedral.

THE CENSUS OF ENGLAND AND WALES

For nearly a hundred and fifty years the census has been taken each ten years. The only ones available for genealogical research are those of 1841 and 1851.

Prior to that time census enumerators listed only the number of people living at a given address. The census of 1841 tells names of family members, the ages of the nearest five years but does not tell the exact place of birth. The census of 1851 gives the names of each member of the family, their relationship to the head of the family, the occupation of each, the age and the parish where born. It is necessary that the approximate address be known before a search can begin.

Information from the 1861 census and later enumerations are not open to the public or their agents. They contain practically the same information as the 1851 census. Upon written application the Register General may make a search for a particular family but it is necessary to give him the precise address, the surname of the person or persons residing there and also a signed statement that the information from the census will not be used for litigation. Also state in your letter that it is for genealogical purposes; your relationship to those who might be named in the record; and whether you know of others more closely or equally related to them. Ask for fees for census research. Information from the 1911 and later censuses is not available for genealogy.

The following is the address of the office in charge of the census, Public Record Office, Chancery Lane, W. C. 2, London, England. They may suggest a professional genealogist if you enclose an international reply coupon which you may buy for 15 cents at your post office.

ENGLAND VITAL STATISTICS

Previous to 1837 the task of keeping a record of vital statistics of England and Wales was left almost entirely to the churches. Beginning on the first day of July, 1837, the government has kept a record of births, deaths and marriages. These records have been gathered in one office and indexed so that anyone born in England or Wales, knowing the date of his birth, can for a small fee obtain a birth certificate, etc. To obtain information from this record write to the Register of Births, Marriages and Death, Somerset House, London, England. The fee for such service is five shillings one penny, (a shilling is about 15¢). Thus if we know the full name of a person and his exact age but do not know his parents or birthplace, the birth certificate will give this information.

If the date is near 1851, you can refer to the census and find the birthplace of the parents and thus open the way for searching the parish register. If you do not know the exact name and date of birth it will be hard to get information from the record.

A research team of the "Institute of Heraldic and Genealogical Studies" at 58 North Gate, Canterbury, Kent, England has undertaken the monumental task of indexing every entry in all the parish and non-parochial registers in England. It might be well to write them if you would like to know more about their plans and subscription rates.

WILLS IN ENGLAND

Wills are the backbone of genealogical research in England. The information they give us is the most reliable, and you can often make up several family group sheets from one will. So far as telling who belongs to which family they are far better than the parish register. After you have examined a will it is well to search a parish register to fill in the dates and complete the record.

NON-PAROCHIAL OR NONCONFORMIST REGISTERS

In England and Wales each church kept its own records. Those who did not belong to the Episcopal Church (Church of England) did not have their names mentioned in the parish registers. The registers of the Nonconformists or Dissenters which included the Methodists, Baptists, Quakers, Presbyterians and some smaller groups were all, as far as possible, gathered up and deposited in Somerset house, London. Most of these records began about 1650 and continued to about 1850. To have these records searched, address: The Registrar General, General Register Office, Somerset House, London, England. When a search is to be made a description of the register must be given, also the name and the location of the chapel. For example, Register of births, from the Baptist Chapel in Dereham, Norfolk, England. Also give the approximate date. Fees vary – we suggest you ask what charges will be asked for each separate search you request. If your ancestor lived in Dereham and you wish to try the other churches you can send and have the Baptist record searched. If that fails you may try the Quakers, etc. There will be a separate charge for each search.

Your research in England will be eased considerably by a study of the following books. Some may be purchased, others you may find in your public or genealogical library.

BERRY, WM., *County Genealogies Pedigrees of Berkshire*, Pub. 1837, Gilbert and Piper, Poternaster Row, London.

COX, J. CHARLES, *Notes on the Churches of Derbyshire*, 4 Vol., Pub. 1875 by Bemrose and Sons, 10, Paternoster Bld. Gives the early history of the ancient churches and chapelries of Derbyshire County.

MARSHAL, DR. G. W., *Marshall's Genealogist's Guide*, 1903, gives a list of publications which have, at various times printed material on English families. The families are arranged alphabetically and the publications are coded with the page, volume, etc. listed, enabling a person to quickly discover if genealogical or historical material on that line has appeared in print. This book along with *A Genealogical Guide*, which is a continuation of this same idea for the period 1903 to 1953 (see Whitmore, J. B., below), are two of the most important books for English researchers.

PALMER, W. M. *Monumental Inscriptions and Coats of Arms from Cambridge*, Pub. by Bowes and Bowes, Cambridge, 1932.

SMITH, FRANK AND GARDNER, DAVID E., *Genealogical Research in England and Wales*, Vol. 1., Pub 1956 and Vol 2., Pub 1959. Bookcraft Publishers, Salt Lake City, Utah. These books can be purchased through most genealogical supply houses, including The Everton Publishers, prices, $3.50 for Vol. 1 and $3.95 for Vol. 2. The authors have been engaged in professional genealogical work for many years. Both were born in England and handled and searched countless parish and archive records in almost every county in England before coming to America to continue their genealogical careers. Their combined effort has brought forth two books that should be in the hands of every person seeking to do research in England and Wales.

THOMPSON, T. R., *A Catalogue of British Family Histories*, 1928, second edition 1935.

WHITMORE, T. R., *A Genealogical Guide*, Pub. 1953, John Whitehead & Son Ltd., Leeds. An index to British pedigrees in continuation of Marshall's Genealogist's Guide, (1903).

WORTHY, CHAS, ESQ., *Devonshire Wills*, Pub. Benrose & Sons Ltd., London, 1896. A collection of annotated testimentary abstracts, together with the family history and genealogy of many of the most ancient gentle houses of the west of England.

Counties and/or Shires of England

Name	Abbreviation	Map Index	County Town
Bedfordshire	Beds.	C7	Bedford
Berkshire	Berks.	F8	Reading

Name	Abbreviation	Map Index	County Town
Buckinghamshire	Bucks.	G7	Buckingham
Cambridgeshire	Cambs.	H7	Cambridge
Cheshire (Chester Co.)	Ches.	E5	Chester
Cornwall	Cornwall	B10	Bodmin
Cumberland	Cumb.	D3	Carlisle

COUNTY MAP OF
ENGLAND
AND
WALES

SCALE OF MILES

Name	Abbreviation	Map Index	County Town
Derbyshire	Derby	F5	Derby
Devonshire	Devon	C9	Plymouth
Dorsetshire	Dorset	E9	Dorchester
Durham	Dur.	F3	Durham
Essex	Essex	H8	Clemsford
Gloucestershire	Glos. (Gloucs.)	E8	Gloucester
Hampshire	Hants.	F9	Winchester
Herefordshire	Herefs.	E7	Hereford
Hertfordshire	Herts.	G8	Hertford
Huntingdonshire	Hunts.	G6	Huntingdon
Kent	Kent	H8	Maidstone
Lancashire (Lancaster Co.)	Lancs.	E4	Lancaster
Leicestershire	Leics.	F6	Leicester
Lincolnshire	Lincs.	G5	Lincoln
London	London	G8	London
Middlesex	Mx.	G8	London
Monmouthshire	Mont.	D8	Monmouth
Norfolk	Norfolk	H6	Norwich
Northamptonshire	Northants.	G7	Northampton
Northumberland	Northumb.	E2	Newcastle
Nottinghamshire	Notts.	F6	Nottingham
Oxfordshire	Oxon.	F7	Oxford
Rutlandshire	Rut.	G6	Oakham
Shropshire	Salop. (Shrops.)	G6	Shrewsbury
Somersetshire	Somerset	D9	Bristol
Staffordshire	Staffs.	E6	Stafford
Suffolk	Suffolk	H7	Ipswich
Surrey	Surrey	G8	Guilford
Sussex	Sussex	H9	Lewes
Warwickshire	War. (Warws.)	E7	Warwick
Westmorelandshire	Westmd.	E3	Appleby
Wiltshire	Wilts.	F8	Salisbury
Worcestershire	Worcs.	E7	Worcester
Yorkshire	York	F4	York

Finland

Administrative Departments of Finland (Suomi).

Department	Map Index	Administrative Center
1 Ahvenanmaa (Åland)	D3	Mariehamn (Maarianhamina)
2 Uusimaa	D4	*Helsinki (Helsingfors)
3 Kymi	C4	Kotka
4 Turu-Pori	C3	Turku (Åbo)
5 Häme	C3	Hämeenlinna (Tavastehus)
6 Mikkeli	C4	Mikkeli (Sankt Michel)
7 Vaasa	C3	Vaasa (Vasa)
8 Kuopio	C4	Kuopio
9 Oulu	B4	Oulu (Uleåborg)
10 Lappi	A4	Kemi

Turku is the oldest Finnish City. It was founded by Swedes in 1157 and was the capital of Finland from 1809 to 1819. Helsinki, the present capital of Finland, was founded by Swedes in 1550. Counties are called Iaani; cities and towns are called kyla, kaupala or kaupunki. SEE MAP PAGE 198

France

The genealogical situation in France is quite different from the conditions in England. We have the noble families in France as in England but unlike England there was no law to prevent any wealthy family from claiming nobility.

The feudal families, the Quasi-feudal, the noblemen created by the King, and the public office holder of old — all claiming nobility — have many descendants. Today it is said that 70,000 Frenchmen assume to be noblemen and not more than 8,000 or 9,000 have any real title to that quality.

The coat of arms, which is so helpful in tracing pedigrees in England, was also greatly overdone in France. The registration of coats of arms was taxed at 20 livres per person. The collector of taxes compelled many persons not connected with the nobility to pay the tax and assume a coat of arms. Over 60,000 coats of arms are recorded.

The earliest parish registers of births, marriages and burials were written about 400 years ago. These registers were kept by the parish priest who, beginning in about 1700 deposited copies of his registers with the Clerk of the Court. At the time of the revolution (1789) the task of recording births, marriages and deaths was transferred to the Mairie (Town Hall) where the parish priests were compelled by law to deposit all the registers in his possession. The new registers (since 1789) are known as Registres de l'Etate Civil. It is therefore to the Town Hall that one should apply to consult the records of births, marriages and deaths either prior to or subsequent to the year 1789. The registers are kept in the Registry Office of the Town Hall or in the Archives or in the Town Hall Library. Occasionally the Departmental Archivist has insisted on the transfer of the old parish registers to his Muniment rooms when they have not been carefully preserved in the Town Hall. There is usually an index provided for each volume. Only rarely is a register found that dates back to 1600. War fires, floods, and the carelessness of parish priests are all responsible for the loss of many parish registers, in Paris the original registers and the duplicates up to 1860 were destroyed by fire. Copies of a few of these registers had been made and these are still preserved. Registers of the Protestants are, relatively speaking, rare. They are found in the Town Hall along with the other registers.

The Registers of "Insinuations" in which all notorial documents that were subject to a tax had to be recorded is another good source of information.

Besides these, the National Library and the National Archives together with the various departmental archives supply inexhaustable sources of information.

In these public archives are preserved thousands of manuscript volumes extending back into the middle ages where the researcher might spend many months and still continue to find new things.

The above information was gleaned from a six page article in the Genealogists' Magazine, published in London, September, 1946.

Regarding printed genealogies the author has this comment: "Finally we have the printed sources, the genealogcial works of the judges of arms and kings genealogists, the monks of St. Maur such as Pere Anselme and a number of professional and amateur genealogists who are more or less reliable, not to say more or less honest or trustworthy . . . Unfortunately the only guide to the printed works on heraldry and genealogy is the Bibliotheque heraldique de la France by Joannis Guigard, published in Paris in 1861. For later works one has to wade through the printed or hand written indexes of the National Library, which from my own experiences is a tedious and not very satisfactory process."

He makes no mention at all of the books which form the great bulk of genealogical literature in England and America. Neither does he mention genealogical libraries which play such an important part in genealogical research in both England and America.

In the closing paragraphs he tells us that the Departmental Archivists are most helpful as also as a rule are the secretaries of the town halls in the important towns all over France where the old parish registers and the modern vital statistics are kept. At the National Library and the National Archives one must rely entirely on the manuscript and printed indexes. A letter of introduction from the Embassy is required of those who would examine these indexes.

Incidentally he gives the name of a firm of genealogists in Paris. Pelletier et Pecquet, 18 Rue de Cherche-Midi, Paris 6, France.

Departments of France
(Departement)

Departments are listed alphabetical with the map index in parenthisis and the department capital following.

Ain (C4) Bourg; Aisne (A3) Laon; Allier (C3) Moulins; Alpes-Maritimes (D4) Nice; Andorra (Autonomous Republic) (D3) Andorra la Vell; Ardeche

(C3) Privas; Ardennes (A3) Mezières; Ariège (D2) Foix; Aube (B3) Troyes; Aude (D3) Carcassonne; Aveyron (C3) Rodez.

Bas-Rhin (B4) Strasbourg; Basses-Alpes (D4) Digne; Basses-Pyrénées (D2) Pau; Belfort (B4) Belfort; Bouches-du-

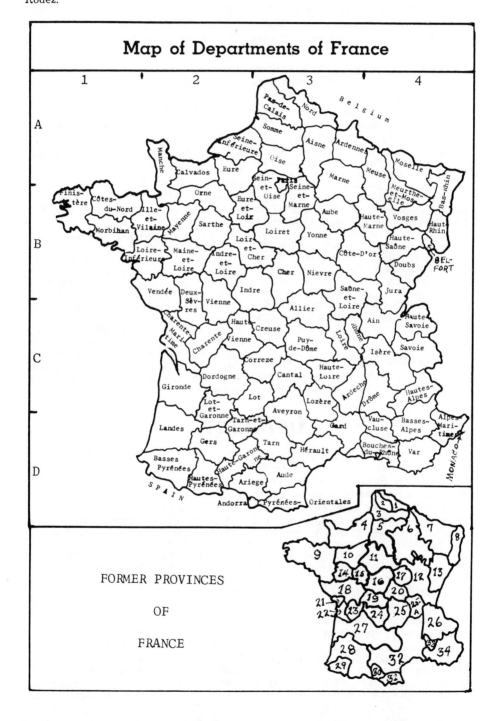

Map of Departments of France

FORMER PROVINCES

OF

FRANCE

Rhône (D4) Marseille; Calvados (A2) Caen; Cantal (C3) Aurillac; Charente (C2) Angoulême; Charente-Maritime (C2) La Rochelle; Cher (B3) Bourges; Corrèze (C3) Tulle; Corse (an island SE of Var) Ajaccio; Côte-D'or (B3) Dijon; Côtes-du-Nord (B1) St. Brieuc; Creuse (C3) Guéret.

Deux-Sèvres (B2) Niort; Dordogne (C2) Périgueux; Doubs (B4) Besancon; Drome (C4) Valence; Eure (A2) Evreux; Eure-et-Loir (B2) Chartres; Finistère (B1) Quimper; Gard (D3) Nimes; Gers (D2) Auch; Gironde (C2) Bordeaux; Haute-Garonne (D2) Toulouse; Haute-Loire (C3) Le Puy; Haute-Marne (B4) Chaumont; Haute-Savoie (C4) Annecy; Haute-Saône (B4) Vesoul; Hautes-Alpes (C4) Gap; Hautes-Pyrénées (D2) Tarbes; Haute-Vienne (C2) Limoges; Haut-Rhin (B4) Colmar; Herault (D3) Montpellier.

Ille-et-Vilaine (B2) Rennes; Indre (B2) Châteauroux; Indre-et-Loire (B2) Tours; Isère (C4) Grenoble; Jura (B4) Lons-le-Saunier; Landes (D2) Mont-de-Marsan; Loire (C3) St. Etienne; Loire-Inférieure (B2) Nantes; Loiret (B3) Orléans; Loir-et-Cher (B2) Blois; Lot (C3) Cahors; Lot-et-Garonne (C2) Agen; Lozère (C3) Mende.

Maine-et-Loire (B2) Angers; Manche (A2) St. Lô; Marne (A3) Chalons-sur-Marne; Mayenne (B2) Laval; Meurthe-et-Moselle (B4) Nancy; Meuse (A4) Bar-le-Duc; Monaco (Principality) (D4) Monaco; Morbihan (B1) Vannes; Moselle (A4) Metz; Nièvre (B3) Nevers; Nord (A3) Lille; Oise (A3) Beauvais; Orne (B2) Alecon; Paris (B3) —; Pas-de-Calais (A3) Arras; Puy-de-Dôme (C3) Clermont-Ferrand; Pyrénées- Orientales (D3) Perpignan.

Rhône (C3) Lyon; Saône-et-Loire (B3) Mâcon; Sarthe (B2) Le Mans; Savoie (C4) Chambery; Seine-et-Marne (B3) Melun; Sein-et-Oise (B3) Versailles; Sein-Inferieure (A2) Rouen; Somme (A3) Amiens; Tarn (D3) Albi; Tarn-et-Garonne (D2) Montauban; Var (D4) Draguignan; Vaucluse (D4) Avignon; Vendée (B2) La Roche-sur-Yon; Vienne (C2) Poitiers; Vosges (B4) Epinal; Yonne (B3) Auxerre.

Former Provinces of France

1, Flanders; 2, Artois; 3, Picardy; 4, Normandy; 5, Ile de France; 6, Champagne; 7, Lorraine; 8, Alsace; 9, Brittany; 10, Maine; 11, Oréanais; 12, Burgundy; 13, Franche-Comté; 14, Anjou; 15, Touraine; 16, Berry; 17, Nivernais; 18, Poitou; 19, Marche; 20, Bourbonnais; 21, Aunis; 22, Saintonge; 23, Angoumois; 24, Limousin; 25, Auvergne; 25A, Lyonais; 26, Dauphin; 27, Guyenne; 28, Gascony; 29, Béarn: 30, Foix; 31, Roussillon; 32, **Languedoc; 33, Comtat; 34, Provence.**

Germany

The German people during the past several centuries have been a record keeping people. Some church records have information since early in the sixteenth century. Birth, Marriage, and death records are generally available since the nineteenth century. Census records have also been kept for many years, as have parish and Protestant church records. In some provinces the real estate records are among the most valuable. Burger rolls, tax lists, and police registers assist in giving accurate identification The German police method of keeping track of every individual arriving in any city or locality, is important in tracing individuals or families from one city to another.

To most Americans interested in German genealogy it is neccessary to employ researchers in Germany. They can be located in many German cities. Care should be taken to secure reliable help. researchers who subscribe to the highest genealogical practices and ideals.

A great deal of information and many records from Germany are now on file in the library of the Genealogical Society of Utah, Salt Lake City, Utah. Those not acquainted with the research situations in Germany may find it advantagous to correspond with that office before employing a researcher.

MILITARY OCCUPATION ZONES OF GERMANY

Some controversy and confusion arises when one attempts to name, locate and established the capitals of the state and zones of Germany. The accompanying map has the boundries and capitols similar to those found in **Hammond's Ambassador World Atlas,** published by C. S. Hammond & Co. Maplewood, N. J., Third Printing 1956. We quote from The New **Funk & Wagnalls Encyclopedia,** Unicorn Publishers, Inc., N. Y., 36 Vols. 1951, **and The Columbia-Viking Desk Encyclopedia,** Published by The Viking Press, N. Y., 2 Vols., 1953.

This from Funk and Wagnalls: **France:** The French zone comprises parts of the former states of Prussia, Baden, Hessen, and Würtemburg, and all of the Saarland. For administrative purposes, the zone has been divided into four states, namely Rhineland - Palatinate, Baden, Würtemberg-Hohenzollern, and the Saar. The capitals of these states are respectively Coblenz, Frieburg, Tübigen, and Saarbrücken . . . **United Kingdom:** The British zone consists of the former state of Hamburg, portions of the former state of Prussia, and the former states of Brunswick, Oldenburg, Schaumburg-Lippe, and Lippe. For administrative purposes the zone has been divided into four states, namely Schleswig-Holstein, Lower Saxony, North Rhine-Westphalia, and Hamburg. The capitals of these states are respectively Kiel, Hanover, Düsseldorph, and Hamburg . . . **Union of**

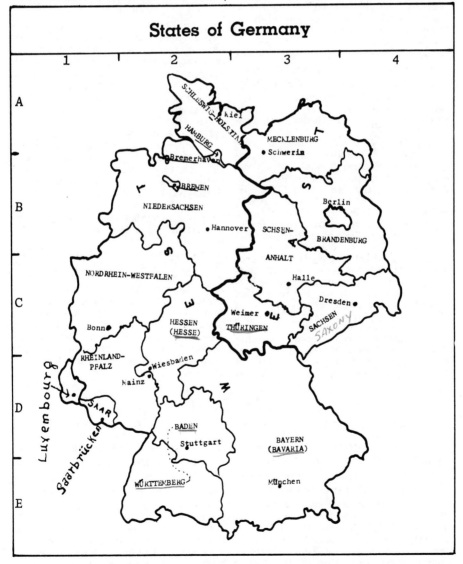

States of Germany

Soviet Socialist Republics: The Soviet zone consists of the former states of Saxony, Thüringia, Mecklenburg and Anhalt, and portions of the former state of Prussia, including the provinces of Silesia and Pomerania. For Administrative purposes, the zone has been divided into five states, namely Brandenburg, Saxony, Saxony-Anhalt, Thüringia, and Mecklenburg. The capitals of these states are respectively, Potsdam, Dresden, Halle, Weimer, and Schwerin . . . **United States:** The American zone comprises the former states of Bavaria and Bremen and parts of the former states of Prussia, Baden, Würtemberg, and Hessen. For administrative purposes, the zone has been divided into four states, namely Bavaria, which consists of the former state of Bavaria, a part of the former Prussian province, the Palatinate, and the town and district of Lindau; Württemberg-Baden; Hessen; and Bremen. The capitals of these states are respectively Munich, Stuttgart, Wiesbaden, and Bremen.

This from Columbia-Viking: in 1949 two separate republics came into existance; (1) Federal Republic of (West) Germany, temporary capital, Bonn, under U. S., British, and French occupation, consisting of the states of Bavaria, Württemberg-Baden, Hesse, and Bremen (U.S. zone); North Rhine-Westphalia, Lower Saxony, Schleswig-Holstein, and Hamburg (British Zone); Rhineland-Palatinate, Württemberg-Hohenzollern, and Baden (French zone); and W. Berlin. (2) (East) German Democratic Republic, capital E. Berlin, under Russian occupation, consisting of the states of Brandenburg, Mecklenberg, Thüringia, Saxony, and Saxony-Anhalt.

It should be remembered regarding Germany and most of the other European countries that the spelling of many of the place names in their native language is different than the English spelling. For instance in Germany Pflaz means the Palatinate; Bayern is Bavaria; München is Munich; Nordrhein is North Rhine; Sachsen is Saxony; Koblenz is Coblenz, etc.

THE THIRD REICH ADMINISTRATIVE DIVISIONS

The sixteen administrative divisions of the Third Reich in 1937 were Anhalt, Baden, Bavaria, Bremen, Brunswick, Hamburg, Hesse, Lippe, Mecklenberg, Oldenburg, Prussia, Saarland, Saxony, Schaumburg-Lippe, Thüringia, and Württemburg. Lübeck, which had held the status of a city-state, was merged with Prussia in March, 1937.

Milton Rubincam, editor of the National Genealogical Society Quarterly, and an expert in many phases of genealogy, has stressed the importance of exhausting both published and unpublished sources in America before attempting research in Germany. The publications of The National Genealogical Society, The New York Genealogical & Biographical Society, The Pennsylvania Genealogical Magazine of History and Biography, and the Pennsylvania Genealogical Magazine abound in material on early German immigrants, as do the very early issues of the publications of the Pennsylvania Dutchman, The Pennsylvania German Folklore Society, the Pennsylvania-German Magazine and the Maryland Historical Magazine, according to Mr. Rubincam.

The National Archives have ship's lists of immigrants of the 19th century; Strassburger & Hinke's "German Pioneers" lists German immigrants in the 18th century; Knittle's Lists gives much information on early Germans to New York State, etc. (See also several chapters in "Genealogical Research Methods and Sources" by the American Society of Genealogists, Edited by Milton Rubincam, 1960, 456 pp.)

Ireland

Capitals: Dublin, Ireland; Belfast, North Ireland

Genealogical Research In Ireland

Only a very few Irish records have been published. Most of the original records were gathered in Dublin. In 1882 a big fire destroyed them. Others were destroyed in the recent civil war in 1922. The Society of Genealogists in London recently wrote us as follows: "Since the destruction of the Four Courts in Dublin, (the equivalent of the Public Record Office in London) in 1922, Irish records have been so sparse that connected research is out of the question, (except in the case of well known families figuring in the standard reference books.)"

A general index for the vital statistics for all of Ireland is at the Custom House, Dublin, Ireland. There are birth, marriage and death records from

1864. Protestant marriage records available only since 1845. Northern Ireland has kept its registers separately since 1922.

Since 1708 land records and deeds have been filed at the Land Registry, Henrietta Street, Dublin. Two Indexes have been made for these records—one under the surname of the grantor, the other under the township or property name. No index has been made of land owners. These records are being microfilmed.

Indexed records of wills filed in the Prerogative Court of Armagh for all Ireland by testators owning land in more than one diocese are available. They are also microfilmed. Wills relating to property in one diocese only were proved in the diocesan court. Each court file is indexed separately.

Mrs Margaret D. Falley, 999 Michigan Ave., Evanston, Illinois, has completed two large volumes on Irish research which every serious Irish researcher should have. Write to her for cost. She

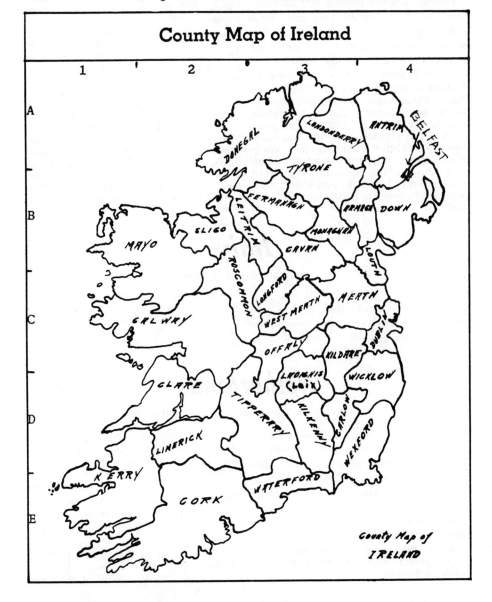

County Map of Ireland

also has collected an excellent library of many rare volumes on Ireland and her people and can probably give help on many phases of research in the Emerald Isle.

The Ulster-Scot Historical Society, Law Courts Bldg. Chichester Street Belfast, Northern Ireland aims to provide facilities for people of Ulster descent to establish connections there. Write to them and ask for initial registration fee.

Ireland Provinces & Counties

Ireland is divided into four provinces which in turn are divided into 32 counties and four county boroughs. Each county borough is a separate administrative district and each one is also the county town of one of the counties.

Ulster Province is divided between N. Ireland (counties Antrim, Down, Armagh, Fermanagh, Tyrone, and Londonderry) and republic (counties Monaghan, Cavan, and Donegal). Other three provinces are in republic—Leinster has counties Louth, Meath, Dublin, Kildare, Wicklow, Carlow, Wexford, Longford; Munster Province has Tipperary, Waterford, Cork, Kerry, Limerick, and Clare; Connaught Province has Leitrim, Roscommon, Galway, Mayo, and Sligo.

Counties and County Boroughs of Ireland

(Counties are listed alphabetical with the map index in parenthisis and the county town following.)

Antrim (A4) Belfast; Armagh (B4) Armagh; Belfast (County Borough) (A4) Belfast; Carlow (D3) Carlow; Cavan (B3) Caven; Clare (D2) Ennis; Cork (E2) Cork; Cork (County Borough (E2) Cork; Donegal (Ancient Name Tryconnel also O'Donnell's Country) (A2) Lifford; Down (B4) Downpatrick; Dublin (C4) Dublin; Dublin (County Borough) (C4) Dublin; Fermanagh (B3) Enniskillen; Galway (C1) Galway; Kerry (E1) Tralee; Kildare (C3) Naas; Kilkenny (D3) Kilkenny; Laoighis (Leix) (Formerly Queen's) (D3) Portlaoighise; Leitrim (B3) Carwick-on-Shannon; Leix (see Laoighis); Limerick (D2) Limerick; Limerick (Luimneach) (County Borough) (D2) Limerick; Londonderry (A3) Londonderry; Longford (C3) Longford; Louth (B4) Dundalk; Mayo (B1) Castlebar; Meath (C4) Trim; Monaghan (B3) Monaghan; Offaly (C3) Tullamore; Roscommon (C2) Roscommon; Sligo (B2) Sligo; Tipperary (D3) Clonmel; Tyrone (B3) Omagh; Waterford (E3) Waterford; West Meath (C3) Mullingar; Wexford (D4) Wexford; Wicklow (D4) Wicklow.

Italy

Capital Rome (Roma)

ITALY

During 1947 and 1948 the records from Piedmont, Italy, were microfilmed for the Genealogical Society of Utah under the personal direction of Archibald F. Bennett, its executive secretary. The records from sixteen parishes were photographed, including the years 1690 to 1940. One film contains as many as 11,896 pages. There are several films available.

Netherlands

Capital — The Hague ('s Gravenhage)

The early history of Holland has been one of troubles and wars, in all of which the determination of the people to rule themselves has been paramount. In religious affairs they have always leaned heavily toward Protestantism. The nation gives financial support to several religious organizations.

Since 1811 vital records have been kept, giving detail information about each individual.

Since 1850 the Bevolkingsregister (population register) has kept information as to the movements of each individual.

Many Hollanders have come to the United States and are now living in various parts of the nation. Michigan and Illinois have many of these industrious people within their borders. Since 1861 more than four thousand Hollanders have made their homes in Utah.

The vital statistics of all of the prov-

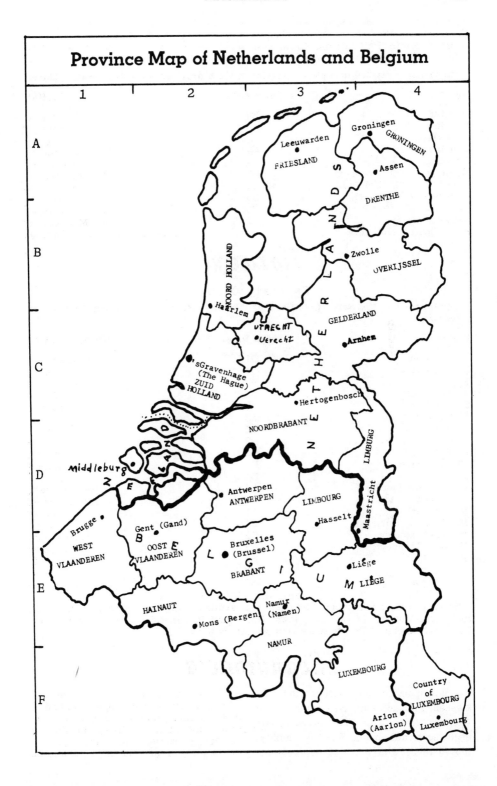

Province Map of Netherlands and Belgium

inces are being microfilmed under the direction of the Genealogical Society of Utah. South Holland and Groningen records have been filmed and work is progressing in other provinces. Several trained Holland researchers are connected with the Genealogical Society of Utah.

Netherlands is divided into eleven provinces. Each province controls its own archive.

Name	Map Index	Capital
Drenthe	B4	Assen
Friesland	A3	Leeuwarden
Gelderland	C3	Arnhem
Groningen	A4	Groningen
Limburg	D4	Maastricht
Noord (North) Brabant	D3	Hertogenbosch
Noord (North) Holland	B2	Haarlem
Overijssel (Overyssel)	B4	Zwolle
Utrecht	C3	Utrecht
Zeeland	D2	Middleburg
Zuid (South) Holland	C2	* 's Gravenhage (The Hague)

Norway

Capital, Oslo

Administrative Districts (Counties) of Norway (Norge) are called Fylkers as follows:

Fylker	Map Index	Administrative Center
1 Vestager	D1	Kristiansand
2 Aust-Agder	D1	Arendal
3 Rogaland	D1	Stavanger
4 Telemark	D1	Skien
5 Vestfold	D2	Tönsberg
6 Östfold	D2	Moss
7 Akershus	D2	*Oslo
8 Oslo	D2	*Oslo
9 Buskerud	D1	Drammen
10 Hordaland	D1	Bergen
11 Bergen	D1	Bergen
12 Sogn og Fjordane	C1	Hermansverk
13 Opland	C1	Lilliehammer
14 Hedmark	C1	Hamar
15 More og Romsdal	C1	Molde
16 Sör-Tröndelag	C2	Trondheim
17 Nord-Tröndelag	C2	Steinkjer
18 Nordland	B2	Bodö
19 Troms	A3	Tromsö
20 Finnmark	A3	Vadsö

SEE MAP PAGE 198
Some Norwegian Pioneer histories are available in the Norwegian–American Historical Museum at Decorah, Iowa. Norwegian Information Service, Washington, D. C. have booklet ''How to trace your ancestors in Norway.''

Scandinavia

Included in this designation should be Sweden, Finland, Norway, Denmark, and Iceland. Years ago Finland was part of Sweden and many Swedish families moved there. They have been perpetuat- ed since then in Finland, and the present generations look upon Finland as their original country. There are also Finns and Russians living in Finland, but their names and languages are entirely different. The present Icelanders have descended from the three Scandinavian peoples, but mainly from the Danish.

At different times over the centuries, Norway has been part of either Denmark or Sweden. It wasn't until 1905 that it became a kingdom of its own, when a Danish prince was invited to become King of Norway.

The three languages are enough alike that they can be understood by people of all three countries, although the dialects in different sections of each one of the three countries vary so much that they are not understood in every section of the country. The dialects of the country sections are nothing like the city dialects, and cities vary in different sections of the country.

Until about 1880 the most common method of giving surnames was for the children to take the father's first name or given name and add to it "ssen", or "sen", or "sson". For instance, if the father's first name was Ronald, his children's surname would be Ronaldssen or Ronaldsson; if Erick, Erickssen or Ericksson; If Johan, Johanssen or Johansson; if Niels or Nils, Nielssen or Nilsson. if Ingvar, Ingvarssen or Ingvarsson, etc.

The patronymic method of naming persons is not so difficult to comprehend as some seem to believe. For instance, if the father's name is Hans Sorensen and son's name is Ola or Jens, or Svend, or Carl, the full name of the son would be Ola Hansen, or Jens Hansen, or Svend Hansen, or Carl Hansen.

The same is true in Swedish families. with the exception that there the name ending is "sson" instead of "sen" as in the Norwegian and the Danish. However, among Scandinavians in America this name ending is not adhered to as strictly as it was years ago. Among Swedish families the "sson" may have become "son," but never "sen". Many Norwegian or Danish name endings, are "son" instead of "sen". In Iceland the name endings are like that in Sweden, "sson," as Gislasson, Thordarsson, Sveinsson, Valgardsson, etc.

Books:

NELSON, O. N., PH.D., *History of the Scandinavians in the United States* 2 Vols. O N. Nelson & Co., Minneapolis, Minn. 1904.

HOKANSON, NELS, *Swedish Immigrants in Lincoln's Time,* Harper & Bros., New York.

Scotland

Capital, Edinburgh

Research In Scotland

Unlike the conditions in England, the parish registers in Scotland have all been gathered in one building in Edinburgh. Besides the parish registers, there is a wealth of other records in Edinburgh which may be searched. Very few of the Scottish records have been printed. It is usually best to hire a genealogist to do the searching.

Before engaging help perhaps you should inquire from the Genealogical Society of Utah, Salt Lake City, what microfilm records from that country are available and if assistance can be obtained to search them.

The Census of Scotland

The census of Scotland was taken the same years and contained the same information as the census of England. In Scotland the census returns of 1841, 1851, 1861 and 1871 may be searched. Written application must be made for permission to search the census. For application blanks write to the Registrar General, New Register House, Edinburgh, Scotland. The fee for a particular search, that is a search for one person or household at one census and at one certain address, is ten shillings. If the address is good enough this search will be made by the office force without extra charge.

Permission for a general search, that is a search that is not limited to one person or to one census will be granted only to responsible officials or local authorities engaged in making search for public purposes, and to other specially approved applicants. A general search must not exceed six hours and must be completed within two days. The cost is One Pound (about $3.00) which covers the cost of the extract. Each additional extract costs two shillings six pence. The office force does not do the searching in a general search. When you write for your application blank ask for the name of a searcher.

The earliest vital registers of Scotland have a starting date of 1538 but most of them did not start until much later, the majority having their inception between 1640 and 1700.

When writing for information it is

County Map of Scotland

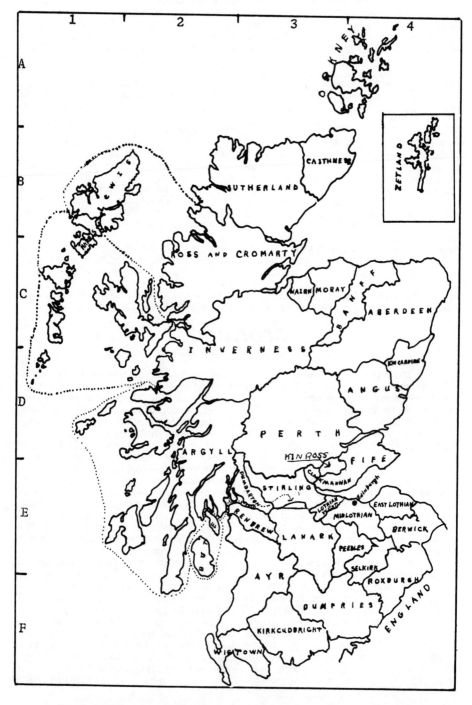

very important that the birth date be given also the locality and occupation of the deceased. The law requiring registration of births, deaths and marriages was passed in 1855.

The Old Registration House in Edinburgh has among others the following records: Wills and Deeds, 1514 to present; Land and Housing records (real estate transfers), 1550 to present; Lyon Court **Records** (King-of-Arms); Guild registrations (tradesmen); Poll Tax (registration of males of over 16 for military service); Registration of University graduates of the Universites of Edinburgh, Glasgow, St. Andrew's and Aberdeene.

COUNTIES OF SCOTLAND

Counties are listed alphabetically with the map index in parenthisis and the county seat following.

1) Aberdeen (C4) Aberdeen; 2) Angus (D4) Forfar; 3) Argyll (D2) Inveraray, includes islands of Jura, Islay, Colonsay, Mull, Coll, Tiree, Scarba, Luing, Siel, Kerrera, Lismore, and others; 4) Ayr (F3) Ayr; 5) Banff (C4) Banff; 6) Berwick (E4) Duns; 7) Bute (E2) Rothesay, includes

islands of Bute, Arran, Gr. Cumbrae, Little Cumbrae, Holy Island, etc.; 8) Caithness (B3) Wick; 9) Clackmannan (E3) Clackmannan; 10) Dumbarton (E2) Dumbarton; 11) Dumfries (F3) Dumfries; 12) East Lotian (E4) Haddington; 13) Fife (D4) Cupar; 14) Inverness (C3) Inverness, includes islands of Skye, Raasay, Muck, Eigg, Rum, Canna, Sanday, Scalpay, Harris, Scalpa, Pabbay, Bernera, Boreray, North Uist, Benbecula, South Uist, Barra, and many little islands; 15) Kincardine (D4) Stonehaven; 16) Kinross (E3) Kinross; 17) Kirkcudbright (F3) Kirkcudbright; 18) Lanark (E3) Lanark; 19) Mid-Lotian (E4) Edinburgh; 20) Moray (C3) Elgin; 21) Nairn (C3) Nairn; 22) Orkney (A3) Kirkwall; 23) Peebles (E4) Peebles; 24) Perth (D3) Perth; 25) Renfrew (E3) Renfrew; 26) Ross and Cromarty (C2) Dingwall, includes Lewis Island; 27) Roxburgh (F4) Jedburgh; 28) Selkirk (E4) Selkirk; 29) Shetland (B4) Lerwick, also called Zetland Islands; 30) Stirling (E3) Stirling; 31) Sutherland (B3) Dornoch; 32) West Lothian (E3) Linlithgow; 33) Wigtown (F3) Wigtown;

South Africa

Capitals, Pretoria and Capetown

The Cape Settlement was established by the Dutch East India Co. as a "half way house" between Europe and India, under the command of Jan van Riebeeck, who arrived in Table Bay on the 6 April, 1652. Ten years later van Riebeeck was appointed commander to the Government at Malacca and the muster rolls of the Cape Settlement showed it had grown to several hundred inhabitants during his tenure of office. The Cape settlement continued under the rule of this trading company for about 140 years, gradually growing from within and without. The Netherlands, of course, supplied most of the immigrants but French refugees also came in considerable numbers as well as numerous Germans, a few Swiss and others.

The first British occupation occurred in 1795 but not until 1806 did they wrest it permanently from the Dutch. In 1820 under sponsorship of the British Government over 3,000 English settlers arrived at Algoa Bay (Port Elizabeth), becoming the nucleus of the English speaking people of South Africa. The start of the

great trek of the Boers (South African descendants of the Dutch), came in 1836. They traveled north and east with the object of settling outside the sphere of British control. Gradually they found their way to Natal, Orange Free State and Transvaal, which with the Cape Province, after much tribulation and war, now form the Union of South Africa.

Published Genealogies

The oldest and largest published genealogical work is that of Christoffel Coetzee de Villiers, **"Geslacht-Register der Oude Kaapsche Familien"** (Generation Index of the Old Cape Families) which was published in three volumes in 1893-4. This is an excellent reference book but should be checked with original or other sources where possible as it has some mistakes. Another useful genealogical work is **"Personalia of the Germans at the Cape, 1652-1806"** by Dr. J. Hoge, which was published as the 1946 issue of the **"Archives Year Book for South African History."** This publication attempts to give a complete list of the Germans and Swiss who came to the Cape in the service of the Dutch East India Co.

during the period 1652 till 1806. It lists as sources manuscripts in the Cape section of the Government Archives and Archives of the Dutch Reformed Church.

Other good sources are: **"The French Refugees at the Cape"** by Col. Graham Botha (1919); **"Precis of the Archives of the Cape of Good Hope"** in two vol., consisting of Requesten (Memorials) 1715-1806; **"De Afkomst der Boeren"** by Dr. H. J. Colenbrander contains a list of many of the early marriages of the settlers, with birthplaces of the wives—sometimes not otherwise obtainable **"The Story of the British Settlers of 1820 in South Africa"** lists all the settlers of 1820 and gives their ages as of that year.

The histories and genealogies of some individual families have been compiled, some of them being: **"Genealogy Jacob Izaak de Villiers and his wife Johanna Margaretha Muller of Waltevreeden, Dist. of Paarl"** by D. F. Bosman; **"History of the Malan de Merindol"** compiled by Henry Victor Malan (1836) and revised by James John Malan (1950); **"Record of the Caldecott Family of South Africa"**; **"Jan Van Riebeeck Zijn Voor-en Nageslacht"** (his ancestors and posterity) published 1952 by the Netherlands government gives many South African descendants of the leader of the first European Colony south of the tropic of Capricorn.

State Records

Laws requiring the registration of births, deaths and marriages were passed in Natal in 1868, in the Cape Province in 1895, in the Orange Free State and Transvaal in 1902. Prior to these dates it was optional with parents as to whether they had the births of their children registered or not. Survivors had the same option with the registration of deaths. The registration of marriages started some years before that of births and deaths in all the provinces except Natal. Births, marriage and death certificates may be obtained from the local registrar or from the Registrar of Births, Marriages and Deaths, Dept. of Int. Pretoria, South Africa. Birth certificates are of little value to the genealogists of South Africa, however, as the information given on them is restricted by law to the name, place and date of birth of the registrant—the price is 2s 6d. Full birth certificates, giving the name, place and date of birth, also the names, ages, place of birth and marriage of parents, may be had only by applicants residing outside the Union of South Africa—the price being 5s. (s—Shilling, abt. 15 cents; d—penny, abt. 1½ cents)

The marriage certificate gives the names of each party, the date and place of marriage, the country of birth and the age of each. The death certificate gives the name, date and place of death, age at death and birthplace. In the case of children who died under 10 years of age, it also gives the names of the parents. The cost of a marriage certificate or death certificate is 2s 6d.

In the Union of South Africa they have what they call a "Death Notice" which is completed on the filing of a will or on the settlement of deceased estate. These are very valuable for genealogists as they list, when properly executed, the following information: name, age, birthplace, date and place of death, names of spouse, parents and children. The law requires that all estates over ten pounds sterling be probated, also that all wills of estates under that amount be filed with the Master of the Supreme Court. The charge made for a certified copy of a Death Notice is 6s 6d. If the complete will is wanted, write for cost. Cape Province wills and Deceased Estate records (Death Notices) from 1689 to 1833 are kept in the Union Archives and from 1834 to date in the Master's Office of the Supreme Court—the address of both is Queen Victoria Street, Capetown, C. P. South Africa. In Natal the Master of the Supreme Court has wills dating back to 1852 and Deceased Estates from 1872 to date — the address is Pietermaritzburg, Natal, South Africa. Deceased Estate records in the Master's Office in the Orange Free State started in 1850 — the address is Bloemfontein, OFS, South Africa. The address of the Master's Office in the Transvaal is Pretoria, Tvl., South Africa. Their records start in 1872.

It must be remembered that sometimes estates are settled many years after death occurred and that most of the estates are indexed according to the year they are filed. Also, none of the public record offices have facilities for doing research, making it necessary to use care in giving information as to what is wanted and what year it may be found when asking for certificates. In the case of birth certificates, the date and place of birth must be given, also the names of parents. If the record is not found in that year, an additional charge of 2s 6d is made for searching the year before and the year following the one given, but no longer search than for the three years will be made on one application.

Church Records

The church records in the Archives of the Dutch Reformed Church (Nederduits-Hervormde of Gereformeerde Kerk, claiming 85% of the membership of the Dutch Reformed Church in South Africa) are of great value to historical and genealogical researchers. They have baptism and other records dating back to 1665 and it has been the aim of the church to gather all their church records up to about 1875 to this repository. However, some of the local churches still have their records from inception and, of course, inquiries on recent records must also be made locally. Baptism Certificates may be had for 2s 6d, membership certificates for 2s 6d, and marriage certificates for 6s 6d. Address inquiries to Dutch Reformed Church Archives, 44 Queen Victoria Street, Capetown, C. P., South Africa, or to locality where your people came from.

The records of other churches are kept mostly in the local churches and inquiries should be directed to them.

The Union Archives at Pretoria, Pietermaritzburg, Bloemfontein and Capetown, though not staffed sufficiently to do research, have many wonderful old records which are veritable "gold mines." In some cases the old church records have been removed to the State Archives as in Pietermaritzburg where they have baptismal and marriage records kept by the "Predikants" as they crossed the plains with the Voortrekkers. Also the Marriage Register—1837 to 1912 of the Dutch Reformed Church of that locality.

The South African Mission of the Church of Jesus Christ of Latter-day Saints, with headquarters at "Cumorah" Main Rd., Mowbray, C. P., South Africa, has a card index file of about 15,000 names which is growing continually as members in South Africa send in all information on their personal lines.

Sweden

Capital, Stockholm

The primary sources of genealogical information in Sweden are the church records. They are recognized as among the best in Europe. The Genealogical Association Library in Salt Lake City has more microfilm records from Sweden than from any other nation, except the United States. If your ancestors lived in Sweden within the past century, their records would be in the church in the parish (församling) in which they lived. If the desired date is older than that, then the search should be conducted in the particular archive (landsarkiv) to which that parish belongs.

There are more than 2,550 parishes in Sweden. The names of the parish and the county (län) in which the ancestor lived must be known before any search can be made. The older records from these parishes are in five archives: Lund, Göteborg, Vadstena, Uppsala, and Härnösand.

Among the records kept by the church are birth and baptism, confirmation, marriage banns (lysing), marriages, incoming and outgoing records, catechetical (husförhörslängder), and deaths.

In 184 communities records are kept of

117 district courts in Sweden (domsagor or häradsrätter). Among them are wills (testamenter), land records (jordeböcker), inventories (bouppteckning or lösöreförteckning), and census (mantalslängder).

Most city or community goverments maintain a taxoffice (uppbördsverket), which keeps yearly lists of taxpayers and their addresses.

One of the difficulties in Swedish research for the novice researcher is the patronymic name system used until about 1890. The surname of the children in any family was the given name of the father plus son or dotter (daughter). Since the Swedish possessive is not indicated by an apostrophe, the son of Peter or Peters son gets the surname Petersson. Similarly Hans son is Hansson, Nils son is Nilsson, Magnus son is Magnusson, etc. In the same way the surname of the daughters became Hansdotter, Nilsdotter, Magnusdotter, etc. If the father had adopted a surname not ending in son, as tens of thousands of them did, the children would use the father's adopted name as their surname.

THE COUNTIES OR LANS OF SWEDEN

Map No.	County (Län)	Administrative Center	Province (Landskap)	Archive (Landsarkiv)
1	Malmöhus	Malmö	Skåne	Lund
2	Kristianstad	Kristianstad	Skåne	Lund
3	Blekinge	Karlskrona	Blekinge	Lund
4	Kronoberg	Växjö	Småland	Vadstena
5	Halland	Halmstad	Halland	Lund
6	Jönköping	Jönköping	Småland	Vadstena
7	Kalmar	Kalmar	Småland	Vadstena
8	Gotland	Visby	Gotland	Vadstena
9	Älvsborg	Vänersborg	Västergötland	Göteborg
10	Göteborg & Bohus	Göteborg	Bohuslän	Göteborg
11	Skaraborg	Mariestad	Västergötland	Göteborg
12	Östergötland	Linköping	Östergötland	Vadstena
13	Södermanland	Nyköping	Södermanland	Uppsala
14	Örebro	Örebro	Närke	Uppsala
15	Värmland	Karlstad	Värmland	Göteborg
16	Västmanland	Västerås	Västmanland	Uppsala
17	Stockholm	Stockholm	Södermanland	Uppsala
18	Uppsala	Uppsala	Uppland	Uppsala
19	Kopparberg	Falun	Dalarna	Uppsala
20	Gävleborg	Gävle	Gästrikland	Härnösand
21	Jämtland	Östersund	Jämtland	Härnösand
22	Västernorrland	Härnösand	Ångermanland	Härnösand
23	Västerbotten	Umeå	Västerbotten	Härnösand
24	Norrbotten	Luleå	Norrbotten	Härnösand

See Map On Page 198

Switzerland

Capital, Bern

Switzerland, anciently known as Helvetia, covers an area about half as large as South Carolina, and into that little space is crowded a population twice that of South Carolina plus half a million. The population 4,700,297, as compared to South Carolina's 2,117, 027. Switzerland is surrounded by France, Germany, Austria, and Italy. Languages represented are German, French, Italian, and Romansch.

Switzerland consists of twenty-two states or cantons which form the Swiss Republic. For administrative purposes three cantons, Appenzell, Basel, and Unterwalden, have been divided into two districts each. The cantons are Aargau, Appenzell, Basselland, Bern, Fribourg, Geneve, Glarus, Grisons, Luzern, Neuchatel, St. Gallen, Schaffhausen, Schwyz, Solothurn, Thurgau, Ticino, Unterwalden, Uri, Valais, Vaud, Zug, and Zurich.

Among the available genealogical sources are the church or parish registers, the baptismal, the confirmation, the marriage, and the death books. The confirmation books contain the names and records of the fifteen-year-old boys and girls who have prepared themselves in special study groups under the direction of the minister prior to their participation for the first time in the Lord's Supper. Among the non-church records are the Burger Rodel (Citizen Roll) in which is recorded the name of each citizen, together with his parents' and grandparents' names, and the Zivilstandsamt (civilian position), containing about the same information.

Of the many European nationalities represented in Utah, none has been more consistent and energetic in their research activities than have the Swiss. As a result voluminous records have been filed with the Genealogical Society of Utah. For instance, one woman has over the years gathered more than 60,000 names of ancestors, all of whom have been thoroughly identified. Several records go back as far as 1520.

People of Swiss descent, regardless of their present residence, may do well to confer with the Genealogical Society of Utah, 80 North Main Street, Salt Lake City 1, Utah, about their research activities before engaging a professional researcher.

Cantons of Switzerland

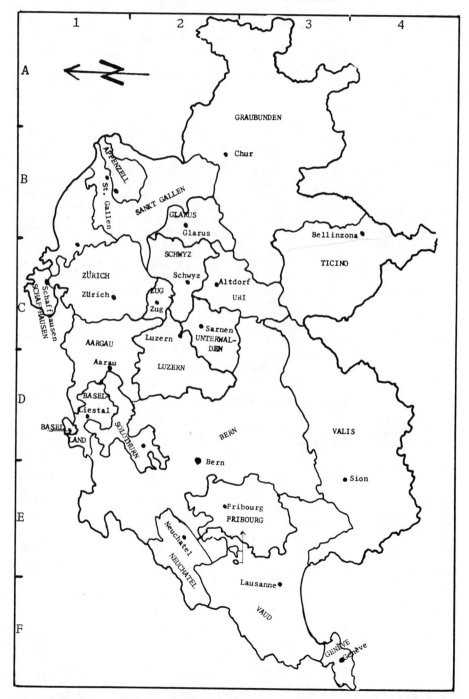

Wales

For nearly five hundred years England and Wales have been one country. The Welsh government affairs have been conducted in London just as those of England. In everything else the two peoples are entirely different. The Welsh, or Cymry, have their own traditions, history, language, literature, and songs.

"English and Welsh records were compiled under the same conditions and laws," says David E. Gardner, an untiring Utah student and teacher of genealogy. "This means that parish registers, probate court wills and administrations, and civil registering of vital statistics (since 1837), taxing, militia records, and overseeng of the poor and highways were practically the same."

Mr. Gardner explains that the language is so difficult that names of days, months, and counties often are mistaken for places of birth. Spelling of names is not always uniform. To add to the difficulty of interpreting the old records, some of the parish vicars or ministers have interchanged Latin and English.

Since many of the surnames were taken from the place of residence, you will find many families with the same name who are unrelated.

The patronymics (father's name) changed with each generation just as in the Scandinavian countries. Until 1850 these changes were common in all families. So, for instance, John son Philip Thomas, is the same as John ap Philip Thomas, which becomes John Philip, or David ab Evan Hugh, becomes David Evan or David Bevan.

The only legal form of marriage from 1754 to 1837 was by the parish minister. If births and burials are not found in parish register, search non-parochial registers, many of which, prior to 1837, are at Somerset House.

Because of the changes of names and frequency of common names, wills may give the only real identification.

Wills and administrations are grouped into four probate courts: (1) Llandaff (South Wales and Monmouth); (2) St. David's (West Wales); (3) Bangor (Central and Northwest Wales); (4) St. Asaph (Northwest Wales). All names in the records are indexed under the first given name.

Unless the researcher is well acquainted with the Welsh language, it may be to his advantage to employ a Welsh professional researcher.

Counties of Wales

Name	Abbreviation	Map Index	County Town
Anglesey	Ang.	C5	Beaurnares
Brecknockshire	Brec.	D7	Brecknock or Brecon
Caernarvonshire (Carnarvon)	Caern.	C6	Caernarvon
Cardiganshire	Card.	C7	Cardigan
Carmarthenshire	Carm.	C7	Carmarthen
Denbighshire	Denb.	D5	Denbigh
Flintshire	Flint.	D5	Flint
Glamorganshire	Glam.	D8	Cardiff
Merionethshire	Meri.	D6	Dolgelly
Montgomeryshire	Mont.	D6	Montgomery
Pembrokeshire	Pemb.	C7	Pembroke
Radnorshire	Rad.	D7	New Radnor

SEE MAP PAGE 202

The Hall of Records, Annapolis, Md.
                    Corner of College Ave. &
                              St. John's St.

"Every State, county, city, town or other public official in Md. is _permitted_ to deposit in the Hall of Records any original papers, official books, records, documents, files, newspapers or printed books, not in current use. He is _required_ to deposit all records in his custody created before the date of the adoption of the Federal Constitution by Md., April 28, 1788. In addition, the Hall of Records has microfilm copies of much county material after 1788, including land and court records at least through 1850 and often beyond; and the major probate series through 1950."

"The Hall of Records will furnish, for a fee, photostatic or microfilm copies of records in its custody. All the materials at the Hall of Records (except those whose use is specifically restricted) are available to the public in the Search Room. Inquiries received by mail will be answered if the research required is confined to the use of our extensive indexes; however, no family lines will be traced. The Hall of Records is open to the public Mondays through Saturdays."

Circuit Court

The justices, or commissioners as they were more commonly called, of the county court were commissioned jointly by the Governor and held office at his pleasure.

In 1790 the State was divided into five judicial districts, each district encompassing [about 4] counties.

A chief justice and two associate justices were appointed for each district and the court terms in the district were staggered so that the full bench could be present in each county when court was held. The judicial districts, now called circuits, have been frequently reorganized and the number of judges increased but the system still prevails.

Clerk of Court

The Clerk of court was responsible for recording the proceedings and actions of the court for recording deeds, conveyances & other papers delivered to him for such purpose and for preserving the records of the court.

Sheriff

He has been described as "the County court's Chief Executive Officer." He served summonses, writs & other process issued by the court. He impaneled juries, apprehended persons accused of crimes & kept them in custody if they were sentenced to the county prison, which was in his charge. He collected & paid out the county levy.

He had certain duties with respect to elections.
He also supervised the work of the constables
in preparing lists of taxables within their area
of responsibility.

Law Jurisdiction

At first the jurisdiction of the county court
was limited to civil cases not exceeding
3,000 # of tobacco & to criminal cases not
jeopardizing life or member. Even in such
cases it shared concurrent jurisdiction with
the Provincial court. In 1785 the county court
acquired full jurisdiction in all civil cases.

Equity Jurisdiction

Throughout the Colonial Period, the Chancery
Court was the major equity court of Md., while
the county court handled the lesser cases. In 1791
the county was granted original equity jurisdiction
in all cases where the value in dispute did not
exceed 10,000 # of tobacco or £100. The Chancery court
was abolished in 1851 & the county court assumed
exclusive original jurisdiction in equity cases.

Baltimore City Courts

Under the Constitution of 1851, Baltimore City was
separated from Baltimore Co. & established as a unit
of government comparable in many respects to a
county.

A. Court of Common Pleas.

This court was created in 1851. It was assigned
civil jurisdiction in all suits where the debt or damage
claim was over $100. & did not exceed $500. Since 1867, the
court has had concurrent civil jurisdiction with the
Superior Court & Baltimore City Court.

B. Superior Court

The constitution of 1851 gave this court civil jurisdiction over all suits where the debt or damage claimed exceeded the sum of $500.

The constitution of 1851 made the clerk of Superior court responsible for receiving & recording "all deeds, conveyances & other papers which are required by law to be recorded."

C. Criminal Court

This court has had exclusive jurisdiction in all criminal cases since its creation in 1851.

d. Circuit Court

This court established in 1853. It had concurrent jurisdiction in equity cases with the Superior court until 1867, when it acquired exclusive jurisdiction. Circuit court #2 was established in 1888 & the two courts have shared (in equity) cases jurisdiction ever since.

E. Baltimore City Court

Created in 1867 & assigned concurrent civil jurisdiction with the court of Common Pleas & the superior court. It has exclusive jurisdiction in cases of appeal from judgments of justices of the Peace, or cases of appeal arising from the ordinances of the mayor & City Council of Baltimore

Orphans Court

During the Colonial period, the settlement of the estates of deceased persons was under the jurisdiction of a central probate court called the Prerogative Court.

NOTES

THE GENEALOGICAL HELPER

A quarterly magazine published since 1947, has aided thousands of people all over the world. It is dedicated to helping more people find more genealogy. It is not confined to any particular section of the country but serves people in every state and many foreign countries. It is edited and published by the same concern publishing this book, THE EVERTON PUBLISHERS, Inc., Box 506, Logan, Utah.

Three of the four yearly issues contain not less than thirty six pages, eight-and-a-half by eleven inches. The September issue contains about 150 pages. The March issue contains a listing of family associations in the United States with the name and address of the president, and some-times the secretary, of the organization. The June issue contains the addresses of genealogical societies and libraries in the various states, and a list of professional genealogists. In each March, June and December issue is a "Question Box" in each one of which generally about sixty or seventy-five researchers ask for information on about two hundred fifty or three hundred different families on which they are working.

The easiest way in which to find relatives is to check your family names in "The Genealogists' Exchange" in the various September issues, which are known as the Annual Exchange Editions, locate the name and address of the registrant or registrants and write them about your problems. These Annual Exchange Editions have been published since 1950.

Hundreds of researchers have extended their pedigrees many generations by utilizing the facilities offered in THE GENEALOGICAL HELPER. It is the most widely read genealogical magazine published. The subscription price is $3.00 per year; $5.50 for two years, and $7.50 for three years, paid in advance. Single copies can be obtained at 50 cents each, with the exception of the Annual Exchange Editions, the September numbers, which are $2.00 each.

SEND FOR A

FREE

CATALOGUE

OF

GENEALOGICAL SUPPLIES

HOBBY KITS

SHEETS

BOOKS

CHARTS

BINDERS

— Send card to —

EVERTON PUBLISHERS, INC.
P. O. Box 506
Logan, Utah 84321

Ask for latest catalogue